Daniela Pettersson-Traba
The Development of the Concept of SMELL in American English

Applications of Cognitive Linguistics

Edited by
Gitte Kristiansen
Francisco J. Ruiz de Mendoza Ibáñez

Honorary editor
René Dirven

Volume 51

Daniela Pettersson-Traba

The Development of the Concept of SMELL in American English

A Usage-Based View of Near-Synonymy

DE GRUYTER
MOUTON

ISBN 978-3-11-163182-0
e-ISBN (PDF) 978-3-11-079229-4
e-ISBN (EPUB) 978-3-11-079236-2
ISSN 1861-4078

Library of Congress Control Number: 2022942664

Bibliographic information published by the Deutsche Nationalbibliothek
The Deutsche Nationalbibliothek lists this publication in the Deutsche Nationalbibliografie;
detailed bibliographic data are available on the internet at http://dnb.dnb.de.

© 2024 Walter de Gruyter GmbH, Berlin/Boston
This volume is text- and page-identical with the hardback published in 2022.
Typesetting: Integra Software Services Pvt. Ltd.

www.degruyter.com

Acknowledgements

This monograph constitutes a revised version of my doctoral thesis, submitted and defended at the University of Santiago de Compostela (Spain) in March, 2021. I am greatly indebted to my supervisor, Professor María José López Couso, for her invaluable advice and guidance throughout the planning and development of this work. I feel immensely privileged to have learnt – and still be learning – from such an exceptional professional. I would also like to express my genuine gratitude to Professors Kathryn Allan, Dirk Speelman, and Augusto Soares da Silva for their expertise and wise counsel received during my research stays at University College London, KU Leuven, and the Catholic University of Portugal. I have also benefited tremendously from the feedback provided by the thesis committee, made up by Professors Kathryn Allan, Pascual Cantos Gómez, and Belén Méndez Naya. In this regard, special thanks are due to Dr. Allan, with whom I was able to further discuss my PhD following the defense, and who was happy to send me all her notes. I also want to thank the research group *Variation and Linguistic Change and Grammaticalization* at the University of Santiago de Compostela, and all its members for their encouragement. For generous financial support, I am grateful to the European Regional Development Fund and the following institutions: The Regional Government of Galicia (grants ED481A–2016/168, ED431B 2017/12, ED431D 2017/09, and ED431B 2020/01) and the Spanish Ministry of Innovation, Science, and Universities (grants FFI2017–86884-P and PID2020-114604GB-100). Finally, I would like to express my profound gratitude to my partner, family, and friends, who have all, in one way or another, played an important part in making this monograph possible with their wholehearted support and commitment over the last few years.

Contents

Acknowledgements —— V

List of figures —— XI

List of tables —— XIII

List of abbreviations —— XVII

1	**Introduction** —— **1**	
1.1	Lexical semantics: Approaches and basic notions —— 3	
1.2	Aims, scope, and contributions —— 9	
1.3	Overview of the book —— 11	
2	**Synonymy** —— **14**	
2.1	Classifications of synonymy —— 15	
2.2	The distributional corpus-based approach and synonymy —— 24	
2.2.1	Two waves of research —— 25	
2.2.2	Near-synonymous adjectives —— 33	
2.3	Synonymy and diachrony —— 38	
3	**The concept PLEASANT SMELLING** —— **48**	
3.1	Introducing the synonym set —— 49	
3.1.1	Why the concept PLEASANT SMELLING —— 49	
3.1.2	Revising reference works —— 51	
3.2	Corpus description and data retrieval —— 61	
3.3	Data annotation —— 65	
3.3.1	Language-internal semantic variables: Sense —— 68	
3.3.2	Language-internal semantic variables: Semantic category —— 71	
3.3.3	Language-internal semantic variables: Animacy, Concreteness, and Countability —— 85	
3.3.4	Language-internal non-semantic variables —— 89	
3.3.5	Language-external variables —— 94	
4	**Semasiological and onomasiological analyses of the synonym set** —— **97**	
4.1	Frequency of the adjectives —— 99	
4.2	The evolution of the concept PLEASANT SMELLING —— 102

4.2.1	Sense —— 103
4.2.2	Semantic category —— 106
4.3	Semasiological analysis —— 110
4.3.1	Sense —— 111
4.3.2	Semantic category —— 114
4.3.3	Interim summary and discussion —— 117
4.4	Onomasiological analysis —— 120
4.4.1	Sense —— 121
4.4.2	Semantic category —— 123
4.4.3	Interim summary and discussion —— 127
4.5	Chapter summary and discussion —— 128
5	**In-depth onomasiological analysis of the synonym set: A multivariate approach —— 131**
5.1	Data and methodology —— 131
5.2	Results —— 136
5.2.1	Multinomial models: Fixed effect structure —— 136
5.2.2	Mixed-effects models: The effects of individual noun collocates —— 154
5.3	Discussion —— 162
6	**Idiosyncratic collocational preferences of the near-synonyms —— 170**
6.1	Data and methodology —— 171
6.2	Results —— 179
6.2.1	Semantic vector space modeling —— 179
6.2.2	Prominent collocates —— 188
7	**The concept PLEASANT SMELLING: A victim of societal change? —— 198**
7.1	Exploring the interconnection between societal and linguistic developments —— 199
7.2	Historical background: First and Second Industrial Revolutions —— 203
7.3	Data and methodology —— 205
7.4	Results —— 210
7.4.1	Dictionary-based approach —— 210

7.4.2	Data-driven approach —— **214**
7.5	Discussion —— **218**

8   Concluding remarks and suggestions for future research —— 220

List of references and sources —— 231
　　　　References —— **231**
　　　　Sources —— **243**

Appendix —— 245

Index —— 267

List of figures

Figure 1 Development of corpus-based research on lexical synonymy over the last 30 years —— 25
Figure 2 Percentages of the five near-synonyms across periods —— 100
Figure 3 Percentages of the concept PLEASANT SMELLING in each sense across periods —— 104
Figure 4 Percentages of the concept PLEASANT SMELLING in each semantic category across periods —— 107
Figure 5 Overall sense distribution (in percentages) per near-synonym —— 112
Figure 6 Sense distribution (in percentages) per adjectival near-synonym across periods —— 113
Figure 7 Overall semantic category distribution (in percentages) per near-synonym —— 115
Figure 8 Semantic category distribution (in percentages) per near-synonym across periods —— 116
Figure 9 Continuum of senses of the five adjectives —— 119
Figure 10 Overall percentages of the five near-synonyms in each sense —— 122
Figure 11 Percentages of the five near-synonyms in each sense across periods —— 123
Figure 12 Overall percentages of the five near-synonyms in each semantic category —— 124
Figure 13 Percentages of the five near-synonyms in each semantic category across periods —— 125
Figure 14 Variable importance of predictors according to random forest analysis —— 140
Figure 15 Effect of Concreteness rating on the probabilities of the adjectives *fragrant*, *perfumed*, and *scented* —— 146
Figure 16 Effect of Degree on the probabilities of the adjectives *fragrant*, *perfumed*, and *scented* —— 147
Figure 17 Effect of Countability on the probabilities of the adjectives *fragrant*, *perfumed*, and *scented* —— 147
Figure 18 Effect of Syntactic function on the probabilities of the adjectives *fragrant*, *perfumed*, and *scented* —— 148
Figure 19 Effect of Text-type on the probabilities of the adjectives *fragrant*, *perfumed*, and *scented* across periods —— 149
Figure 20 Effect of Sense on the probabilities of the adjectives *fragrant*, *perfumed*, and *scented* across periods —— 150
Figure 21 Effect of Semantic category on the probabilities of the adjectives *fragrant*, *perfumed*, and *scented* across periods —— 152
Figure 22 Collocational preferences of *fragrant* —— 157
Figure 23 Collocational preferences of *perfumed* —— 158
Figure 24 Collocational preferences of *scented* —— 160
Figure 25 The use of *fragrant*, *perfumed*, and *scented* in the artificial, indeterminate, and natural senses over time —— 165
Figure 26 Dendrogram of the collocational preferences of *fragrant*, *perfumed*, and *scented* throughout the period 1810–2009 —— 180

https://doi.org/10.1515/9783110792294-204

Figure 27 Two-dimensional MDS map of the collocational preferences of *fragrant*, *perfumed*, and *scented* throughout the period 1810–2009 —— **181**

Figure 28 Significant correlations between MDS dimensions and semantic categories in *USAS* —— **186**

Figure 29 Mean NFs of the prototypically artificial semantic categories (1820s–2000s) —— **211**

Figure 30 Mean NFs of the prototypically natural semantic categories (1820s–2000s) —— **213**

Figure 31 Percentage of artificial second-order collocates in the prototypically artificial semantic categories CLEANING, COSMETICS, and TEXTILE AND CLOTHING —— **215**

Figure 32 Percentage of natural second-order collocates in the prototypically natural semantic categories EARTH, ATMOSPHERE, AND WEATHER, FOOD AND DRINK, and PLANTS AND FLOWERS —— **216**

Figure 33 Percentage of artificial second-order collocates in the semantic categories BODY AND PEOPLE, OBJECT, SUBSTANCE AND MATERIAL, SENSATION, and SPACE —— **217**

List of tables

Table 1	Classifications of synonymy by Lyons and Cruse —— 19	
Table 2	Sense division of the five adjectives according to nine dictionaries and thesauri —— 56	
Table 3	Number of instances retrieved per query —— 64	
Table 4	Major semantic classes in *USAS* —— 71	
Table 5	Major semantic classes in the *HTOED* —— 73	
Table 6	Classification of nouns into semantic categories —— 81	
Table 7	Variables in the first dataset and their levels —— 95	
Table 8	Absolute and relative frequencies of the five near-synonyms —— 99	
Table 9	Chi-square residuals of the frequency of the five adjectives in the period 1810–2009 —— 101	
Table 10	Frequency clines of the five adjectives in the period 1810–2009 —— 102	
Table 11	Distribution of the concept PLEASANT SMELLING across senses —— 104	
Table 12	Chi-square residuals of the frequency of the concept PLEASANT SMELLING across senses in the period 1810–2009 —— 105	
Table 13	Distribution of the concept PLEASANT SMELLING across semantic categories —— 107	
Table 14	Chi-square residuals of the frequency of the concept PLEASANT SMELLING across semantic categories in the period 1810–2009 —— 109	
Table 15	Absolute and relative frequencies of *fragrant*, *perfumed*, and *scented* —— 135	
Table 16	Model summary of multinomial logistic regression Model A (Sense) —— 136	
Table 17	Model summary of multinomial logistic regression Model B (Semantic category) —— 138	
Table 18	Model summary of multinomial logistic regression with only semantic predictors (Sense) —— 138	
Table 19	Model summary of multinomial logistic regression with only semantic predictors (Semantic category) —— 138	
Table 20	Model A coefficients (Sense) —— 141	
Table 21	Model B coefficients (Semantic category) —— 142	
Table 22	Model summary of the binary mixed-effects logistic regression (*fragrant*) —— 155	
Table 23	Model summary of the binary mixed-effects logistic regression (*perfumed*) —— 155	
Table 24	Model summary of the binary mixed-effects logistic regression (*scented*) —— 155	
Table 25	Structure of the dataset —— 172	
Table 26	Similarity matrix based on cosine similarity scores for the data —— 175	
Table 27	Distance matrix for the data —— 176	
Table 28	Settings for the analysis of prominent collocates —— 178	
Table 29	AU *p*-values for the five-cluster solution in Figure 26 —— 180	
Table 30	Significant correlations between the dimensions in Figure 27 and semantic categories in *USAS* —— 184	
Table 31	Examples of types of noun collocates in the semantic (sub)-categories in *USAS* —— 184	

Table 32	Number and percentage of consistent, initiating, terminating, and transient noun collocates of *fragrant*, *perfumed*, and *scented* —— 189
Table 33	Consistent, initiating, terminating, and transient noun collocates of *fragrant* —— 189
Table 34	Consistent, initiating, terminating, and transient noun collocates of *perfumed* —— 192
Table 35	Consistent, initiating, terminating, and transient noun collocates of *scented* —— 194
Table 36	PMI scores over time of *fragrant*, *perfumed*, and *scented* with shared collocates in P4 —— 195
Table 37	Semantic classes in *USAS* representing the artificial-natural continuum —— 208
Table 38	Period contrasts in fiction —— 245
Table 39	Period contrasts in non-fiction —— 246
Table 40	Period contrasts in periodicals —— 247
Table 41	Period contrasts in the artificial sense —— 248
Table 42	Period contrasts in the figurative sense —— 249
Table 43	Period contrasts in the indeterminate value —— 250
Table 44	Period contrasts in the natural sense —— 251
Table 45	Period contrasts in the semantic category ABSTRACT —— 252
Table 46	Period contrasts in the semantic category BODY AND PEOPLE —— 253
Table 47	Period contrasts in the semantic category CLEANING —— 254
Table 48	Period contrasts in the semantic category COSMETICS —— 255
Table 49	Period contrasts in the semantic category EARTH, ATMOSPHERE, AND WEATHER —— 256
Table 50	Period contrasts in the semantic category FOOD AND DRINK —— 257
Table 51	Period contrasts in the semantic category OBJECT —— 258
Table 52	Period contrasts in the semantic category PLANTS AND FLOWERS —— 259
Table 53	Period contrasts in the semantic category SUBSTANCE AND MATERIAL —— 260
Table 54	Period contrasts in the semantic category SENSATION —— 261
Table 55	Period contrasts in the semantic category SPACE —— 262
Table 56	Period contrasts in the semantic category TEXTILE AND CLOTHING —— 263
Table 57	Number and percentage of artificial and natural second-order collocates in the semantic category BODY AND PEOPLE —— 264
Table 58	Number and percentage of artificial and natural second-order collocates in the semantic category CLEANING —— 264
Table 59	Number and percentage of artificial and natural second-order collocates in the semantic category COSMETICS —— 264
Table 60	Number and percentage of artificial and natural second-order collocates in the semantic category EARTH, ATMOSPHERE, AND WEATHER —— 264
Table 61	Number and percentage of artificial and natural second-order collocates in the semantic category FOOD AND DRINK —— 264
Table 62	Number and percentage of artificial and natural second-order collocates in the semantic category OBJECT —— 265
Table 63	Number and percentage of artificial and natural second-order collocates in the semantic category PLANTS AND FLOWERS —— 265
Table 64	Number and percentage of artificial and natural second-order collocates in the semantic category SUBSTANCE AND MATERIAL —— 265

Table 65	Number and percentage of artificial and natural second-order collocates in the semantic category SENSATION —— 265
Table 66	Number and percentage of artificial and natural second-order collocates in the semantic category SPACE —— 265
Table 67	Number and percentage of artificial and natural second-order collocates in the semantic category TEXTILE AND CLOTHING —— 266

List of abbreviations

Corpora, dictionaries, and thesauri

AHDOE	American Heritage Dictionary of the English Language
CD	Cambridge Dictionaries
COCA	Corpus of Contemporary American English
CoD	Collins Dictionary
COHA	Corpus of Historical American English
HTOED	Historical Thesaurus of the Oxford English Dictionary
LDOCE	Longman Dictionary of Contemporary English
MD	MacMillan Dictionary
MW	Merriam-Webster
NHDAE	Newbury House Dictionary of American English
OED	Oxford English Dictionary
USAS	UCREL Semantic Analysis System

Semantic categories

ABS	ABSTRACT
B&P	BODY AND PEOPLE
CL	CLEANING
COS	COSMETICS
EAW	EARTH, ATMOSPHERE, AND WEATHER
F&D	FOOD AND DRINK
OBJ	OBJECT
P&F	PLANTS AND FLOWERS
S&M	SUBSTANCE AND MATERIAL
SEN	SENSATION
SPACE	SPACE
T&C	TEXTILE MATERIAL AND CLOTHING

USAS Semantic tags (only those referred to in the text)

B	THE BODY AND THE INDIVIDUAL
B1	ANATOMY AND PHYSIOLOGY
B3	MEDICINE AND MEDICAL TREATMENT
B4	CLEANING AND PERSONAL CARE
B5	CLOTHES AND PERSONAL BELONGINGS
F1	FOOD
F2	DRINKS

F3	CIGARETTES AND DRUGS
F4	FARMING AND HORTICULTURE
H	ARCHITECTURE, BUILDINGS, HOUSES AND THE HOME
H3	AREAS AROUND OR NEAR HOUSES
H5	FURNITURE AND HOUSEHOLD FITTINGS
I4	INDUSTRY
L1	LIFE AND LIVING THINGS
L2	LIVING CREATURES GENERALLY
L3	PLANTS
M3	MOVEMENT/TRANSPORTATION (LAND)
M7	PLACES
O1	SUBSTANCES AND MATERIALS GENERALLY
O1.1	SUBSTANCES AND MATERIALS GENERALLY: SOLID
O2	OBJECTS GENERALLY
O3	ELECTRICITY AND ELECTRICAL EQUIPMENT
Q1	COMMUNICATION
Q1.2	PAPER DOCUMENTS AND WRITING
Q4	THE MEDIA
S2	PEOPLE
W	THE WORLD AND OUR ENVIRONMENT
W3	GEOGRAPHICAL TERMS
W4	WEATHER
X3	SENSORY
Y	SCIENCE AND TECHNOLOGY

Other

AU	Approximately Unbiased p-values
HAC	Hierarchical Agglomerative Cluster
HCFA	Hierarchical Configural Frequency Analysis
MDS	Multidimensional Scaling
NFs	Normalized frequencies
PMI	Pointwise Mutual Information
POS	Part of speech
SVS	Semantic Vector Space

1 Introduction

What exactly is a synonym? This is a question that has excited much interest among linguists and laymen alike and for which slightly different answers have been proposed in the literature through the years. Even a cursory glance at definitions of the term *synonym* in dictionaries reveals that there is yet no agreement regarding exactly what constitutes synonymy. Despite the fact that all sources coincide in characterizing this semantic relation in terms of similarity of meaning, two groups of definitions emerge. While some dictionaries define the term *synonym* as "[. . .] a word or expression which means the same as another word or expression" (*Collins Dictionary*, s.v. *synonym* n.), in other sources a partial degree of similarity is considered sufficient for a word or expression to constitute a synonym of another item: "a word having the same or *nearly* the same meaning as another word or other words in a language" (emphasis mine; *American Heritage Dictionary of English*, s.v. *synonym* n. 1). As has been argued by many scholars (e.g., Cruse 2000: 157–158; Taylor 2003: 264; Divjak and Gries 2006: 24; Liu 2010: 56–57), absolute synonymy, that is, complete identity of meaning, is an extremely rare, if not a non-existent, phenomenon in language, as opposed to near-synonymy, which is exceedingly common. This can easily be experienced by considering for a moment the use of any pair or larger group of synonymous expressions in a given language. Regardless of the synonym set one selects, the most likely scenario is one in which there exist some contexts of use where one of the terms is either the only possible choice or at least a more suitable option.

Such an impressionistic experiment suggests that, in all probability, the great majority of synonyms differ in one way or another, which prevents them from being completely interchangeable in all contexts of use. As argued by the philosopher Thomas Reid, "[m]ost synonimes [sic] have some minute distinction that deserves notice" (1785: 14; quoted in the *OED*, s.v. *synonym* n. 1a). Therefore, perhaps the most interesting question which arises when dealing with synonyms is not what makes them similar but, on the contrary, where exactly their differences reside. This is an issue which has fascinated not only linguists, but also ordinary speakers. As a matter of fact, as shown by Murphy (2013: Section 3), one of the most frequent uses of dictionaries and thesauri is precisely to search for synonyms, especially in language production, in order to avoid repetition, achieve a more sophisticated writing, or adjust the style employed, among others. In fact, selecting the most appropriate word from a set of candidate synonymous expressions is a notoriously difficult task, both for non-native and for native language users, because synonyms can vary along a great number of dimensions – up to 35 according to Edmonds (1999: Chapter 3) – and differences are often multidimensional in nature (e.g., Cruse 1986: 284–289; 2000: 159–60; Murphy 2003: 154–157). In view of this, it is not surprising that research on synonymy has recently moved away from an excessive emphasis on the classification of synonyms into types and subtypes to a focus on the identification of the factors underlying their choice, thus zooming in on the differences between synonymous expressions. To this purpose, innovative methods and techniques have been employed in neo-structuralist and cognitive semantics to capture precisely the dimensions along which particular pairs or sets of lexical synonyms vary, with successful results (e.g., Persson 1989; Arppe 2002; 2008; Taylor 2003; Divjak 2006; 2010; Divjak and Gries 2006; 2008; Gries and Otani 2010; Liu 2010; 2013; Liu and Espino 2012; Desagulier 2014; Krawczak 2014; 2018). Such studies have proven the suitability of these approaches to uncover fine-grained differences among synonyms through the use of corpus data and in-depth analyses of the contexts in which these words are used, including semantic, lexical, morphosyntactic, and stylistic ones, among others.

Despite the usefulness of such approaches for the study of synonymy, most research of this type adopts a synchronic perspective, thus examining the set of factors that are thought to influence the alternation between synonymous lexical expressions at a particular point in time, most typically the present day. On the contrary, diachronic usage-based studies on how the relation between members of a lexical synonym set gradually changes over time are relatively scarce, with only a handful of such investigations over the last two decades (e.g., Kaunisto 2001; Primahadi-Vijaya-R and Rajeg 2014; Baker 2017: 95–101). In addition, the underlying motivations for changes in the internal semantic structure of such semantically related words have traditionally been reduced to the so-called *no-synonymy rule* (e.g., Samuels 1972: 65; Bolinger 1977: ix–x, 9; Wierzbicka 1988: 13–14; Croft 2000: 176; Nuyts and Byloo 2015: 62–63), whereby languages are assumed to work against absolute synonymy. In particular, synonyms are expected to become increasingly differentiated over time or, if this is not the case, one or more of the terms from a given set are expected to drop out of use so as to ensure that languages remain efficient and economic systems of communication. However, it has recently been claimed that this theory of competition is insufficient to account for all changes undergone by synonymous expressions and that other diachronic processes may also be at play (De Smet et al. 2018). Besides differentiation and substitution, it has been proposed that synonyms can also increasingly converge in functional terms as time passes. However, this process of attraction has thus far not received as much attention in semantic research as the more well-understood competition phenomena. Against this backdrop, the present monograph aims at further contributing to our knowledge of the factors influencing lexical choice in English, as well as whether and how their effects fluctuate over time and the motivations behind such changes. In the remainder of this chapter, a brief description of the main approaches to and basic notions in lexical semantics, the field in which the study of synonymy is encompassed, is first provided in Section 1.1. Then, the aims, scope, and contributions of the monograph are discussed in Section 1.2, followed by an outline of its structure in Section 1.3.

1.1 Lexical semantics: Approaches and basic notions

Lexical semantics has been a prominent discipline within linguistics since the beginning of the nineteenth century when it emerged as an established field of study. From a historical perspective, the research conducted in this field can be classified into five broad theoretical movements: historical-philological semantics, structuralist semantics, generative semantics, neostructuralist semantics, and cognitive semantics. Some scholars (e.g., Geeraerts 2010: 277) suggest that the historical development of this field can be characterized on the basis of a series of oppositions that serve to describe the main interests of each of these five movements. First, the schools' approaches to the study of word meaning vary depending on whether meaning is conceptualized as a purely linguistic entity, separate from general human cognition, or whether the latter, in the form of encyclopedic knowledge, should also be contemplated in semantic description. Second, the five movements diverge in terms of the prominence they assign to language use (i.e., *parole* and *performance* in the parlance of Saussure 1916 and Chomsky 1965, respectively). A third dimension along which the traditions differ is that of *semasiology* (i.e., from word form to meaning) vs. *onomasiology* (i.e., from meaning to word form), with some schools focusing primarily on the study of the former and others on the latter. Lastly, the emphasis given to either synchronic or diachronic research varies from one school to another. These five schools should, however, not be considered in isolation but rather in relation to one another, as the transition from one movement to the next can be characterized either in terms of continuation or of reaction along the four dimensions just described. Therefore, to understand the concepts and principles present in one tradition, it is often necessary to have some knowledge of the key developments in the preceding ones.

The historical-philological school takes a diachronic perspective towards semantics and displays a great interest in meaning change, especially at the level of individual words, thus focusing mainly on semasiological structures in the lexicon. As such, it is unsurprising that one of the major contributions of this tradition concerns the various classifications of semantic change postulated (e.g.,

Carnoy 1927; Stern 1931). Language use is key within this school to understand semantic change, since it is argued that new meanings of a word can only emerge as a result of the repeated use of specific contextual readings of that same word, which may become conventionalized over time (Paul 1920). Lastly, historical-philological semantics is also characterized by its psychological conceptualization of meaning in which language is seen as being closely connected to our general cognitive abilities (Bréal 1897). Despite the widespread acceptance of these tenets by scholars in this tradition, the movement, while usage-based in theory, cannot in practice be characterized as a fully usage-based approach due to the lack of systematic semantic analyses of concrete texts and explicit reference to the actual contexts of use of words. Nevertheless, historical-philological semantics has still greatly contributed to many of the most important principles of cognitive semantics, and it is in this sense that we can certainly regard the latter tradition as a continuation of the main ideas of the prestructuralist semantic movement.

The emergence of the structuralist movement, which followed historical-philological semantics, is typically contemplated as a direct reaction against all of the main assumptions of the prestructuralist tradition: it adopts a primarily synchronic approach to meaning, it focuses on onomasiological structures in language, and it considers the language system in isolation without reference to language use, that is, as an autonomous system with its own rules and principles, where meaning is conceptualized as a non-psychological entity. Given the onomasiological orientation of the structuralist school, relations between concepts within the system are considered of paramount importance since it is argued that related words lie at the basis of the creation and demarcation of meaning (Saussure 1916). For this reason, one prominent branch of structuralism known as relational semantics was devoted to the identification and classification of semantic relations, including synonymy and antonymy, among others (e.g., Lyons 1963, 1967). This line of research can in fact be said to have provided lexical semantics with a theoretical framework to understand the relations between neighboring words in the language system, which had not received sufficient attention before. However, the excessive focus on the language system and the general lack of concern that the structuralist onomasiological orientation towards meaning shows for actual usage and language context is highly problematic. This creates major complications when it comes to explaining the existence of alternative forms such as synonyms, since it leads to descriptions which are too restrictive. For an in-depth analysis of the relations of particular synonym sets, it is certainly not sufficient to state that such relations exist between the members of the set, but an analysis of the multiple factors determining the choice between such expressions is also required. This change of perspective, however, involves usage considerations and requires a shift to a usage-based onomasiological orientation, which emerges in later traditions of semantics (cf. for instance, Grondelaers, Speelman, and Geeraerts 2007). The lack of examination of the motivations underlying lexical variation is one of the main causes for the abandonment of the structuralist view of onomasiology by current scholars in the field.

The school known as neostructuralist semantics comprises a series of approaches which are possibly of a more heterogenous nature than those discussed so far. This is because they do not adhere to any particular theoretical framework, but are instead grouped under the label of neostructuralism due to their affinity with structuralism. Within this group of approaches, the distributional corpus-based method is undoubtedly one of the most prominent in the field of synonymy and is thus of particular relevance for the purposes of this monograph. Even though Sinclair (1966; 1987; 1991; 2004) is considered to be the pioneer of this approach, its main principles are based on ideas already present in earlier work, particularly that of Firth (e.g., 1935; 1957). Firth is thought to be one of the founding fathers of this approach as he believed distributional patterns and, in particular, *collocations*, to be crucial in lexico-semantic analysis. This idea is reflected in his famous quote "you shall know a word by the company it keeps" (1957: 11), in which he highlights the correlation existing between the semantic and functional features of lexical items and their distributional patterns. Sinclair (1966) extends Firth's ideas by stating that the principal duty of researchers devoted to lexico-semantic analysis is to describe the collocational tendencies of lexical items by means of the examination of large collections of natural language data, i.e., corpora.

The distributional corpus-based method rests on three major tenets, namely, a radical usage-based orientation, a paramount importance of collocation, and a strong link with statistical analysis (cf. Geeraerts 2010: 167). The first of these tenets reflects the assumption that it is only by adopting a usage-based perspective that we can reach an adequate description of meaning. Distributionalists thus reject introspective analysis of invented sentences presented in isolation and emphasize the need to analyze central and recurrent usage patterns of words to uncover their internal semantic structure. In fact, results of studies employing this radical usage-based methodology came to challenge previous assumptions about both linguistic data and form-meaning associations by demonstrating the untrustworthiness of intuitive judgements about the frequency and distribution of particular words and word senses. The second tenet, that is, the importance of collocation, was first emphasized by advocates of the distributional approach, but has since then become one of the central notions in lexical semantics. The notion of collocation, which can be preliminarily defined as the co-occurrence of two or more lexical items that commonly appear juxtaposed in a text or utterance, is a central one in this monograph and will be further discussed in Chapter 2.

Finally, the use of statistical analysis also constitutes one of the main principles of distributionalism and is closely related to collocational analysis. Major advancements concerning information technology and statistics in the last decades have led to the emergence of different association measures that allow the objective identification of collocation and the quantification of collocational strength between co-occurring lexical items (e.g., Church et al. 1991; Clear 1993), including Pointwise Mutual Information (PMI), *t*-score, log-likelihood, and ΔP (e.g., Gries 2013), among others.

The distributional corpus-based approach has been successfully applied not only to lexical semantics, but also to research in other fields such as language teaching and learning (cf. for instance, Gablasova, Brezina, and McEnery 2017) and computational linguistics (cf. e.g., Schulz and Aziz 2016). More importantly for our purposes, an ever-increasing number of studies have shown that the distributional corpus-based approach is a particularly useful one to reveal fine-grained semantic and usage distinctions between near-synonyms. A detailed overview of such research is provided in Sections 2.2 and 2.3, which deal with synonymy in depth. Despite the methodological strengths of the approach, it is ultimately, as argued by Geeraerts (2010: 177–178), a method rather than a theory, as it is not always clear how the distributional patterns uncovered relate to theoretical issues in lexical semantics. Therefore, distributional methods have recently been adopted for semantic analysis under the theoretical framework of cognitive semantics, which embeds the study of meaning in the study of human cognition in general, as is done in the present monograph.

Cognitive semantics, which emerged in the 1980s, is probably the approach that enjoys the widest currency in contemporary semantic research, given that it brought the study of meaning back to the fore in linguistic research, particularly in comparison with previous movements such as generativism.[1] Cognitive semantics adopts a maximalist perspective in which many of the oppositions mentioned above are completely abolished (namely, semantic vs. encyclopedic knowledge and use vs. system), whereas others are maintained (namely, semasiology vs. onomasiology and synchrony vs. diachrony) but none is given priority over the other. For this reason, semantic descriptions within this school are more comprehensive than in previous traditions and many of the problems encountered before disappear or are minimized.

---

[1] Generative semantics is not discussed here given that meaning was relegated to a secondary role within this approach, which focused mainly on the study of syntax and issues of semantics considered important within this school are in fact closely related to syntax (e.g., Lakoff 1970; Fillmore 1968).

Four central principles lie at the core of the conception of meaning in cognitive semantics (Geeraerts 2006: 3–6):
(i) Linguistic meaning implies perspectivization.
(ii) Linguistic meaning is characterized by its dynamicity and flexibility.
(iii) Linguistic meaning is encyclopedic and therefore not independent from the rest of human cognition.
(iv) Linguistic meaning is experiential in nature and heavily dependent on actual use.

These four central tenets constitute the foundation of the major models and theories within cognitive semantics, such as the conceptual theories of metaphor and metonymy, idealized cognitive models, frame theory, and prototype theory. Prototype theory, which is especially important for the purposes of the present monograph, emerged and gained importance in the 1970s in the work of Rosch (e.g., 1973) due to the limitations of the models based on the classical orientation to category structure postulated by Aristotle. The most essential notion is that of *prototypicality*, which basically refers to the degree of representativeness of the members of categories: whereas some members are more central and therefore more prototypical, others are more peripheral and therefore less prototypical. In this view, categories are said to exhibit a number of prototypicality effects that can help us explain how they are organized. The first is *non-equality* or *gradience*, which means that there is no clear-cut delimitation between neighboring linguistic concepts, but instead a cline. Therefore, we talk about degrees or gradience of membership within categories. Closely related to this is *non-discreteness* of categories, which entails that the limits between concepts are only clear-cut in the center not in the periphery, where membership is often uncertain. Another prototypicality effect is that of *family resemblance*, that is, category membership depends on a series of features, but most members only exhibit a subset of these features and do therefore not coincide in all of them. Therefore, within this view there is no set of necessary and sufficient characteristics that define all members of a given category or concept (for more information on these prototypicality effects, cf. for instance Geeraerts 1997: 11; 2010: 187–189; Grondelaers, Speelman, and Geeraerts 2007: 989–990).

Related to the notion of prototypicality just described are those of *entrenchment* and *salience*. Entrenchment refers to the process whereby a linguistic unit, such as a new word or a new sense of an already existing word, becomes more cognitively established in the grammar or lexicon due to its more frequent occurrence in actual language use (Langacker 1987: 59). However, the concept does not typically refer to the overall frequency of a word, but rather to its frequency with respect to a particular sense or function, especially when alternative choices exist to express that same sense or function (e.g., Schmid 2007: 119). Therefore, entrenchment is particularly relevant when dealing with onomasiological processes such as the relation of synonymy as members of a synonym set commonly exhibit different degrees of entrenchment or *onomasiological salience* (cf. Chapter 4).

Given that categorization processes are experientially based, we can easily observe how features such as prototypicality and entrenchment may vary across both space and time depending on the different experiences of language users. For instance, varying degrees of exposure to objects or situations lead to differences in prototypicality and entrenchment. A case in point, which shows the influence of time on changes in prototypicality, is that of the concept or category SHIP. This is so because its prototypical members nowadays probably differ substantially from those in the Middle Ages, even though the core meaning is still 'vehicle for transportation across masses of water' (Kay and Allan 2015: 39). This example demonstrates how sociocultural changes and technological advances lead to differences in degrees of prototypicality. Such changes and advances often bring about modifications of an existing category, the disappearance of some concepts associated with a given category, or the incorporation of new categories (Blank 1999: 71–73). Given the impact of experience on category structure, research within cognitive semantics has attempted to account for semantic variation and change by means of usage-based corpus approaches that allow the quantification of features such as the prototypicality and entrenchment of specific concepts and categories, as well as the items employed to refer to them (e.g., Geeraerts 1988; Soares da Silva 2015). These approaches can be said to constitute a continuation of the diachronic semantic research set out in the historical-philological tradition briefly discussed above, given that they echo many of the principles of this school.

The contributions of cognitive semantics are numerous and are primarily due to its maximalist stance to meaning, as it allows for new ways to systematically explain issues which had only exerted a minor influence in preceding schools, such as the apparent fuzziness of concepts and categories and their structure around prototypical centers. Similarly, a close link between meaning and sociocultural aspects, which is also a fundamental principle of cognitive semantics, offers a suitable framework to explain semantic change by resorting to the study of non-linguistic history. However, cognitive semantics is certainly not devoid of problems, but the many benefits of the approach demonstrate its great potential for semantic description. New developments are constantly appearing and improving semantic analysis within this tradition. In fact, Geeraerts (2010: 240–266) identifies a set of interesting research areas in need of further refinement. Among these, one particular line of research is related to the analyses provided in the present monograph, namely usage-based approaches to the study of onomasiological variation which focus on the identification of factors that underlie the choice between synonymous expressions by employing electronic corpora (see also Grondelaers, Speelman and Geeraerts 2007). Although these factors are commonly of an internal nature (e.g., Divjak 2006; 2010; Divjak and Gries 2008; Liu 2010), many studies also focus on extralinguistic factors, and thus have a more sociolinguistic orientation (e.g., Speelman, Grondelaers, and Geeraerts 2003; Levshina 2011). Many of the internal factors studied in research of this type are related to co-occurrence features of the synonyms, including collocational patterns, which, in turn, points to a close link between this line of research and the neostructuralist distributional corpus-based approach. It is, therefore, at the crossroads of the distributional approach, usage-based onomasiology, and historical linguistics that the analyses in this book are located.

1.2 Aims, scope, and contributions

The main goal of the present monograph is to fill a gap in the specialized literature on synonymy by conducting a usage-based corpus study of a set of near-synonymous adjectives from the relatively little studied semantic domain of SMELL in nineteenth- and twentieth-century American English, namely, *fragrant*, *perfumed*, *scented*, *sweet-scented*, and *sweet-smelling*, which designate the concept PLEASANT SMELLING. The five adjectives are illustrated in examples (1)–(5):

(1) They made campfires with top-quality hardwood, which released **fragrant** smoke, to cook for their families. (*COHA*, 2009, FIC, FarawayWarNovel)

(2) Dellius had seen enough easterners to know that the curls were not dirty greasy; easterners pomaded their locks with **perfumed** creams. (*COHA*, 2007, FIC, ColorsInsulting)

(3) Avoid chemical irritants in bubble baths and heavily **scented** soaps, and don't let her sit in a wet bathing suit for too long. (*COHA*, 2009, MAG, COCA)

(4) As his eyes adjusted ever so slowly to the gloom, he saw looming shadows, blurred shapes like enormous trees that stirred not at all in the gentle **sweet-scented** wind. (*COHA*, 2005, FIC, FantasySciFi)

(5) Route 214 turned out to be a winding lane through **sweet-smelling** fields long abandoned to goldenrod and blackberry brambles. (*COHA*, 2008, FIC, BookOldHouses)

The reasons for choosing this specific synonym set are twofold. First, the *Historical Thesaurus of the Oxford English Dictionary* (*HTOED*) lists an extremely great amount of words in the semantic domain of SMELL, a large number of which are in fact adjectives. Many of these adjectives are defined in a similar way in dictionaries, with some minor variations. Therefore, this seems to be a particularly rich semantic field for the study of near-synonymy. Second, the rather low degree of polysemy of the near-synonymous adjectives at issue here constitutes an advantage for a study focusing on synonymy. If a highly polysemous set had been selected instead, the study would not have been focused exclusively on the semantic relation of synonymy, since polysemy would also play a prominent role in the discussion.

The data used is drawn from the *Corpus of Historical American English* (*COHA*; Davies 2010–), which covers the time span 1810–2009 and contains over 400 million words, thus being one of the largest structured historical corpora to date (Davies 2012, 2019). The focus is on the distributional patterns of the selected near-synonymous expressions as a proxy to quantify their functional (dis)similarity. Therefore, following recent synchronic approaches to synonymy, this semantic relation is here measured in quantitative terms by examining a series of factors which have been shown to play an important role in lexical choice. The factors analyzed represent both language-internal semantic and non-semantic contexts of use, as well as language-external variables. The influence of these factors is examined over the time span covered by the corpus, which is divided into four 50-year periods, namely, 1810–1859, 1860–1909, 1910–1959, and 1960–2009, in order to capture how each lexical item, as well as the relation between the members of the set, evolves over time. To this purpose, the data is submitted to both univariate and multivariate statistical techniques which have been previously employed to measure the semantic (dis)similarity of near-synonymous expressions from a synchronic perspective. Consequently, a secondary objective of the present monograph is to assess the usefulness for diachronic research on lexical synonymy of these primarily synchronic quantitative methods. Furthermore, given the nature of the source of data examined and the methods employed, the studies included in this book also showcase how big data (cf. Renouf 2019) can be fruitfully analyzed to dig deeper into lexico-semantic change undergone by relatively low-frequency items, thus complementing work in the same field which employs smaller datasets and/or qualitative and classical philological approaches.

From a theoretical perspective, the analyses in the present monograph are grounded on the tenets of neostructuralist and cognitive semantics, both of which emphasize the utmost importance of actual use in language structure. In addition, the study draws on insights from theories of semantic change by considering the various processes at work in the development of the internal semantic structure of synonym sets, particularly those of differentiation and substitution, but also that of attraction, as well as the underlying motivations of such processes and their connection with the extralinguistic reality. Therefore, yet another aim of this monograph is to determine whether the traditional theory of competition and substitution is sufficient to account for the changes taking place in the selected synonym set, or whether, on the contrary, it is necessary to resort also to other processes of semantic change such as attraction.

In sum, by adding a diachronic dimension to the quantitative study of lexical near-synonymy, this monograph provides one of the first applications of primarily synchronic methods to historical research on the semantic relation of synonymy. Moreover, the study considers a larger set of near-synonymous expressions from the same domain than is typically examined in the specialized literature and these near-synonyms are analyzed across a wide variety of contexts of use. Therefore, despite the relatively long research tradition on synonymy, this work provides an innovative approach to the study of this semantic relation, as well as new and interesting findings regarding the development of near-synonyms over time.

1.3 Overview of the book

The present monograph is divided into eight chapters, organized as follows. Chapter 2 provides a review of the relevant literature on synonymy. Chapter 3 explains the data used for the analyses conducted, focusing on the near-synonyms object of study and the corpus employed, as well as the data extraction and annotation processes. Chapters 4–6 present the results of three separate corpus-based studies on the concept PLEASANT SMELLING and the items denoting this concept. Chapter 7 provides a hypothesis to account for the existent variation of the concept PLEASANT SMELLING over time. Finally, Chapter 8 offers some concluding remarks and suggestions for future research.

Chapter 2 zooms in on the semantic relation of synonymy. First, the most relevant classifications of synonyms into types are discussed in Section 2.1. The main conclusion drawn from these classifications is that a distinction between absolute synonymy and near-synonymy is the most adequate for an empirical investigation into the semantic phenomenon of synonymy. Then, Section 2.2 moves on to an in-depth review of synchronic usage-based corpus studies on specific pairs or groups of near-synonyms that have been published over the last 30 years. Two separate waves of research are first identified and explained in Section 2.2.1, which suggest that considerable developments have recently taken place in this area of research. Then, in Section 2.2.2, the focus turns to studies on near-synonymous adjectives, since the items belonging to the synonym set analyzed in this study are precisely adjectives. Finally, Section 2.3 provides an overview of diachronic research on lexical synonymy by first considering the few usage-based corpus studies on the historical development of particular pairs or groups of near-synonyms, and then shifting the attention to general processes of semantic change relevant for the diachronic study of synonymy.

Chapter 3 is concerned with issues related to the data employed in the analyses provided in subsequent chapters. The chapter opens with a description in Section 3.1 of the synonym set object of study; it outlines the main motivations for its selection and then reviews the information on these lexical items in various present-day and historical dictionaries and thesauri. Next, Section 3.2 discusses the corpus used as a source of data, as well as the data retrieval process. Lastly, Section 3.3 deals with the data annotation process. Considerable space is devoted here to the explanation of the language-internal and language-external variables used for the codification of the data.

Chapter 4 moves on to the first corpus-based study presented in the monograph, which constitutes a descriptive univariate analysis of the data. The chapter is divided into four sections, each focusing on a different aspect of the synonym set. Section 4.1 provides the overall frequency of the five near-synonyms, as well as their frequency developments over the time span 1810–2009. Then, Section 4.2 turns to the concept PLEASANT SMELLING as a whole, that is, as designated by the five adjectives, and its distribution across senses and semantic categories of modified nouns. Next, Section 4.3 examines the behavior of each adjective separately, thus offering a semasiological perspective of the data. Finally, Section 4.4 deals with the competition between the near-synonyms in different semantic contexts, hence adopting an onomasiological orientation.

Chapter 5 delves deeper into the onomasiological structure of the synonym set. This is done by measuring the competition between the near-synonyms across a large number of intralinguistic and extralinguistic factors. Here, the perspective adopted is a multivariate one and hence a series of more sophisticated statistical techniques are employed. These statistical methods are explained in Section 5.1, together with the dataset used for this particular analysis. Section 5.2, in turn, discusses the results of the study by first focusing on the effects of the predictors included (Section 5.2.1) and then offering a preliminary enquiry into the collocational behavior of the adjectives (Section 5.2.2), where their individual noun collocates are taken into consideration. The chapter closes with a discussion of the main findings in Section 5.3, highlighting the importance of the idiosyncratic collocational preferences of the adjectives under scrutiny, a topic which is taken up in Chapter 6.

Chapter 6 opens with a description of the dataset and the methods used in the collocational analyses (Section 6.1). Section 6.2 deals with the results of these analyses and their discussion. A bird's-eye view of the collocational behavior of the near-synonymous adjectives is provided in Section 6.2.1 by having a look at their general co-occurrence patterns before moving to a more qualitative examination of the most prominent individual noun collocates in Section 6.2.2.

Chapter 7 provides a hypothesis to account for the existent variation of the concept PLEASANT SMELLING over time that has been uncovered in previous chapters of the monograph. This hypothesis is postulated on the basis of the social and technological transformations experienced by American society over the period analyzed in the studies presented in Chapters 4–6. Section 7.1 offers a review of recent research on the interplay between social and linguistic changes which provides interesting insights both on the possibilities and limitations of using corpus data to explore how extralinguistic changes at the cultural and social levels are reflected in language. In Section 7.2 the focus is on particular changes that took place in American society following the First and Second Industrial Revolutions as it is hypothesized that they might well have steered the semantic changes undergone by the near-synonymous adjectives. Section 7.3 turns the attention to the data and methodology of the analyses conducted to verify or refute the hypothesis postulated. First, a dictionary-based approach is adopted, the results of which are complemented by a more data-driven approach investigating the conceptualization of a series of semantic domains that might reflect the aforementioned extralinguistic changes. Section 7.4 presents the findings, which are then discussed in Section 7.5.

The monograph concludes with Chapter 8, a summary of the most relevant generalizations that can be drawn from the studies conducted in the preceding chapters and the identification of some areas that can be further improved and taken up in future research on the topic.

2 Synonymy

In the introductory chapter synonymy was defined as a relation of identity of meaning between two or more words or word senses. However, it was claimed that a less strict definition is more suitable for this semantic relation, as words are rarely – if ever – completely identical in meaning. In fact, different types of synonyms can be distinguished depending on which aspects of meaning they share, i.e., whether they match only in denotative meaning or whether they coincide also in other dimensions, such as connotation, style, and/or collocation (cf. Section 2.1 below). This implies that different degrees of synonymy exist, and it appears to be the case that competent language users have an intuition about some words or word senses being more synonymous than others (e.g., Lyons 1968: 447; Cruse 1986: 265–268). Even within a specific set of synonyms, speakers commonly have the feeling that some members of a synonym set share more semantic features than others and can thus be interchanged in more contexts of use. However, although synonymy is typically defined and viewed as a semantic relation of similarity, it is also crucial to consider the differences between synonymous words in order to provide a comprehensive picture of the semantic relation that holds between them. This is so because, as has already been pointed out, a great majority of synonyms, despite being semantically similar in one or more aspects, also differ in other respects, which prevents them from being freely interchangeable when used.

Once the focus shifts from concentrating solely on the similarities to considering also the level of contrast between synonymous words, it becomes evident that the way in which synonyms differ from each other varies from synonym set to synonym set, as well as from synonym to synonym. Edmonds (1999: Chapter 3) claims that there are at least 35 ways in which synonyms can differ and provides evidence of the complex and intriguing nature of synonymy. In fact, research on synonymy has been and continues to be a rich field of study in many areas of linguistics, including lexicography (e.g., Atkins and Levin 1995; Bergenholtz and Gouws 2012; Murphy 2013), computational linguistics (e.g., Edmonds 1999; Edmonds and Hirst 2002; Inkpen and Hirst 2006), and language learning and teaching (e.g., Martin 1984; Xiao and McEnery 2006; Liu and Zong 2016), among others. Giving a detailed account of all the research conducted on this semantic relation therefore lies beyond the scope of the present monograph, which analyzes a specific set of synonyms from the perspective of the distributional corpus-based approach. Instead, the focus of this chapter is exclusively on studies employing such a methodology to examine the internal semantic structure of pairs or sets of synonyms, either in a strict neostructuralist fashion or by resorting also to concepts and theories from cognitive semantics. Additionally, the emphasis is mainly on lexical synonymy, thus excluding most of the literature on constructional synonymy, though some studies of the latter kind are considered for methodological reasons.

However, before reviewing existing research on individual groups of synonyms, I describe in more detail the different types of synonyms identified mainly in structuralist work. As such, this chapter is structured as follows. Section 2.1 is concerned with the classifications of types of synonymy, with a special emphasis on three types that are most recurrent: absolute synonymy, cognitive synonymy, and near-synonymy. Then, in Section 2.2, previous work on specific pairs and sets of synonyms employing the corpus-based contextual approach is summarized and assessed, focusing particularly on methodological aspects such as the number and types of factors analyzed to determine the choice between synonyms, the statistical techniques applied, but also relevant findings and contributions of such studies. While Section 2.2 deals exclusively with synonymy from a synchronic perspective, Section 2.3 considers the few corpus-based studies on lexical synonyms that have been conducted from a diachronic viewpoint.

2.1 Classifications of synonymy

As mentioned above, synonymy is a linguistic phenomenon which has been widely researched in different subfields of linguistics and which has also been studied from a broad variety of perspectives and theoretical frameworks. One early research area, primarily within the structuralist school, aimed at providing classifications of synonyms, in which different types were identified depending on the extent and kind of semantic overlap that exists between two or more words or word senses. However, to fully understand these classifications, a succinct summary of the different dimensions of meaning that are typically distinguished seems in order here.

Although at least seven types of meaning are distinguished in the specialized literature (cf. for instance, Leech 1974: Chapter 2), four of these are especially relevant for our purposes: *denotational meaning*, *expressive meaning*, *stylistic meaning*, and *collocational meaning*. Denotational meaning refers to what a word designates in the extralinguistic world, be it an entity, an event, an action, or a process, which is said to be the reference or *denotatum* of that particular word. Expressive meaning, on the other hand, is used to refer to the overtones carried by words (i.e., connotations) as well as to speakers' positions and evaluative judgements toward words and their referents (i.e., affect). This dimension of meaning allows language users to regard lexical items as more or less neutral, negative, or positive. The third type, stylistic meaning, concerns aspects such as formality, discourse field, and medium of production. Additionally, relationships between the participants in a linguistic exchange are also of fundamental importance for this dimension, since familiarity and social distance play a crucial role when it comes to stylistic choices. Collocational or collocative meaning, i.e., the dimension of meaning which concerns the way in which lexical items are used in combination with other items in the lexicon, is probably the most important dimension for the purposes of the present monograph and is therefore discussed more thoroughly.

The term collocation refers to the co-occurrence of two or more lexical items that commonly appear juxtaposed in a text or utterance: the individual lexical items making up a collocation are known as *nodes* and *collocates*. The former term designates the lexical item which is the object of study, while the latter relates to the items that appear together with a node (e.g., Sinclair 1991: 115; Stubbs 2002: 29–30). However, the notion of collocation has received various slightly different interpretations over the years, which have led to the existence of a number of distinct definitions in the specialized literature.[2] Here, we emphasize three of the most important types of definitions of the term, labeled *textual*, *statistical*, and *associative* or *psychological* (cf. for instance, Partington 1998: 15–16).

Starting with the textual definition, this interpretation views collocation as a syntagmatic relation of co-occurrence of lexical items appearing within a short span of words in any given text (e.g., Sinclair 1991: 170; Partington 1998: 15; Stubbs 2002: 24). As such, two words, lemmas, or more complex structures are said to form a collocation when they occur together in a textual unit such as a phrase, a clause, a sentence, or a larger discourse segment. A proximity limit is often set to establish which co-occurring items are to be contemplated as collocates of a node. Such a proximity limit typically involves a context window of a given number of words to the left and to the right of the node. For instance, a restriction of four or five words – often calculated in terms of lexical words – is a typical measurement and is often formalized as L4–R4 and L5–R5. A further refinement of the textual interpretation is to use a more specific context window in which only immediately adjacent or syntactically related lexical items of the node are included. To illustrate this, if one is interested in researching adjectival nodes, especially when used in attributive function, it is probably more elucidating to analyze their noun collocates as they reveal more about the function of the adjectives than other types of collocates. By means of illustration, consider

---

[2] Gries (2013) provides a comprehensive overview of the work done on collocation over the last half century and how research in this field can be improved.

the example provided by Geeraerts (2086: 282–284). In this study, he examines *vers(e)*, a Dutch polysemous adjective which can be translated as 'fresh' in English and demonstrates that depending on the nouns with which *vers(e)* co-occurs it means either fresh in the sense of 'recent', as in *verse wond 'fresh wound'*, or fresh in the sense of 'pure, optimal, untainted', as in *verse lucht 'fresh air'*.

Moving on to the statistical definition this view assumes that only those lexical items that co-occur with a node often enough to be statistically significant, that is, those that occur more often than is expected by chance, should be included in collocational analysis (e.g., Hoey 1991: 7–8). As Sinclair notes (1991: 170), this definition of collocation is perhaps the most widely used in contemporary semantic studies, especially since an ever-increasing quantity of corpus data is nowadays available, thus enabling the research community to calculate the association of strength between lexical items through measurements such as PMI, among others. Such means allow researchers to draw detailed conclusions about how lexical items behave in discourse and, more importantly, to explain their particular collocational preferences (e.g., Partington 1998: 16).

The last definition of collocation to be discussed is the associative or psychological one. It is commonly known as the associative definition because, as native speakers of a specific language, our mental lexicon contains information about which collocations are typical and untypical in particular contexts of use. This is what Leech (1974: 17) calls *collocative meaning* and it contributes information regarding how lexical items are used, enabling speakers to correctly combine words and preventing them from making certain combinations.

Besides differing in collocational preferences, lexical items can also diverge as regards their *collocational range*. This term refers to the amount of types – as opposed to tokens – of collocates that a given lexical item co-occurs with. For instance, the adjective *bad* can modify a much wider range of nouns than the semantically similar but much more specific adjective *substandard*.

As we have seen, the notion of collocation is a rather vast one and can therefore be understood in different ways. As such, it also takes several different forms. Besides collocation, Sinclair (1991; 1996) establishes three additional important levels of co-occurrence, namely, *colligation*, *semantic preference*, and *semantic prosody*. Colligation refers to the co-occurrence of a particular lexical item with grammatical or function words, thus being opposed to collocation, which is a co-occurrence relation between lexical words. Semantic preferences, in turn, have to do with the semantic features that the collocates of a particular node share with one another. For instance, many of the typical noun collocates of *large* refer to amounts and sizes, including the lemmas *number*, *scale*, and *part*. Many of the collocates of *large* can therefore be said to belong to the same semantic field (Stubbs 2002: 65). It is important to note here that two or more lexical items, for instance, synonyms, may have the same semantic preferences, but still differ as regards collocational preferences, that is, as regards the specific collocates with which they occur within a particular semantic category. Finally, semantic prosody relates to the connotations of the typical collocates of a node, that is, whether they express negative or positive overtones. We thus speak about lexical items as having a positive, negative, or neutral semantic prosody depending on the evaluative attitudes conveyed by its neighboring words (cf. e.g., Stubbs 2002: 64–66; Geeraerts 2010: 170–173).

Out of the four dimensions of meaning discussed (i.e., denotational, expressive, stylistic, and collocational), many scholars agree that denotational meaning is the most relevant dimension (e.g., Murphy 2003: 137). In fact, two or more words must share the same denotation and thus refer to the same concept in the extralinguistic reality, to be regarded as synonymous, while they are allowed to vary in other aspects of meaning. To provide an example, *woman* and *lady* are considered synonyms as they both denote an 'adult human female'. Nevertheless, the two words differ as regards expressive meaning: whereas *woman* is fairly neutral, connoting a vast set of properties, *lady* is expressively more restricted, since it is closely associated with features such as class, status, elegance, and manners, and thus carries a positive connotation (Leith 1983: 70–72). However, as shown by this example, all non-denotational dimensions of meaning are crucial when an onomasiological orientation is adopted, since as Grondelaers, Speelman, and Geeraerts (2007: 994) point out, "[. . .] the very definition of nonreferential [i.e., non-denotational] meaning involves the concept of onomasiological alternatives". It is precisely along these other dimensions of meaning that the great majority of synonyms differ and, consequently, they must be accounted for in a semantic analysis of synonymy.

Different classifications of synonymy have been put forward in the literature and, as a result, a variety of labels have been used to refer to the same types of synonyms. Here, we focus exclusively on the different types of synonymy established in the most important works on the topic, namely those by Lyons (1968; 1981a; 1981b; 1995) and Cruse (1986; 2000; 2002), but also that of Murphy (2003).

Lyons' (1968) early classification is probably the most comprehensive one as it distinguishes between two dimensions: total synonymy, that is, those words which are interchangeable in all contexts of use, and complete synonymy, i.e., those words which are equivalent both on the denotative and connotative dimensions of meaning. By crossing these two dimensions, four types of synonyms can be established, namely (i) complete and total synonyms, (ii) complete and non-total synonyms, (iii) incomplete and total synonyms, and (iv) incomplete and non-total synonyms. For example, the first type, complete and total, includes those synonyms which share both their denotational and expressive meanings and are interchangeable in all contexts. This type refers to what is usually termed absolute synonymy. However, although this classification is the most exhaustive one, it can also be said to provide unnecessary divisions. This is so because type (iii), incomplete and total synonymy, would refer to words or word senses which are interchangeable in all contexts of use without being denotationally and expressively equivalent. Such a relation is quite unlikely – if not impossible – to occur in language.[3] Lyons' (1995) latest classification differs considerably from his previous ones (i.e., 1968; 1981a; 1981b), as he establishes a different division into absolute synonymy, cognitive synonymy, near-synonymy, and partial synonymy. *Partial synonymy* roughly corresponds with type (ii) in his early classification (i.e., complete and non-total). The reason for drawing a distinction between absolute and partial synonyms, according to Lyons, is that whereas absolute synonyms are most certainly non-existent in language, partial synonyms, though infrequent, do exist. This is because, in contrast to absolute synonyms, partial synonyms are equivalent both as concerns denotational and expressive meaning, but need not be interchangeable in all contexts.

Cruse (1986), in turn, proposes a three-way split into absolute synonymy, cognitive synonymy, and plesionymy, which partially overlap with Lyons' (1995) typology.[4] In subsequent classifications by Cruse (2000; 2002), the same three types of synonyms are present, although the labels for the latter two vary. Table 1 below summarizes the various classifications of synonymy by the two authors and the terminology discussed so far:

Table 1: Classifications of synonymy by Lyons and Cruse.

Definition \ Author	Lyons (1968)	Lyons (1995)	Cruse (1986)	Cruse (2000; 2002)
Identical on all dimensions of meaning and interchangeable in all contexts of use	Complete & total	Absolute synonymy	Absolute synonymy	Absolute synonymy
Identical on all dimensions of meaning but not interchangeable in all contexts of use	Complete & non-total	Partial synonymy	–	–

---

3 Some subsequent formulations of Lyons' classification overlap substantially with the original one while at the same time differing in certain respects, both regarding the labels used and the types identified (for more details, cf. 1981a; 1981b).
4 Near-synonymy, rather than plesionymy (e.g., Storjohann 2009), is the label adopted here as it is the most frequent term employed in contemporary research on synonymy.

Table 1 (continued)

Author / Definition	Lyons (1968)	Lyons (1995)	Cruse (1986)	Cruse (2000; 2002)
Not identical on all dimensions of meaning but interchangeable in all contexts of use	Incomplete & total	–	–	–
Identical on the denotative dimension of meaning, but not on other dimensions, and not interchangeable in all contexts of use	Incomplete & non-total	Cognitive synonymy	Cognitive synonymy	Propositional synonymy
Similar but not identical on the denotational dimension of meaning and not interchangeable in all contexts of use		Near-synonymy	Plesionymy	Near-synonymy

In addition to Lyons' and Cruse's classifications of synonymy, Murphy (2003) postulates yet another typology, in which she distinguishes between synonyms in terms of denotative meaning only and synonyms which share more than their denotation. As regards denotative meaning, she considers two dimensions, namely (i) how many senses synonymous words share and (ii) how similar the shared senses are. *Full synonyms* are those which share all their senses and these senses are all identical (e.g., *groundhog* and *woodchuck*). *Sense synonyms*, in turn, are those which share one or more senses, but not all. As in the case of full synonyms, the shared senses are also identical. One example would be *couch* and *sofa*, which share the sense '[a] long, stuffed seat with a back and ends or end, used for reclining' (*OED* s.v. *sofa* n. 2), but not the meaning '[a] couch upon which a patient reclines when undergoing psychoanalysis or psychiatric treatment' (*OED*, s.v. *couch* n. 3b), which only the former term can designate. Full synonyms and sense synonyms are included within the general category of cognitive synonyms, or *logical synonyms* in Murphy's terminology. Finally, lexical items that are similar, but not identical in their senses are called near-synonyms, as in the case of *fog(gy)* and *mist(y)*, which differ as regards the density of the weather phenomenon they denote (see below). Concerning non-denotative dimensions, synonyms may also differ. According to Murphy (2003: 151), such aspects of meaning can either enhance or diminish their degree of similarity. For instance, the sense synonyms *drunk* and *inebriated*, despite sharing the sense '[a]ffected by alcohol to the extent of losing control of one's faculties or behavior' (*Lexico*, s.v. *drunk* adj. 1), differ in register, the former being more informal than the latter.

Notwithstanding the existence of these and other classifications of synonymy, what is relevant here is that three types are recurrently mentioned in most classifications: absolute synonymy, cognitive synonymy, and near-synonymy. The first of these three types is thought to constitute one of the endpoints of the synonym continuum, namely that of absolute identity of meaning. Exactly what counts as absolute identity of meaning depends largely on the types of meaning that are considered to be relevant. Nevertheless, most scholars agree that absolute synonymy refers to those words or word senses which are identical on all four dimensions of meaning mentioned above. Ullmann (1957: 109–110), for instance, claims that two criteria need to be met for absolute synonymy to occur. On the one hand, absolute synonyms must be able to substitute for each other in all contexts of use and, on the other, they must not differ in neither denotational nor non-denotational aspects of meaning. Cruse (1986; 2000) adds yet a third criterion, that of contextual normality, which particularly useful for a contextual approach such as the one adopted in the present monograph. According to such a perspective, in addition to being interchangeable, absolute synonyms must also be *equinormal* in all contexts of use. Along these lines, Cruse (2000: 157) argues that

> [. . .] absolute synonyms can be defined as items which are equinormal in all contexts: that is to say, for two lexical items X and Y, if they are to be recognized as absolute synonyms, in any context in which X is fully normal, Y is, too; in any context in which X is slightly odd, Y is also slightly odd, and in any context in which X is totally anomalous, the same is true of Y.

This definition evidences that very severe requirements are imposed on words or word senses for them to comply with the criteria for absolute synonymy and demonstrates why this type of synonymy is very rare – if not inexistent – in language. Cruse (2000: 268–269) tests some plausible candidates, for instance, *begin* and *commence*, and *almost* and *nearly*, and draws the conclusion that for all these synonymous pairs contexts in which one of the members is more normal than the other can be observed. In fact, it is commonly claimed that there is no reason why a semantic relation of this type should exist and be maintained in language, as it goes against the economy principle. As Taylor (2003: 264) states, "[absolute] synonymy would have to be regarded as an extravagant luxury, even dysfunctional, in that limited symbolic resources get squandered on the designation of one and the same semantic unit." In this statement, Taylor indirectly refers to the well-known *no-synonymy rule* or *isomorphic* state of languages, i.e., one form, one meaning (e.g., Bolinger 1977: ix–x, 9; Wierzbicka 1988: 13–14; Croft 2000: 176; Nuyts and Byloo 2015: 62–63), which makes languages work against absolute synonymy if it at some point comes to exist. This is an issue that has clear diachronic implications and is therefore further discussed in Section 2.3 below.

Concerning cognitive synonymy, this is a relation which holds between words or word senses that are identical on the denotational dimension and therefore mutually entail one another. In other words, cognitive synonyms, if substituted for one another in a particular context of use, generate clauses or sentences with the same truth-values. Nevertheless, such pairs or groups of synonyms do not meet the criteria for absolute synonymy because they differ in non-denotational traits, for instance, connotation (e.g., *firm* and *stubborn*), register (e.g., *drunk* and *pissed*), or style (e.g., *kick the bucket*, *die*, and *pass away*), or the language variety in which they occur, such as British English *autumn* and American English *fall* (Cruse 1986: 278–280; Desagulier 2014: 153). Given that cognitive synonyms differ in non-denotational traits, they are typically used in different speech situations, text-types, or discourse fields, and using one word in a context in which its synonym is more typical will probably result in an odd sentence.

Finally, near-synonymy, which is undoubtedly the most frequent type of synonymy in language, refers to those words or word senses that differ slightly in conceptual content and are thus not denotationally identical. As such, if substituted for one another, the generated sentences yield somewhat different truth-conditions. However, near-synonyms are still sufficiently semantically similar to be interchanged in many contexts of use. The denotational traits in which near-synonyms vary must, according to Cruse (2000: 159), "[. . .] be either minor or backgrounded". Differences between near-synonyms include, but are not limited to, aspects such as the following (examples taken from Cruse 2000: 157–160; Murphy 2003: 147; Divjak 2010: 3–4; Desagulier 2014: 153):

(i) Contiguity on a gradable continuum or degree, e.g., *fog(gy)* and *mist(y)*: Both *fog* and *mist* refer to '[a] cloud of water substance present in the atmosphere at or close to the surface of the earth' (*OED*, s.v. *fog* n. 2, I 1a; *mist*. n. 1, I 1a). However, *fog* is denser and thicker than *mist*, the latter being lighter and therefore not limiting visibility to the same extent as the former.

(ii) Nuances involving specialization, e.g., *laugh* and *giggle*: the verb *laugh* denotes any type of spontaneous movement of the lower part of the face, accompanied by an explosive vocal sound, to display emotions such as joy or amusement, arising in a wide variety of situations (*OED*, s.v. *laugh* v. 1a). In turn, the verb *giggle* is more specialized, as it refers to a particular way of laughing, namely a light and foolish type which occurs in a more restricted set of circumstances, including amusement but also uneasiness and embarrassment (*OED*, s.v. *giggle* v.1, a).

(iii) Prototypicality, e.g., *brave* and *courageous*: While *brave* is used to describe a fearless person in physical terms, *courageous* emphasizes the moral or intellectual dimension.

(iv) Viewpoint or connotation, e.g., *slim/slender* and *skinny*: The three terms are all used to refer to people who are thin, but whereas *slim* and *slender* have positive connotations, being associated with grace and elegance, *skinny* has a clearly negative connotation, being linked to unattractiveness.
(v) Aspectual variation, e.g., *calm* and *placid*: The former adjective is used to denote a determinate state, which is ephemeral, while the latter refers to a more inherent feature of a person or entity.

In contrast to absolute synonyms, near-synonyms cannot be considered uneconomical and unnecessary, especially since language users are more likely to devise differences between such related words than to abandon one or more of the terms. In fact, a great majority of scholars claim that near-synonyms add substantially to the lexical expressivity of language, as they enable speakers to convey different nuances of meaning in a very precise manner (cf. for instance, Edmonds and Hirst 2002: 107–108; Murphy 2003: 165–166). However, given that near-synonyms can vary on any dimension of meaning and since that variation is frequently multidimensional, even native speakers sometimes find it difficult to master the fine-grained differences that exist between them.

Although the distinction between cognitive synonyms and near-synonyms appears to be clear in theory, the boundary between the two types becomes much more problematic in practice. This is so because it is not often obvious whether two or more words differ solely in their non-denotational semantic traits or whether, on the contrary, slight differences in denotation also exist between them. Due to the difficulty in distinguishing between cognitive synonymy and near-synonymy when specific pairs or sets of synonyms are concerned, some scholars have argued for a two-fold division into synonym types, namely absolute synonymy vs. non-absolute synonymy or near-synonymy, thus dismissing the distinction between cognitive synonyms and near-synonyms. This is the standpoint adopted by Edmonds and Hirst (2002: 116–117) and Desaguliers (2014: 153), among others, and the one followed in the present analyses.

A great amount of research has been conducted on specific near-synonymous pairs or groups in the last few decades. Given that near-synonyms differ in one or more aspects of meaning, it is certainly not sufficient to state that a relation of partial equivalence exists between the members of a synonym set, but it is also necessary to examine the multiple factors determining the choice between them to reach a comprehensive understanding of their semantic relation. Such an approach is the only one which allows us to know for certain in which contexts and the reasons why we use one word instead of another one. Disentangling the differences between near-synonyms, which are often multivariate and related to semantic, stylistic, and morphosyntactic dimensions, among others, has been and continues to be the main aim of many studies with a usage-based onomasiological orientation. The remainder of this chapter is concerned with a review of such studies. Section 2.2. discusses synchronic research on lexical synonymy, while Section 2.3 considers studies with a diachronic perspective.

2.2 The distributional corpus-based approach and synonymy

Although synonymy in general has figured prominently in theories of lexical semantics, dating back to the structuralist school, the semantic structure of specific pairs or sets of lexical near-synonyms had until quite recently not received much attention, especially if compared to constructional near-synonyms and other semantic phenomena such as metaphor and polysemy, which have been the subject of an ever-increasing body of literature (Taylor 2003: 264; Geeraerts 2010: 264; Liu 2010: 57). Consequently, several scholars have lately stressed the need for more research in this field, which has led to the emergence over the last 30 years of studies following diverse types of methodologies within the distributional approach originally set out by Firth and Sinclair. The aim of this section is to offer an overview of the existing synchronic corpus-based research on specific synonym sets that has been carried out since the 1980s and the evolution of this line of research on methodological grounds. A detailed account of all studies is not provided here because not all the methods proposed in the literature are equally relevant for our purposes. This is so because the approach adopted in such studies differs widely depending on the specific groups of synonyms analyzed, the POS the synonyms belong to, and the factors that significantly influence the choice between them. This is to be expected since, as argued by Liu (2010: 61),

> [. . .] the use of diverse procedures makes perfect sense in the study of internal structures of near-synonym sets because the way near synonyms differ often varies from synonym to synonym and from set to set. [. . .] Thus a researcher has to decide, based on a close scrutiny of the features of the synonyms being examined, what micro-procedures to employ.[5]

Therefore, the next section provides some generalizations extracted from previous studies, primarily focusing on those dealing with adjectival near-synonyms, as the factors they consider have more in common with the analyses conducted in this monograph (cf. Chapters 4–6).

---

5 For a similar argument, cf. also Hanks (1996: 92; 96).

2.2.1 Two waves of research

The research reviewed in this section can be classified into different groups depending on three parameters related to the scope of the analyses and to methodological issues:

(i) Number of synonyms examined: pairs vs. larger sets (i.e., three or more synonyms).
(ii) Amount and type of factors conditioning the choice between synonyms, ranging from collocational and/or stylistic patterns only to a wider array of determinants of variation which include semantic, morphosyntactic, and/or extralinguistic factors.
(iii) Statistical techniques and measures used: from mere frequencies and percentages, to association measures of collocational strength (e.g., PMI, t-score), multivariate tests (e.g., Hierarchical Configural Frequency Analysis (HCFA), logistic regression analysis, multiple correspondence analysis), and clustering techniques (e.g., HAC).

Along these parameters, corpus-based synonymy research can be divided, with some exceptions, into two main waves. The first one includes mainly those studies published approximately before the mid-2000s, most of which focus on pairs of near-synonyms by making use of raw frequencies, percentages, or association measures in order to examine their collocational and stylistic patterns. By contrast, in the second wave, which can be said to take off with the works of Divjak (2006) and Divjak and Gries (2006; 2008), the focus shifts to larger groups of near-synonyms. Here, in addition to accounting for collocational and stylistic behavior, further factors from different linguistic levels are also considered, including semantics and morphosyntax. A direct corollary of this multidimensional perspective is the use of more advanced and sophisticated techniques, which allow for the inclusion of a larger number of variables. The development of corpus-based research on lexical synonymy over the last 30 years can thus be summarized as shown in Figure 1.

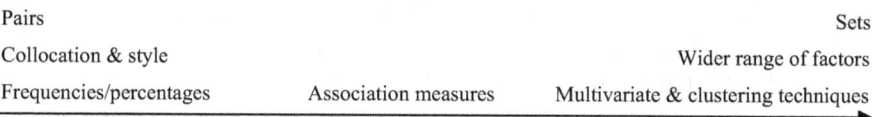

Figure 1: Development of corpus-based research on lexical synonymy over the last 30 years.

As has already been mentioned, most of the early research in this field considered pairs of near-synonyms (cf. for instance, Persson 1989; Church et al. 1991;

Kennedy 1991; Gries 2001; 2003; Arppe 2002; Kjellmer 2003; Taylor 2003). One case in point is Biber, Conrad, and Reppen (1998: Section 4.3), who analyzed the grammatical preferences of the verbs *begin* and *start*. Although *begin* and *start* can be used in exactly the same syntactic structures, both intransitive and transitive, and even with the same type of objects when used transitively (i.e., noun phrases, *to*-clauses, and *-ing* clauses), closer inspection of their distributional patterns in such contexts reveals that the way in which they are typically used in actual discourse differs considerably. While the frequency of *start* almost doubles that of *begin* in intransitive structures in fictional texts, *begin* is three times more common than *start* with *to*-clauses as objects. In fact, in fictional texts more than half of the total examples of *begin* are transitive uses followed by *to*-clauses. By contrast, *start* occurs in this particular structure in only 17% of the cases, which demonstrates that it is preferred in other patterns, be it intransitive structures or transitive ones with other types of direct objects. Therefore Biber, Conrad, and Reppen (1998) show that by examining the valency of the two verbs, remarkable differences in use emerge. Their results point to a division of labor between the two verbs: despite being interchangeable in most cases, each verb is clearly the preferred option in different contexts of use. Additionally, language users are not able to predict the individual preferred grammatical associations of the two verbs, which they generally consider to be completely interchangeable. It is therefore only by means of detailed analyses of usage data such as that in Biber, Conrad, and Reppen (1998) that these preferred structures can be discovered, while native speaker intuitions are often unreliable.

Despite the valuable findings of studies on near-synonymous pairs such as the one conducted by Biber, Conrad, and Reppen (1998), it is clear from the information presented in dictionaries and thesauri that most lexical items have more than one synonym and thus synonyms typically come in larger groups (e.g., Divjak 2006; Gries 2010). For instance, the verb *commence* is also listed as a synonym of both *begin* and *start* in dictionaries and thesauri (e.g., *MW*). Analyzing only pairs of synonyms could therefore be considered reductive and insufficient to offer a complete picture of the semantic structure of specific concepts. This is the principal motivation for the analysis of larger sets of near-synonyms in the studies belonging to the second wave of research mentioned above (e.g., Divjak 2006; 2010; Divjak and Gries 2006; 2008; Arppe and Järvikivi 2007; Arppe 2008; Gries and Otani 2010; Liu 2010; 2013; Liu and Espino 2012; Desagulier 2014; Krawczak 2014; Yatandu Uba 2015).[6] For instance, Divjak and Gries (2006) examine the dis-

---

[6] Research before the mid-2000s that did focus on larger groups of near-synonyms include Hanks' (1996) on the verb *urge* and its near-synonyms (e.g., *request, order, command, incite,* and

tributional profiles of nine Russian verbs of trying: *probovat'* ('try'), *pytat'sja* ('try, attempt'), *starat'sja* ('try, endeavor'), *silit'sja* ('try, make efforts'), *norovit'* ('try, strive to, aim at'), *poryvat'sja* ('try, endeavor'), *tščit'sja* ('try, endeavor'), *pyžit'sja* ('go all out'), and *tužit'sja* ('make an effort, exert oneself'). This is done by means of cluster analysis to determine whether synonyms are structured in pairs, as assumed in earlier research, or in larger groups. Three clearly delineated clusters emerge from their analysis, each containing three verbs:

(i) *Probovat'*, *pytat'sja*, and *starat'sja* belong to the first cluster and are typically used to designate 'a human who is strongly encouraged to try to physically move himself or others'.
(ii) The verbs *tščit'sja*, *pyžit'sja*, and *tužit'sja* form the second cluster and are most commonly used to refer to 'an inanimate subject which tries very hard (without succeeding) to undertake "metaphorical extensions of physical actions"' (Divjak and Gries 2006: 42).
(iii) The third cluster, formed by the remaining three verbs, *silit'sja*, *norovit'*, and *poryvat'sja*, signals 'an inanimate entity that repeatedly, but not very intensely, tries but fails to perform a physical action'.

Divjak and Gries (2008) test the corpus-based results in their 2006 paper by means of experimental data with the aim of validating their claim that humans categorize synonyms into groups rather than pairs. Their findings, for the most part, point to a significant correlation between the corpus-based analysis and the experimental data. They thus conclude that "[. . .] there seems to be a psychological reality corresponding to clusters of near synonyms" and that "[. . .] speakers group these near synonyms into clusters, not pairs. Hence near synonymy is not about pairs of words that entertain dichotomous, dyadic relations [. . .] but about groups of words that are more similar to each other than to (words belonging to) other groups of semantically similar words" (2008: 208).

These two studies by Divjak and Gries constitute a clear break with the first wave of research and most subsequent studies in the field focus on larger groups of near-synonyms. However, regardless of whether pairs or larger groups of near-synonyms are analyzed, most corpus-based onomasiological research conducted during the last three decades have the same goal, namely, to identify how particular near-synonyms differ from each other. As such, the focus is on the factors determining the choice between near-synonyms.

---

encourage), Biber, Conrad, and Reppens' (1998: Section 2.6) analysis of the adjectives *big*, *large*, and *great*, and Partington's (1998: Sections 2.4 and 3.6) investigation into the adjectives *sheer*, *pure*, *complete*, and *absolute* and the adverbs *absolutely*, *completely*, and *entirely*.

Closely related to the amount and types of factors included in the analyses are the specific methods used to evaluate the differences between near-synonyms. If only one or two factors, such as collocational and/or stylistic patterns are considered, it may be sufficient to use frequencies and percentages or association measures of collocational strength. However, including a wider range of factors in the analysis requires the use of more sophisticated multivariate techniques in order to disentangle the individual effects of the factors as well as the possible interactions between them. Consequently, parameters (ii) and (iii) mentioned above, i.e., amount and types of factors and statistical techniques and measures, are here jointly discussed.

The main focus of most corpus-based studies on near-synonyms during the 1990s and early 2000s was on collocational preferences (e.g., Persson 1989; Church et al. 1991; Biber, Conrad and Reppen 1998; Partington 1998; Gries 2001; 2003; Kjellmer 2003). As mentioned above (cf. Section 2.1), in collocational analyses, a proximity limit is often determined to restrict the number of collocates of a node and that such a limit often takes the form of a context window of *x* words to the left and to the right of the node. However, whereas some studies use a rather wide context window, others consider only direct adjacent collocates of the node. Typically, adjacent collocates are examined to search for collocates which are considered to be more informative. Within the first wave of corpus-based studies on near-synonymy, we find collocational analyses of both types. For instance, Kjellmer (2003), in his work on *almost* and *nearly*, opts for a context window of L4–R4 and focuses on the type of individual collocates that occur with these adverbs in terms of their POS. Kjellmer draws the conclusion that *almost* and *nearly* differ considerably in collocational behavior: while the former is mainly followed by adverbs, adjectives, pronouns, and prepositions (e.g., *almost immediately, almost identical, almost all,* and *almost by definition*), post co-occurring collocates of *nearly* are primarily numerals (e.g., *nearly 50 years* or *nearly two thousand*). In turn, most studies on near-synonymous adjectives that focus on collocational behavior tend to consider exclusively their right-side collocates, particularly those immediately following the adjectives, i.e., R1 collocates. This is so because, in most cases, the nouns modified by adjectives appear in this particular slot, at least when used attributively. Such studies include, among others, Persson (1989) on *deep* and *profound,* Church et al. (1991) on *strong* and *powerful,* Biber, Conrad, and Reppen (1998: Section 2.6) on *big, large,* and *great,* and Gries (2001; 2003) on *-ic* and *-ical* pairs, for instance, *alphabetic(al), economic(al),* and *classic(al).*

Much of this line of research focuses not only on the individual lexical words that co-occur with the near-synonyms object of study, but also on more schematic aspects of the notion of collocation, namely colligation, semantic preference, and semantic prosody. In some studies, for instance Kjellmer (2003) on *almost* and *nearly*, function words such as pronouns and prepositions, but also determiners and conjunctions, are included in the collocational analysis; these are in fact colligations of the near-synonyms.

Other studies abstract away from individual lexical collocates by grouping them into semantic categories, thus focusing on their semantic preferences. One case in point is Gries' (2001) analyses on adjectival *-ic* vs. *-ical* pairs. He claims that in order to obtain a clearer insight into differences in collocational behavior of near-synonyms, it is sometimes necessary not only to focus on their specific collocates but also to consider their discriminating features or indicator attributes. By doing so, for the pair *magic(al)*, Gries is able to determine that while *magic* is commonly used to modify concrete nouns (e.g., *carpet, lantern*, and *sword*), *magical* is more typically used with abstract nouns (e.g., *power, mystery*, and *healing*). Similarly, in the pair *electric(al)*, *electric* is significantly more frequent with specific or basic-level nouns of a concrete nature (e.g., *kettle, sunroof*, and *toothbrush*), while *electrical* appears to a greater extent with more general or superordinate nouns, including both concrete and abstract entities (e.g., *appliances* and *equipment*).

Finally, some scholars also include information pertaining to semantic prosody in their collocational analyses. For example, Hanks (1996; cf. also 2013: Section 5.2.6) examines the contexts in which *urge* and two of its near-synonyms, *incite* and *encourage*, are used in British English. He finds that *urge* and *encourage* are neutral, while *incite* has a negative semantic prosody, being used in the great majority of cases to refer to an action that someone is persuaded to carry out and which tends to have negative or unpleasant effects in society.

Another important distinction to draw in research on the collocational behavior of near-synonyms concerns how collocational preferences are measured: by means of frequencies and percentages only or by making use of association measures. This methodological issue is closely related to how collocation is defined, that is, in textual or statistical terms. If a textual definition is adopted, mere frequencies or percentages are enough to compute the collocational strength between a node and its collocates. Analyses on near-synonyms adopting this perspective include, for instance, Persson (1989), Kennedy (1991), Biber, Reppen, and Conrad (1998), Taylor (2003), and Chung (2011). However, a great amount of research in the field embrace a statistical definition of collocation, thus considering only those collocates which occur with a node significantly more often than expected by chance. To this end, association measures such PMI, *t*-score, or log-likelihood are applied. All these measures have in common that they compare the likelihood of two words co-occurring with the likelihood of the respective individual items. However, they differ in the specific calculations they perform, which makes each of them suitable for different purposes. For instance, PMI favors words with a generally low frequency in a corpus but that tend to collocate with a particular node; it is therefore more adequate for the analysis of content words, as opposed to *t*-score, which performs better with function words (Church et al. 1991; Church et al. 1994; Liu 2010).[7] Studies on near-synonyms using association measures are Church et al. (1991), Gries (2001; 2003), Arppe (2002), Kjellmer (2003), and Arppe and Järvikivi (2007), among others. The use of association measures undoubtedly meant an improvement over that of mere frequencies and percentages, as the former allow to distinguish between those words that significantly collocate with a node from those that merely have a high overall frequency in a corpus, and therefore also co-occur frequently with the node.

The main goal of collocational analysis is certainly to establish the collocational preferences of lexical items, in this case of particular near-synonyms, and whether they differ or not in this respect. However, by recurring to collocational analysis it is also possible to extract additional and valuable information about the node words. For instance, collocational patterns can serve as indicators of the distribution and frequencies of different senses of lexical items. A case in point is Taylor's (2003) study of the adjectives *high* and *tall*. While these two near-synonyms can be used in the same senses, both literal ones pertaining to the spatial domain (e.g., *high/tall building*) and non-spatial metaphorical ones (e.g., *high temperature* or *tall order*), a collocational analysis of the two terms reveals that *high* is much more frequent than *tall* in the latter sense. Moreover, collocational analysis can also serve as an indicator of the syntactic function of node words. Gries (2001) points out that by analyzing the R1 collocates of adjectives, it is possible to ascertain whether they are used attributively or in other functions, most commonly predicatively. He shows that attributive adjectives are frequently immediately followed by a noun while predicative uses can be identified because other POS, particularly function words, occur directly after them in textual units. In this way, Gries is able to identify significant differences in syntactic distribution between particular pairs of *-ic* and *-ical* adjectives. An example concerns the pair *politic* and *political* as the former is often followed by the function words *to*, *for*, and *not*, and is thus frequent in predicative function, whereas the latter is hardly ever followed by collocates other than nouns (Gries 2001: 88).

Many of the studies on collocational behavior that have been discussed so far also examine stylistic differences between near-synonyms. Analyses such as those by Persson (1989), Biber, Conrad, and Reppen (1998: Section 2.6), Kjellmer (2003), Arppe (2008), Liu (2010), and Liu and Espino (2012) examine the stylis-

---

[7] PMI is further discussed in Section 6.1, where it is used to measure collocational strength.

tic preferences of pairs or larger groups of near-synonyms, mainly to determine whether they differ in formality. To this end, the distribution of near-synonyms in different text-types is typically explored. For example, on the basis of data from the *Corpus of Contemporary American English* or *COCA* (Davies 2008–), which comprises five different text-types showing different degrees of formality, namely, spoken, fiction, newspaper, magazine, and academic writing, Liu (2010) establishes a cline of formality for the near-synonymous adjectives *main*, *major*, *chief*, *principal*, and *primary*, with *main* being the most informal and *primary* the most formal.

While most corpus-based studies on near-synonyms during the 1990s and early 2000s exclusively examined collocational and/or stylistic preferences, a majority of studies from the second wave analyze a wider range of factors and therefore go far beyond previous corpus-based research on synonymy. Again, Divjak (2006) and Divjak and Gries (2006; 2008) represent a clear break with previous analyses, this time in the sense that they examine a large number of factors.[8] In fact, Divjak and Gries proposed a new approach to the study of semantic phenomena, mainly synonymy and polysemy, which they called the *Behavioral Profile* (BP) approach, following Hanks (1996: 79), the first author to use this label to refer to the typical patterns and contexts in which a given word is used. In brief, the BP approach consists in analyzing sets of near-synonymous words or senses of a polysemous word by considering many different types of co-occurrence information (e.g., morphological, syntactic, semantic, and stylistic) in order to determine their conventional uses. This is done by means of different types of statistical techniques, such as correlations, HAC, and logistic regression (Gries and Divjak 2009; Gries 2010).[9] In one of the earliest BP studies, namely Divjak and Gries (2006), referred to earlier on in this section, the usage patterns of nine near-synonymous verbs in Russian with the meaning 'to try' are examined on the basis of 87 different variables pertaining to the different linguistic levels. Many of these variables concern the morphosyntactic features of the near-synonymous verbs themselves, that is, the aspect, mood and tense they are used in, but others also consider features related to the clause in which the verbs appear or to the subjects of the near-synonymous verbs. Semantic variables

---

8 Even though some earlier studies (e.g., Hanks 1996; Biber, Conrad, and Reppen 1998: Sections 4.2 and 4.3; Arppe 2002), also include some syntactic and morphological co-occurrence features, the amount of factors considered in these works cannot be compared to those by Divjak (2006) and Divjak and Gries (2006; 2008), who include 47 and 87 variables, respectively.
9 These two papers constitute in-depth summaries of the BP approach. The reader is referred to them for further details on the steps and procedures used, as well as for examples of variables to be included in such analyses.

are also accounted for in their study, focusing particularly on the semantic features of the subjects of the near-synonymous verbs, which are operationalized on the basis of distinctions such as animate vs. inanimate and concrete vs. abstract, among others. Finally, the individual verb collocates which appear in close proximity to the verbs of trying are classified into broad semantic domains, including PHYSICAL ACTION, PHYSICAL PERCEPTION, SPEECH, and INTELLECTUAL ACTIVITY, among others, thus paying special attention to the complementation patterns and argument structures of the verbs under analysis. As mentioned above, the results point to the existence of three clearly delineated clusters within this synonym set, each of them containing three of the verbs. The pioneering study by Divjak and Gries (2006) demonstrated that the so-called BP approach is particularly useful to explore the internal semantic structure of sets of near-synonyms and can be said to have opened up new avenues of research in distributional corpus-based semantics, not only leading to further BP studies being conducted on near-synonymous verbs (Divjak and Gries 2008; Divjak 2010), but also on other POS: adjectives (e.g., Gries and Otani 2010; Liu 2010; Yatandu Uba 2015), nouns (e.g., Liu 2013), and adverbs (e.g., Liu and Espino 2012).

The BP approach is not the only existing corpus-based distributional method in cognitive semantics that has been used to analyze a wider range of contextual factors that determine the choice between near-synonyms. Other methods can be found which share the same main goals, but differ in the specific procedures employed along three stages distinguished by Levshina (2011: 24–29). These stages are data collection, data exploration, and confirmatory testing. Within the first stage, we find methods in which the data is collected manually, as in most BP studies, as opposed to automatically, as in SVS modeling (e.g., Heylen et al. 2008). SVS can be used to model the behavior of polysemous or near-synonymous words by analyzing their collocational patterns with the help of association measures. In the second stage, the data is explored. Depending on the method adopted, different statistical techniques can be used to visualize the results. For instance, BP studies tend to use dimensionality-reduction techniques, such as HAC, Multidimensional Scaling or MDS for short (Wickelmaier 2003; Levshina 2015: Chapter 17), and (multiple) correspondence analysis (e.g., Desagulier 2014; Krawczak 2018). Finally, in the third stage statistical tests are applied to determine whether the results can be generalized to other data. Logistic regression analysis is most commonly employed to see which variables and variable interactions have a statistically significant effect on the choice between near-synonyms (e.g., Arppe 2008; Krawczak 2014; 2018), but other tests can also be used, for instance, HCFA (e.g., Liu 2010; Liu and Espino 2012; Liu 2013). Many BP studies do not include this last stage, mainly due to the extremely large number of variables to be analyzed, and are therefore of a more exploratory nature (but cf. Divjak 2010 for an exception). Some of the techniques mentioned here are further explained in Chapters 5 and 6, where they are used to examine the adjectives *fragrant*, *perfumed*, *scented*, *sweet-scented*, and *sweet-smelling*.

2.2.2 Near-synonymous adjectives

The distributional corpus-based research reviewed in the previous section reveals that synonym sets belonging to different POS have been analyzed over the last few decades, including verbs (Hanks 1996; 2013; Biber, Conrad, and Reppen 1998: Section 4.3; Arppe 2002; 2008; Divjak 2006; 2010; Divjak and Gries 2006; 2008; Arppe and Järvikivi 2007; Chung 2011), nouns (Liu 2013), adjectives (Persson 1989; Church et al. 1991; Biber, Conrad, and Reppen 1998: Sections 2.6 and 4.2; Partington 1998: Section 2.4; Gries 2001; 2003; Taylor 2003; Gries and Otani 2010; Liu 2010; Krawczak 2014; 2018; Yatandu Uba 2015), adverbs (Partington 1998: Section 3.6; Liu and Espino 2012; Desagulier 2014), and prepositions (Kennedy 1991). As such, a wide variety of different types of factors from different linguistic levels (e.g., semantic, syntactic, and morphological) have been examined in order to determine their effect on the choice between particular near-synonyms. However, not all factors are equally relevant for all studies, since the way synonyms differ from one another depends largely on their POS and conceptual nature. Thus, most studies on near-synonymous verbs, besides including collocational patterns and semantic features in the analysis, also consider a great amount of morphosyntactic contextual clues, for instance, tense, aspect, and mood, or sentence and clause type in which the verbs occur. In fact, in many of these cases the morphosyntactic variables have proven to be of utmost importance to distinguish between near-synonymous verbs (cf. for instance, Divjak 2010: 183–193). On the other hand, studies on adjectives and adverbs generally consider fewer morphosyntactic factors, whereas semantic features seem to play a more crucial role in determining the choice between near-synonyms belonging to these POS, for instance, semantic preference regarding the elements they modify (e.g., Gries 2001; Liu 2010; Liu and Espino 2012). In what follows, studies on near-synonymous adjectives are dealt with in more depth, concentrating on the types of factors that are typically included in these analyses, as such determinants are the most relevant for our purposes in the present work.

A great majority of the existing distributional corpus-based research on pairs or sets of near-synonymous adjectives consider their collocational and/or stylistic behavior only. More specifically, as has already been mentioned in Section 2.2.1, such studies tend to focus on the R1 collocates of the adjectives in order to concentrate on the nouns they modify. This is so because, as has been demonstrated in previous research on adjectives in general, analyzing the nouns that adjectives modify is one of the best ways to reveal the nature of the semantic content of the adjectives (e.g, Geeraerts 1986: 282–284). However, other studies go beyond mere individual collocates and consider other features of the modified nouns, including primarily semantic aspects, but also morphological ones. For example, as mentioned earlier, Gries (2001; 2003) includes information concerning the dichotomies concrete vs. abstract and specific/basic level vs. general/superordinate level of the modified nouns of *-ic* and *-ical* adjectival pairs, but he also contemplates that of animacy (i.e., animate vs. inanimate) for those adjectives in which such a division is relevant, as in the case of *optic* vs. *optical*. In his study on *chief, main, major, primary*, and *principal*, Liu (2010) discovers a division of semantic labor between the five adjectives by classifying their noun collocates into six semantic categories:[10]

(i) ABSTRACT: *change, problem*, and *reason*.
(ii) CONCRETE: *dish, entrance*, and *street*.
(iii) DUAL (can be either concrete or abstract): *character, component*, and *source*.
(iv) INSTITUTION: *city, corporation*, and *school*.
(v) POSITION TITLE: *deputy, investigator*, and *officer*.
(vi) NON-POSITION TITLE: *author, owner*, and *sponsor*.

By doing so, Liu concludes that while abstract and dual nouns frequently co-occur with all five adjectives, the nouns in the remaining four semantic categories are modified mainly by one or two of the near-synonyms: for example, while nouns classified as CONCRETE prefer *main* (e.g., *main entrance*), nouns belonging to the category POSITION TITLE are dominated by *chief* (e.g., *chief deputy*). Furthermore, as all five adjectives seem to converge in meaning when they modify dual and abstract nouns, Liu investigates whether other fine-grained differences exist between them when used with nouns belonging to these two semantic categories. To this end, he explores two morphological features of the modified nouns, that is, number (singular vs. plural) and definiteness (indefinite vs. definite). This is relevant for the adjectival synonyms object of study to establish the degree of importance that they convey: *one main issue* is more important than *two main issues* and *the main issue* is more important than *a main issue*. Thus, Liu identifies a cline of importance, with *primary, chief*, and *main* being used to refer to entities that are considered to be more important by speakers, followed by *major*, and lastly *principal*.

---

10 For further information about the nouns belonging to each category and the decisions regarding specific nouns, see Liu (2010: 84).

By far the most comprehensive work on synonymous adjectives is the BP study conducted by Gries and Otani (2010), in which they examine two sets of near-synonymous from the semantic domain of SIZE, namely *big*, *great*, and *large*, on the one hand, and *little*, *small*, and *tiny*, on the other. They analyze a great amount of factors from different linguistic levels, including morphological, syntactic, and semantic ones. Among morphological factors, they consider the aspect, tense, voice, and transitivity marking of the finite verb of the clause in which the adjectives occur. As regards syntactic factors, these are similar to those considered in BP studies on near-synonymous verbs, for instance, the type (i.e., main vs. dependent) and function (e.g., direct object, noun phrase postmodifier) of the clauses where the adjectives are located. This syntactic information is automatically retrieved, as Gries and Otani use the British component of the *International Corpus of English*, which is a parsed corpus. Another syntactic feature that they examine, which is also present in other studies on adjectival near-synonyms (e.g., Biber, Conrad, and Reppen 1998: Section 2.6; Gries 2001; 2003; Liu 2010), is the syntactic function of the adjectives, that is whether they are used in attributive, predicative, or adverbial function. Finally, Gries and Otani analyze several semantic features of the noun collocates, such as countability (count vs. non-count) and a wide range of semantic categories including, among others, CONCRETE, ABSTRACT, HUMAN, ORGANIZATION/INSTITUTION, and QUANTITY. Another semantic feature they consider is how SIZE is modified, i.e., literally, metaphorically, quantitatively, or evaluatively. The results for each of the variables are then aggregated by means of HAC and visualized with the use of dendrograms. Findings point to a clustering solution according to different parameters, including both sameness of meaning, so that *tiny* and *smallest* are grouped together, and oppositeness of meaning, with *big* and *little* forming one cluster, and *large* and *small* another. Although Gries and Otani's (2010) study includes a wide range of different types of factors, the effects of each of the levels of the variables are not discussed. This is so because it is practically impossible to statistically test for all the variables included in their analysis without an extremely large amount of data for each of the six adjectives at issue. This is, in fact, a recurrent problem in many BP studies, as the third step of analyses of this type, i.e., testing for significance, is unviable (cf. Section 2.2.1 above). Therefore, even though such studies provide valuable results concerning the general behavior of the synonyms examined, specific details about exactly how they differ from one another are seldom offered. However, it must be borne in mind that the goal of many BP studies is not that of giving an in-depth description of each of the variables explaining the choice between near-synonyms, but rather that of presenting a bird's-eye view of their contextual behavior.

Finally, some studies on near-synonymous adjectives, besides considering intralinguistic factors pertaining to their co-occurrence preferences, also examine the effects of extralinguistic variables. This is the case of, for instance, Krawczak (2014; 2018), who analyzes adjectives from the semantic domain of SHAME. Her (2014) paper examines three lexical items, namely *ashamed*, *embarrassed*, and *humiliated*, in both American and British English to verify Wierzbicka's (1992; 1999) claims as to their semasiological and onomasiological structures. To this end, Krawczak includes three different semantic features, namely, cause of emotion (e.g., bodily causes, insecurity, and social failure), type of emotion (i.e., internal vs. external), and temporal scope of the emotion (present, past, and general). Moreover, she includes the factor dialect to ascertain whether there exist extralinguistic usage differences. By means of two multivariate methods, namely correspondence analysis and multinomial logistic regression, she establishes three clearly delineated usage-profiles for the three adjectives: *ashamed* is connected to internal and atemporal causes related to insecurities of social status, emotional or bodily problems, and social failures; *embarrassed*, in turn, is associated with interactive factors, for instance, self-esteem difficulties or deviation from social conventions regarding politeness; finally, *humiliated* is linked to damages to one's social status due to external motivations. With regard to the extralinguistic variable examined (i.e., dialect), no significant differences are found, as the lexical items display basically the same behavior in the two reference varieties of English.

Krawczak's (2018) study constitutes a continuation of the author's previous research. She adopts a cross-linguistic and cross-cultural perspective to the same social emotion, namely SHAME, but restricts the analysis to two of the adjectives: *ashamed* and *embarrassed*, and their counterparts in French (i.e., *honteux* and *embarrassé*) and Polish (i.e., *zazenowany* and *zawstydzony*). The same factors are examined, with the exception of dialect, which is replaced by country and language, and a variable coding for whether an audience is present or absent from the speech situation in which the social emotion emerges. The findings point to the existence of a cline of communities from Poland through France to the United Kingdom and the United States that is linked to their respective cultures and, more particularly, to whether the societies are more collectivist, as in the case of Poland, or more individualistic, as in the case of the United Kingdom and the United States. France, in turn, occupies an intermediate position. Krawczak thus finds a significant effect of the extralinguistic factors on the choice between the two near-synonymous terms in the different languages. Consequently, although the concept EMBARRASSED in general is more interactive than that of ASHAMED, being closely linked to the presence of an audience, this is not the case in Polish, where the line between the two emotions is not as clear-cut. Krawczak's (2018) findings may indeed be relevant for the present study since, in addition to intralinguistic factors of a primarily contextual nature, extralinguistic ones may need to be considered in order to reach a full understanding of onomasiological structure.

As we have just seen, some studies resort to sociolinguistic and cultural aspects to explain onomasiological variation. However, many of the works that have been reviewed throughout this section, despite offering valuable descriptive information about differences between near-synonyms, do not connect the patterns uncovered to a specific theoretical framework, nor do they discuss the implications of their findings. Geeraerts (2010: 177–178) states that the distributional corpus-based approach is ultimately a method rather than a theory, given that it is not always evident how the distributional patterns relate to theoretical issues in lexical semantics. Similarly, Gries (2010: 324–325) points to several areas in which this line of research could be further improved, one of which has to do precisely with the lack of theoretical background in many of these studies. Therefore, such distributional methods have recently tended to adopt the framework of cognitive semantics and make use of concepts and principles within this theory, such as prototypicality and entrenchment, to explain the findings obtained.

One rather early corpus-based study on near-synonymy which provides a cognitive explanation for its findings is Taylor (2003) on the adjectives *high* and *tall*. Both terms are positive polarity items indicating the extent of an entity on the vertical dimension. However, while *high* dates back to the Old English period, having been inherited from Germanic, the spatial sense of *tall* is rather recent, approximately from the mid-sixteenth century according to the *OED* (*OED*, s.v. *tall* n. II, 6). The adoption of *tall* to denote an entity of great vertical extent did not imply a decrease in the usage range of *high*, which was retained for all types of entities with which it was used before. The adjective *tall*, on the other hand, offered a new way of conceptualizing positive polarity verticality that is specific to the human body (e.g., *tall man, tall girl*). In order to explain this distribution, Taylor makes use of the so-called vantage theory (e.g., MacLaury 1997), originally applied to the semantic domain of COLOR, in which a distinction is made between *dominant* and *recessive* terms. A dominant term within a pair is that which can be applied to a wide range of entities or situations, as it emphasizes the similarities between them. On the other hand, a recessive term emphasizes their differences, and as such can only be applied to a narrow range of entities or situations (Taylor 2003: 280). By using this distinction, Taylor concludes that *high* is the dominant term in the pair, while *tall* is the recessive one, as it is limited to denote a specific type of verticality, i.e., that of the human body. Taylor (2003) thus demonstrates how findings from distributional corpus-based studies on near-synonymy can be embedded within a theoretical framework on language and human cognition in general, and lexical semantics, in particular.

Even though Taylor (2003) briefly considers the diachronic development of *tall* and *high* in his discussion of the findings, the rest of the studies reviewed until now adopt a fully synchronic orientation towards lexical onomasiological variation due to the scarcity of diachronic studies on lexical near-synonymy from the perspective of usage-based onomasiology with a cognitive stance. The next section deals with the scant diachronic corpus-based analyses on pairs or sets of lexical near-synonyms, as well as with some generalizations about synonymy and diachrony that have been proposed in the specialized literature, including the types of semantic change that near-synonymous words have been said to undergo over time.

2.3 Synonymy and diachrony

Both synchronic and diachronic approaches to the study of meaning abound within cognitive semantics. However, while a considerable amount of diachronic work within this tradition has recently been devoted to constructional synonymy and other morphosyntactic changes (e.g., Shank, Plevoets, and Cuyckens 2014; Hilpert 2016; De Smet et al. 2018; Hilpert 2021), we find only a handful of diachronic studies on lexical synonymy from a distributional corpus-based perspective. In what follows, a brief summary of this research is provided.

Kaunisto (2001) investigates the evolution of twelve pairs of *-ic* and *-ical* adjectives from the second half of the sixteenth century to the first half of the nineteenth century by drawing on data from the prose section of *Chadwyck-Healey Literature Online* (1996–2000): *angelic(al)*, *authentic(al)*, *comic(al)*, *domestic(al)*, *fantastic(al)*, *heroic(al)*, *magic(al)*, *majestic(al)*, *philosophic(al)*, *poetic(al)*, *tragic(al)*, and *tyrannic(al)*. First, he analyzes the productivity of each of the two suffixes from the 1300s to the present-day by counting the number of first attestations of *-ic/-ical* adjectives in the *OED*. By doing so, Kaunisto is able to determine that, whereas until the seventeenth century both suffixes are approximately equally productive, from 1750 and until about 1900 *-ic* is used considerably more often to coin new adjectives, especially in scientific domains such as chemistry (e.g., *acidic, cyanic*). Nevertheless, in the twentieth century the productivity of both suffixes becomes similar again. As regards the specific diachronic patterns of pairs of *-ic/-ical* near-synonyms, Kaunisto identifies five evolutionary trends:

(i) First, in some pairs, which are all characterized by exhibiting the semantic feature NOBILITY (e.g., *angelic(al)*, *heroic(al)*, *majestic(al)*), there is a move from *-ical* to *-ic* mainly in the seventeenth century. Moreover, in previous periods, when adjectives with both suffixes are common, there appears to be

no change in meaning between them, as they are used with the same senses and in the same syntactic functions and even seem to collocate with the same types of nouns.
(ii) Second, pairs such as *comic(al)*, *fantastic(al)*, and *magic(al)* come to be more often used with *-ic* in the eighteenth century.
(iii) Third, in the case of *tyrannic(al)*, the number of occurrences with *-ic* increase as in the preceding two cases, but the *-ical* form remains the most frequent.
(iv) Fourth, *philosophic* becomes more common at the expense of *philosophical* in the second half of the eighteenth century, when the two near-synonyms seem to undergo a process of differentiation: the former has a more popular meaning (e.g., *philosophic look*), while the latter occurs mainly with nouns referring to science, such as *research* and *theory*. Nevertheless, the two terms then converge again in meaning and *philosophic* became the dominant adjective in both uses.
(v) Finally, *tragic(al)* undergoes a change from *-ical* to *-ic*, but much later than the rest of the terms discussed, after the first half of the nineteenth century.

Thus, in almost all cases we witness a shift from *-ical* to *-ic*, although at different points in time. In some *-ic/-ical* pairs semantic differentiation takes place in a given period. However, Kaunisto (2001) concludes that, in the end, the main result of these changes seems to be that of discarding one of the options rather than maintaining both forms with different meanings and/or functions.

Primahadi-Vijaya-R. and Rajeg (2014) examine the nominal collocational profiles of two near-synonymous adjectives from the domain of TEMPERATURE, namely *hot* and *warm*, in American English throughout the last one and a half centuries (i.e., 1860s–2000s) by drawing on data from *COHA* (Davies 2010–). To this purpose, they extract the top 100 R1 noun collocates of the two adjectives, excluding those that appear less than five times in each decade in the corpus. The data is visualized by means of motion charts (Hilpert 2011; 2013: 66–74), which is a method to display a series of graphs in order to plot the diachronic changes of a given phenomenon. Primahadi-Vijaya-R. and Rajeg show, for each decade, the absolute co-occurrence frequencies of the different R1 noun collocates and identify several diachronic trends that have contributed to the differential use of these two near-synonyms in present-day American English. Whereas in the 1860s some nouns, for example, *blood*, *water*, and *weather*, are commonly modified by both *hot* and *warm* in the literal sense 'of high temperature', other nouns are already clearly associated with one of the two adjectives. For instance, *warm* typically collocates with nouns such as *smile*, *heart*, *affection*, and *friend*, thus pointing to its frequent use in the metaphorical extension of 'friendliness'. On the other hand, *hot* seems to be typically used in the 1860s in another metaphorical sense, viz.

that of 'excitement' and 'intensity', as in *hot haste* or *hot pursuit*. With the passing of time, the collocational profile of *hot* changes somewhat. First, from the 1920s onwards, it undergoes a lexicalization process with the noun *dog* (i.e., *hotdog*), which is today a compound noun rather than a combination of an adjective and a head noun. This is also the case of *hotspot*, in which the original meaning of *hot* is no longer transparent. Second, from the 2000s onwards, *hot* becomes strongly associated to nouns denoting people (e.g., *girl*, *guy*, and *woman*) in order to refer to 'sexually attractive' individuals, thus indicating a rise in this particular sense of the adjective. Primahadi-Vijaya-R. and Rajeg (2014) thus uncover some interesting differentiating patterns of the two near-synonymous adjectives and how they develop through time, especially concerning the lexicalization processes of the nouns *hotdog* and *hotspot*.

Baker (2017) uses another useful visualization method for diachronic collocational changes of lexical near-synonyms known as collocational networks (Brezina, McEnery, and Wattam 2015). Put briefly, this approach consists in plotting the most important collocates of lexical items in networks in which the collocates are connected to their nodes by means of arrows. Baker (2017: 95–101) adapts this method to diachronic analysis by plotting different collocational networks in separate periods, thus revealing how particular nodes attract but also lose collocates over time. In particular, he analyzes the near-synonyms *on* and *upon*, on the one hand, and *round* and *around* in the recent history of British English (1930s–2000s). In the case of *on* and *upon*, Baker finds that with time *on*, which was already more frequent in the 1930s, draws away collocates from *upon*, for instance, the adjective *dependent*. In other words, several collocates which were previously shared by the two near-synonyms or which were only associated with *upon* in the 1930s are exclusive to *on* in 2006. This particular development is considered to illustrate a linguistic process termed densification, whereby shorter words, clauses, sentences, or other discourse units are preferred to longer ones (Baker 2017: 24). By contrast, the opposite process is identified in the development undergone by the lexical items *round* and *around*: whereas in 1931 *round* has a greater amount of collocates than *around*, with time the latter attracts many new collocates and becomes the preferred variant in 2006. As shown by Baker, diachronic collocational networks are valuable assets in order to zoom in on the competition between near-synonyms as they help to determine which collocates are shared by them at different points in time and to identify the potential variations in the relation between the near-synonyms. Therefore, this approach allows for the examination of changes at a lower level of granularity.

Finally, Pettersson-Traba (2021) conducts a pilot study on the diachronic development of the attributive uses of an adjectival synonym set which designates the concept PLEASANT SMELLING, i.e., *fragrant*, *perfumed*, *scented*, and *sweet-smelling*, in the history of American English (1850–2009). On the basis of data extracted from *COHA* analyzed by means of a HCFA, she examines the usage patterns of these four near-synonyms. In particular, she focuses on their modified nouns, which are classified into nine semantic categories: BODY, CLEANING, EARTH, ESTHETICS, FOOD AND DRINK, MATTER, PLANTS AND FLOWERS, SENSATION, and TEXTILE AND CLOTHING. The findings suggest that major changes took place in the period examined, whereby the concept PLEASANT SMELLING went from being used mainly to modify nouns referring to entities which emanate natural pleasant aromas (e.g., *plant* and *flower*) to co-occurring more frequently with nouns designating objects which are artificially sweet-scented (e.g., *soap* and *candle*). This change is hypothesized to be a result of extralinguistic factors, that is, socio-economic changes such as industrialization and mass production that took place during the period examined, in particular at the end of the nineteenth century, which led to an ever-increasing need to refer to artificially scented soaps and candles rather than naturally fragrant plants and flowers. However, this hypothesis was not empirically tested, but merely suggested. This idea is taken up in the present monograph, which constitutes a continuation of the line of research initiated in Pettersson-Traba (2021), here considerably extended and refined.

Though not a study on near-synonymy, it is worth mentioning here Jansegers and Gries' (2020) work on the semantic evolution of the polysemous verb *sentir* 'feel' in Peninsular Spanish, as it constitutes the first diachronic application of the BP approach, thus providing an interesting methodological avenue in distributional lexical semantics. Jansegers and Gries (2020) follow the ordinary steps of the BP approach (cf. Section 2.2), but repeat the procedure for each of the five historical periods that they examine, namely the thirteenth, fifteenth, seventeenth, nineteenth, and twenty-first centuries. As in the case of Primahadi-Vijaya-R. and Rajeg (2014), they use motion charts to visualize their results, but do so by means of a more sophisticated technique, namely MDS. This is a dimensionality-reduction technique common in many fields of linguistics to visualize, in a simple and straightforward way, the degree of (dis)similarity between two or more objects, senses in this particular study. The (dis)similarity between the objects is computed on the basis of a series of parameters selected by the researcher(s), for instance, a series of contextual cues of either a semantic or a morphosyntactic nature. The output of MDS is a two- or – in some cases – three-dimensional map on which these objects are situated, either close to or further apart from one another, on the basis of how (dis)similar they are in terms of the parameters selected for inclusion in the model: the closer two objects are to each other on the MDS map, the more similar. Following Hilpert (2011; 2013), who has recently adapted this technique to diachronic data to visualize language change, Jansegers and Gries (2020) use MDS instead of HAC, the more typical clustering technique in BP studies, which is employed in Divjak and Gries (2006; 2008), among others. The reason for this methodological shift is that MDS is semantically more realistic than HAC, since it does not suppose a categorical either/or split between individual clusters, but instead displays a more precise and continuous cline of semantic (dis)similarity (Jansegers and Gries 2020: 158). In this way, they discover the evolution of the three different broad semantic domains of *sentir*, namely direct physical, cognitive, and emotional perception. First, they identify the distributional patterns of these three uses of the verb in different periods and then trace their frequency development over time, concluding that *sentir* evolves from being used primarily as a physical perception verb in the earliest periods, specifically in the thirteenth and the fifteenth centuries, to being used mostly in the emotional sense in later stages. Moreover, the MDS maps also display an interesting development in recent times, namely the emergence and rise of *lo siento* 'I'm sorry' as a discourse marker. In this way, the MDS maps also serve to ascertain from which particular senses of *sentir* this discourse marker originates, namely its use with the meaning 'regret', belonging to the emotional perception domain, on the one hand, and its cognitive use 'consider, judge', on the other. Consequently, Jansegers and Gries (2020) demonstrate the usefulness of examining the diachronic evolution of distributional patterns of lexical items by means of a technique which had until then been primarily used for morphosyntactic research, both of a synchronic and a diachronic nature.

The usage-based studies reviewed in this section so far show that lexical semantic relations do not, in many cases, remain stable over time, neither when it comes to the association between semantically related words such as near-synonyms nor in the case of the senses of a particular polysemous word. In other words, by using a distributional corpus-based approach, both onomasiological and semasiological changes can be successfully tracked over time, and this method can even help reveal their possible underlying motivations. Nevertheless, the idea that modulations of meaning occur over time is a well-established one in the specialized literature, and much research has been devoted to the identification of the principal mechanisms of semantic change, as well as to classifications of such regular patterns into different types (cf. for instance, the pioneering work of Carnoy 1927, Stern 1931, Ullmann 1962).

Absolute synonymy is considered to go against language economy. Therefore, as mentioned earlier in this chapter (Section 2.1), a well-established belief in the specialized literature is that if two words become absolute synonyms, for instance, as a result of borrowing, they enter into competition until at least one of them undergoes some semantic change (e.g., specialization) to become differentiated from the other; this is known as the no-synonymy rule or isomorphic state of languages (e.g., Bolinger 1977: ix–x, 9; Wierzbicka 1988: 13–14; Croft 2000: 176; Nuyts and Byloo 2015: 62–63). In the words of Samuels (1972: 65), "if [. . .]

two exact synonyms exist for a time in the spoken chain, either one of them will be less and less selected and eventually discarded, or a difference of meaning, connotation, nuance or register will arise to distinguish them". In the former case, one of the alternatives progressively takes over more and more of the original shared semantic ground and, consequently, the other variant becomes less frequent until it stops being used altogether in the shared sense(s). This process is known as substitution. An example drawn from the history of English concerns the lexical items *guard* (*OED*, s.v. *guard* n. 7a) and *ward* (*OED*, s.v. *ward* n.1), which shared the sense '[a] person who keeps, protects, or defends; a watchman' during the latter part of the Midde English period. *Ward* has its origins in the Old English noun *weard* and was used in this sense until the end of the fifteenth century, as its last attestation from the year 1472 in the *OED* demonstrates. Interestingly, this is precisely the same century in which the noun *guard*, coming from French *garde*, was borrowed into English with the same meaning. The two terms coexisted in Middle English for a while, but eventually *guard* replaced *ward*, as the latter fell into disuse in this sense. In the second scenario mentioned by Samuels (1972: 65), the synonyms instead become differentiated because at least one of them experiences some change in meaning, such as *specialization* or *generalization* (cf. for instance, Kay and Allan 2015: 75–76). Specialization refers to the process whereby a word or a particular word sense becomes increasingly narrower or more specific, so that the number of referents which the word can denote is reduced. On the other hand, generalization is the opposite process, that is, when a word or a word sense becomes increasingly broader or more general, thus coming to designate a wider number of referents. The nouns *bird* and *fowl*, which could at one point in history be used interchangeably, exemplify the two processes. *Bird*, which dates back to Old English, was originally used to denote a specific type of bird, namely a young one (*OED*, s.v. *bird* n. 1a). Nevertheless, in the Middle English period it underwent a process of generalization and came to be used to refer to any type of bird, including both young and adult members of the species. In turn, *fowl*, of Germanic origin, was a general term during the Old English period, being used for '[a]ny feathered vertebrate animal' (*OED*, s.v. *fowl* n. 1a), much as its present-day counterparts in other Germanic languages (e.g., German *Vogel* and Swedish *fågel*). Once *bird* began to be used in the more general sense, the two terms progressively became differentiated, as *fowl* underwent a process of specialization and was established with a narrower sense in the Early Modern English period, namely that of '[a] domestic bird (e.g., turkey or hen)' (*OED*, s.v. *fowl* n. 3). Consequently, the relationship between *bird* and *fowl* can be characterized as hyponymy in Old English and part of Middle English (*bird* being a hyponym of *fowl*), followed by a period of synonymy in Middle English and Early Modern English, and then again hyponymy in Present-day English (*fowl* being a hyponym of *bird*).

Two additional and related semantic changes often mentioned in the literature are *amelioration* and *pejoration* (cf. for instance, Kay and Allan 2015: 77–81), which pertain to the connotative dimension of meaning explained earlier (cf. Section 2.1). Amelioration refers to a change from a more negative to a more positive meaning, while pejoration entails the opposite development, i.e., a change from a more positive to a more negative meaning. The Present-Day English terms *quean* and *queen*, which can be traced back to the same Indo-European root, could be used with the meaning 'woman' in Old English, thus being interchangeable sometimes, although *queen* was more commonly employed to denote a specific type of woman, namely a noble one. With time the nouns underwent differentiation, as *quean* became more negative (i.e., pejoration) and *queen* more positive (i.e., amelioration), so that already in Middle English the two terms were not regarded as synonymous. Nowadays, *quean* is used almost exclusively – except in Scottish English – to refer to a woman of lower status, namely a bold or impudent one, or a prostitute. *Queen*, on the other hand, though associated with positive undertones already in Old English, has become further ameliorated over time, its predominant sense in Present-day English being that of 'a female ruler'. The case of pejoration can be exemplified also by means of the two nouns *stench* and *odor* from the semantic domain of SMELL, which were formerly synonymous with *smell*. Both nouns were originally used to denote any type of smell, be it an unpleasant or a pleasant one, but eventually they became increasingly associated with negative undertones and finally used either exclusively (in the case of *stench*) or almost exclusively (in the case of *odor*) to refer to disagreeable or even disgusting smells. The pejoration of *stench* took place already after the Old English period (*OED*, s.v. *stench* n. 1 and 2). In the case of *odor* the change occurred only rather recently, but the process of pejoration can be said to be more dramatic, as the early uses of this noun in Middle English were typically of a positive nature, referring to sweet and pleasing aromas (*OED*, s.v. *odour* n. I. 1). These examples demonstrate that amelioration and pejoration do not exclude other types of semantic changes pertaining to the denotative domain, such as specialization, which is also present in the cases of *queen*, *quean*, *stench*, and *odor*.

The view of competition between synonyms just exemplified is prevalent in the specialized literature as it is considered that the avoidance of absolute synonymy is an inherent characteristic of languages. In fact, the literature is full to the brim with examples of synonymous expressions that have ultimately become more differentiated, particularly via the process of specialization which, as argued by Kay and Allan (2015: 32), "[. . .] is one of the commonest forms of semantic change among words which start off as synonyms". The English vocabulary was greatly extended after the Norman Conquest which took place in 1066 due to the borrowing of French terms, in many cases even when an Anglo-Saxon term for the same concept already existed. Well-known examples are the pairs *pig/pork*, *cow/beef*, and *sheep/mutton*, the first term of each pair being Anglo-Saxon and the second term originating in French. At first, these words in each pair were absolute synonyms, denoting both the animal and the flesh of the animal, conceptualized as food, but as time passed they underwent a process of differentiation by becoming specialized (e.g., Jackson 1988: 66; Murphy 2003: 161): whereas the Anglo-Saxon term became restricted to designating only the animal, the French one retained only the 'meat' sense. The reasons behind this semantic change have been thoroughly discussed in the specialized literature and have often been linked to the notion of prestige.[11] French was the prestigious language throughout the Middle English and part of the Early Modern English period and therefore it was connected to the more sophisticated spheres of life, including that of "fine dining" (Murphy 2003: 161).

Anglo-Saxon and French pairings also serve as examples of synonyms becoming differentiated not concerning their denotative meaning, but as regards style. For instance, in the cases of Anglo-Saxon *begin/start*, *ask*, and *hearty* vs. French *commence*, *demand*, and *cordial*, respectively, the French loanwords came to be associated with formal and literary styles, whereas the Anglo-Saxon counterparts are more colloquial or neutral and thus used in a wider range of stylistic contexts (Jackson 1988: 66–67; Kay and Allan 2015: 12).

Although the competition theory is widespread and has proved successful to understand many changes in language, not only at the lexical level but also at the syntactic, morphological, and phonological ones (cf. for instance, Mondorf 2010; Berg 2014), some scholars have recently suggested that this competition metaphor represents an oversimplification. This is so because it does not make room for scenarios where synonyms converge rather than diverge in meaning. This process, referred to as attraction by De Smet et al. (2018) is thought to underly many semantic developments. In fact, De Smet et al. (2018) show how pairs of constructional near-synonyms have become functionally more and more similar over time (cf. also Hilpert 2021 for additional examples of constructional synonyms that have experienced attraction). One of the pairs of constructions De Smet et al. (2018) analyze is the alternation between *-ing* and *to*-infinitive clauses as complements of the verb *begin*. Whereas *begin* occurred mainly with *to*-infinitive complements in the 1840s, particularly with non-agentive subjects but also with agentive ones, later on *-ing*-clauses progressively gained ground at the expense of *to*-infinitive clauses. At first, this replacement occurred only with agentive sub-

---

11 But cf. Kornexl and Lenker (2011) for a different account on the motivations underlying this semantic shift.

jects, but over time it spread also to non-agentive subjects. In a typical scenario of differentiation, we would expect *to*-infinitive complements to retreat from agentive contexts. However, this did not happen as the decrease of *to*-infinitive complements following *begin* was mainly limited to non-agentive contexts. All of these developments therefore led to a functional convergence of the two constructions, both being more commonly used with agentive subjects. In other words, while this development represents an instance of ongoing replacement of *to*-infinitive clauses by *-ing*-clauses it also constitutes an example of attraction. De Smet et al. (2018) argue that for substitution to occur some degree of attraction is possibly necessary, as for one construction to be the target for replacement by another, the two constructions first need to share some semantic or functional space.

According to De Smet et al. (2018: 204, 217), analogical change, that is, the process whereby one form becomes more similar to another which it already resembled, usually from a formal perspective (Trask 2007: 15–16), lies at the core of attraction. However, analogy in this case is considered to include also functional beside formal or structural similarity (see also Nuyt and Byloo 2015: 36). De Smet et al (2018) therefore claim that synonyms, be they lexical or constructional, can mirror each other's functional and semantic behavior.[12] This hypothesis receives support for instance from the fact that synonymous lexical expressions can adopt the same figurative senses apart from their literal ones, thus coming to share more senses over time (e.g., Stefanowitsch 2008; Turkkila 2014). An example is provided by Stefanowitsch (2008: 96–99), who shows that the synonymous nouns *joy* and *happiness*, besides sharing the literal sense 'the emotion or state of being highly pleased or delighted', occur also in similar metaphorical mappings where the feeling of happiness is conceptualized as a liquid or as a source of heat (e.g., *river of joy/happiness* or *sparks of joy/happiness*).

De Smet et al. (2018: 205) argue that differentiation and attraction cannot occur simultaneously within one synonym set. This might well be true when synonymous pairs are analyzed, as in their case studies, but if one adopts a broader perspective and considers larger synonym sets of three or more elements, it might be possible to encounter both processes at play at the same time.[13] This is so because the members making up a synonym set do not necessarily have to relate to one another in the same way. As an illustration, consider the following hypothetical scenario where words A, B, and C are near-synonyms. By examining solely the evolving relation between A and B, we might find that they undergo a process

---

[12] For a similar explanation of the process of attraction cf. Hilpert (2021).
[13] Yet another possibility is that of stability, i.e., when no functional changes occur in a synonym set over time.

of attraction, that is, converging semantically over time. This of course entails that A and B cannot become differentiated during the same period. However, if we analyze also the relations between A and C or B and C, we might find the process of differentiation occurring besides that of attraction, given that either A and C or B and C (or both) may become less rather than more similar diachronically. Therefore, by adopting a broader perspective and including larger groups of near-synonyms in the analysis, both types of changes can be found to be at work in one and the same synonym set. This is an issue that has, to my knowledge, not yet been explored, and that can be of crucial importance for lexical synonymy, where, as discussed in Section 2.2.1, near-synonyms tend to come in larger groups rather than in pairs.

Despite the studies summarized in this section, there is still an evident shortage of diachronic research on lexical synonymy, which shows that there is a clear need for more analyses of this nature. In this context, the present monograph aims at partially filling this existing gap by analyzing in the recent history of American English a set of adjectival near-synonyms from the olfactory domain, namely *fragrant*, *perfumed*, *scented*, *sweet-scented*, and *sweet-smelling*. Chapters 4–6 present the results of corpus-based analyses of this synonym set. First, however, Chapter 3 introduces the synonyms object of study, as well as the reasons for the selection of this particular near-synonym set. Moreover, the data retrieval and annotation processes of the databases employed in the subsequent corpus-based analyses in Chapters 4–6 are also explained in detail.

3 The concept PLEASANT SMELLING

As became evident in the previous chapter, although absolute synonyms are virtually nonexistent, languages abound in near-synonyms, that is, words with similar, though not identical meanings. This is particularly true for English, which, due to its long history of borrowing from other languages, such as French and Latin in Middle and Early Modern English, displays an exceptionally large number of roughly synonymous expressions (Kay and Allan 2015: 12, 31, 88). Consequently, the task of selecting one specific synonym for the analysis is not an easy one. As seen in Sections 2.2 and 2.3, where previous studies of individual pairs and sets of adjectives were reviewed, certain tendencies are observed, with some semantic domains and even specific synonyms receiving particular attention. Thus, for instance, several analyses have focused on *-ic* and *-ical* adjectives (i.e., Gries 2001; 2003; Kaunisto 2001) and others have paid attention to basic descriptive adjectives from the domains of SIZE and AMOUNT, namely Biber, Conrad and Reppen (1998: Section 2.6) on *big*, *large*, and *great*, Taylor (2003) on *high* and *tall*, and Gries and Otani (2010) on the following two sets: *big*, *large*, and *great*, on the one hand, and *little*, *small*, and *tiny*, on the other. This work, however, sets out to examine a set of adjectival near-synonyms from the relatively little studied semantic domain of SMELL: *fragrant*, *perfumed*, *scented*, *sweet-scented*, and *sweet-smelling*, which designate the concept PLEASANT SMELLING. Section 3.1 is devoted to a description of this synonym set, drawing on data from different dictionaries and thesauri, and to an explanation of the motivations for selecting this particular group of adjectives.

Different analyses conducted on this synonym set are presented in subsequent chapters (i.e., Chapters 4–6) on the basis of corpus data. For the purposes of the present study and due to the relatively low frequency of some of the items in the synonym set object of study (cf. Section 4.1), a rather large corpus is desirable in order to achieve a representative sample. The corpus used here is *COHA* (Davies 2010–), which contains more than 400 million words. A description of this corpus is provided in Section 3.2, together with the data retrieval process of the occurrences of the near-synonyms employed in the case studies in Chapters 4, 5, and 6. The resulting databases were annotated for a series of language-external and language-internal variables pertaining to the contextual features of each attestation of the five near-synonyms. This annotation process is described in depth in Section 3.3.

3.1 Introducing the synonym set

Five adjectival near-synonyms from the olfactory domain are the object of study of the analyses conducted in the present monograph, namely *fragrant, perfumed, scented, sweet-scented,* and *sweet-smelling*. These five items are exemplified in (6)–(10):

(6) It had rained a little last night, and the moist earth was **fragrant**. (*COHA*, 2009, FIC, WifeGodsNovel)

(7) Jake touched warm, breathing woman, inhaled her freshly bathed scent and found her primal essence beneath the **perfumed** soap and body lotion. (*COHA*, 2007, FIC, WolfTalesIII)

(8) You can think of this smoky entre from W. Park Kerr's "Burning Desires: Salsa, Smoke and Sizzle From Down by the Rio Grande," as pork chops with red-hot **scented** applesauce all grown. (*COHA*, 2007, NEWS, Denver)

(9) As his eyes adjusted ever so slowly to the gloom, he saw looming shadows, blurred shapes like enormous trees that stirred not at all in the gentle **sweet-scented** wind. (*COHA*, 2005, FIC, FantasySciFi)

(10) Tapping one slim cigarette out of the pack, she brought the **sweet-smelling** tobacco to her lips and searched blindly for her lighter [. . .]. (*COHA*, 2003, FIC, RoomService)

The main motivations for selecting these particular lexical items are explained in Section 3.1.1. Section 3.1.2, in turn, offers a review of the existing descriptions of these adjectives as provided in dictionaries and thesauri, concentrating specifically on their etymology, different senses, and examples of use.

3.1.1 Why the concept PLEASANT SMELLING

As mentioned in the introduction to this chapter, the semantic domain of SMELL has hitherto been relatively understudied in semantic research, especially in the domain of synonymy. In later years, with the increased interest in perception in the field of cognitive linguistics, a considerable number of studies on the senses have seen the light. This branch of investigation has been labeled sensory linguistics by Winter (2019). In the olfactory domain, several studies have focused on the role of smell in figurative language, both as a target and source domain (cf. for instance, Ibarretxe-Antuñano 1999; Digonnet 2018; Kövecses 2019) and recently an edited volume including work on the lexicon of olfaction in different languages has been published (cf. contributions in Jędrzejowski and Staniewski 2020). A common claim in the literature is that humans, despite being able to identify and discriminate a wide range of smells, experience difficulties when having to name them (e.g., Ibarretxe-Antuñano 1999: 36; Yeshurun and Sobel 2010: 216). This can be one of the reasons why the odor vocabulary has not been researched to the same extent as other domains of perception such as that of COLOR (e.g., Berlin and Kay 1969; Wright 2011; Biggam 2012; Sandford 2016; 2018; 2021) or the lexicon related to the other four senses (i.e., hearing, vision, taste, and touch), which have been claimed to be much more extensive and precise in English and other Germanic languages (e.g., Sperber 1975: 115–116; Digonnet 2018: 178–179; Winter 2019: 94, 171). This does not mean, however, that humans have a poor sense of olfaction. On the contrary, the sense of smell is considered to be one of the most diverse ones, with up to one trillion olfactory stimuli being discriminated by humans vs. for instance, only half a million different auditory tones (Bushdid et al. 2014; McGann 2017). In fact, it has been demonstrated that languages outside those belonging to the Indo-European family (e.g., Tsimané and Seri, spoken in Bolivia and Mexico, respectively) have a much richer terminology to refer to olfaction (Majid and Burenhult 2014; Jędrzejowski and Staniewski 2020: 3–5). Despite the claim of English, among other Germanic languages, having a rather poor lexicon to refer to olfaction, especially when it comes to denoting agreeable smells (Winter 2019: 206–207), the semantic classification offered by the *HTOED*, which groups all senses of words into semantic categories, includes more than 900 word senses in the category labelled SMELL AND ODOUR.[14] The great number of words belonging to this semantic class therefore seems to go against previous claims about the extensiveness and precision of this semantic domain in English. In fact, a substantial number of the words in SMELL AND ODOUR are adjectives, many of which are closely related to the near-synonymous adjectives object of study in the present monograph, with some minor variations in definition or use. Therefore, this semantic field seems to be a specially interesting one for research on synonymy. Examples of these semantically related adjectives include *aromatic* (*OED*, s.v. *aromatic* adj. 1), *balmy* (*OED*, s.v. *balmy* adj. 3), *odoriferous* (*OED*, s.v. *odoriferous* adj. 1), *odorous* (*OED*, s.v. *odorous* adj.), *perfumy* (*OED*, s.v. *perfumy* adj), *redolent* (*OED*, s.v. *redolent* adj. 1 and 2), and *sweet*

---

[14] Although American English orthographic conventions are used in the present monograph, the British spelling of the labels of semantic categories in the *HTOED* is retained to maintain the original nomenclature.

(*OED*, s.v. *sweet* adj. 2), among others, many of which are loanwords from French and/or Latin that entered English between the fifteenth and the seventeenth centuries (cf. also Durkin 2014: 413–414).

Second, as demonstrated in a previous pilot study on this synonym set (Pettersson-Traba 2021), there seem to be some intriguing diachronic developments regarding the relationship between the selected adjectives in the latter part of Late Modern and Present-Day American English. By analyzing the noun collocates of the adjectives in attributive function, Pettersson-Traba discovers in her analysis a tendency for the adjectives to be increasingly used to modify artificial, as opposed to natural, smells. Additionally, *fragrant* and *perfumed*, which were initially the most frequent adjectives, are gradually replaced by *scented*, thus reflecting a change, which still seems to be ongoing, in the relation between the near-synonyms over time. The concept PLEASANT SMELLING therefore appears to be a particularly interesting and relevant object of study for the purposes of the present work, which aims at uncovering the semantic processes that specific lexical synonyms undergo with time, as well as the underlying motivations for such processes.

Finally, another crucial reason for selecting this synonym set is its rather low degree of polysemy, which is advantageous for the innovative approach adopted here. Given that the main focus is on the semantic relation of synonymy, examining a set of lexical items that, besides being synonymous, are also highly polysemous would result in an extremely complex and almost unfeasible study. For example, analyzing a highly polysemous synonym set would require a great amount of manual pruning to ensure that the final dataset contained exclusively those instances which are truly synonymous and therefore interchangeable. This would entail a great deal of "donkey work" as, to my knowledge, no semantically tagged diachronic corpora exist to date.[15] Nevertheless, the semantic structure of the selected five near-synonymous adjectives is not devoid of complexity, with at least three senses being shared by all of them, including a figurative one. This issue is further discussed in the next section.

3.1.2 Revising reference works

The information about the near-synonyms reviewed in this section is based on different English dictionaries and thesauri, both historical and present-day. The list

---

15 It is even difficult to find semantically tagged synchronic corpora, although a few do exist. One example is the *English SemCor Corpus* (Landes, Leacock, and Fellbaum 1998), which includes semantic annotations for sense.

of present-day dictionaries includes the following: *American Heritage Dictionary of the English Language* (*AHDOE*), *Cambridge Dictionary* (*CD*), *Collins Dictionary* (*CoD*), *Lexico*, *Longman Dictionary of Contemporary English* (*LDOCE*), *MacMillan Dictionary* (*MD*), *Merriam-Webster* (*MW*), and *Newbury House Dictionary of American English* (*NHDAE*). All of them offer information about the current senses of the adjectives and examples of use. Moreover, several of the dictionaries contain a thesaurus section, thus providing synonyms and antonyms of words. *CoD*, which uses data from the *COBUILD Corpus* to exemplify the different meanings of words, also gives information about their usage frequency, not only in Present-Day English but also in earlier periods of the language. The reference work therefore serves to shed light on the different senses and uses of the near-synonyms at issue in contemporary English. In addition, historical information has been drawn from the *OED*, which is considered to be the largest and most comprehensive dictionary of English (e.g., Hoffmann 2004: 18). The *OED* constitutes an unparalleled database when it comes to tracking the history of English words and their meanings from the time when they entered the language until the present-day, thus serving as an essential guide for research on historical English. As such, it includes earlier meanings and etymology alongside current meanings. Each entry in the *OED* provides information about the pronunciation, spelling, frequency band in Present-Day English etymology, POS, and senses of a word. By making use of the examples of usage one can ascertain the first known attestation of the different meanings of a word and, in many cases, it is also possible to establish the relation between senses.

The *OED* makes evident that *fragrant*, *perfumed*, and *scented* are loanwords that were borrowed from French in Early Modern English, specifically during the first half of the sixteenth century (cf. examples (11)–(13) below), as is the case of many words in this particular semantic domain (Durkin 2014: 414; cf. Section 3.1.1 above). However, despite this common origin, the way they entered the English language differs. *Fragrant*, which comes from the French adjective *fragrant*, ultimately derives from Latin *frāgrant-em*, the present participle of *frāgrāre* 'to smell sweetly.' However, although it stems from a participial form, when *fragrant* was borrowed into English, the participial nature of this word was no longer recognizable. Both *perfumed* and *scented*, in turn, were formed through the process of derivation by adding the suffix *-ed* (*OED*, s.v. *-ed* suffix[1]) to the verbal base forms *perfume* and *scent*, which had previously entered English through borrowing from French.[16] Given that the process of derivation took place in English, *perfumed* and

---

16 Another possibility, according to the *OED*, is that *perfumed* and *scented* derive from the nominal forms *perfume* and *scent* plus the suffix *-ed* (*OED*, s.v. *-ed* suffix[2]).

scented, unlike *fragrant*, retained their participial form. For this reason, it can be safely hypothesized that these two adjectives still maintain at least some of their verbal semantic functions today, namely that of 'denoting a process or action' (Biber et al. 1999: 63).This may also be the case of the adjective *sweet-scented*, first attested at the end of the sixteenth century (cf. example (14)), given that it is a compound formed by the loanword *scented* and the Old English adjective *sweet*. On the other hand, *sweet-smelling* is a composite form first attested in the early fifteenth century that combines the adjective *sweet* and the gerund form of *smell*, also of Old English origin (cf. example (15)). Therefore, as on many other occasions in the history of English, near-synonymy arises in this specific case as a result of borrowing from Latin and French in the Early Modern English period, with loanwords —*fragrant, perfumed, scented*, and, to a certain extent, *sweet-scented*— coming to be established in the language alongside an already existing native expression with the same meaning, that is, *sweet-smelling*.

(11)   The **fragraunt** odour, and oyntment of swete flour (c.1530. *OED*, s.v. *fragrant* adj.)

(12)   Suffitus, **perfumed**. (1538. *OED*, s.v. *perfumed* adj. 1)

(13)   Many here smell strong but none so ranke as he A stronger **sented** knaue [knave] then he was cannot bee. (?c.1562. *OED*, s.v. *scented* adj. 1)

(14)   **Sweet sented** Roe (1591. *OED*, s.v. *sweet-scented* adj. a)

(15)   A place..Y-set aboute with floures so **swete smellyng**. (c.1400. *OED*, s.v. *sweet-smelling* adj. 1)

Although not all the dictionaries consulted distinguish the same senses for the five near-synonyms, they all provide the same basic meaning 'having a sweet pleasant smell' for the five adjectives. This general sense is in fact the only definition provided for *sweet-scented* and *sweet-smelling* in the *OED*, *Lexico*, and *CoD*, which include an independent entry for these two compound words.[17] Similarly,

---

17 *MW* does not provide an entry for *sweet-smelling*, only for *sweet-scented*. *MW* and the *OED* also offer an additional sub-sense for *sweet-scented*, namely 'in names of species or varieties of plants having sweet-smelling flowers, leaves, etc.,' (*OED*, s.v. *sweet-scented* adj. b), as in *sweet-scented pea* or *sweet-scented geranium*. Examples exhibiting this sense are excluded from the present study as the adjective in this case forms part of the vernacular name of the plants. None of the other four adjectives seem to be used in this sense according to the reference material consulted here.

fragrant occurs only with this sense in all eight Present-Day English dictionaries, while the *OED* points out that this adjective can also be used figuratively to mean simply 'sweet or pleasant', as in example (16), where *fragrant* co-occurs with the noun *fame*, which refers to an abstract entity and can therefore not emit an odor:[18]

(16) In Basil He did end his days, as full of yeeres, as **fragrant fame**. (1651. *OED*, s.v. *fragrant* adj.)

Whereas a few dictionaries also define *perfumed* and *scented* exclusively in the general and figurative senses just mentioned, others make a distinction between two senses, which will here be labeled 'natural' and 'artificial'.[19] This is the case of, for instance, *MD*, which lists the following two definitions for *perfumed* and thus serves to illustrate these two senses:
(i) '[P]leasant to smell because of natural qualities' (*MD*, s.v. *perfumed* adj.)
(ii) '[P]leasant to smell because perfume has been added or used' (*MD*, s.v. *perfumed* adj.)

Therefore, the dictionaries that make such a distinction assume that there is a difference in meaning depending on whether the source of the smell is natural, in which case nouns modified by the adjectives denote entities which can emit a smell on their own, such as *wallflowers* in (17), or artificial, where the adjectives

---

18 This figurative meaning is argued to have emerged through the conceptual association between sweetness and pleasure and many adjectives which imply sweetness, not just in the domain of olfaction, but also in that of taste (e.g., *sugary* and *honeysome*) have developed a similar figurative meaning whereby they designate pleasure in general terms (Bagli 2021: 119–120). The conceptual mapping underlying this figurative meaning has been explained in different ways in the specialized literature: whereas, for instance Kövecses (2019) analyze such instances through the conceptual metaphor PLEASURE IS SWEET, Bagli (2021: 119–120) claims that they originate via the conceptual metonymy SWEET FOR PLEASANT as the basis for the mapping lies in "[. . .] the embodied value of sugars and perception of sweetness".
19 Moreover, two additional senses are provided for *scented* in the *OED*:
(i) 'Of tea, tobacco, etc.,: flavoured with an aromatic ingredient. Also: having a fragrant taste as if flavoured by an aromatic ingredient. [. . .]' (*OED*, s.v. *scented* adj. 2b)
(ii) 'With modifying word. Chiefly of an animal: having a sense of smell of the specified kind. [. . .]' (*OED*, s.v. *scented* adj. 3)

The former meaning is classified in the *OED* as a subsense of the artificial sense and, since the other adjectives have also been found to collocate with tea- and tobacco-related nouns, for instance *sweet-smelling tobacco* in example (15) above, examples featuring this sense are included in the subsequent corpus analyses. Meaning (ii), on the contrary, is exclusive to *scented* and is therefore excluded here.

collocate with nouns referring to entities which can acquire a pleasant smell only by being impregnated by a pleasantly smelling substance, as in the case of *bath products* in (18).

(17) I planted some wonderful, dark-red, **scented wallflowers.** (*CD*, s.v. *scented* adj.)

(18) Indulge in your favorite **scented bath products.** (*CD*, s.v. *scented* adj.)

In fact, in the *OED* the primary and first attested sense of *perfumed* is '[i]mpregnated with perfume; wearing perfume; scented with a (usually pleasant) odour' (*OED*, s.v. *perfumed* adj. 1), exemplified in (12) above. Therefore, as concerns the prototypicality or onomasiological salience of the near-synonyms, the reference works seem to indicate that artificially pleasant aromas are more likely to be referred to by using the adjectives *perfumed* and *scented* rather than *fragrant*, *sweet-scented*, and *sweet-smelling*. In other words, the former two adjectives are in all likelihood more prototypical in the artificial sense. This state of affairs may be a result of the etymological roots of the adjectives. As previously mentioned, *perfumed* and *scented* retain their participial form and thus probably also some of their original verbal functions, even when used as adjectives, namely '[t]o impregnate with a (usually pleasant) odour; to impart a (sweet) smell to [. . .]' (*OED*, s.v. *perfume* v. 2). However, it is important to note that *fragrant*, *sweet-scented*, and *sweet-smelling* can also be used in the artificial sense (cf. examples (19)–(21)), as proved by several instances of these three adjectives in the dictionaries. Moreover, *sweet-smelling*, in contrast to *sweet-scented*, also appears in the figurative sense, although no dictionary mentions this particular sense for this adjective (cf. example (22)).

(19) With soap still to be invented, the **fragrant oils** and **waters** were used in bathing and for perfuming hair. (*Lexico*, s.v. *fragrant* adj.)

(20) A scrumptious dinner with some **sweet-scented candles** and flowers is really worth coming home to. (*Lexico*, s.v. *sweet-scented* adj.)

(21) A light, **sweet-smelling formula** to support soft, fine curls that are prone to drooping. (2009. *CoD*, s.v. *sweet-smelling* adj.)

(22) But the **project's success** is not that **sweet-smelling**. (2007. *CoD*, s.v. *sweet-smelling* adj.)

In (19)–(21), *fragrant*, *sweet-scented*, and *sweet-smelling* collocate with nouns referring to entities that need to be impregnated by an artificial substance so as to release an aroma, namely *oils* and *waters* (19), *candles* (20), and *formula* (21).[20] In (22) *sweet-smelling* co-occurs with the noun phrase *project's success*, where the head noun *success* refers to an abstract entity that, as in the case of *memory* in (16) above, cannot emit an odor, and thus has to be interpreted as a metaphorical use of the adjective with the meaning 'pleasant or agreeable' through the pattern PLEASURE IS SWEET or SWEET FOR PLEASANT. Table 2 summarizes the division into senses provided by each of the dictionaries and thesauri consulted for each of the five near-synonymous adjectives.

Table 2: Sense division of the five adjectives according to nine dictionaries and thesauri.

Senses \ Synonyms	Fragrant	Perfumed	Scented	Sweet-scented	Sweet-smelling
General basic sense 'Emitting a sweet or pleasant odor' / 'Having a pleasant or sweet smell'	AHDOE, CD, CoD, LDOCE, Lexico, MD, MW, NHDAE, OED	CD	CD, LDOCE, Lexico, MD, MW	CoD, Lexico, MW, OED	CoD, Lexico, OED
Natural sense 'Naturally having or producing a sweet, pleasant smell'	–	CoD, Lexico, MD, OED	CD, CoD, OED	–	–
Artificial sense 'Impregnated or scented with a sweet-smelling substance'	–	CoD, Lexico, MD, OED	CD, CoD, OED	–	–
Figurative sense 'Sweet, pleasant; cloying; made to seem sweet, disguised'	OED	OED	OED	–	–
NO ENTRY	–	AHDOE, LDOCE, MW, NHDAE	AHDOE, NHDAE	AHDOE, CD, LDOCE, NHDAE, MD	AHDOE, CD, LDOCE, MD, MW, NHDAE

---

20 Note that in example (20), *sweet-scented* also modifies the noun *flowers*, which refers to an entity that can release a smell on its own (cf. Section 3.3 below for an explanation of how coordinated nouns modified by the adjectives under analysis are treated in the data annotation process).

Concerning the thesauri sections in the reference works, five out of the eight Present-Day English dictionaries include such a section in which synonyms are provided: *CD, CoD, Lexico, MD,* and *MW*. Most of them list the five adjectives as synonymous, with the exception of *sweet-smelling*, for which a thesaurus entry is not included in any of the dictionaries consulted. However, in both *CoD* and *Lexico*, *sweet-smelling* is registered as a synonym of *fragrant, perfumed, sweet-scented,* and *scented*.

As can be observed in most thesauri entries, several other adjectives are also listed as being synonymous with the five selected items, including the seven mentioned in Section 3.1.1 above, that is, *aromatic, balmy, odoriferous, odorous, perfumy, redolent,* and *sweet*, together with *fragranced*. Nevertheless, after careful examination of the definitions and examples of usage provided by the Present-Day English dictionaries and the *OED*, these adjectives have been excluded from the analysis for different reasons:

(i) In the case of *aromatic* (*OED*, s.v. *aromatic* adj. 1), its definition mentions a nuance of meaning which is not present in the definitions of any the five adjectives selected: if something is described as *aromatic* it entails that its scent stems from spices or herbs ('[h]aving the fragrant smell, and warm slightly pungent, taste, of spice [. . .]'). This is not always the case with *fragrant, perfumed, scented, sweet-scented,* and *sweet-smelling*.

(ii) The polysemous word *balmy*, although included in the *HTOED* in the category of SMELL AND ODOUR in one of its senses (i.e., *OED*, s.v. *balmy* adj. 3), seems to be more often used in other senses in Present-Day English, as this particular meaning, namely '[d]elicately and deliciously fragrant', is not often listed in the contemporary dictionaries (cf. for instance, the entries for *balmy* in *CD, Lexico, LDOCE, MD,* and *MW*). In fact, in most of the Present-Day English reference material only the sense '[o]f wind, air, weather, etc., Deliciously mild, fragrant, and soothing' (*OED*, s.v. *balmy* adj. 5) is included, and most examples of usage are illustrations of this particular sense, which indicates that *balmy* is today more semantically specialized than the five selected near-synonyms.

(iii) The two adjectives *odoriferous* and *odorous*, which originally shared the same definition as *fragrant, perfumed, scented, sweet-scented,* and *sweet-smelling*, have become generalized with time to denote unpleasant smells alongside pleasant ones. Moreover, in the case of *odorous*, it seems to have undergone recently a process of pejoration, just as the related noun *odor* discussed in Section 2.3, so that many of the Present-Day English dictionaries point out that it is now mostly used in the sense of 'malodorous' (e.g *CD*, s.v. *odorous* adj.; *Lexico*, s.v. *odorous* adj. 1). The recently acquired negative semantic prosody of *odorous* becomes evident if its noun collocates are compared in a historical corpus such as *COHA* and a contemporary one such as *COCA*: whereas the top noun collocates of *odorous* in the former include words such as *blossom*, *perfume*, *sweets*, and *breezes*, in the latter they include items such as *emissions*, *stinkweed*, and *toxin*, which clearly have negative connotations, as well as more neutral ones, for instance, *air* and *compound*. Such preliminary analyses of *odorous* suggest that it is an antonym rather than a synonym of *fragrant*, *perfumed*, *scented*, *sweet-scented*, and *sweet-smelling* in Present-Day English.

(iv) A similar scenario is found for *redolent*, which originally also shared the same definition as the five selected near-synonyms (*OED*, s.v. *redolent* adj. 1a), but which over time became differentiated from them. Although its first attested sense is 'of a pleasant sweet smell', it has come to acquire a different nuance of meaning and is nowadays more often used to denote a strong smell, thus being synonymous with *pungent*. Moreover, *redolent*, as evinced in most dictionaries, is most typically used in Present-Day English in the constructions *redolent with* or *redolent of*, which suggests that it is contextually more restricted.[21] When followed by *with* or *of*, *redolent* can also be used in the figurative sense '[i]mbued with or rich in a quality, a feeling, etc.; strongly suggestive or reminiscent of a particular thing', as in *[t]his dingy street was redolent with history* [. . .] (1989. *OED*, s.v. *redolent* adj. 2b), which does not belong to the semantic field of SMELL AND ODOUR. In fact, this particular sense seems to be one of the most common of *redolent* nowadays, given that it is the meaning that is first mentioned in many of the Present-Day English dictionaries (e.g., *CoD*, *LDOCE*, *Lexico*, and *MD*), and therefore its most the basic sense.

(v) The adjective *sweet* has been excluded from the analysis primarily due to the fact that it is a highly polysemous word with eleven different main senses and a large number of subsenses in the *OED*, of which only one belongs to the olfactory domain (*OED*, s.v. *sweet* adj. 2). In a recent analysis of the adjective *sweet*, Bagli (2021:130-135) shows that more than 50% of the occurrences examined of this word in *COCA* correspond to non-literal senses of the word whereby it is used to refer for instance to the semantic domain LOVE, including conceptualizations such as kindness, cuteness, sex, gentleness, innocence, among others. Given the extensive polysemy of the adjective and its large number of occurrences in *COHA* (41,970) it would have been extremely time-consuming to go through them manually in order to select only those which correspond to the meaning 'of a pleasant sweet smell'. Additionally, the difficulty of teasing apart some of the other senses of *sweet*, particularly that in which the adjective is used to designate a pleasant taste (*OED*, s.v. *sweet* adj. 1), from the one of interest here would further complicate the task

---

21 Out of the 452 occurrences of the adjective *redolent* in *COHA*, 378 instances, that is, 83.7%, are followed by either *with* or *of*.

(cf. Durkin and Allan 2016 for a similar argument). Consider examples (23) and (24), in which *sweet* and *fragrant* modify the noun *tea*. Whereas *fragrant* in (24) is most probably used to refer to the smell of the tea, *sweet* in (23) is more ambiguous and could refer either to the taste or to the aroma of the tea, or to both at the same time.

(23) Recovering her composure in the servant's parlor, watched by Mr. Grove's kind eyes as she sipped at her second cup of **sweet tea**, Mrs. France tried once again to explain to him the swirl of feelings that were in her head. (*COHA*, 1995, FIC, FantasySciFi)

(24) Greer nodded a greeting to Blythe as the other woman sipped a **fragrant tea** from a delicate china cup. (*COHA*, 2006, FIC, MatchMaker)

The difficulty of separating examples in which *sweet* refers to taste and smell might be due to the fact that olfaction is considered to be essential in the perception of flavor: many so-called flavors are in reality smells so some perceptions we classify as taste when ingesting something are in fact aromas (Bagli 2021: 23).[22]

(vi) Finally, the two adjectives *fragranced* and *perfumy*, while sharing the same definition as the five near-synonyms at issue, seem to be relatively infrequent in English. *Fragranced* is classified as rare in several of the dictionaries and, in fact, it is not attested in *COHA*. In turn, although *perfumy* occurs in *COHA*, there are only 15 instances of this adjective in the corpus. Such a small number of instances are not enough to extract any generalizations about the contextual behavior of *perfumy*, which has therefore been left out.

In conclusion, although *aromatic, balmy, odoriferous, odorous, redolent, sweet, fragranced*, and *perfumy* are all still semantically related to *fragrant, perfumed, scented, sweet-scented*, and *sweet-smelling*, with some of their senses belonging to the domain of SMELL AND ODOUR, their descriptions in the reference material suggest that they are not as prototypical to denote the concept PLEASANT SMELLING as the five selected adjectives. Therefore, the degree of synonymy holding between *fragrant, perfumed, scented, sweet-scented*, and *sweet-smelling* is probably higher, as they seem to be interchangeable in most, if not all, contexts of use. This is so

---

22 This is due to the so-called retronasal receptors, located in the nasal cavity, that identify smells emitted by food when ingesting it and send this information to the brain which in turn identifies it as taste (for more information on this process, cf. Smith 2015: 325-326).

because (i) they are defined in practically the same way in all dictionaries, (ii) the examples of usage provided are very similar, with some nouns appearing with all of them (e.g., *flower, smell,* and *water*), (iii) they are practically always listed as synonyms of one another, and (iv) they are sometimes defined in terms of each other.

Nonetheless, the dictionaries also point to some differences between the five terms at issue here concerning their frequency of use. The *OED*, which provides a frequency range between 1 (very low frequency) to 8 (very high frequency) for words in Present-Day English, assigns a rating of 5 to *fragrant* —that is, between 1 and 10 times per million words—, a rating of 4 to *perfumed, scented,* and *sweet-smelling* —that is, between 0.1 and 1 times per million words—, and a rating of 3 to *sweet-scented*— that is, between 0.01 and 0.1 times per million words. This suggests that *fragrant* is probably the dominant term in the set in Present-Day English. Additionally, *CoD* includes information regarding the frequency of four out of the five adjectives, namely *fragrant, perfumed, scented,* and *sweet-scented,* across time, particularly from the year 1708 to 2008. According to this data, based on *Google Ngrams, fragrant* and *perfumed* have decreased in frequency over time from 2.62 and 0.48 instances per million words in 1708, respectively, to 0.54 and 0.23 in 2008. Similarly, *sweet-scented* has gone from a frequency of 0.2 in 1720 to 0.01 in 2008. On the contrary, *scented* has increased in frequency throughout the same period, from 0 to 0.4 instances per million words. Interestingly, most changes seem to have taken place from approximately the nineteenth century onwards, precisely the time span covered in the present study. Despite this valuable frequency information for Present-Day English and earlier periods of English, neither the *OED* nor *CoD* shed any light on the distribution of the adjectives in different senses and more specific contexts of use.

The dictionaries and thesauri reviewed in the present section offer some important insights into the relation between the five near-synonymous adjectives *fragrant, perfumed, scented, sweet-scented,* and *sweet-smelling* regarding both their similarities and possible differences in terms of frequency and semantic characteristics. However, the information provided by these reference works is still insufficient in order to acquire a full understanding of the structure of the concept PLEASANT SMELLING and of the degree to which the five adjectival near-synonyms are interchangeable. As such, some questions are yet left unanswered:

(i) Are *perfumed* and *scented* the only adjectives of the set that are used in the artificial sense, i.e., 'pleasant to smell because perfume has been added or used', or do *fragrant, sweet-scented,* and *sweet-smelling* also appear in such semantic contexts?

(ii) If *fragrant, sweet-scented,* and *sweet-smelling* are also used in the artificial sense, is there any difference in their distribution, both in this and in the other senses (i.e., natural and figurative) of the adjectives?

(iii) Does the distribution of the five adjectives across senses remain stable over time or does it fluctuate? In other words, are the apparent changes in frequency of the adjectives revealed in *CoD* specific to one or several contexts of use or do they, on the contrary, occur equally across all contexts?
(iv) The reference works point to some semantic (dis)similarities among the adjectives, but do differences concerning, for instance, connotation, style, and/or morphosyntactic features also exist?

The analyses in the present monograph are designed in order to try to answer these research questions. However, before moving on to the results of these analyses, Sections 3.2 and 3.3 offer a description of the corpus used, as well as the data retrieval and annotation processes.

3.2 Corpus description and data retrieval

Given the relatively low frequency of the five near-synonymous adjectives object of study, a large corpus is necessary to carry out the analyses in Chapters 4–6. As has already been noted by other scholars (e.g., Baker 2011; Davies 2019), small corpora do not contain enough data to conduct lexico-semantic research unless the lexical items object of study are highly frequent. This problem is further aggravated when diachronic work is carried out as the research has to divide the data into different periods (with even less data) to trace the development of the linguistic phenomenon under investigation. For this reason, the data used was drawn from *COHA*. Released in 2010, *COHA* is one of the largest structured historical corpus of English to date, containing about 400 million words of running text from more than 100,000 individual texts, which are divided into four different genres or text-types: fiction, popular magazines, newspapers, and non-fiction (Davies 2012).[23] *COHA* covers the period 1810–2009 in American English, and this time span of 200 years is split into 20 decades. However, *COHA* is not a balanced corpus in terms of number of words, neither across decades nor across genres, as it contains considerably more data for the later decades than for the earlier ones, and fiction accounts for a much higher percentage of the data than the other three genres.[24] For instance, until the 1850s there are less than 17 million words per decade, whereas the last two decades, 1990s

---

23 Unless otherwise specified, the analyses in the present monograph are based on the pre-2021 version of the corpus, not the updated version, released in 2021, which contains more data from additional text-types.
24 Cf. the following webpage for a table displaying the number of words across the different decades and text-types: https://varieng.helsinki.fi/CoRD/corpora/COHA/basic.html.

and 2000s, include nearly double the amount of running text, almost 28 and 30 million words, respectively. Despite the unequal distribution of the data, an effort was made by the corpus compilers to keep the distribution of the different genres even through the 20 decades. For instance, fiction totals between 48–55% of the data in each decade. Similarly, roughly the same percentage of popular magazines, non-fiction, and newspapers is maintained over time, with the exception of newspapers in the first six decades. This distribution ensures that possible changes are not just a byproduct of fluctuations in the number of words per genre over time, but that they reflect actual changes (Davies 2012: 124).

Two separate databases were created from the data in *COHA*, given that the aims of the case studies in Chapters 4 and 5, on the one hand, and Chapter 6, on the other, differ and thus impose distinct requirements on the data. For the first database the following queries were made by using *COHA*'s online interface: 'fragrant_j*', 'perfumed_j*', 'scented_j*', 'sweet-scented_j*', 'sweetscented_j*', 'sweet scented', 'sweet-smelling_j*', 'sweetsmelling_j*', and 'sweet smelling', where the POS-tag '_j*' indicates that only adjectives were searched for. The strings 'sweet scented' and 'sweet smelling', written as two separate words without hyphenation, were not specified for POS because it is not possible to add one POS-tag to two separate words, as the tag would only affect one of them. In addition, the instances of *perfumed* and *scented* tagged as verbs in *COHA* were also retrieved, that is, 'perfumed_v*' and 'scented_v*', where '_v*' stands for verb. This step was taken in order to identify possible adjectival uses of these lexical items which had been erroneously tagged as verbs.

The instances of the adjectives *sweet-scented* and *sweet-smelling* were retrieved by means of three distinct search strings given that, although the two compounds are mostly spelt with a hyphen, alternative spellings exist, as in many other cases of compounds (Huddleston and Pullum et al. 2002: 451).[25] It is a well-known fact that it is often very difficult to disambiguate between compound words and syntactic constructions formed by two independent lexical items (e.g., *a blackbird* vs. *a black bird*), given that there is not a clear-cut division between the two, but rather a cline (e.g., Biber et al. 1999: 589–590; Huddleston and Pullum et al. 2002: 1644). This problem is further aggravated when texts from different historical periods are considered, as in the present analyses, because as pointed out by Quirk et al. (1985: 1569), it is usually the case that compounds first occur as individual words and only once they become more established and lexicalized are they written as hyphenated or even as single words. Although

---

[25] For the sake of convenience, throughout the present monograph, these two compounds are always referred to by means of the hyphenated alternative, that is, *sweet-scented* and *sweet-smelling*, as the vast majority of examples retrieved from *COHA* correspond to these spellings (cf. Table 3 below).

alternative interpretations may exist for such ambiguous cases, the decision was taken to include in the analysis the examples corresponding to the search strings 'sweet scented' and 'sweet smelling' because they seem to behave exactly as those instances in which the adjectives are written with a hyphen or as one word. Consider in this connection examples (25)–(27):

(25) Before it lay a neat smooth little court, surrounded by a close hedge, of a **sweet scented** red and white **flower**, resembling the honeysuckle in shape. (*COHA*, 1828, MAG, NorthAmRev)

(26) It has white, **sweetscented flowers**, arranged in the same manner as the last; stem without spots. (*COHA*, 1851, NF, FlowerGardenBrecks)

(27) Bladder Senna. Colutea, an ancient name of a bush with **sweet-scented flowers**. (*COHA*, 1851, NF, FlowerGardenBrecks)

In all three examples, *sweet(-)scented* modifies the noun *flower(s)* without any discernible difference in meaning. It is worth mentioning here that a series of criteria, both syntactic and non-syntactic, have been used to distinguish between a true compound and a mere combination of two independent words (Biber et al. 1999: 589–590; Huddleston and Pullum et al. 2002: 448–451). Among syntactic criteria, combinations of two words can be individually coordinated with and modified by a different word, whereas this is not possible in the case of compounds. As to non-syntactic criteria, compounds are typically stressed on the first element, are spelt as one word (either without or with a hyphen), and have a non-transparent meaning. Combinations of two independent words, in turn, are typically stressed on the second element, are written as two separate words, and have a transparent meaning. These syntactic and non-syntactic criteria, however, were not easily applicable to the current dataset for various reasons. First, given that *COHA* contains only written language, it is not possible to know the stress patterns of the relevant examples. Second, orthography is not a reliable clue, as many compounds have alternative spellings and, as mentioned above, compounds are typically first written as separate words and later on as hyphenated or single words as they become more accepted and established. Moreover, hyphenation is claimed to be less common in American English (Quirk et al. 1985: 1569). Finally, meaning is also problematic in this case, given that the semantics of the compounds *sweet-smelling* and *sweet-scented* are highly transparent in the sense that they are the sum of their components, namely 'that smells sweet' and 'that has a sweet scent', respectively. Therefore, their meaning is the same if they are spelt as two separate units. Considering the difficulty of applying these criteria to the data from *COHA*, the decision to include in the analyses all instances corresponding to the search queries 'sweet scented' and 'sweet smelling' was further reinforced.

Table 3 summarizes the data retrieval process of the first database, relevant to the analyses in Chapters 4 and 5, and the initial number of examples extracted by means of each query.

Table 3: Number of instances retrieved per query.

Query	Number of instances retrieved
fragrant_j*	3,374
perfumed_j*	792
scented_j*	792
sweet-scented	173
sweetscented_j*	5
sweet scented	37
sweet-smelling_j*	207
sweetsmelling_j*	4
sweet smelling	37
perfumed_v*	340
scented_v*	577
Total	6,338

The second database, relevant for the discussion in Chapter 6, does not include the instances of the adjectives, but their noun collocates. Therefore, the collocates option in *COHA* was used to retrieve the lemmas of the collocates of *fragrant*, *perfumed*, *scented*, *sweet-scented*, and *sweet-smelling* by means of the POS-tag _nn* in an L5–R5 context window. An L5–R5 context window was selected in this case since it has been shown that tighter windows, such as one or two words to the left and to the right of the node word, often lead to data sparseness, especially if low frequency items are considered (Sahlgren 2006). In addition, tighter context windows (e.g., L1-R1 or L2-R2) are considered to be more suitable if one is interested in extracting semantically (dis)similar items of the node, including its synonyms and antonyms (Peirsman, Heylen, and Geeraerts 2008: 40). In turn, a slight loosening of the context window, for instance, to L5-R5, is desirable if one wants to retrieve a greater variety of typical collocates of the target word. Yet another possibility is to analyze solely those words or phrases which are syntactically connected to the node, in the present study those nouns which are modified, either syntactically —or semantically— by the adjectives (e.g., *the scented candle*; *the candle is scented*). Nevertheless, retrieving only the modified nouns of the adjectives would again cause data sparseness as a much lower number of collocates would be included in the analysis. In the present study, the decision was taken to analyze only the noun collocates of the adjectives because, as argued by several scholars, including Geeraerts (1986) and Gries (2001; 2003), nouns are more informative than other types of collocates when delineating the semantic structure of adjectives (cf. Section 2.2.2). The second database did not require further annotation due to the fact that it is used only in the analyses of individual collocates in Chapter 6. On the contrary, the instances retrieved for the first database were manually pruned and subsequently annotated for a number of variables, both language-external and language-internal ones. The pruning and annotation processes of the first database are the focus of the next section.

3.3 Data annotation

Prior to the annotation process, the instances in the first database were revised one by one to exclude false positives, as well as other problematic examples. First, in the case of duplicated occurrences, that is, when the same instance appeared more than once in the corpus, only one of them was maintained in the database. Second, three cases of *perfumed* from the same source (for instance, example (28)) were used in a metalinguistic context and were therefore excluded, as they are not actual instances of the adjective:

(28)   Note also the magical use of the "f's" and "v's" in "**perfumed**," "love," and "silver," and of the "m's" in "**perfumed**," "them," "made," and "amorous." (*COHA*, 1909, MAG, Harpers)

Third, two instances of *perfumed* and two of *fragrant* were also removed given that they were part of the title of a book (29) and of the name of a brand (30):

(29)   She burned your translation of **The Perfumed Garden**, claiming you would not have wanted to publish it unless you needed the money for it, and you didn't need it, of course, because you were now dead. (*COHA*, 1971, FIC, YourScatteredBodies)

(30)   She had given him a bottle of **Arkady Ferson's Fragrant Goddess**, prepared by him and described in his 1969 treatise [...]. (*COHA*, 2007, FIC, FantasySciFi)

Fourth, during the course of the manual revision, some false positives of 'perfumed_j*'and 'scented_j*' were identified, that is, examples which were erroneously tagged as adjectives, but in fact corresponded to verbal uses. This is the case of, for instance, examples (31) and (32):

(31) He was determined to have a luxurious bath, to be shaved and **perfumed**, to leave behind him the very dust of his past life. (*COHA*, 1893, FIC, SingerFromSea)

(32) The cops had heard that one before, and **scented** trouble. One of them began to advance. (*COHA*, 1970, MAG, Time)

In (31), *perfumed* is a past participle in a verb phrase in the passive voice, with the meaning '[t]o impregnate with a (usually pleasant) odour; to impart a (sweet) smell to; to apply perfume to' (*OED*, s.v. *perfume* v. 2). In (32), *scented* is the past participle or past simple of the verb *scent*, used figuratively to mean '[t]o perceive or discover as if by smell; to detect or discern instinctively or from subtle indications; to intuit' (*OED*, s.v. *scent* v. I. 2b).

Among the instances of *perfumed* and *scented* tagged as verbs, that is, those retrieved by means of the queries 'perfumed_v*' and 'scented_v*', some were in fact tagging errors, as *scented* and *perfumed* were used as adjectives rather than verbs. As is well-known, it is not always easy to determine whether a particular instance of words such as *scented* or *perfumed* functions as a past participle or as a participial adjective. In fact, several such ambiguous instances were identified in the database and for this reason, it was necessary to resort to some criteria to determine whether such cases counted as adjectival uses or as verbal uses. A number of different criteria have been put forward in the literature (e.g., Quirk et al. 1985: Section 7.16; Biber et al. 1999: 505–506; Huddleston and Pullum et al. 2002: 78–79) to decide whether these ambiguous instances were located closer to the adjectival end or closer to the verbal end of the continuum. Even though participial adjectives are not considered prototypical instances of the adjectival class, a participle is regarded more adjective-like than verb-like if:[26]

(i) the focus is more on the state resulting from an action rather than on the action itself, as in example (33), where the emphasis is on the look of the man, not on the process whereby he acquired his *barbered and perfumed* appearance;
(ii) it can occur with lexical copular verbs such as *appear*, *feel*, or *seem* (cf. example (34));
(iii) it can be modified by adjectival intensifiers such as *very* (cf. example (35));

---

[26] It is worth noting here that these criteria are postulated to disambiguate between past participles and participial adjectives in Present-Day English. Therefore, it is not entirely clear whether they can also be safely applied to data from earlier periods in the history of English. However, these criteria are often the only way of reaching a relatively objective decision regarding such ambiguous cases.

(iv) it can be inflected for degree, either comparative or superlative (cf. examples (33) and (36)); and
(v) it can be coordinated with central or true adjectives (cf. examples (34) and (37)).

(33) And, oddly enough, this **look** of premature senility was not masculine but feminine. Though no more barbered and **perfumed** than the next Italian man, he evoked the black mass of the dressing-table and the hand-mirror. (*COHA*, 1950, FIC, CastColdEye)

(34) Our voices **seemed low** and **scented** with fragrant incense, hidden behind the static-cracked passion of the Baptists, the Pentecostal brimstone and fury [. . .]. (*COHA*, 1998, FIC, MassachRev)

(35) They did, however, keep up a suspicious intimacy with a brilliantly lighted, though not **very** fragrantly **scented**, saloon on the left. (*COHA*, 1858, FIC, LifeAdventures)

(36) The breezes that bore them were **more** exquisitely **scented** than those which had soothed my doubts, bad stimulated my imagination on her feast-days. (*COHA*, 1922, MAG, Atlantic)

(37) She was a frail, stern-voiced patridge of a woman, always **perfumed** and **attractive**, but unlike Anda, she looked as if she might come off in peeling with her clothes. (*COHA*, 1968, FIC, Bloodline)

Examples of *perfumed* and *scented* which met any of these criteria were consequently kept in the database and subsequently included in the analyses.

Finally, some occurrences of the five near-synonyms were counted more than once. This is the case of examples in which the adjectives modify two or more coordinated nouns, as in (38):

(38) For years Italy led in perfuming; it supplied the rest of Europe with sweet bags, perfume cakes for throwing on fires, **fragrant candles** and **cosmetics**, **scented gloves** and **pomanders**. (*COHA*, 1922, MAG, Mentor)

Four entries in the database were derived from example (38): two instances of *fragrant* and two of *scented*. This was so because both adjectives here modify more than one noun, which appear in coordination, namely, *candles and cosmetics*, in the case of *fragrant*, and *gloves and pomanders*, in the case of *scented*. The reasons for taking this decision were two. First, in many such cases, the coordinated nouns belong to different semantic domains and even instantiate different senses of the adjectives, which poses problems for the annotation of the variables Sense (cf. Section 3.3.1) and Semantic category (cf. Section 3.3.2). In (38), for instance, the nouns modified by *fragrant*, namely, *candles* and *cosmetics*, were classified as belonging to the semantic categories OBJECT and COSMETICS, respectively. Similarly, the nouns modified by *scented*, *gloves* and *pomanders*, were categorized as TEXTILE AND CLOTHING and COSMETICS, respectively. Second, given that one of the variables for which the data was annotated included the specific nouns modified by the adjectives (cf. Section 3.3.2 below), coordinated nouns had to be kept separate.

As mentioned in Section 3.2, the data retrieval process resulted in a total of 6,338 instances (cf. Table 3 above). Following the manual pruning discussed in the preceding paragraphs, 5,764 occurrences of the five adjectives remained in the first database. These examples were subsequently annotated for eleven variables of different types, including language-internal semantic (Sections 3.3.1–3.3.3) and non-semantic factors (Section 3.3.4), as well as language-external ones (Section 3.3.5).

3.3.1 Language-internal semantic variables: Sense

As argued in Section 2.2, the variables which influence the choice between near-synonyms vary from one set to another, depending on factors such as their POS or their semantic domain (cf. for instance, Hanks 1996: 92, 96; Liu 2010: 61). Previous studies on adjectival near-synonyms reveal that semantic factors are the most significant, particularly those pertaining to the nouns that the adjectives modify, such as animacy, concreteness, countability, and more specific semantic categorizations (e.g., Gries 2001; 2003; Gries and Otani 2010; Liu 2010). Therefore, in the present monograph, the semantic factors examined also focus on features of the nouns modified by *fragrant*, *perfumed*, *scented*, *sweet-scented*, and *sweet-smelling*. In fact, out of the eleven variables for which the data was annotated, five are language-internal semantic factors which directly or indirectly relate to the modified nominal elements. These are Sense, Semantic category, Animacy, Concreteness, and Countability.

The first of these five variables is Sense. The basic meaning of all five adjectives is 'having a sweet pleasant smell' but, as discussed in Section 3.1 above, some dictionaries distinguish between two related senses, namely the artificial and the natural senses, depending on the source of the smell. While this distinction is made explicit only in the entries for *perfumed* and *scented*, we saw that *fragrant*, *sweet-scented*, and *sweet-smelling* could also be used to denote both natural and artificial smells (cf. examples (19)–(21)). Moreover, a figurative sense, 'sweet or pleasant', was also distinguished in the *OED* for *fragrant, perfumed*, and *scented*, and instances of *sweet-smelling* in this sense also occurred in examples of usage offered in the dictionaries (cf. example (22)). Although a considerable amount of information is provided in the dictionaries and thesauri, one issue that is yet not clear concerns the distribution of the adjectives across these three senses (i.e., natural, artificial, and figurative). Therefore, the data was first annotated for a variable called Sense, which contained these three senses as levels. Examples (16)–(18) in Section 3.1.2 which represent the figurative, natural, and artificial, senses, respectively, are here reprinted as (39)–(41) for the sake of convenience:

(39) In Basil He did end his days, as full of yeeres, as **fragrant fame**. (1651. *OED*, s.v. *fragrant* adj.)

(40) I planted some wonderful, dark-red, **scented wallflowers**. (*CD*, s.v. *scented* adj.)

(41) Indulge in your favorite **scented bath products**. (*CD*, s.v. *scented* adj.)

During the annotation process, it became clear that many cases could not be safely assigned to any of the three aforementioned senses, given that their interpretation was ambiguous between the natural and artificial readings.[27] Consider in this respect example (42):

(42) Floyd turned off the engine and put his arm around Lizette, kissing the top of her head, right where her **fragrant hair** was parted. "Why we stopped here?" she asked, looking at the flat fields around the car. (*COHA*, 1994, FIC, WomenLanguage)

In (42), *fragrant* could be interpreted as referring either to the natural scent of Lizette's hair or to an artificial fragrance, for instance, that left by shampoo or another cleansing agent which Lizette uses to wash her hair, or even to a mixture of artificial and natural smells. In fact, there is nothing in the context which can help in disambiguation. It may well be the case that the specific nature of the smell was not relevant or important for the author of this particular text at the point of writing.

---

27 The high number of ambiguous occurrences may well be one of the reasons why many dictionaries do not contain separate senses for what we call here the natural and artificial senses, but include just one basic or general sense.

Even though ambiguity introduces more complexity to the annotation process and subsequent analyses, it is rampant in the lexicon. As demonstrated by advocates of the prototype theory (e.g., Taylor 1995: Chapters 2 and 3; Geeraerts 1997: 11), vagueness is widespread in language and communication, particularly in lexical semantics, where the limits between one meaning and another are not always clear-cut. The specific type of vagueness involved in examples such as (42) is what Geeraerts (2010: 197) denominates *interpretative indeterminacy*, which refers to instances that are impossible to disambiguate contextually and can thus not be interpreted through the information available. Geeraerts gives the example of the adjective *plain* in *she is a plain girl*, where we cannot be certain whether *plain* is used in the sense of 'simple' or rather in that of 'ugly'. Therefore, it was necessary to add a further level to the variable Sense to account for instances in which it was not possible to identify the source of the smell. By making use of the notion introduced by Geeraerts, this level was called 'indeterminate'. Besides examples of the type illustrated in (42), this level also includes those in which there exists a mixture of natural and artificial aromas, as in (43).[28]

(43) The air was **fragrant with incense and lilies**. Incense burned before the gods, and lilies bloomed in the court. (*COHA*, 1946, FIC, PavilionWomen)

The smell of the air described in (43) clearly comes from both artificial and natural sources, as proved by the prepositional complement of *fragrant*, namely *with incense and lilies*, where incense is artificially fragrant, and lilies naturally so.

Indeterminate cases were maintained in the count because of two main reasons. First, given that vagueness is a pervasive feature in the lexicon, excluding such cases would result in a rather incomplete and unrealistic reflection of the near-synonyms in particular, and of language in general. Second, and more importantly for our purposes, excluding indeterminate instances from the analysis would certainly skew the results for other variables, particularly Semantic category, as many of the ambiguous cases belong to the semantic categories BODY AND PEOPLE and SPACE, which comprise, respectively, more than half and almost one third of the indeterminate examples in the corpus (cf. Section 4.2.2). The semantic categorization of modified nouns is discussed next.

---

28 The extremely low number of examples in the corpus where there is clearly a mixture of natural and artificial aromas made it inefficient to have an independent level for such instances.

3.3.2 Language-internal semantic variables: Semantic category

As seen in Section 2.1, besides individual collocates, Sinclair (1991; 1996) identifies three additional levels of co-occurrence: colligation, semantic preference, and semantic prosody. Semantic preference concerns more schematic semantic features of the collocates of a particular node, in this case the five near-synonymous adjectives. Drawing on this notion, the data was annotated for a variable called Semantic category, which classifies the nouns modified by the adjectives according to the semantic domain to which they belong.[29] This variable thus provides a more fine-grained picture than Sense regarding the contexts of use in which the adjectives occur. In fact, this variable is the most complex of those considered in the analysis, given that it contains twelve different levels or semantic categories. The identification of semantic classes is often highly subjective and far from being straightforward. Consequently, to achieve a certain degree of objectivity, two well-known systems of semantic classification were used, namely the *UCREL Semantic Analysis System* or *USAS* for short (Archer, Wilson, and Rayson 2002; Rayson et al. 2004) and the *HTOED*.

USAS contains twenty-one major semantic classes, displayed in Table 4, which are then further divided into more specific subclasses.[30]

Table 4: Major semantic classes in *USAS*.

A	B	C	E
GENERAL AND ABSTRACT TERMS	THE BODY AND THE INDIVIDUAL	ARTS AND CRAFTS	EMOTION
F	G	H	I
FOOD AND FARMING	GOVERNMENT AND PUBLIC	ARCHITECTURE, HOUSING AND THE HOME	MONEY AND COMMERCE IN INDUSTRY
K	L	M	N
ENTERTAINMENT, SPORTS AND GAMES	LIFE AND LIVING THINGS	MOVEMENT, LOCATION, TRAVEL AND TRANSPORT	NUMBERS AND MEASUREMENTS
O	P	Q	S
SUBSTANCES, MATERIALS, OBJECTS AND EQUIPMENT	EDUCATION	LANGUAGE AND COMMUNICATION	SOCIAL ACTIONS, STATES AND PROCESSES

---

29 Whenever a pronoun was modified by any of the near-synonymous adjectives at issue, its antecedent was used for the semantic classification.
30 For more detailed information about the different semantic classes and subclasses, see the official *USAS* website, available at: http://ucrel.lancs.ac.uk/usas/.

Table 4 (continued)

T	W	X	Y
Time	World and Environment	Psychological actions, states and processes	Science and technology

Z			
Names and grammar			

Each semantic tag groups together semantically related items which are associated with the same mental concept, including synonyms and antonyms. *USAS* allows researchers to input up to 100,000 words of running text, which it then automatically tags according to their semantic category. Given enough context for a word, *USAS* is in some cases able to identify its correct sense. However, on many occasions this is not possible and the tagger then provides a list of tags for the same word, ranked according to their frequency order, with the most probable tag first. To illustrate this point, consider the word *bath* in *[h]e had imprudently taken a bath at too high a temperature* (1837. *OED*, s.v. *bath* n.[1] I. 1). *USAS* analyzes *bath* as belonging to two different categories, namely H5: FURNITURE AND HOUSEHOLD FITTINGS and B4: CLEANING AND PERSONAL CARE, even though in this particular instance the noun *bath* does not refer to the receptacle for bathing, which would be considered a piece of furniture. Therefore, it is often necessary to manually verify the semantic classification provided by *USAS* with the help of a more precise database such as the *HTOED*. This second source also offers a taxonomic classification of semantic classes, with the great majority of word senses in the *OED* being categorized into semantic domains which are hierarchically ordered (Kay 2010; 2012). At the most schematic level, three divisions are made between THE EXTERNAL WORLD, THE MIND, and SOCIETY. These three general levels are then subdivided into specific classifications, which in turn display even more specific subclasses. Table 5 provides an overview of the major semantic classes within each of the three most schematic levels.

For instance, the noun *bath*, as used in the example discussed above, is classified in the *HTOED* as follows, thus providing a number of semantic categories for this word at different degrees of granularity:

THE EXTERNAL WORLD → PHYSICAL SENSATION → CLEANNESS AND DIRTINESS → CLEANING → WASHING → WASHING ONESELF OR BODY → [noun] → BATHING.

The semantic classes are ordered in chronological order, that is, words in a particular class are ordered by date of first attestation. Therefore, even obsolete or rare senses are included in the classification, which is important for a study of a diachronic nature such as the present one. Additionally, in the more specific

Table 5: Major semantic classes in the *HTOED*.

THE EXTERNAL WORLD	THE MIND	SOCIETY
THE UNIVERSE	MENTAL CAPACITY	SOCIETY AND COMMUNITY
THE EARTH	ATTENTION AND JUDGEMENT	INHABITING AND DWELLING
LIFE	GOODNESS AND BADNESS	ARMED HOSTILITY
HEALTH AND DISEASE	EMOTION	AUTHORITY
PEOPLE	WILL	LAW
ANIMALS	POSSESSION	MORALITY
PLANTS	LANGUAGE	FAITH
FOOD AND DRINK		COMMUNICATION
TEXTILES AND CLOTHING		COMPUTING AND INFORMATION TECHNOLOGY
PHYSICAL SENSATION		TRAVEL
MATTER		OCCUPATION AND WORK
EXISTENCE AND CAUSATION		TRADE AND FINANCE
SPACE		LEISURE
TIME		
MOVEMENT		
ACTION OR OPERATION		
RELATIVE PROPERTIES		
THE SUPERNATURAL		

categories, it is possible to retrieve only the words belonging to a given POS, such as noun in the case of *bath*.

Both *USAS* and the *HTOED* provide detailed hierarchies of semantic classes and domains, which in fact overlap to a large degree. For instance, both sources distinguish categories for body parts, people, plants, time, and weather. However, some important differences between them are worth highlighting, especially concerning their respective advantages and disadvantages. On the one hand, whereas *USAS* automatically tags words according to their semantic category — albeit with a certain degree of manual editing—, the *HTOED* is less automatic, as the researcher has to select manually the correct sense for the lexical items of interest in the *OED* before being able to retrieve its semantic classification.[31] On

---

[31] One can also use the *HTOED* directly by searching for all the items included in a given semantic class (for such use of the *HTOED*, cf., for instance, Allan 2015a on EDUCATION). However, in order to do so, it is first necessary to know which specific category or categories to examine,

the other hand, while the *HTOED* is extremely sense specific, that is, the same word typically occurs in many different semantic classes, this is often not the case of *USAS*, which commonly provides only one or two tags for each word. In fact, many examples of metonymies and metaphors are not captured by *USAS*, while they do appear in the *HTOED*.[32] To illustrate this point, consider example (44):

(44) Down in the vale where cowslips are growing, Where violets breathe thro' **sweet scented lips**, Where brook o'er the bright pebbly bottom is flowing, And bee of the nectar of columbine sips. (*COHA*, 1895, FIC, OurProfession-Other)

In (44), the noun *lips* is a typical example of metaphorical sense extension, in which it is used to refer to a part of a flower, rather than to a body part, thus being used with the meaning '[s]omething resembling the lips of the mouth', specifically '[o]ne of the two divisions of a bilabiate corolla or calyx' (*OED*, s.v. *lip* n. II. 5c). The *HTOED* provides an entry for this sense of the noun, whereas *USAS* classifies this instance of *lip* as a body part (i.e., B1: ANATOMY AND PHYSIOLOGY), even when access is given to the whole context in (44) and even though this is a fairly well-established metaphor.[33]

The classification of nouns modified by *fragrant*, *perfumed*, *scented*, *sweet-scented*, and *sweet-smelling* resulted in a total of twelve semantic categories: (i) ABSTRACT; (ii) BODY AND PEOPLE; (iii) CLEANING; (iv) COSMETICS; (v) EARTH, ATMOSPHERE, AND WEATHER; (vi) FOOD AND DRINK; (vii) OBJECT; (viii) PLANTS AND FLOWERS; (ix) SENSATION; (x) SPACE; (xi) SUBSTANCE AND MATERIAL; and (xii) TEXTILE AND CLOTHING.

The category ABSTRACT groups together under one single heading all abstract nouns, such as those denoting actions, processes, beliefs, and states. These are all entities which cannot emit an odor and thus the five adjectives, when modifying such nouns, must be interpreted in the figurative sense 'sweet or pleasant', which originates through the pattern PLEASURE IS SWEET or SWEET FOR PLEASANT. An example is provided in (45):

---

which is not the case in the present dissertation, whose goal is to discover to which category the modified nouns belong in a particular context of use.
32 The definitions of metaphor and metonymy followed here are those of conceptual approaches within cognitive semantics (cf. for instance, Lakoff 1993; Lakoff and Johnson 2003 for metaphor and Panther and Radden 1999; Kövecses 2010 for metonymy).
33 In fact, body parts constitute a very common source of conventional metaphors, as they represent familiar concepts, e.g., *head/foot of a mountain* or *mouth of a cave* (Kay and Allan 2015: 159–160; cf. also Kövecses 2010: 18).

(45) When she slips away in the dusk to-night I shall put a period to my thought of Maria de Guadalupe Rosalia Merced Castello. I want to keep this **fragrant memory** of her. (*COHA*, 1922, FIC, JaneJourneysOn)

The category BODY AND PEOPLE contains nouns designating human beings and human body parts, together with proper nouns and pronouns that refer to people. Both *USAS* and the *HTOED* propose separate classes for body (i.e., B1: ANATOMY AND PHYSIOLOGY and THE BODY, respectively), on the one hand, and for people (i.e., S2: PEOPLE in *USAS* and PEOPLE in the *HTOED*), on the other. However, in the present study the decision was made to keep the two together due to the similarities of the examples, which all refer to the pleasant smell people exhibit, either coming from a specific body part, as in (46), or in general, as in (47).

(46) Then I felt a soft little hand slip into mine; a **perfumed hair tress** touched my cheek; and the sweetest voice, to me, on earth whispered in my ear. (*COHA*, 1906, FIC, ColonelRedHuzzars)

(47) Tea and toast unobserved before them, music drifting unheard about them, furred and **fragrant women** coming and going. (*COHA*, 1921, FIC, BelovedWoman)

A few instances of specific contextual readings of the meaning of clothing nouns which present extensions of meaning via the metonymical pattern PIECE OF CLOTHING FOR PERSON (e.g., Nyrop 1913 and Paul 1920) or OBJECT USED FOR USER (Lakoff and Johnson 2003: 38; Kövecses 2010: 172) were also categorized as BODY AND PEOPLE. This is the case of (48), where *bodice* does not refer to the piece of clothing, but to the person wearing it:

(48) Hooped petticoat and **fragrant bodice** found reason for whispering to laced coat and periwig; significant glances traveled from every quarter of the building toward the tall pew where, collected but somewhat palely smiling, sat Mistress Evelyn Byrd beside her father. (*COHA*, 1902, FIC, Audrey)

Nouns referring to cleaning and personal care products were classified into two separate categories, following the organization in the *HTOED*, but contrary to that in *USAS*, which keeps the two together under the label CLEANING AND PERSONAL CARE (i.e., class B4). These two categories are (i) CLEANING, which encompasses those products whose essential purpose is that of cleansing, either the body or areas and objects which people inhabit or use on a daily basis, and (ii) COSMETICS, which includes those products used mainly to enhance physical appearance, that is, for beautification purposes. Examples of *perfumed* and *sweet-smelling* modifying a CLEANING and a COSMETICS noun are provided in (49) and (50), respectively:

(49)   The **soap** was **perfumed**. She inhaled deeply." Luxury is everywhere." (*COHA*, 1973, FIC, EagleEye)

(50)   One whiff of the **sweet-smelling cologne** was enough for Bragdon and he bolted up the companionway, leaving the stateroom door wide open and the prisoner free to go where he pleased. (*COHA*, 1902, FIC, BrewstersMillions)

Apart from instances like (49), CLEANING also comprises cases such as (51), where *tub* represents an instance of a conceptual metonymic mapping, namely that known as CONTAINER FOR CONTENTS (e.g., Kay and Allan 2015: 165). Here what is fragrant is not the tub itself, but the water it contains, which has been impregnated with a cleansing agent of some type.

(51)   Sherry, always an early riser, had already breakfasted in her chamber and was, Adam knew, even now sunk deep in a hot, **fragrant tub**. Washing herself clean of him, arming herself for another day of battle. (*COHA*, 2000, FIC, ComeNearMe)

Nouns referring to natural geographical terms, expressions related to the weather, and atmospheric conditions were coded as EARTH, ATMOSPHERE, AND WEATHER. A great majority of the nouns belonging to this category are grouped into the rather general class THE EARTH in the *HTOED*, particularly within the subclasses LAND, WATER, and WEATHER AND THE ATMOSPHERE. In *USAS* nouns of these types are included in the category W: THE WORLD AND OUR ENVIRONMENT, particularly in W3: GEOGRAPHICAL TERMS and W4: WEATHER. Thus, the decision of maintaining such nouns together in one individual category is well justified, as they in fact belong to the same general semantic domain in both the *HTOED* and *USAS*. An example of this category is given in (52):

(52)   Turning from the mountain scenes we have described, let us back once more to Constantinople, and direct our footsteps up the **fragrant valley** where the Barbyses threads its meandering course. (*COHA*, 1851, FIC, CircassianSlave)

In this category we also find a wide range of metonymical or metaphorical extensions of meaning in which temporal expressions and states are used to refer to the surrounding environment and atmospheric conditions of an outdoor location, and sometimes even to the characteristic actions and processes of the natural entities present in those locations. Consider (53) and (54):

(53) And how we used to drive the sleepy old cows through the wood and meadow land, wading knee deep in the clover that seemed to be holding up its red lips to be kissed, while the wild flowers like gossamer chalices filled with dew, made the rosy **morning fragrant.** (*COHA*, 1873, FIC, WhiteSlave)

(54) Accordingly, she had attired herself in a becoming negligee, and had spent the fore part of the night somewhat restlessly, occasionally emerging on the veranda and gazing down into the **perfumed gloom** of the garden. (*COHA*, 1892, FIC, GoldenFleeceRomance)

In (53), the noun *morning* does not denote '[...] the early part of the day, esp. from sunrise until noon or lunchtime' (*OED*, s.v. *morning* n. A 1a), but instead refers to '[...] the early part of a day as characterized by the particular weather, conditions, sentiments, etc., prevailing or experienced during that time' (*OED*, s.v. *morning* n. A 2). Therefore, *morning* is in this instance not just an abstract temporal expression, but it also refers to the concrete surroundings and atmospheric conditions of *the wood and meadow land* through which the narrator drives the cows. In fact, it is evident that the smell stems from the *wild flowers* mentioned in the example. Consequently, instances of the type in (53) would correspond to the metonymical pattern TIME PERIOD FOR A CHARACTERISTIC ACTIVITY IN THAT PERIOD (Kövecses 2010: 258), in which the characteristic activity could be that of the flowers blooming again in the morning after closing at night. Note that TIME is a particularly complex concept. In fact, it is one of the most common target domains in metaphor and metonymy and thus appears in a wide range of different mappings (Kövecses 2010: 26), which makes it particularly difficult to pinpoint the exact pattern of such examples. Similarly, in (54), *gloom* does not just refer to the darkness of the garden, but also to the garden itself, which is most probably filled by flowers and plants. The conceptualization of the state as a space is reinforced by the preposition *into* (*into the perfumed gloom of the garden*), which expresses motion or direction. As in (53), difficulties arise when trying to characterize the mapping, given that SPACE is also a common target domain. However, one possibility could be that of the metaphorical pattern STATES ARE LOCATIONS, where a more abstract aspect is understood in terms of physical location (Kövecses 2010: 163). Be that as it may, the importance here lies not in identifying the specific figurative pattern at stake, which is beyond the purposes of the present study, but in the fact that when the adjectives modify such nouns, these nouns are often not used literally but figuratively.

Within the category FOOD AND DRINK we find nouns corresponding to the semantic class with the same label in the *HTOED* and to the F1: FOOD and F2: DRINKS *USAS* categories, which include edible and drinkable products, as well as nouns referring to different meals of the day (e.g., *breakfast*). Example (55) was, therefore, grouped into this category:

(55) Every morning believers came to offer Han-shan a bowl of **fragrant soup** that steamed his face as if to make him sweat. (*COHA*, 1970, NF, BuddhistLeader)

Moreover, the category FOOD AND DRINK also comprises several metonymic examples corresponding to the conceptual metonymy CONTAINER FOR CONTENTS (e.g., Kay and Allan 2015: 165), already discussed above, in which the near-synonymous adjectives occur with nouns denoting containers (e.g., *bowl* and *cup*) but modify the contents within them, as in (56):

(56) Two learned but despondent university professors met, not long ago, at an afternoon "coffee," and drew sympathetically together in a corner. "What a world this would be," said one, "without coffee!" "Yes," replied the other, stirring the **fragrant cup** in a dejected aspect, - "yes; but what a H. of a world it is with coffee!" (*COHA*, 1883, MAG, Atlantic)

A relatively general category is that of OBJECT, as it contains a mixture of concrete nouns referring to material things which can be seen and touched, including furniture (e.g., *bed* and *couch*), paper documents (e.g., *envelope* and *book*), and other objects (e.g., *box* and *candle*). Many of these nouns belong to the semantic classes MATTER in the *HTOED* and O2: OBJECTS GENERALLY, Q1.2: PAPER DOCUMENTS AND WRITING, and Q4: THE MEDIA in *USAS*, among others. The decision was made to group these more specific classes into a more general one due to data sparseness, as retaining the more specific categories would yield very low figures, which would make it difficult to obtain significant results. An example of OBJECT is shown in (57):

(57) We who produce the world where Heirston finds John Robshaw pillows along with Calypso's own Pom Pom cotton throws and **scented candles** ($38 each) in eleven fragrances. (*COHA*, 2009, MAG, COCA)

Categories L3: PLANTS in *USAS* and PLANTS in the *HTOED* were here classified under the label PLANTS AND FLOWERS. This category is illustrated in (58):

(58) […] he came to a beautiful rose-bush upon which bloomed a **rose** lovelier and more **fragrant** than any of her kind. (*COHA*, 1896, FIC, SecondBookTales)

Again, we find several metonymical instances in this semantic category. In this case, the metonymical extension follows the pattern CHARACTERISTIC FOR CHARACTERIZED ENTITY (e.g., Nyrop 1913 and Paul 1920), in which the near-synonymous adjectives modify a noun that denotes an attribute of a plant or a flower. Such an example is illustrated in (59):

(59)   The woman sprang back from the flowers as though a poisonous serpent, hidden in their **fragrant beauty**, had struck her. (*COHA*, 1912, FIC, Their-Yesterdays)

In this example, even though *fragrant* modifies the noun *beauty*, the pleasant and sweet smell applies to the flowers, since *beauty* here is clearly a characteristic of the flowers.

The ninth category, SENSATION, includes nouns referring to any of the five physical senses, that is, smell (e.g., *aroma* and *scent*), taste (e.g., *flavor* and *taste*), hearing (e.g., *music* and *voice*), sight (e.g., *look*), and touch (e.g., *kiss*). Evidently, the great majority of the nouns in the data correspond to the sense of smell, since the adjectives under analysis belong to this particular semantic domain, as in example (60):

(60)   He spread the faded army blanket, which was old but clean, on the straw of the second loft. The **smell** was **fragrant** and sweet. (*COHA*, 1979, FIC, SilverGhost)

Nevertheless, several instances of nouns belonging to one of the other four senses were also found in the data and were therefore included in this category, which corresponds to the broad semantic classes PHYSICAL SENSATION in the *HTOED* and x3: SENSORY in *USAS*. In general, when the adjectives at issue here modify any of the senses apart from smell, they are used in the figurative sense 'pleasant or agreeable', as in example (61), where *perfumed* modifies the noun *murmur*:

(61)   There was a rustle among the girls and a **perfumed murmur** of "Everything?" "Everything." he said firmly. (*COHA*, 1958, FIC, Maggie-Now)

Examples such as (58) are instances of *synesthetic metaphors*, which describe one sensory domain on the basis of another one (e.g., Geeraerts 2010: 35). Here, an adjective from the olfactory domain is used to describe a noun from the auditory domain.

While the category EARTH, ATMOSPHERE, AND WEATHER included, as seen above, natural geographical terms, among other types of nouns, the category SPACE contains nouns referring to indoor locations, such as *room* and *kitchen*, as well as those denoting human —as opposed to natural— geographical terms, for instance, *avenue* and *city*. The principal reason for maintaining these two categories separate is that whereas the category EARTH, ATMOSPHERE, AND WEATHER contains instances of the adjectives solely in the natural sense, SPACE comprises also occurrences of the adjectives in the artificial sense, as well as indeterminate cases. Additionally, while the great majority of nouns in the former group are classified as THE EARTH in the *HTOED* and in W3: GEOGRAPHICAL TERMS and W4: WEATHER in *USAS*, this is not the case of nouns in the category SPACE. Instead, these nouns appear mainly in the general category SOCIETY, especially within the more specific classes INHABITING AND DWELLING and TRAVEL, in the *HTOED*, and in H: ARCHITECTURE, BUILDINGS, HOUSES AND THE HOME and in M3: MOVEMENT/TRANSPORTATION (LAND) and M7: PLACES in *USAS*. An example of the category SPACE is given in (62):

(62)   As he and Jock left the warm, **scented room** behind them, and faced the white, still cold of an apparently dead St. Ange, the boy turned a drawn face upon Jock, and cried tremblingly, "Say, you". (*COHA*, 1911, FIC, Joyce-NorthWoods)

As in the case of EARTH, ATMOSPHERE, AND WEATHER, the category SPACE also contains instances of metaphors following the pattern STATES ARE LOCATIONS, but in which the space is an indoor location, as in example (63):

(63)   Look, there are orchids and camellias and oleanders.' He was silent so long that she thought he hadn't heard her. She looked up inquiringly and saw that he was staring not into the **perfumed dampness** of the hall but at her. (*COHA*, 1944, FIC, Dragonwyck)

Similarly to example (54) above, *dampness* does not just refer here to the condition or state of the hall, but also to the hall itself, that is, an indoor space, where there are several flowers.

The category SUBSTANCE AND MATERIAL includes nouns referring to liquid, solid, or gaseous substances (e.g., *ash*, *liquid*, and *steam*), and to materials from which objects are made (e.g., *amber* and *wood*). Moreover, this category also contains nouns referring to drugs, especially tobacco (e.g., *cigar* and *tobacco*). These drug-related nouns, very few in number, were included here as they are in fact substances of a kind. In *USAS* most of the nouns belonging to SUBSTANCE AND MATERIAL are grouped into the semantic class O1: SUBSTANCES AND MATERIALS GENERALLY, whereas they mainly correspond with the general category MATTER in the *HTOED*. Example (64) illustrates this semantic category:

(64) Most wood gives off a pleasant aroma when it's cut, but **wood dust** is more than just **fragrant** - it's also hazardous to your health. (*COHA*, 2003, MAG, MotherEarth)

Finally, the last category, TEXTILE AND CLOTHING, comprises nouns referring either to textile material (e.g., *linen* and *wool*) or to different types of clothing (e.g., *garment* and *glove*). These nouns all belong to the categories TEXTILES AND CLOTHING in the *HTOED* and B5: CLOTHES AND PERSONAL BELONGINGS, in the case of clothing, and O1.1: SUBSTANCES AND MATERIALS GENERALLY: SOLID, in the case of textile material, in *USAS*. An example is provided in (65), where *perfumed* collocates with the noun *gloves*:

(65) [...] and lay piled in heaps beneath the Sand Hill fort-many youthful gallants from Spain and Italy among them, noble volunteers recognized by their **perfumed gloves** and golden chains. (*COHA*, 1868, NF, HistoryUnitedNetherlands)

The twelve semantic categories distinguished and illustrative examples of nouns belonging to each of them are provided in Table 6.

Table 6: Classification of nouns into semantic categories.

Semantic Category	Examples of nouns
ABSTRACT (ABS)	*charm, darkness, fear, knowledge, memory, personality*
BODY AND PEOPLE (B&P)	*arm, bodice, cheek, girl, hair, lock, woman, wrist*
CLEANING (CL)	*bath, deodorant, disinfectant, shampoo, soap, tub, water*
COSMETICS (COS)	*cologne, cosmetics, cream, gloss, oil*
EARTH, ATMOSPHERE, AND WEATHER (EAW)	*air, breeze, darkness, gloom, hill, mist, morning, rain, summer, valley, water*
FOOD AND DRINK (F&D)	*apple, beverage, bowl, chicken, coffee, cup, glass, rice*
OBJECT (OBJ)	*book, box, candle, couch, lamp, letter, notepaper, stationary*
PLANTS AND FLOWERS (P&F)	*beauty, bloom, bud, flower, leaf, loveliness, pine, rose, shrub, tree*
SENSATION (SEN)	*aroma, flavor, kiss, look, music, odor, scent, smell, taste, tone*
SPACE (SPA)	*avenue, bakery, boudoir, chamber, city, dampness, house, room*
SUBSTANCE AND MATERIAL (S&M)	*amber, dust, fume, liquid, oil, smoke, steam, vapor, water, wood*
TEXTILE AND CLOTHING (T&C)	*cambric, cloth, dress, glove, linen, pillow*

Since the classification was made on the basis of the referents of the nouns, which may vary from instance to instance, some of the nouns, especially those which are highly polysemic, such as *breath*, *darkness*, *lip*, *oil*, and *water*, were grouped into several semantic categories (cf. Table 6). First, the near-synonymous adjectives serve as modifiers of more than one sense of some nouns. For instance, consider examples (66) and (67), where *fragrant* and *perfumed*, respectively, modifies the noun *breath*.

(66) When she was there, sitting with me at her mother's feet, sometimes so near that her dark, shining hair brushed against my cheek, and her **fragrant breath** came on my face. (*COHA*, 1906, FIC, CrystalAge)

(67) Although one window was open, and the mild air laden with the **perfumed breath** of spring, a bright wood fire flashed on the hearth, near which Miss Jane sat in her large, cushioned rocking-chair [. . .]. (*COHA*, 1869, FIC, WashtiQuotUntil)

Whereas in (66) *breath* designates '[t]he air exhaled from the lungs' (*OED*, s.v. *breath* n. 3a), in (67) it is used in the sense '[t]he air exhaled from anything, or impregnated with its exhalations, and retaining its characteristic odour' (*OED*, s.v. *breath* n. 2b). These two senses of *breath* belong to different semantic categories in HTOED and in the present study, namely BODY AND PEOPLE (sense 3a) and SENSATION (sense 2b). The same is true of nouns which have developed figurative meanings besides their literal ones, as is the case of conventional metaphors. This happens with, for instance, the noun *lip*, which appears in the category BODY AND PEOPLE, as in (68), and in PLANTS AND FLOWERS, as in (44) above, reprinted here as example (69):

(68) Her body met his, yielded; her face was upturned; her **fragrant**, half-opened **lips** were crushed to his in a fierce, impassioned kiss of genuine ecstasy. (*COHA*, 1917, FIC, LaughingBillHyde)

(69) Down in the vale where cowslips are growing, Where violets breathe thro' **sweet scented lips**, Where brook o'er the bright pebbly bottom is flowing, And bee of the nectar of columbine sips. (*COHA*, 1895, FIC, OurProfessionOther)

Another example is that of the noun *darkness*, which, similarly to its near-synonym *gloom* (cf. example (54)), can be used figuratively to denote a location along the mapping STATES ARE LOCATIONS. This is the case of example (70), where *darkness* has been grouped into the category EARTH, ATMOSPHERE, AND WEATHER, as it does not only refer to the darkness of the place Natasha is entering, but also to the place itself:

(70) Entering steamy **perfumed darkness**, dimly lit by sunlight coming through slits in the stone, Natasha stripped before a hot foamy cascade, sponging away the sweat and grime of travel [. . .]. (*COHA*, 2003, FIC, FantasySciFi)

Darkness in (71), in turn, belongs to the semantic category ABSTRACT, since it here refers to a psychological condition, namely that of '[g]loom of sorrow, trouble, or distress' (*OED*, s.v. *darkness* n. 5).

(71) She might be grave by nature, she might be sad by circumstance, she might have secret doubts and pangs, but she was essentially young and strong and fresh and able to enjoy [. . .]. Rowland felt that it was not amusement and sensation that she coveted, but knowledge -- facts that she might noiselessly lay away, piece by piece, in the **perfumed darkness** of her serious mind [. . .]. (*COHA*, 1876, FIC, RoderickHudson)

Second, non-conventional meanings of nouns emerged in specific contexts, which led to the classification of some of them into semantic categories to which their conventional meanings do not belong. A case in point is (72), where the noun *sister* refers to a flower (i.e., *sassafras*) and is thus coded as PLANTS AND FLOWERS:

(72) It was a swell of land, on the summit very rocky, covered with beech and maple trees, and with an undergrowth of spice-wood and its **fragrant sister**, the sassafras. (*COHA*, 1835, FIC, HawksHawk-Hollow)

Similarly, many of the types of metonymical extensions of meaning mentioned throughout this section (e.g., CONTAINER FOR CONTENTS, CHARACTERISTIC FOR CHARACTERIZED ENTITY) also result in a deviation from the conventional semantic categorization of nouns. By way of illustration, *tub* was categorized as CLEANING rather than as OBJECT in example (51) above. An even more complex deviation from the conventional meaning of a noun is displayed in (73), where *fragrant* modifies the noun *womb*:

(73) "I have brought down all of the old homestead that I could," said Martha, who had her **willow basket** at the bedside; "and it is here." She unclasped it; and as Fob glanced down into its **fragrant womb**, his eyes shone with a new light. He saw whole tracts and acres there. "These, you know," continued Martha, producing a handful of **green cresses**, "I plucked them from the Mower's Nook in the wood, so calm and shady in the summer time. (*COHA*, 1842, FIC, CareerPufferHopkins)

Here, *womb* is used metaphorically to denote a specific part of the *willow basket* mentioned in the previous sentence, namely its interior. This metaphorical extension of *womb* corresponds to the meaning '[s]omething likened to the uterus (†or belly) in being hollow or enveloping; a hollow space or cavity' (*OED*, s.v. *womb* n. 4). However, in this instance a metonymy following the pattern CONTAINER FOR CONTENTS is also present, with *womb* referring not to the actual *willow basket*, which is here a container, but to its contents, namely the *green cresses* that Martha plucked from the wood and which she now has in her willow basket.[34] Therefore, *womb* in this instance was classified as PLANTS AND FLOWERS. This example demonstrates that the semantic categorization of nouns is sometimes not straightforward and that the extended context must necessarily be analyzed in depth to reach an adequate classification.

A further complication in the categorization process that needs to be acknowledged is the lack of a clear-cut distinction between some of the twelve semantic categories, with some nouns being located at the periphery of more than one category. This is in line with the non-discrete nature of semantic categories demonstrated by prototype theory (cf. Section 1.1). For instance, nouns such as *berry*, *orange*, and *herb* can be said to lie at the border between the categories FOOD AND DRINK, on the one hand, and PLANTS AND FLOWERS, on the other. Such nouns can therefore be conceptualized either as food or as parts of plants (most commonly the former in my data), and again the context of use must therefore be carefully examined to reach a decision. Similarly, the distinction between the categories CLEANING and COSMETICS is not devoid of problems either. Consider in this connection example (74):

(74) [. . .] or spread over and between the hair some drying and cleansing powder before going to bed, and remove it in the morning with a comb.17 **Powder** had, in fact, already enjoyed a lasting success at the court of Henri III. **Sweet-smelling**, it was no longer only a means of washing the hair, but had become a hair cosmetic. (*COHA*, 1988, NF, ConceptsCleanliness)

The noun *powder* is almost always conceptualized as a cleansing agent in my data, thus belonging to the category CLEANING. However, (74) is somewhat ambiguous, showing that the noun could also be regarded as a hair cosmetic, thus maybe belonging to the category COSMETICS as well. Given that in all other cases analyzed, *powder* is clearly a CLEANING noun and that the context in (74) does not help to disambiguate, this example has been categorized as such.

---

34 The interaction of the two cognitive processes of metaphor and metonymy has been labeled *metaphtonymy* (Goossens 1990).

Finally, it is worth mentioning that a correspondence can be established between the variables Semantic category, discussed in this section, and Sense (cf. Section 3.3.1). Of the twelve categories, three comprise only nouns which refer to entities that can release a smell on their own, namely EARTH, ATMOSPHERE, AND WEATHER, FOOD AND DRINK, and PLANTS AND FLOWERS. In other words, these three categories correspond with the natural sense. On the other hand, CLEANING, COSMETICS, and TEXTILE AND CLOTHING include only nouns which exhibit artificial smells, thus corresponding with the artificial sense. Moreover, the category ABSTRACT displays a one-to-one correspondence with the figurative sense. The five remaining categories, that is, BODY AND PEOPLE, OBJECT, SENSATION, SPACE, and SUBSTANCE AND MATERIAL, include nouns which can denote either an artificial or a natural smell depending on the context in which they are used, as well as indeterminate instances (cf. example (42)). For instance, the noun *smoke*, which belongs to SUBSTANCE AND MATERIAL, can refer either to a natural or to an artificial smell:

(75) They made campfires with top-quality hardwood, which released **fragrant smoke**, to cook for their families. (*COHA*, 2009, FIC, FarawayWarNovel)

(76) He was pulling dreamily at the corncob pipe; the **fragrant** blue **smoke**, drifting toward the open fireplace, was suddenly caught by the draft and drawn stringily into the hot cavern where it was lost in the hickory volume that swept up the chimney. (*COHA*, 1922, FIC,ViolaGwyn)

In (75), *fragrant* designates a natural aroma, namely that of the smoke emanated from the hardwood which makes up the campfire and has been cut from broadleaved trees (e.g., elms and birches). In (76), in turn, *fragrant* co-occurs with the same noun but denotes an artificial smell, as in this example the smoke springs from the tobacco contained in the corncob pipe of the man mentioned in the text. This correspondence between the two variables Semantic Category and Sense poses a problem for the type of analysis carried out in Chapter 5, where this issue is further discussed (cf. Section 5.1).

3.3.3 Language-internal semantic variables: Animacy, Concreteness, and Countability

The nouns modified by the adjectives *fragrant, perfumed, scented, sweet-scented*, and *sweet-smelling* were also annotated for three additional semantic factors, namely, Animacy, Concreteness, and Countability, which provide relatively schematic semantic classifications.

Following, for instance, Gries (2001) on adjectival *-ic* and *-ical* pairs (cf. Section 2.2.2), the variable Animacy contains two levels: animate and inanimate nouns.[35] The value animate refers to nouns denoting living entities, an overwhelming majority of which are human beings in my data (e.g., *women* in example (77)).

(77) The whispers of the **perfumed** mascaraed **women** rose to an excited buzz. (*COHA*, 1945, MAG, TIME)

However, following scholars such as Yamamoto (1999: 23), some typically inanimate nouns, such as those referring to weather or plants and flowers, were also sometimes classified as animate when they were personified, that is, given human or animate characteristics, especially in highly figurative texts. This is the case in example (78), where all plants mentioned (e.g., *Marigolds* and *Mr. Thistle*), including the *fragrant Lily*, are described as people. In all other cases, PLANTS AND FLOWERS nouns were classified as inanimate, as in animacy hierarchies they tend to be given a fairly low animacy score (cf. for instance, Yamamoto 1999: 16, 38).

(78) Ragged Ladies and **Marigolds** clustered together, And gossiped of scandal, the news, and the weather -- What dresses were worn at the wedding so fine Of sharp **Mr. Thistle** and sweet Columbine [. . .]. In a snug little nook sate the Jessamine pale, And that pure **fragrant Lily**, the gem of the vale. (*COHA*, 1834, FIC, Poems)

On the contrary, the value inanimate was given to those nouns denoting non-living entities. An example is provided in (79):

(79) Blue-Eyes propped her up, which hurt terribly, and held a **sweet-smelling clay jar** to her lips. (*COHA*, 2003, FIC, FantasySciFi)

---

35 I am well aware that conceptualizing animacy as a binary choice between animate and inanimate referents is probably too limiting in contrast to animacy scales such as human, animal nouns, collective nouns, temporal nouns, locative nouns, and common inanimate nouns (e.g., Rosenbach 2008: 153). However, for the purposes of the analyses in the present study, the data was annotated only for a binary distinction to avoid data sparsity as a fine-grained classification of nouns according to their semantic category with twelve different levels is used (cf. Section 3.3.2), which makes it inadvisable to consider further variables with a high number of levels (cf. Section 5.1).

As regards the degree of concreteness of a noun modified by the adjectives at issue, this was coded for in two different variables, Concreteness rating and Concreteness binary. Brysbaert, Warriner, and Kuperman (2014) provide a concreteness rating of about 40,000 English lexical items: by means of an online survey, they asked 4,000 participants to rate a series of lexical items according to how concrete they thought the items were, ranging from 1 (abstract) to 5 (concrete). Explicit instructions were given to the participants to consider all five physical senses when giving a rating, rather than basing their decisions on only one or two of them (e.g., sight and touch). The average rating for each word was included in a database.[36] The concreteness ratings of the nouns modified by the near-synonymous adjectives analyzed in this work were extracted from this database. For instance, a concrete noun like *handkerchief* was given an average rating of 5, whereas an abstract noun such as *gloom* was given a rating of 1.86. Even though most modified nouns in my data were found in the database, some were not included. In those cases, the rating of a semantically related word, most typically a hyperonym, was used instead to retrieve the rating. By way of illustration, on one occasion *fragrant* modified *wildrose*, which was not included in Brysbaert, Warriner, and Kuperman (2014). Therefore, the rating for the hyperonym of *wildrose*, that is, *rose* (i.e., 4.9), was used instead.

Despite the fact that the participants were asked to bear all five physical senses in mind when providing a rating, the authors conclude that participants attach more importance to sight and touch than to the other three senses. Given that the present analyses focus on adjectives from the olfactory domain and that context of use is of crucial importance here, the data was annotated for an additional variable, namely, Concreteness binary. This variable offers a more qualitative assessment of the concreteness of the modified nouns, since it takes into account the sense in which each noun is used as well as the referent it denotes in each particular context. As the label itself suggests, Concreteness binary comprises two levels, namely concrete, that is, entities which can be perceived by any of the five senses, and abstract, that is, those which cannot be experienced directly through the senses. Examples (80) and (81) show an instance of a concrete (*apple*) and of an abstract noun (*malice*), respectively:

---

36 The database with the average concreteness rating for the almost 40,000 English lexical items is available at: http://crr.ugent.be/archives/1330.

(80) Their return from these visits was still more grotesque, for their family-carriage generally trundled into town garnished with baskets of fresh, **sweet-scented apples**, and a pair or two of tender poultry, presented by the kindly farmer friends whom they had visited, hanging at the sides, enlivened at times by a gay string of onions, or an ambitious head of cabbage. (*COHA*, 1843, FIC, VariousWritings)

(81) Finally, the late Richard Burton as O'Brien, the couple's betrayer and interrogator, gives a last performance that is all silky corruption, **perfumed malice** in every beautifully measured phrase. (*COHA*, 1985, MAG, Time)

The last variable pertaining to the semantics of the nouns modified by the adjectives at issue here is Countability. Following, for instance, Gries and Otani (2010), two types of common nouns were distinguished, namely count nouns and non-count nouns (cf. Section 2.2.2). As the labels of the values indicate, the former group contains common nouns referring to entities that can be counted, whereas the latter comprises common nouns denoting entities which cannot be counted (Huddleston and Pullum et al. 2002: Section 5.3.1). A count noun modified by *scented* is seen in (82), while a non-count noun co-occurring with *sweet-smelling* is found in (83):

(82) [...] she taught him to dance the "Boston," and the Frenchman, who it turned out was a duke or a baron or something, kept offering him drinks and cigars and **scented cigarettes**. (*COHA*, 1930, FIC, 42ndParallel)

(83) A breeze blew in through the opened hay door, and the **hay** was clean and fresh and **sweet-smelling**. (*COHA*, 1961, FIC, JourneyMatecumb)

As in the case of the other variables discussed so far, it is crucial to consider the context of use to reach a decision regarding the countability of some nouns. This is specially so with nouns which are countable in some of their senses, and uncountable in others. A case in point is *air*, which is modified by *scented* in (84) and (85):

(84) At the town florist's he rapped a timid signal to the driver to stop, and, glowing with anticipation, spryly shuffled into the warm, **scented air** of the little shop. (*COHA*, 1913, FIC, UncleNoahsChristmas)

(85) **Scented airs** which had swept all the way from distant blue hills over countless orange, olive, and mulberry groves filled the room, and fluttered the paper upon which the girls were writing [...]. (*COHA*, 1899, FIC, BarbarasHeritage)

In (84), *air* is used in the sense '[a] special state, condition, or quality of the atmosphere, as affected by temperature, moisture, etc., or as modified by time or place' (*OED*, s.v. *air* n¹. I. 4), i.e., a non-count noun. In (85), in turn, *air* refers to the '[a]ir in motion; a current or draught of air; (esp. in the context of sailing) a breeze, a light wind' (*OED*, s.v. *air* n¹. I. 6), i.e., a count noun. Therefore, although we speak of count and non-count nouns, we in fact mean count and non-count uses of nouns.

Given that the five near-synonymous adjectives also co-occur with proper nouns (cf. example (86)) and pronouns (cf. example (87)), it was necessary to add a third value to the variable Countability, labelled 'other'.[37] Although not applicable to these two types of nominal elements, the decision was taken to maintain the semantic variable Countability because proper nouns and pronouns account only for a relatively low amount of the modified entities in the data, namely 5.7%, of which about 0.9% are proper nouns and about 4.8% are pronouns. This means that over 94% of the modified nominal elements are common nouns which can be characterized as either count or non-count.

(86) Pearl, "a lovely, listless sister, a too mellow fruit"; **Richmiel**, sleek and **perfumed**, "whose body had seemed nine-tenths of her being." (*COHA*, 1923, MAG, TIME)

(87) This shrub is in bloom early in April. **It** is **sweet-scented**; and, where there are many together, they will perfume the air to a considerable distance. (*COHA*, 1851, NF, FlowerGardenBrecks)

3.3.4 Language-internal non-semantic variables

Besides the semantic features pertaining to modified nouns, the data was also annotated for morphosyntactic characteristics of the five near-synonyms under analysis. As mentioned in Section 2.2.2, previous studies on adjectival synonym sets have shown that morphological and/or syntactic factors in some cases determine the choice between the members of a synonym set (e.g., Gries 2003; Gries and Otani 2010; Liu 2010). The most common syntactic feature examined for adjectives is their syntactic function, but others, such as degree, have also been

---

37 The three reference grammars consulted make a distinction between common and proper nouns. Whereas the former can be further divided into count and non-count nouns, the latter cannot (Quirk et al. 1985: 245–247; Biber et al. 1999: 241; Huddleston and Pullum et al. 2002: 328).

considered. Therefore, these two factors were also included in the present analyses under the labels 'Syntactic function' and 'Degree'.

Most reference grammars agree as to the number and types of syntactic functions of adjectives. The three basic functions of adjectives are attributive, predicative complement, and postpositive (e.g., Huddleston and Pullum et al. 2002: 528–529).[38] While we here speak of adjectives as being attributive, postpositive, and predicative, it is not the adjectives alone that perform these functions, but rather the adjective phrases in which they serve as heads (Quirk et al. 1985: 416–417; Biber et al. 1999: 101–102; Huddleston and Pullum et al. 2002: 529).

Attributive adjectives are those that serve as premodifiers of the head of a noun phrase (Quirk et al. 1985: 417; Biber et al. 1999: 510; Huddleston and Pullum et al. 2002: 528). In (88), for instance, *sweet-smelling* occurs in attributive position as a premodifier of the noun *wind*:

(88) The **sweet-smelling** warm **wind** moved gently in Francie's hair. (*COHA*, 1943, FIC, TreesGrowInBrooklyn)

As to predicative adjectives, two types can be distinguished. Subject predicatives function as complements of copular verbs, such as *appear* and *be*, among others, and qualify the nominal expression in subject position (cf. example (89)). Moreover, non-copular verbs which fulfil similar functions to copular verbs in particular contexts, such as *grow* and *come*, can also take predicative complements. Object predicatives, in turn, typically occur with verbs such as *declare* and *make*, and characterize the direct object of the clause, as in (90) (Quirk et al. 1985: 417; Biber et al. 1999: 515–516; Huddleston and Pullum et al. 2002: 528; 530).

(89) Two of them were the kind he got in every town; the paper of one **was** pink and **scented**, the other pale violet. (*COHA*, 1949, FIC, BraveBulls)

(90) The apple-trees **made** the air **fragrant**, and some of the delicate pink of their blossoms was in Mousie's cheeks. (*COHA*, 1885, FIC, DrivenBackEden)

Besides the prototypical cases of predicative complements just exemplified, some examples featured adjectives in predicative complement function in constructions in which the subject and the verb of the clause were omitted. Such examples

---

38 Although different labels are used to refer to the different syntactic functions of adjectives, the nomenclature employed in Huddleston and Pullum et al. (2002) is followed here.

occurred mostly in recipes, a genre which exhibits a high incidence of ellipsis (e.g., Brown and Yule 1983: 174–176; Culy 1996). In particular, ellipsis is highly frequent in adverbial clauses with *until* (Klenová 2010: 90–91), as in (91), where we find an instance of *fragrant* in a context of this type:

(91) Let mixture bubble and sizzle **until fragrant**, another 2 minutes. (*COHA*, 1997, NEWS, SanFran)

The example of *fragrant* in (91) was classified as a predicative complement in a construction which shows the omission of both the subject *mixture* and the verb of the clause, probably *be*. Compare (91) to (92), where *fragrant* occurs in a non-elliptical adverbial clause introduced by *until* and functions as a prototypical predicative subject complement:

(92) Add onion paste, paprika and pepper flakes and cook, stirring, **until** mixture is **fragrant** and begins to brown, about 5 minutes. (*COHA*, 2000, MAG, VegTimes)

Postpositive adjectives immediately follow the nominal element they modify, thus serving as postmodifiers (Quirk et al. 1985: 418–419; Biber et al. 1999: 519; Huddleston and Pullum et al. 2002: 528–529). They are frequently found following indefinite pronouns such as *something, somebody*, and *no one* (cf. example (93)).

(93) Sky Eyes took hot water from a kettle near the fire and mixed it with cold in a large, shallow bowl, then dripped **something** light green and **fragrant** into it. (*COHA*, 1991, FIC, FantasySciFi)

Apart from these three basic syntactic roles, adjectives can also occur in a number of minor functions, including predicative adjunct, fused modifier-head, and predeterminer (Quirk et al. 1985: 421–428; Biber et al. 1999: 519–521; Huddleston and Pullum et al. 2002: 529). Predicative adjuncts qualify a nominal element, but do so from a syntactically freer position than predicative complements (Quirk et al. 1985: 424–426; Biber et al. 1999: 520–521; Huddleston and Pullum et al. 2002: 529). Consider in this connection (94), where the predicative adjunct *sweet-smelling or odoursome* is separated by means of commas from the rest of the clause and is thus detached from it:

(94) Breezes, **sweet-smelling or odoursome**, would come off the water towards him. (*COHA*, 1988, FIC, "E"IsEvidence)

Predicative adjuncts can occur in different positions in the sentence and are therefore mobile. For instance, in example (94) it is possible to move the adjunct to clause-initial or to clause-final position.

Adjectives serving as fused modifier-heads function simultaneously as modifiers and as heads of the noun phrase. Fused modifier-head adjectives behave almost like nouns but do not exhibit the typical morphological characteristics of nouns, such as inflection for number (Quirk et al. 1985: 421–424; Biber et al. 1999: 519–520; Huddleston and Pullum et al. 2002: 415–418). An example is provided in (95):

(95) Of natural **odors** the most agreeable are **the aromatic and fragrant** that emanate from plants. (*COHA*, 1922, MAG, Century)

In this example, *the aromatic and fragrant* refers to the noun *odors*, which is mentioned in the preceding context. However, in order to avoid repetition of the noun, and since it is clear from the context which noun the two adjectives qualify, *odors* is omitted. Consequently, *aromatic* and *fragrant* combine simultaneously the role of premodifier and that of head of the noun phrase.

Finally, predeterminer adjectives function as external modifiers of noun phrases. According to Huddleston and Pullum et al. (2002: 550–551), adjectives in this function have to fulfil two criteria: first, they must precede the indefinite article *a*/*an* and, second, the adjective phrase in which they appear must either begin with any of the modifiers *how*, *as*, *so*, *too*, *this*, or *that*, or contain *such* or exclamatory *what* as head. In (96), *fragrant* is a predeterminer of the noun phrase *an odor*, and is preceded by the modifier *so*:

(96) She could not understand it, but concluded that it must be some great delicacy among the vessel's stores lying on the bank, which had **so** very **fragrant an /z/ odor**. (*COHA*, 1869, NF, BookBoys)

The variable Syntactic function therefore comprises the following values: attributive, predicative complement, postpositive, and a level labelled 'other', with all the minor functions explained in the preceding paragraphs grouped together, given their low frequency of occurrence (less than 5% of the data).

The second syntactic variable coded for was the degree of the adjective, with three levels: positive, comparative, and superlative, exemplified in (97)–(99), respectively:

(97) Sympathizing friends from his own and distant cities sent fresh, **fragrant** flowers he loved so well. (*COHA*, 1855, MAG, NorthAmRev)

(98) For Persian mythology, like Persian wines and Persian roses, is richer, more subtle, **more fragrant**, more glowing than any other. (*COHA*, 1869, FIC, VashtiQuotUntil)

(99) "I think," said Barker, "she is the prettiest and **most fragrant** bud I have seen; a very rare specimen." (*COHA*, 1902, FIC, CaliforniaGirl)

Even though many adjectives can be morphologically marked for the comparative and superlative degrees through the suffixes *-er* and *-est*, respectively, all five near-synonymous adjectives examined in the present monograph are always marked via analytical means, that is, with the adverbs *more* and *most*.

In addition to the six semantic and two syntactic factors discussed, the data was also annotated for a language-internal lexical variable termed Collocate. This variable contains the specific semantically modified nouns of the adjectives in each instance and allows us to control for lexical effects. Previous studies on near-synonyms have shown the importance of including the specific collocates of nodes, as members of synonym sets often display their own idiosyncratic lexical behavior (e.g., Gries 2003; Liu 2010; 2013; Desaulier 2014; cf. Section 2.2.2 above). In the case of adjectives, noun collocates seem to be more informative than other POS. In particular, many studies on attributive adjectives consider their R1 collocates, that is, the head nouns they modify (e.g., Church et al. 1991; Gries 2001). In the present analyses, modified nouns include head nouns modified by attributive adjectives, which often occur directly to their right (but cf. *wind* in (88) above), but also subjects and objects qualified by predicative complements, as *paper* in (89) and *air* in (90), and nominal elements modified by postpositive adjectives (cf. example (93)), among others. In most cases, the task simply entailed retrieving the specific noun collocate from each example. However, in a few cases this was not possible, as in (100), where the nominal element modified by *fragrant* is the pronoun *something*:

(100) In the kitchen, Coxie was waiting. She handed me a napkin wrapped around **something warm and fragrant**. And a mug of tea. "Breakfast. You'd best be goin' afore that hellcat up there wakes up an' thinks of some errand fer you." (*COHA*, 1993, FIC, SplitHeirs)

Whenever a pronoun was modified by any of the adjectives at issue, its antecedent was retrieved from the context. By way of illustration, in example (101), the pronoun *it* is used as an anaphor for (*lavender-colored*) *letter*, and consequently *letter* is considered to be the noun collocate of *scented* in this particular instance.

(101) "Who was your lavender-colored **letter** from?" Eleanor said, yawning; "I forgot to ask you. **It** was awfully **scented**!" (*COHA*, 1992, FIC, Vehement-Flame)

In some cases, it was not possible to locate the precise referent of anaphoric or cataphoric pronouns. For instance, in (100), even when the extended context in *COHA* is examined, it is impossible to identify the exact referent of *something* in *something warm and fragrant*. We know that it is used to denote an edible item of some kind, which Coxie gives to the narrator as breakfast, but we cannot know for sure exactly what type of food it is. Consequently, the collocate of *fragrant* in example (100) has been taken to be the generic noun *food*. Similarly, in contexts such as instructional discourse segments (e.g., recipes), where ellipsis is very frequent, it is difficult to pinpoint the exact source of the smell, as the near-synonyms usually qualify a mixture of ingredients. This the case in examples (91) and (92) above, where *fragrant* does not refer to one specific ingredient, but to the resulting mixture of all of them. Therefore, the generic noun *food* was also selected as the collocate of *fragrant* in these two examples.

Even though most studies on near-synonyms focus on language-internal variables such as those considered so far, language-external factors have also been shown to exert a strong influence on lexico-semantic variation and change (cf. for instance, Levshina 2011). Therefore, variables of an extralinguistic nature were also included in the analyses of the present study. These are explained in the next section.

3.3.5 Language-external variables

Since the main aim of the present monograph is to analyze the diachronic development of the five near-synonymous adjectives *fragrant*, *perfumed*, *scented*, *sweet-scented*, and *sweet-smelling*, a variable that must necessarily be included in the analyses is Period. As mentioned in Section 3.2, *COHA* covers the time span 1810–2009 in American English and is divided into 20 decades. However, given the relatively low frequency of the adjectives examined, especially *sweet-scented* and *sweet-smelling* (cf. Table 3 above and Table 8 in Section 4.1), it would have been difficult to identify changes in their distributional behavior if decades or years had been considered. For this reason, the temporal span covered by the corpus was divided into four fifty-year periods, which are the values of the variable Period: 1810–1859 (period 1 or P1), 1860–1909 (P2), 1910–1959 (P3), and 1960–2009 (P4).

The second language-external factor is Text-type, which refers to the genre in *COHA* to which each of the examples belong. As mentioned earlier, *COHA* distinguishes four major text-types: fiction, non-fiction, magazines, and newspapers. In the analyses in this work, however, magazines and newspapers were merged into one single category, labelled 'periodicals', due to the low number of instances of the adjectives at issue in newspapers and to the fact that *COHA* does not contain texts from this genre until the 1860s. Therefore, Text-type is here a categorical variable with three levels: fiction, non-fiction, and periodicals. Table 7 summarizes the eleven variables included in the study which, together with their values, have been described in the present section.

Table 7: Variables in the first dataset and their levels.

Variable types	Variable	Variable levels
Language-internal semantic variables	Sense	Natural
		Artificial
		Figurative
		Indeterminate
	Semantic category	ABSTRACT
		BODY AND PEOPLE
		CLEANING
		COSMETICS
		EARTH, ATMOSPHERE, AND WEATHER
		FOOD AND DRINK
		OBJECT
		PLANTS AND FLOWERS
		SENSATION
		SPACE
		SUBSTANCE AND MATERIAL
		TEXTILE AND CLOTHING
	Animacy	Animate
		Inanimate
	Concreteness rating	Average rating of concreteness from 1 to 5
	Concreteness binary	Concrete
		Abstract
	Countability	Count
		Non-count
		Other
Language-internal non-semantic variables	Syntactic function	Attributive
		Predicative complement
		Postpositive
		Other
	Degree	Positive
		Comparative
		Superlative

Table 7 (continued)

Variable types	Variable	Variable levels
	Collocate	Specific noun collocate (lemma)
Language-external variables	Period	Period 1 (1810–1859)
		Period 2 (1860–1909)
		Period 3 (1910–1959)
		Period 4 (1960–2009)
	Text-type	Fiction
		Non-fiction
		Periodicals

The remaining chapters of the present monograph provide the results of three separate analyses. The findings in Chapters 4 and 5 are based on the first dataset (cf. Section 3.2), and thus focus on the effects of the variables in Table 7 on the choice between the five near-synonyms. Chapter 4 is of a more descriptive and univariate nature, including both semasiological and onomasiological perspectives of the adjectives, while Chapter 5 presents a confirmatory multivariate analysis in which the emphasis lies on the differences between the members of the synonym set over time. Chapter 6, in turn, offers a more detailed account of the idiosyncratic collocational patterns of *fragrant, perfumed, scented, sweet-scented*, and *sweet-smelling*, by zooming in on their specific noun collocates, thus employing the second database described in Section 3.2 above.

4 Semasiological and onomasiological analyses of the synonym set

Before the emergence of cognitive linguistics, different theoretical frameworks in lexical semantics tended to focus almost exclusively on either semasiological or onomasiological structures: whereas, for instance, the historical-philological school was mainly devoted to the former, structuralist scholars primarily paid attention to the latter. Semasiology refers to the study of particular words and the senses or concepts that they designate, thus being closely associated with polysemy. A typical semasiological study would therefore consider a polysemic word such as *water* in isolation and its different senses. Conversely, onomasiology takes a particular concept or category as a starting point and examines the various expressions which are used to designate it, hence being closely related to synonymy. A typical onomasiological study would therefore select a concept such as PLEASANT TO THE TASTE and analyze the different lexical items that can be used to refer to it, for instance, *delicious*, *luscious*, *delectable*, and *tasty*. As argued by Levshina (2011: 11–12), analyses which consider both perspectives are few and far between. However, both semasiological and onomasiological descriptions are necessary to reach a full understanding of the semantics of individual lexical items, the concepts they denote, and the relationship between neighboring categories. This is so because, depending on the perspective one adopts, prototypicality and salience effects may vary. In other words, what is semasiologically salient or prototypical is not necessarily onomasiologically so.

Salience is in itself a very complex concept, which refers to the degree of typicality of the members of a given category. This category can be an individual word, in which case the emphasis is on the typicality of its different senses, or a larger linguistic category, in which case the focus is on the typicality of the words used to denote it. In this line, semasiological salience, when applied to the phenomenon of polysemy, refers to how central a specific sense or reading of a concrete lexical item is. Central or salient senses are usually those from which other senses derive and those that are more frequent (e.g., Levshina 2011: 13; Kay and Allan 2015: 41). This is the reason why metaphorically extended senses are often less salient, as they tend to derive from literal ones and are, at the same time, often less common. The noun *bird* serves to illustrate this point: besides its literal meaning in Present-Day English '[a]n animal of the vertebrate class Aves [. . .]' (*OED*, s.v. *bird* n. II 3), *bird* can also be used metaphorically to denote 'A vehicle designed to travel through the air; an aircraft; esp. an aeroplane or helicopter' (*OED*, s.v. *bird* n. II 7a.). The latter reading is in fact a metaphorical extension of the former and is less salient, both logically and diachronically, as it originates from the 'biological species' sense, but also statistically, as it is much less frequent (Lewandowska-Tomaszcyk 2007: 147). Onomasiological salience, on the other hand, refers to the degree of entrenchment of a lexical item used to designate a particular semantic concept or category in comparison with other alternatives, be they synonyms or hyponyms/hypernyms. Onomasiological salience can be operationalized as "the ratio between (a) the frequency with which the members of a category are named with an item that is a unique name for that category, (b) and the total frequency with which the category occurs in a corpus" (Geeraerts 2010: 202). Salience is not a static but a dynamic phenomenon and, as such, can vary over time, since the experiences of language users often change due to, for instance, transformations in culture and society, and the fact that categorization processes are experientially based. This applies both to semasiological salience, and thus senses can become more or less prototypical over time, and to onomasiological salience, where the competing alternatives may differ as regards entrenchment from one period to another.

The previous chapter offered an overview of the semantics of the selected adjectival near-synonyms *fragrant*, *perfumed*, *scented*, *sweet-scented*, and *sweet-smelling*, as described in existing reference works. This overview provided some preliminary clues as to the frequency and prototypicality of the five adjectives, as well as to their possible usage patterns in terms of the senses that they share. This information led us to formulate some research questions, some of which are explored in the present chapter (cf. Section 3.1.2).

The goal of this chapter is to analyze the first database described in Section 3.2, focusing on the language-internal semantic variables Sense and Semantic category. This allows us to contrast the information provided by the reference material against actual corpus data. To this purpose, the absolute and relative frequencies of the five adjectives at issue in different periods are examined, first generally, and then in particular contexts of use, that is, across senses and semantic categories. Only minor confirmatory testing—namely, chi-square tests of independence— is carried out in this chapter, as the main objective here is to provide a more descriptive analysis of the data. Chi-square tests are conducted to determine if there is a significant association between two categorical variables. The test compares the observed frequencies in a contingency table with the expected frequencies that would be found if the variables were independent. If the observed frequencies differ significantly from the expected frequencies, this means that the variables are correlated (cf. for instance, Levshina 2015: 210–213).[39] Multivariate analyses of the data are, in turn, carried out in Chapter 5, which offers a more sophisticated quantitative approach.

---

[39] All statistical procedures conducted were computed in *R* (R Core Team 2017).

Chapter 4 is structured as follows. Section 4.1 presents the overall frequency in *COHA* of the concept PLEASANT SMELLING and of the five adjectival near-synonyms, as well as their frequency over the time span 1810–2009. Then, Section 4.2 provides an account of the semantics of the concept PLEASANT SMELLING as a whole, that is, as designated by the five near-synonyms, both generally and diachronically throughout the four historical periods distinguished. Section 4.3 focuses on the semasiological structure of each of the five adjectives individually in order to identify their prototypical uses. Section 4.4, in turn, deals with the onomasiological structure of the concept PLEASANT SMELLING, exploring the competition between the synonyms in different contexts of use.

4.1 Frequency of the adjectives

Out of the initial 6,338 hits, a total number of 5,764 tokens of the five adjectival near-synonyms remained in the database following the manual pruning, and were subsequently analyzed (cf. Section 3.3). The frequency distribution is provided in Table 8, which shows the absolute and relative frequencies of the concept PLEASANT SMELLING and of the individual adjectives in general and over time. The percentages display the relative frequencies of the adjectives with respect to one another, thus comparing the frequency of the five synonyms in each period. Therefore, the percentages have to be interpreted vertically in Table 8, that is, they total 100% in each period.

Table 8: Absolute and relative frequencies of the five near-synonyms.

Synonym	Period	P1 (1810–1859)	P2 (1860–1909)	P3 (1910–1959)	P4 (1960–2009)	Total
Fragrant	N	804	1291	712	588	3,395
	%	66.83	64.87	52.88	48.32	58.90
Perfumed	N	193	333	227	224	977
	%	16.04	16.73	16.77	18.41	16.95
Scented	N	109	235	296	301	941
	%	9.06	11.81	21.86	24.73	16.33
Sweet-scented	N	78	78	29	13	198
	%	6.48	3.92	2.14	1.07	3.44
Sweet-smelling	N	19	53	90	91	253
	%	1.58	2.66	6.65	7.48	4.39
Total	N	1,203	1,990	1,354	1,217	5,764
	%	100	100	100	100	100

Starting with the overall frequency, the findings evince major differences among the synonyms, with *fragrant* being considerably more frequent than the other four adjectives, followed by *perfumed* and *scented*, which display a similar frequency, and finally *sweet-smelling* and *sweet-scented*, which together account for less than 8% of the data. In fact, out of the total 5,764 occurrences, more than half, namely 3,395 (58.90%), correspond to instances of *fragrant*, while 977 (16.95%), 941 (16.33%), 198 (3.44%), and 253 (4.39%) are cases of *perfumed*, *scented*, *sweet-scented*, and *sweet-smelling*, respectively. This considerable variation in frequency among synonyms is not uncommon, since synonym sets often contain one or more dominant expressions.

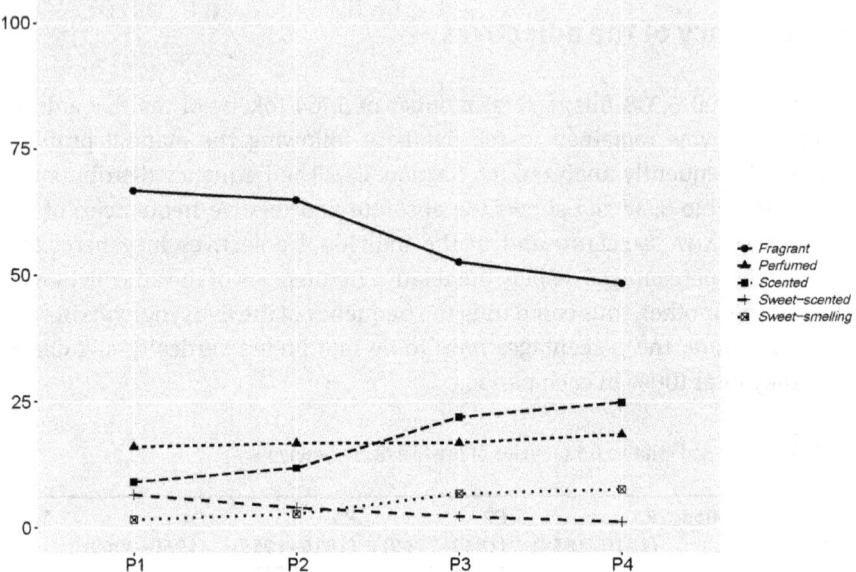

Figure 2: Percentages of the five near-synonyms across periods.

In addition, the frequency distribution of the five adjectives varies greatly over time, as shown in Figure 2. While *fragrant* clearly decreases diachronically, from 66.83% in P1 to 48.32% in P4, *scented* increases substantially, from 9.06% of the total occurrences in P1 to 24.73% in P4. Similarly, *sweet-scented* and *sweet-smelling*, despite their low overall frequency, also fluctuate considerably over time. The former displays an important downward tendency, from 6.48% in P1 to 1.07% in P4, and the latter an important upward tendency, from 1.58% in P1 to 7.48% in P4. Conversely, *perfumed* remains rather stable diachronically, with only a minor increase of approximately 2.5 percentual points. The distribution of the five near-synonyms across the four periods is statistically significant, as proved by a chi-square test of independence ($\chi^2 = 338.94$, df = 12 $p < 0.001$). By examining the residuals calculated by the test, it is possible to identify which specific changes contribute the most to the obtained chi-square value and its significance. The residuals constitute the differences between the observed and expected frequencies, with positive and negative values indicating a higher and a lower observed frequency than expected, respectively (Levshina 2015: 218; Desagulier 2017: 183–185). Residuals are to be interpreted as follows: the degree of contribution of a particular cell in the contingency table to the obtained chi-square value depends on the absolute size of its residual, so that the larger the residual, the higher the contribution. As a rule of thumb, residual values that are larger than +2 or lower than −2 are considered to contribute substantially to the distribution (Levshina 2015: 220–221; Desagulier 2017: 185). Here, the residuals demonstrate that both *fragrant* and *sweet-scented* are considerably more frequent than expected in P1, and *fragrant* also in P2, but less frequent than expected in P3 and P4, while the opposite tendency is true for *scented* and *sweet-smelling*. The distribution of *perfumed*, in turn, does not seem to change much over time. These chi-square residuals are provided in Table 9.

Table 9: Chi-square residuals of the frequency of the five adjectives in the period 1810–2009.

Period Synonym	P1 (1810–1859)	P2 (1860–1909)	P3 (1910–1959)	P4 (1960–2009)
Fragrant	3.59	3.47	−3.03	−4.81
Perfumed	−0.76	−0.23	−0.17	1.23
Scented	−6.24	−4.99	5.04	7.26
Sweet-scented	5.71	1.17	−2.57	−4.46
Sweet-smelling	−4.65	−3.68	3.97	5.14

The frequency fluctuations over time evince a competition between the five synonyms, with some of them converging in frequency as time passes. In fact, in a few cases one adjective comes to overthrow another. For instance, *scented*, which in P1 is less frequent than *perfumed*, becomes more frequent over time. Similarly, *sweet-smelling* starts out as being approximately four times less common than *sweet-scented*, but in P4 it is seven times more common. The increase of *scented* and the decrease of *fragrant* also lead to a gradual convergence in the frequency of the two adjectives: while *fragrant* is seven times more frequent than *scented* in P1, in P4 it is only twice as frequent. This convergence between the two synonyms is particularly pronounced from P2 to P3, that is, in the transition from the nineteenth to the twentieth century.

The frequency clines in Table 10 summarize the data in Table 8 and Figure 2 above, where '>' stands for 'more frequent than'.

Table 10: Frequency clines of the five adjectives in the period 1810–2009.

P1 (1810–1859): *fragrant* > *perfumed* > *scented* > *sweet-scented* > *sweet-smelling*
P2 (1860–1909): *fragrant* > *perfumed* > *scented* > *sweet-scented* > *sweet-smelling*
P3 (1910–1959): *fragrant* > *scented* > *perfumed* > *sweet-smelling* > *sweet-scented*
P4 (1960–2009): *fragrant* > *scented* > *perfumed* > *sweet-smelling* > *sweet-scented*

Therefore, although *fragrant* maintains its dominance over time, the other four adjectives change positions in the frequency cline throughout the period 1810–2009. In particular, *scented* displaces *perfumed*, and *sweet-smelling* displaces *sweet-scented*. These changes take place especially between P2 and P3.

The findings obtained regarding the frequency of the five near-synonyms are mostly in line with the information provided in the *OED* and *CoD* discussed in Section 3.1.2. First, *fragrant* is the most common adjective in Present-Day English, followed by *scented*, *perfumed*, and *sweet-smelling*, and lastly *sweet-scented*, thus coinciding with the frequency ranges provided in the *OED*. Second, the diachronic tendencies in *CoD*, which are based on *Google Ngrams*, correspond with the frequency fluctuations obtained here: *fragrant*, *perfumed*, and *sweet-scented* all decrease, while *scented* increases somewhat.[40]

In sum, this section has demonstrated that the concept PLEASANT SMELLING and the five adjectives *fragrant*, *perfumed*, *scented*, *sweet-scented*, and *sweet-smelling*, which are used to designate it, experience changes over time. However, it is not clear whether these fluctuations in frequency occur across the board, that is, in all contexts of use, or whether different patterns emerge depending on the senses in which the adjectives are used or on the semantic categories of the nouns which they modify. The remainder of this chapter delves into these issues and tries to uncover the underlying motivations for the changes identified in the present section, starting with the concept PLEASANT SMELLING as a whole.

4.2 The evolution of the concept PLEASANT SMELLING

This section considers the diachronic development of the concept PLEASANT SMELLING across senses and semantic categories. Given that Sense represents

---

[40] Nothing can be said about *sweet-smelling* in this respect, since *CoD* does not include information regarding the frequency of this adjective over time (cf. Section 3.1.2).

a rather coarse-grained distinction, while Semantic category represents a more fine-grained classification of the data, the former is first discussed in Section 4.2.1. Then, to further localize the possible changes of the concept across senses, the different semantic categories are analyzed in Section 4.2.2. Chi-square tests are again conducted, in this case to determine if there is a significant association between the variables Sense and Period, on the one hand, and between Semantic category and Period, on the other. As the focus here lies on the concept in its entirety, the five near-synonyms are considered together at this point.

4.2.1 Sense

Figure 3 displays the distribution of the concept PLEASANT SMELLING across senses and periods: each bar represents one period, and within each period the senses are signaled by different shades of grey. Table 11 provides the specific figures per period, as well as the overall frequency of the concept in each sense. Again, the percentages are to be interpreted vertically. Overall, the concept is much more commonly used to denote natural smells (Na), with a general frequency of 3,844 instances, equaling 66.69% of the total data. The other three senses (i.e., artificial, figurative, and indeterminate) are much less common. The concept is used in the artificial sense (Art) in a total of 1,211 instances, representing 21.01% of the cases. The figurative (Fig) and indeterminate (Indet) senses together account for less than 15% of the data, with the former amounting to 235 instances (4.08%) and the latter to 474 instances (8.22%).

As mentioned in Section 3.3.1 above, the value 'indeterminate' groups together those instances which could not be safely assigned to either the natural or artificial senses. An instance was provided in example (42) in Section 3.3.1, which is here reprinted as (102) for the sake of convenience:

(102)   Floyd turned off the engine and put his arm around Lizette, kissing the top of her head, right where her **fragrant hair** was parted. "Why we stopped here?" she asked, looking at the flat fields around the car. (*COHA*, 1994, FIC, WomenLanguage)

Note that indeterminate cases such as this one are more frequent in the data than occurrences illustrating the figurative sense.

If the distribution of the concept across senses is analyzed over time, considerable changes are identified. This is so because, even though the natural sense remains the most common one throughout the time span 1810–2009, this sense displays a major downward tendency as time passes, from about four fifths of the

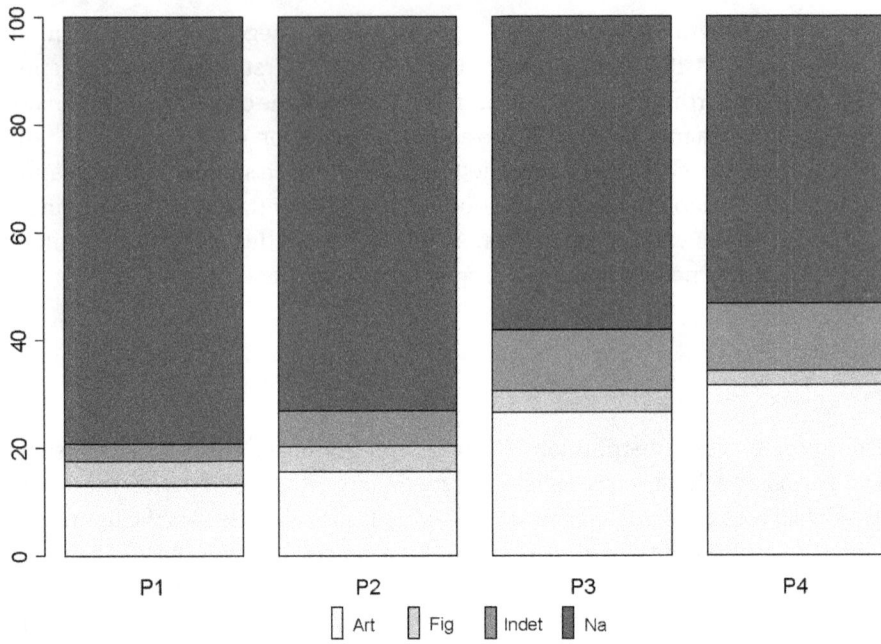

Figure 3: Percentages of the concept PLEASANT SMELLING in each sense across periods.

Table 11: Distribution of the concept PLEASANT SMELLING across senses.

Sense	Period	P1 (1810–1859)	P2 (1860–1909)	P3 (1910–1959)	P4 (1960–2009)	Total
Artificial	N	157	309	360	385	1,211
	%	13.05	15.53	26.59	31.64	21.01
Figurative	N	54	95	54	32	235
	%	4.49	4.77	3.99	2.63	4.08
Indeterminate	N	39	131	153	151	474
	%	3.24	6.58	11.30	12.41	8.22
Natural	N	953	1455	787	649	3,844
	%	79.22	73.12	58.12	53.33	66.69
Total	N	1,203	1,990	1,354	1,217	5,764
	%	100	100	100	100	100

data in P1 (79.22%) to only about half in P4 (53.33%). The figurative sense, despite its overall low frequency, also decreases in use from P1 to P4, from 4.49% to 2.63%. The artificial sense and indeterminate examples, in turn, show the opposite trend, becoming more and more frequent with each subsequent period. Concerning the artificial sense, it totals only 13.05% of the data in P1, while it rises up to 31.64% in P4. In the case of the value 'indeterminate', we see an upward tendency from 3.24% in P1 to 12.41% in P4. These changes lead to a convergence of the senses in terms of frequency, especially in the case of the natural and artificial senses. In other words, whereas in P1, the concept PLEASANT SMELLING is mainly used to refer to natural aromas, in P4 this predominance is not as strong. In fact, whereas in P1 the natural sense is about six times more common than the artificial one, in P4 it is only around two times more common. Crucially, both the decrease of the natural sense and the increase of both the artificial sense and indeterminate uses are particularly pronounced from P2 to P3, that is, around the transition from the nineteenth to the twentieth century. Interestingly, it is precisely at this point in time that most fluctuations in the frequency of individual adjectives takes place (cf. Section 4.1), thus suggesting the existence of some underlying motivation(s) for change.

A chi-square test of independence confirms that the distribution of the concept PLEASANT SMELLING across senses and periods shown in Table 11 and Figure 3 is statistically significant (χ^2 = 331.76, df = 9, p < 0.001). In this case, the residuals indicate that the natural sense is considerably more frequent than expected in both P1 and P2, but less frequent than expected in P3 and P4. The opposite trend emerges in the case of the artificial sense and of indeterminate uses, both of which are substantially less frequent than expected in P1 and P2, but more so in P3 and P4. Some of the changes undergone by the figurative sense are also quite notable, as this sense is considerably less frequent than expected in P4. The residuals of this statistical analysis are provided in Table 12.

Table 12: Chi-square residuals of the concept PLEASANT SMELLING across senses in the period 1810–2009.

Period Sense	P1 (1810–1859)	P2 (1860–1909)	P3 (1910–1959)	P4 (1960–2009)
Artificial	−6.02	−5.34	4.48	8.09
Figurative	0.71	1.54	−0.16	−2.50
Indeterminate	−6.03	−2.55	3.95	5.09
Natural	5.32	3.51	−3.86	−5.71

The findings presented in this section have uncovered rather general diachronic tendencies regarding the distribution of the concept PLEASANT SMELLING as a whole across senses. In the next section we turn to the distribution of the concept across semantic categories to identify whether these changes occur with specific types of nouns or whether, on the contrary, they are equally distributed across the natural, artificial, figurative, and indeterminate uses.

4.2.2 Semantic category

As mentioned in Section 3.3.2, there is a one-to-one correspondence between some of the four senses discussed in the previous section and the twelve semantic categories. The reader might recall that in seven of the twelve semantic categories distinguished (i.e., ABSTRACT, CLEANING, COSMETICS, EARTH, ATMOSPHERE, AND WEATHER, FOOD AND DRINK, PLANTS AND FLOWERS, TEXTILE AND CLOTHING), we witness a complete match between the two variables. On the contrary, in none of the five remaining categories, namely BODY AND PEOPLE, OBJECT, SENSATION, SPACE, and SUBSTANCE AND MATERIAL, is there an exact parallelism between the variables, although some clear tendencies can be observed. First, SENSATION and SPACE are overall 'natural' categories, as more than half of the instances occur in this sense, 79.69% in the former case and 54.12% in the latter. On the contrary, OBJECT and SUBSTANCE AND MATERIAL are mainly 'artificial,' with 69.92% and 61.38% of cases, respectively, corresponding with this sense. Finally, BODY AND PEOPLE is a more heterogenous category, exhibiting a great deal of ambiguity (51.53% of indeterminate instances). Similarly, SPACE, although chiefly a 'natural' category, also displays a high percentage of indeterminate cases (30%).

Figure 4 shows the distribution of the concept PLEASANT SMELLING across semantic categories per period: each bar represents a separate period, and within each of them the semantic categories are signaled by different colors. Table 13 provides the specific figures for each period and the overall frequency of the concept with respect to the twelve semantic categories, both in absolute numbers and in percentages. As in previous cases, the percentages should be interpreted vertically.

Starting with the overall frequencies, which are shown in the rightmost column, it is evident that some semantic categories of nouns are modified by the concept under analysis much more frequently than others. For instance, PLANTS AND FLOWERS and EARTH, ATMOSPHERE, AND WEATHER represent 28.57% and 19.52%, respectively, while nouns belonging to COSMETICS and CLEANING correspond to just 2.31% and 3.09%. Overall, the prototypically 'natural' categories are much more common than the prototypically 'artificial' ones.

If the diachronic evolution of the concept is considered, some clear trends can be observed. On the one hand, the frequency of the concept decreases in four categories, namely ABSTRACT, EARTH, ATMOSPHERE, AND WEATHER, PLANTS AND FLOWERS, and SENSATION. The downward tendency seems to be particularly pronounced in the latter two categories, from 41.65% and 7.40% in P1 to 16.43% and 2.88% in P4, respectively. Interestingly, both PLANTS AND FLOWERS and SENSATION are mainly 'natural' categories: PLANTS AND FLOWERS corresponds completely with the natural sense, while in approximately 80% of the instances of SENSA-

4.2 The evolution of the concept PLEASANT SMELLING — 107

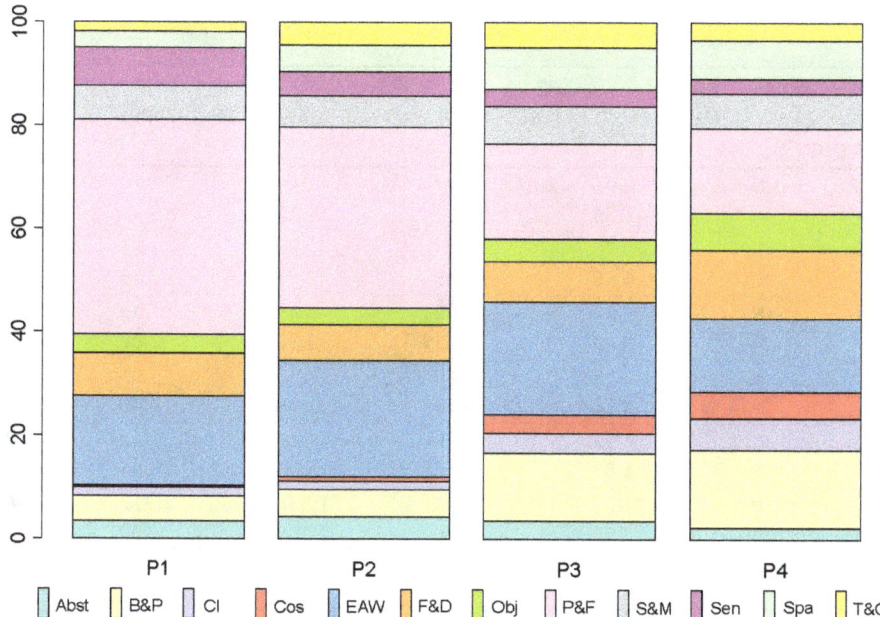

Figure 4: Percentages of the concept PLEASANT SMELLING in each semantic category across periods.

Table 13: Distribution of the concept PLEASANT SMELLING across semantic categories.

Sem. category	Period	P1 (1810–1859)	P2 (1860–1909)	P3 (1910–1859)	P4 (1960–2009)	Total
ABS	N	40	84	48	27	199
	%	3.33	4.22	3.55	2.22	3.45
B&P	N	59	104	177	184	524
	%	4.90	5.23	13.07	15.12	9.09
CL	N	20	32	52	74	178
	%	1.66	1.61	3.84	6.08	3.09
COS	N	4	17	49	63	133
	%	0.33	0.85	3.62	5.18	2.31
EAW	N	208	448	296	173	1,125
	%	17.29	22.51	21.86	14.22	19.52
F&D	N	100	138	105	160	503
	%	8.31	6.93	7.75	13.15	8.73
OBJ	N	44	66	59	87	256
	%	3.66	3.32	4.36	7.15	4.44

Table 13 (continued)

Period Sem. category		P1 (1810–1859)	P2 (1860–1909)	P3 (1910–1859)	P4 (1960–2009)	Total
P&F	N	501	697	249	200	1,647
	%	41.65	35.03	18.39	16.43	28.57
S&M	N	78	120	99	81	378
	%	6.48	6.03	7.31	6.66	6.56
S<small>EN</small>	N	89	92	45	35	261
	%	7.40	4.62	3.32	2.88	4.53
S<small>PA</small>	N	38	103	108	91	340
	%	3.16	5.18	7.98	7.48	5.90
T&C	N	22	89	67	42	220
	%	1.83	4.47	4.95	3.45	3.82
Total	N	1,203	1,990	1,354	1,217	5,764
	%	100	100	100	100	100

TION the concept is used to denote natural aromas. Therefore, the considerable decrease of the natural sense uncovered in the previous section is mainly located in these two semantic categories. On the other hand, seven semantic categories exhibit an upward tendency over time; these are BODY AND PEOPLE, CLEANING, COSMETICS, FOOD AND DRINK, OBJECT, SPACE, and TEXTILE AND CLOTHING. Note that three of these, CLEANING, COSMETICS, and TEXTILE AND CLOTHING, display a one-to-one correspondence with the artificial sense. Additionally, OBJECT is also a prototypically 'artificial' category, given that almost 70% of the instances of the concept with nouns belonging to this class are used in this sense. In other words, the substantial increase of the artificial sense discussed earlier (cf. Section 4.2.1) seems to occur in most prototypically 'artificial' semantic categories. The only exception to this trend is SUBSTANCE AND MATERIAL (61.38% in the artificial sense), which remains rather stable over time. In turn, BODY AND PEOPLE, the semantic category which displays the highest degree of ambiguity, also increases considerably, from 4.90% in P1 to 15.12% P4. Although this semantic category contains a large amount of indeterminate cases, the percentage of uses in the artificial sense (i.e., 38.93%) is still substantially greater than that in the natural one (8.59%). In the case of BODY AND PEOPLE, the upward tendency may be related to the growing use of lotions, perfumes, cleansing agents, and other artificial products that are often applied to the body. This would also go a long way towards explaining the increase in both the CLEANING and COSMETICS categories.

These results are mostly in line with the distribution of the concept PLEASANT SMELLING across senses discussed in Section 4.2.1. However, despite the decrease over time in the frequency of the concept in the natural sense, two semantic categories that are placed close to the natural end of the continuum do in fact increase. First, FOOD AND DRINK, a category which comprises only natural uses of the concept, rises from 8.31% in P1 to 13.15% in P4. Second, SPACE, a category used in almost 55% of instances in the natural sense, also increases, from 3.16% in P1 to 7.48% in P4. These findings, however, do not necessarily contradict the ones obtained in the previous section, namely that the concept decreases in the natural sense and rises in the artificial sense and in indeterminate uses. This is so because, although FOOD AND DRINK is prototypically 'natural', it could be argued that food and drinks have progressively become less 'natural' over time with the growing addition of food coloring, sweeteners, and preservatives. In the case of SPACE, the increase is attested mainly in the indeterminate uses, going from 15.79% in P1 to 32.97% in P4, but not in the natural sense, which decreases from 63.16% in P1 to 46.15% in P4.

Many of diachronic tendencies discussed in the previous paragraphs are statistically significant according to a chi-square test of independence ($\chi^2 = 686.41$, df = 33, $p < 0.001$). The residuals of the test confirm the following important tendencies over the period 1810–2009 (cf. Table 14):

(i) Substantial downward tendency over time: ABSTRACT; PLANTS AND FLOWERS; EARTH, ATMOSPHERE, AND WEATHER; and SENSATION.
(ii) Substantial upward tendency over time: BODY AND PEOPLE; CLEANING; COSMETICS; FOOD AND DRINK; OBJECT; SPACE; and TEXTILE AND CLOTHING.

Table 14: Chi-square residuals of the frequency of the concept PLEASANT SMELLING across semantic categories in the period 1810–2009.

Period Sem. Category	P1 (1810–1859)	P2 (1860–1909)	P3 (1910–1859)	P4 (1960–2009)
ABS	−0.24	1.85	0.18	−2.32
B&P	−4.82	−5.72	4.86	6.97
CL	−2.81	−3.76	1.58	5.94
COS	−4.51	−4.27	3.18	6.59
EAW	−1.75	3.02	1.95	−4.19
F&D	−0.49	−2.71	−1.21	5.22
OBJ	−1.29	−2.38	−0.15	4.48
P&F	8.48	5.38	−7.01	−7.92
S&M	−0.10	−0.92	1.08	0.13
SEN	4.68	0.20	−2.08	−2.71
SPA	−3.91	−1.33	3.15	2.27
T&C	−3.53	1.50	2.13	−0.65

As in the case of the distribution across senses shown in Table 11 and Figure 3 (cf. Section 5.2.1), the respective decreases and increases in frequency of the concept across semantic categories are particularly pronounced from P2 to P3, i.e., in the transition from the nineteenth to the twentieth century, especially in the following categories: BODY AND PEOPLE, CLEANING, COSMETICS, PLANTS AND FLOWERS, SENSATION, and SPACE.

In conclusion, the distributional changes experienced by the concept PLEASANT SMELLING throughout the time span 1810–2009 uncovered in the previous section and in the preceding paragraphs indicate that the concept undergoes a change from being used mainly to denote natural smells to becoming more and more frequent to refer to artificial ones. In other words, we witness a change as regards the kinds of nouns typically modified by the concept. Between 1810 and 1909 (i.e., in P1 and P2), the concept chiefly appears with nouns referring to entities with a natural pleasant smell, especially those belonging to the categories PLANTS AND FLOWERS and EARTH, ATMOSPHERE, AND WEATHER. However, from 1910 onwards (i.e., in P3 and P4), the concept increasingly collocates with nouns referring to entities with an agreeable aroma by virtue of having been impregnated by a pleasantly smelling synthetic substance. In Chapter 7, this change is hypothesized to have been caused principally by language-external motivations, specifically, the social and technological transformations experienced by American society after the First and Second Industrial Revolutions.

In the next section, a more detailed analysis of each of the five selected adjectival near-synonyms is offered separately to identify how the changes in the concept uncovered here are distributed across the different members of the synonym set. To this purpose, a semasiological perspective is adopted, thus accounting for the prototypical uses of each adjective across senses and semantic categories, both generally and over time.

4.3 Semasiological analysis

In Section 3.1.2, an overview of the sense division of the near-synonymous adjectives *fragrant*, *perfumed*, *scented*, *sweet-scented*, and *sweet-smelling* was provided on the basis of a series of dictionaries and thesauri (cf. Table 2). It was shown there that while the reference works provided the same basic meaning 'having a sweet pleasant smell' for the five adjectives, a few also explicitly distinguished between the artificial and the natural senses in the case of *perfumed* and *scented*. Therefore, it was hypothesized that *perfumed* and *scented* could be more prototypical than the three remaining adjectives to refer to artificial, as opposed to natural, aromas. In this section, the distribution of the five adjectives across the different senses and semantic categories is examined from a semasiological perspective, that is, considering each adjective separately to identify their prototypical uses. In addition, the adjectives are analyzed over time to uncover possible changes in their prototypical structure and to determine whether the changes in the concept PLEASANT SMELLING as a whole may be due to only one or a few of the adjectives or whether, on the contrary, all five near-synonyms undergo similar diachronic semantic developments. The structure of this section mirrors that of the previous one in that the distribution of the adjectives across senses is first analyzed in Section 4.3.1 and then across semantic categories in 4.3.2. The section closes with a discussion of the findings in 4.3.3.

4.3.1 Sense

Figure 5 displays the overall distribution of each adjective, represented by a separate bar, across the four senses distinguished.[41] Each shade of grey stands for a different sense. Starting with *fragrant*, it is used to refer to natural smells in 79.18% of the cases, while artificial smells amount to only 9.75% of the data.[42] Similarly, *sweet-scented* is also predominantly 'natural', with 86.36% of the instances of this adjective occurring in this particular sense. On the contrary, both *perfumed* and *scented* are common in both the artificial and natural senses. *Perfumed* is more frequent in the artificial sense (44.32%) vs. natural (36.85%), while *scented* is used somewhat more frequently in the natural (50.58%) than in the artificial sense (39.21%). Lastly, *sweet-smelling*, although more prototypically 'natural' (58.89%), also displays a considerable proportion of artificial uses (25.69%), at least if compared to *fragrant* and *sweet-scented*. The figurative and indeterminate senses are not particularly frequent for any of the adjectives. Nevertheless, the value 'indeterminate' is generally more common with the three adjectives that occur relatively frequently in both the natural and artificial senses, that is, *perfumed*, *scented*, and *sweet-smelling*. The low overall frequency of the figurative

---

[41] No chi-square tests are conducted in this section because (i) the overall distributions of the adjectives across senses and semantic categories are not compared to one another, as a semasiological perspective is adopted here; and (ii) on some occasions, the frequency of some of the adjectives over time across senses and semantic categories is lower than 5. The chi-square test requires that at least 80% of cells in tables larger than 2 by 2 exhibit a frequency of 5 or higher and no cells with zero (Levshina 2015: 213–214).

[42] In the remainder of this chapter, only figures are provided, as it would require a vast number of tables to show all the absolute and relative frequencies of the different adjectives overall and across senses and semantic categories. However, some data is discussed in the running text to support the tendencies visualized in the figures provided.

sense is not entirely surprising since metaphorical extensions are often less salient than the literal senses from which they originate, just as in the case of the noun *bird* discussed above.[43]

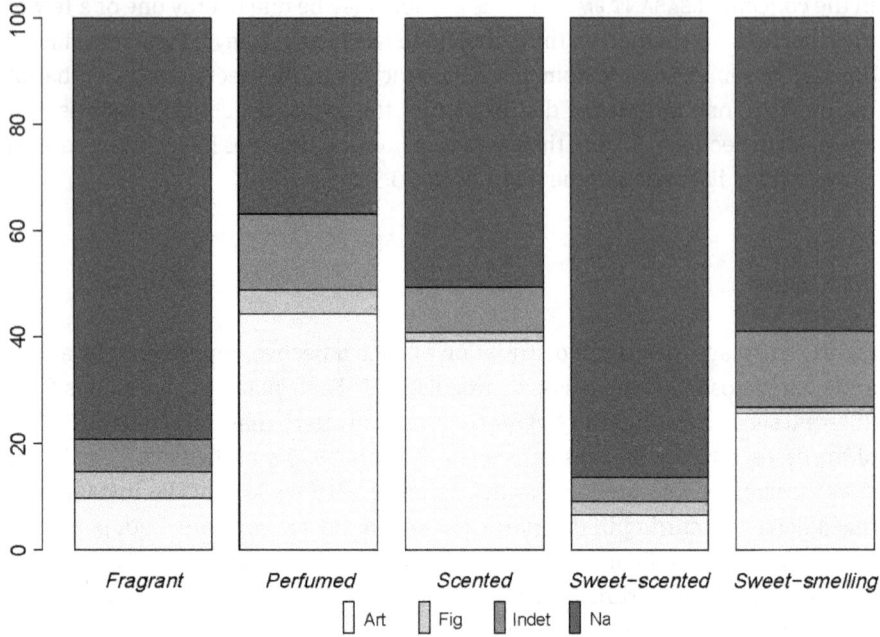

Figure 5: Overall sense distribution (in percentages) per near-synonym.

If the distribution of each adjective across senses in the four periods is examined, some interesting developments seem to be at play, as shown in Figure 6 below, which includes five independent plots, one per adjective, with the bars representing the four periods and a different shade of grey for each sense.

As regards *fragrant*, although it remains prototypical in the natural sense, its use in such contexts decreases over time, from 87.19% in P1 to 73.47% in P4. Similarly, we also witness a decrease of this adjective in the figurative sense

---

43 However, this is not to say that the figurative senses of a word or expression cannot come to be more salient than its literal ones, even when the former originate from the latter (Allan 2021: 287). A case in point is the adjective *ardent* (cf. Allan 2014: Section 5; Allan 2015b: Section 4) as the etymologically literal meaning 'burning', which is still attested in Present-Day English though classified as rare or archaic in most dictionaries, is less salient than the metaphorical sense 'passionate or very enthusiastic', which is the most frequently used sense of the word today.

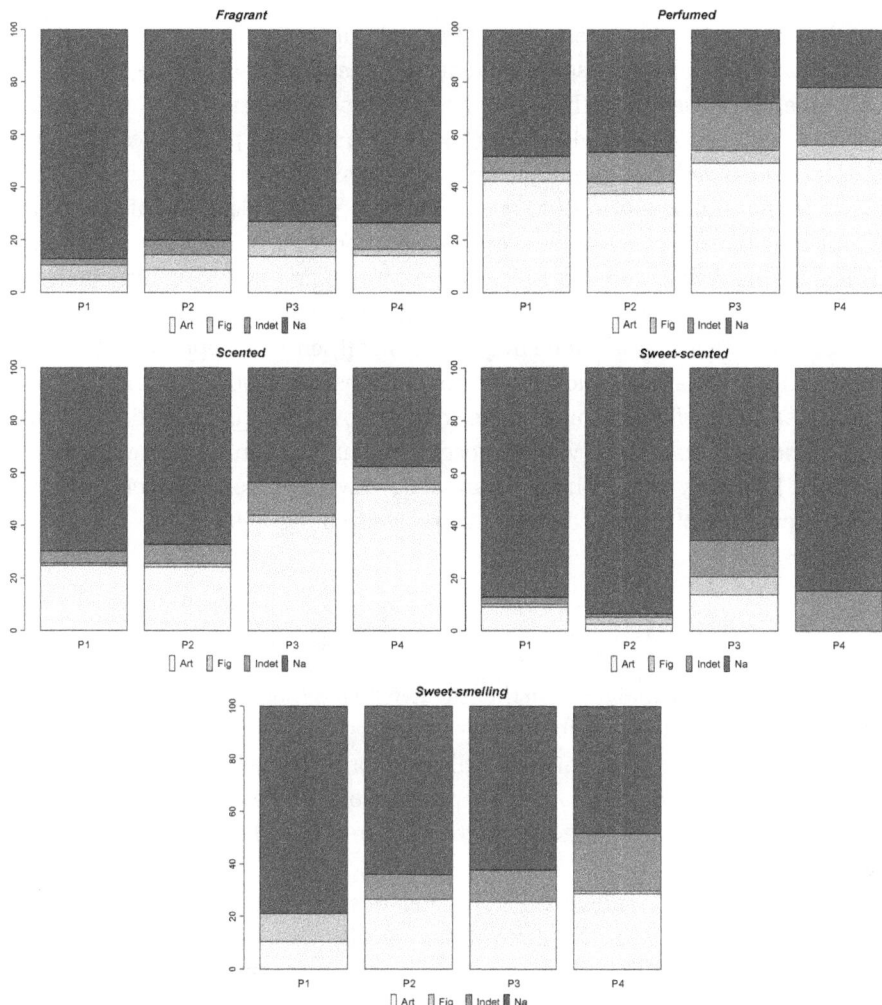

Figure 6: Sense distribution (in percentages) per adjectival near-synonym across periods.

across periods, while it becomes more common in both the artificial and indeterminate senses throughout the period 1810–2009, from 4.85% and 2.49% in P1 to 14.12% and 10.03% in P4, respectively. In the case of *perfumed*, we observe an increase in three of the four senses, namely artificial, figurative, and indeterminate, although this upward tendency is much more pronounced in indeterminate cases, from 6.22% in P1 to 21.88% in P4. The use of this adjective to denote natural aromas, in turn, declines substantially, as it is used in the natural sense more than twice as frequently in P1 (48.19%) than in P4 (21.88%). Similar trends emerge concerning the development of *scented*: it increases in the artificial, figurative, and indeterminate senses and decreases substantially in the natural one over time. Nevertheless, in this case, the rise in use is most noticeable in the artificial sense, from 24.77% in P1 to 53.82% in P4. In fact, the prototypical structure of *scented* changes throughout the time span considered, from being used mostly to denote natural smells in P1 to becoming more prototypically 'artificial' in P4. Concerning the adjective *sweet-scented*, it experiences less fluctuations over time as regards its distribution across senses, as it remains predominantly 'natural' throughout the period 1810–2009, with only an increase in indeterminate uses. However, due to its low absolute frequencies in all senses except the natural one, specifically in P3 and P4, no reliable conclusions can be drawn from the data. Finally, *sweet-smelling* becomes more frequent over time in the artificial sense and in indeterminate uses, while its occurrence in the natural sense drastically declines. However, despite this substantial downward tendency, *sweet-smelling* is still more prototypically used in the natural sense in P4.

4.3.2 Semantic category

The present section analyzes whether the five near-synonymous adjectives occur as modifiers of some specific types of nouns by considering their distribution across the twelve semantic categories. Figure 7 provides the overall tendencies of the adjectives individually. Each bar represents one of the adjectives and, within the bars, the colors indicate the proportion of use of the adjectives with particular semantic categories.

The overall trends shown in Figure 7 demonstrate that *fragrant*, as expected, is most often used with the three prototypically natural semantic categories PLANTS AND FLOWERS (36.29%), EARTH, ATMOSPHERE, AND WEATHER (20%), and FOOD AND DRINK (12.05%), while it almost never occurs with nouns belonging to CLEANING (0.80%), COSMETICS (1.09%), and TEXTILE AND CLOTHING (1.38%), that is, the prototypically 'artificial' categories. Similarly, *sweet-scented* is also very frequently used with PLANTS AND FLOWERS and EARTH, ATMOSPHERE, AND WEATHER nouns, which together account for more than 70% of its total occurrences. In the remaining semantic categories this adjective is relatively uncommon, with less than 10 instances in each of them, except in SUBSTANCE AND MATERIAL (16 examples; 8.08%). In turn, the three categories of nouns with which *perfumed* collocates mostly are BODY AND PEOPLE (21.29%), EARTH, ATMOSPHERE, AND WEATHER (18.12%), and TEXTILE AND CLOTHING (10.44%). In the other nine categories *perfumed* occurs with a lower frequency and with a rather balanced distribution. In the case of *scented*, the order of semantic categories according

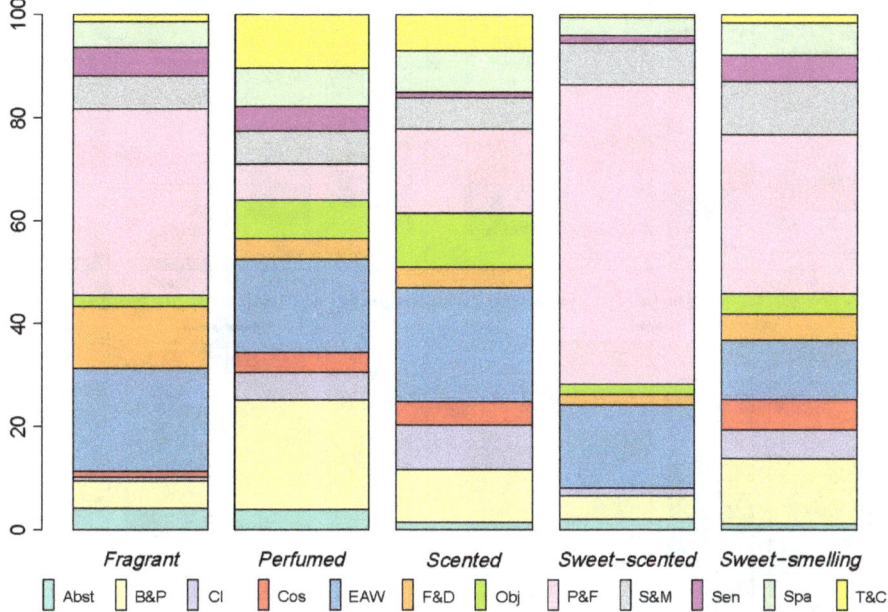

Figure 7: Overall semantic category distribution (in percentages) per near-synonym.

to frequency is as follows: EARTH, ATMOSPHERE, AND WEATHER (22.10%), PLANTS AND FLOWERS (16.37%), OBJECT (10.41%), and BODY AND PEOPLE (10.20%). In ABSTRACT and SENSATION, the use of *scented* is, on the contrary, only residual, with 13 (1.38%) and 10 (1.06%) instances, respectively. Lastly, *sweet-smelling* is most commonly used with nouns denoting PLANTS AND FLOWERS (30.83%). Additionally, this adjective is also relatively frequent in the semantic categories BODY AND PEOPLE (12.65%), EARTH, ATMOSPHERE, AND WEATHER (11.46%), and SUBSTANCE AND MATERIAL (10.28%).

Figure 8 shows the distribution of each adjective across semantic categories in the four periods. Again, five separate plots, one per adjective, are included, with the bars representing the four periods and, within each period, one color standing for each semantic category.

In the case of *fragrant*, the most prototypical semantic category in P1 is clearly PLANTS AND FLOWERS, with a relative frequency of 49.88%, followed by EARTH, ATMOSPHERE, AND WEATHER (16.17%) and FOOD AND DRINK (9.95%). However, this state of affairs changes substantially over time: *fragrant* decreases considerably with PLANTS AND FLOWERS nouns, and increases considerably with FOOD AND DRINK nouns, to the point that both categories are almost equally frequently modified by this adjective in P4 (23.13% and 21.94%, respectively). The category

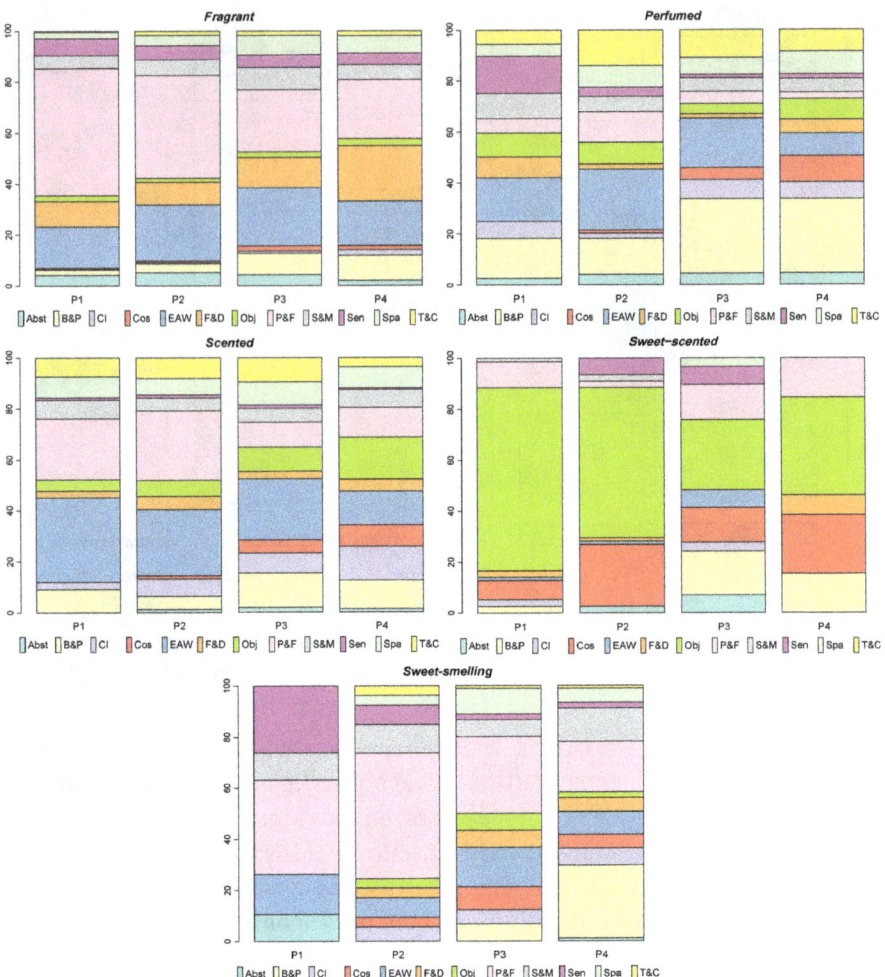

Figure 8: Semantic category distribution (in percentages) per near-synonym across periods.

EARTH, ATMOSPHERE, AND WEATHER, on the other hand, remains rather stable. Interestingly, two categories of nouns which are very infrequent with *fragrant* in P1 become more common by the end of the time span considered. These are BODY AND PEOPLE and SPACE, which go from 2.11% and 2.49% in P1 to 9.69% and 6.97% in P4, respectively.

In the case of *perfumed*, the following semantic categories experience noticeable fluctuations diachronically. On the one hand, BODY AND PEOPLE, COSMETICS, SPACE, and TEXTILE AND CLOTHING increase greatly in frequency over the period 1810–2009. The increase is particularly pronounced in the case of BODY AND

PEOPLE and COSMETICS, which go from 15.54% and 0% in P1 to 29.02% and 10.27% in P4, respectively. On the other hand, four categories exhibit a downward tendency with this adjective, namely EARTH, ATMOSPHERE, AND WEATHER, FOOD AND DRINK, PLANTS AND FLOWERS, SUBSTANCE AND MATERIAL, and SENSATION. In the case of SENSATION, there is a sharp decrease from P1 to P2 (from 14.51% to 3.60%). However, the high frequency of this category in P1 is due to just three particular texts in *COHA* in which SENSATION nouns are commonly modified by *perfumed*.[44]

Several categories of nouns also become either more or less frequently modified by *scented* over time. The most noticeable changes in the case of this adjective occur in the categories CLEANING, COSMETICS, and OBJECT, on the one hand, which increase substantially from P1 to P4, and EARTH, ATMOSPHERE, AND WEATHER and PLANTS AND FLOWERS, on the other, which decrease considerably.

Concerning the evolution of *sweet-scented*, although the scarcity of data did not allow to draw reliable conclusions, one interesting trend is observed: this adjective becomes a much less common modifier of nouns belonging to the category PLANTS AND FLOWERS, from 71.79% in P1 to 38.46% in P4. Nevertheless, PLANTS AND FLOWERS is still the category which is most often modified by *sweet-scented* in P4.

Similarly to *sweet-scented*, *sweet-smelling* also exhibits a low frequency in some semantic categories and thus the reliability of the results is at least questionable. However, some types of nouns do undergo changes over time, although only in relative, rather than absolute, terms. A considerable increase is observed in the semantic category BODY AND PEOPLE, from 0% in P1 to 28.57% in P4, while an important decrease takes place with PLANTS AND FLOWERS (from 36.84% to 19.78%) and SENSATION (from 26.32% to 2.20%).

4.3.3 Interim summary and discussion

This section has focused on the semasiological patterns of the five near-synonymous adjectives individually, both in general and throughout the time span 1810–2009. Their distribution across the four senses and twelve semantic categories uncovers some interesting differences, but also some similarities in their semasiological structures. First, we have seen that, overall, two of the adjectives, namely *fragrant* and *sweet-scented*, are prototypically used in the natural sense, whereas they are not very frequent in the artificial one. *Sweet-smelling* is also predomi-

---

[44] In these texts a total of 14 instances of *perfumed* occur as modifier of the SENSATION noun *flavor*.

nantly used in the natural sense, but, contrary to *fragrant* and *sweet-scented*, it is not so uncommon in the artificial sense. Finally, *perfumed* and *scented* are more evenly distributed across the natural and artificial senses, with *perfumed* coming closer to the artificial end of the semantic spectrum and *scented* to the natural one. Figurative and indeterminate uses display a much lower frequency, and none of the adjectives are particularly salient in any of these two uses. This is not surprising, given that it is not uncommon for figurative senses to be less salient than the literal ones from which they derive, and since the value 'indeterminate' does not, as explained earlier (cf. Section 3.3.1), constitute a separate sense, but merely groups together ambiguous examples.

A more fine-grained picture of the semasiological structures of the adjectives was obtained by examining their distribution across the semantic categories of nouns, though similar tendencies were observed: *fragrant* and *sweet-scented* occur mostly in the prototypically 'natural' categories, particularly in PLANTS AND FLOWERS, EARTH, ATMOSPHERE, AND WEATHER, and, in the case of *fragrant*, also in FOOD AND DRINK. Two of these semantic categories of nouns, that is, PLANTS AND FLOWERS and EARTH, ATMOSPHERE, AND WEATHER, are in fact also among the most common contexts of use with the remaining three adjectives, *perfumed*, *scented*, and *sweet-smelling*, with the exception of *perfumed* in the former. The fact that these two semantic categories of nouns are frequently modified by all five adjectives explains the very high proportion of these particular categories with the concept PLEASANT SMELLING as a whole (cf. Figure 4 in Section 4.2.2). In addition, *perfumed*, *scented*, and *sweet-smelling* are also relatively salient in the categories BODY AND PEOPLE, TEXTILE AND CLOTHING (in the case of *perfumed*), OBJECT (in the case of *scented*), and SUBSTANCE AND MATERIAL (in the case of *sweet-smelling*). The remaining five categories of nouns, i.e., ABSTRACT, CLEANING, COSMETICS, SENSATION, and SPACE, are not particularly typical with any of the five adjectives and therefore display a much lower overall frequency.

These results seem to be mostly in line with the definitions provided by the reference material (cf. Section 3.1.2), as *fragrant* and *sweet-scented* are both infrequent to refer to artificial aromas. Nevertheless, even though an artificial sense is not provided for *sweet-smelling* in any of the dictionaries consulted, this adjective does occur in this sense relatively frequently in the data. As hypothesized in Section 3.1.2, *perfumed* and *scented* are the two adjectives with the highest proportion of uses in the artificial sense, which may explain why some of the dictionaries distinguish between a natural and an artificial sense for these two items. It is plausible that this state of affairs, i.e., *perfumed* and *scented* being the most 'artificial' adjectives of the synonym set, derives from their etymology. As mentioned in Section 3.1.2, both *perfumed* and *scented* are derivatives formed by the suffix *-ed* (*OED*, s.v. *-ed* suffix[1]), which were coined after their base form *perfume* and *scent* had already been borrowed into English. Therefore, *perfumed* and *scented* still retain their participial shape and also possibly part of their verbal semantic functions, namely, denoting a process or action whereby something is impregnated with a pleasant smell. Consequently, it is not at all surprising that *perfumed* and *scented* are more salient in the artificial sense than the three remaining adjectives.

Regarding the diachronic evolution of the semasiological structure of the adjectives, similar trends can be observed for several of the five near-synonyms. First, four of the five adjectives, namely *fragrant*, *perfumed*, *scented*, and *sweet-smelling*, become more frequent in the artificial sense and, to a certain extent, in indeterminate uses, while they undergo a considerable decrease in the natural sense. Such tendencies seem to be more pronounced in the case of *perfumed* (particularly in the natural sense and indeterminate cases) and of *scented* (particularly in the natural and artificial senses). On the other hand, *sweet-scented* constitutes an exception, since it remains rather stable over time and is mainly used to refer to natural aromas, with more than 80% of its occurrences corresponding to this specific sense in three of the four periods and only a slight dip in P3. Consequently, the diachronic trend across senses uncovered in Section 4.2.1 regarding the concept PLEASANT SMELLING as a whole seems to be relatively general, occurring across the board, with the exception of *sweet-scented*. Second, in Section 4.2.2 two main diachronic trends were identified with respect to the distribution of the concept as a whole across semantic categories: (i) a substantial decrease with nouns belonging to PLANTS AND FLOWERS, and (ii) an increase with BODY AND PEOPLE, CLEANING, and COSMETICS. The findings of the semasiological analysis demonstrate that whereas the decrease in PLANTS AND FLOWERS affects all five adjectives, the increase in BODY AND PEOPLE is restricted mainly to the adjectives *fragrant*, *perfumed*, and *sweet-smelling*. Similarly, the upward tendency in COSMETICS is witnessed mostly with *perfumed* and *scented*, and that of CLEANING only with *scented*.

In conclusion, the findings in Section 4.3 suggest the existence of a continuum of senses with *sweet-scented* and *fragrant* being located at or towards the natural end of the cline and *perfumed* at the artificial end. *Sweet-smelling* and *scented*, in turn, occupy intermediate positions on the cline, since although both exhibit the same preference for the natural sense overall, they are also quite salient in the artificial sense, especially in the case of *scented*. Figure 9 visualizes this cline:

+ natural   *sweet-scented – fragrant – sweet-smelling – scented – perfumed*   **+ artificial**

Figure 9: Continuum of senses of the five adjectives.

Interestingly, there seems to exist a correlation between the position occupied by the adjectives on the continuum of senses and the diachronic frequency fluctuations identified in Section 4.1 (cf. Figure 2 and Table 8): *sweet-scented* and *fragrant*, the prototypically 'natural' adjectives, are the only near-synonyms in the set that undergo a significant decrease in frequency from P1 to P4. On the contrary, the adjectives occupying intermediate positions on the continuum, i.e., *scented* and *sweet-smelling*, are the only ones that increase significantly in frequency over time, while *perfumed*, the prototypically 'artificial' member of the set, remains rather stable in terms of frequency. It may be the case that the relative neutrality of *scented* and *sweet-smelling*, not being restricted to particular semantic categories, enables them to occur relatively often in a wider range of contexts than the other adjectives. This, in turn, may explain why they are the only adjectives that increase diachronically, given that the natural and artificial senses seem to even out progressively in terms of frequency over time. However, it is surprising that *perfumed*, the prototypically 'artificial' adjective, remains stable even though the artificial sense becomes diachronically more and more salient at the expense of the natural one.

So far, attention has been paid to the distribution of the concept PLEASANT SMELLING as a whole (cf. Section 4.2), as well as to the semasiological structure of each adjective individually (cf. Section 4.3). Nonetheless, given that the five lexical items are semantically related and occur in very similar contexts of use, the analysis of the competition between them in such contexts may help to reach a fuller understanding of their relation. To this purpose, an onomasiological perspective is adopted in which the five near-synonymous adjectives are compared to one another. As mentioned previously, semasiological and onomasiological analyses offer only a partial picture, since prototypicality and salience effects may vary if either one or the other perspective is adopted. Therefore, leaving out one of the two perspectives could lead to an incomplete interpretation of the data. In this context, the next section deals with the onomasiological structure of the synonym set.

4.4 Onomasiological analysis

To analyze the onomasiological structure of the synonyms in different contexts of use, the different senses and semantic categories constitute the point of departure in this section. Within each sense and semantic category, the proportions of use of the five adjectives are compared, first generally and then across time. As argued by Schmid (2007: 119), the degree of onomasiological salience —or entrenchment— of a lexical item with respect to other competing forms depends on its frequency in a particular sense or function rather than on its overall frequency. Thus, despite the general dominance of *fragrant* in terms of frequency, equaling 58.90% of the total data (cf. Table 8 in Section 4.1), it may well be the case that *fragrant* is outperformed by some of the other adjectives in specific contexts of use. In particular, both *perfumed* and *scented* are relatively semasiologically salient in the artificial sense, as opposed to *fragrant*, which is more semasiologically salient in the natural sense (cf. Section 4.3.1). Therefore, if an onomasiological perspective is adopted, *perfumed* and/or *scented* may surpass *fragrant* in 'artificial' contexts of use. As in the case of the two preceding sections, the adjectives are first examined across senses in Section 4.4.1, and then across semantic categories in 4.4.2. Finally, the results are discussed in Section 4.4.3.

4.4.1 Sense

Figure 10 provides the overall proportion of the five adjectives across each of the four senses with respect to one another.[45] In this figure, therefore, each bar represents one of the four senses, and within each bar, a different shade of grey stands for one of the near-synonymous adjectives.

As was to be expected due its overall much higher frequency, *fragrant* is the most entrenched variant in three of the four senses, namely figurative, indeterminate, and natural. Its dominance is particularly pronounced in the figurative and natural senses, where it accounts for 70.64% and 69.93% of the cases, respectively. In the indeterminate sense, *fragrant* also dominates (44.30%), but *perfumed* is relatively common as well (29.32%). However, despite its overall predominance in terms of frequency, *fragrant* is outperformed by both *perfumed* and *scented* in the artificial sense (35.76% and 30.47%, respectively vs. 27.33%). Nevertheless, the difference between these three adjectives in the artificial sense is not particularly large. Finally, neither *sweet-scented* nor *sweet-smelling* seem to be especially entrenched in any of the four senses, as is to be expected due to their overall low frequency (cf. Table 8 in Section 4.1).

Figure 11 offers the proportions of the five adjectives with respect to the different senses in the four periods to identify potential differences concerning their distribution over time. In this case, four separate plots, one per period, are provided. Again, the bars stand for the different senses and within them, the various shades of grey represent the near-synonymous adjectives.

---

[45] As in the previous section, no chi-square analyses are conducted here for similar reasons, the low frequency of certain semantic categories.

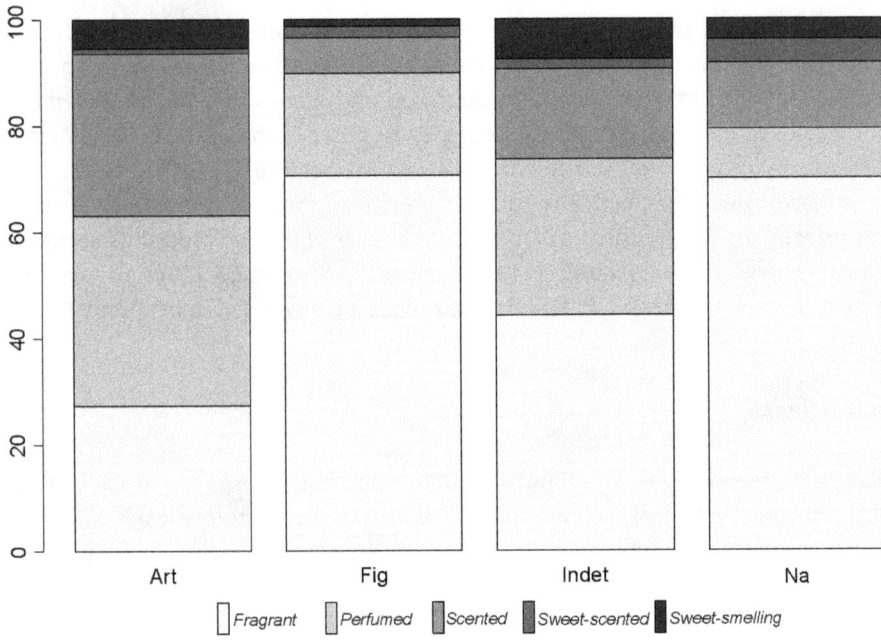

Figure 10: Overall percentages of the five near-synonyms in each sense.

Several changes seem to have taken place over the period 1810–2009 as concerns the proportions of the five adjectives across the different senses. First, in the artificial sense we observe a change in the frequency order of the adjectives over time: in P1 *perfumed* is clearly dominant as it accounts for 52.23%. However, from P2 onwards, its proportion gradually decreases, first in favor of *fragrant* in P2, and then mainly in favor of *scented* in P3 and P4. In fact, in P4, *scented* totals 42.08% of the data in the artificial sense, while *perfumed* amounts to 29.61%. As regards the figurative sense, *fragrant* continues to be the most frequent member of the set throughout the time span but, with each subsequent period, *perfumed* takes up more and more ground. In P4, for instance, *perfumed* is almost as frequent as *fragrant* in this sense (37.50% vs. 43.75%). Similarly, in the value 'indeterminate' *fragrant* decreases in favor of *sweet-smelling*, which is the only adjective that increases considerably with respect to the others in this use, from 0% in P1 to 13.25% in P4.[46] Lastly, in the natural sense, no remarkable changes can be observed, except for a moderate decrease of *fragrant* in favor of *scented*, with the

---

[46] The proportions of *perfumed* and *scented* also increase marginally in the value 'indeterminate' over time, from 30.77% and 12.82% in P1 to 32.45% and 13.91% in P4, respectively.

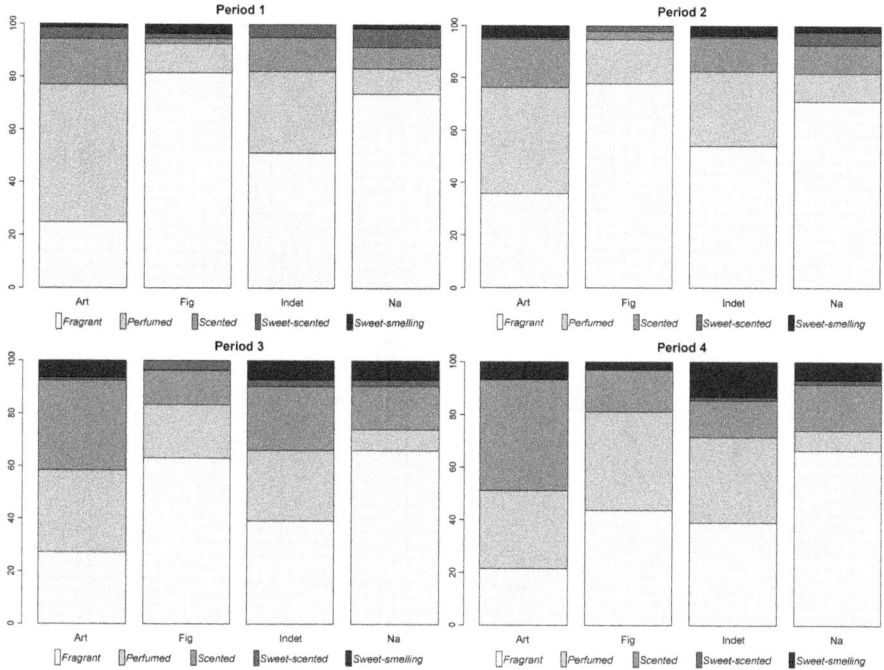

Figure 11: Percentages of the five near-synonyms in each sense across periods.

latter increasing from 7.97% in P1 to 17.41% in P4. Nevertheless, *fragrant* is still clearly predominant in the natural sense even in P4, totaling 66.56% of the data.

In sum, the data suggests an overall reorganization in the onomasiological structure of the set over time, which results in (i) *fragrant* no longer being markedly dominant in the figurative sense and in indeterminate uses by P4 and (ii) *scented* surpassing *perfumed* in the artificial sense at the end of the time span considered here. In what follows, the proportions of use of the near-synonyms across semantic categories are examined.

4.4.2 Semantic category

Figure 12 presents the overall proportions of the five near-synonyms across the twelve semantic categories distinguished. In this case, each bar represents one semantic category, and within each of them, a different shade of grey stands for the proportion of use of each adjective.

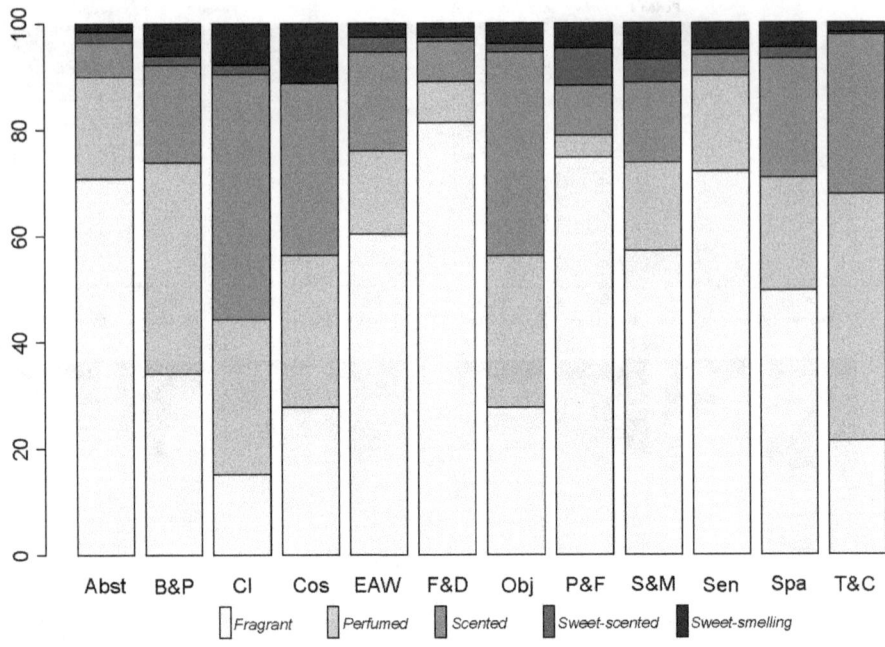

Figure 12: Overall percentages of the five near-synonyms in each semantic category.

As can be seen, *fragrant* is overall the default choice in seven out of the twelve categories, namely ABSTRACT (70.85%); EARTH, ATMOSPHERE, AND WEATHER (60.36%); FOOD AND DRINK (81.31%), PLANTS AND FLOWERS (74.80%); SUBSTANCE AND MATERIAL (57.14 %); SENSATION (72.03%); and SPACE (49.71%). It is also relatively frequent, although surpassed by *perfumed* and/or *scented*, in BODY AND PEOPLE (34.16%), COSMETICS (27.82%), OBJECT (27.73%), and TEXTILE AND CLOTHING (21.36%). Finally, in CLEANING *fragrant* exhibits its lowest proportion of use, accounting for only 15.17% of the total instances in this semantic category. In turn, *perfumed* is the dominant adjective with two semantic types of nouns, namely, BODY AND PEOPLE (39.69%), where it is closely followed by *fragrant* (34.16%), and TEXTILE AND CLOTHING (46.36%). In addition, it is also relatively common in CLEANING (29.21%), COSMETICS (28.57%), OBJECT (28.52%), and SPACE (21.18%). *Scented* surpasses the other adjectives in the set in the categories CLEANING (46.07%), COSMETICS (32.33%), and OBJECT (38.28%), and is reasonably frequent in SPACE (22.35%) and TEXTILE AND CLOTHING (30%). Finally, *sweet-scented* and *sweet-smelling* do not stand out in any of the twelve semantic categories. Nevertheless, the former reaches its peak in PLANTS AND FLOWERS (6.98%), where it is more frequent than both *perfumed* and *sweet-smelling* (4.13% and 4.74%, respectively), and the latter in COSMETICS (11.28%), followed by CLEANING (7.87%), SUBSTANCE AND MATERIAL (6.88%), and BODY AND PEOPLE (6.11%).

Therefore, from an onomasiological perspective, *fragrant* is most salient in all five prototypically 'natural' semantic categories (i.e., EARTH, ATMOSPHERE, AND WEATHER, FOOD AND DRINK, PLANTS AND FLOWERS, SENSATION, and SPACE), as well as in the 'figurative' category ABSTRACT and in the relatively 'artificial' category SUBSTANCE AND MATERIAL. On the contrary, both *perfumed* and *scented* display a clear preference for 'artificial' categories, as the former dominates in TEXTILE AND CLOTHING and the latter in CLEANING, COSMETICS, and OBJECT. In addition, *perfumed* is the most salient adjective in BODY AND PEOPLE, a mixed category with an extremely high proportion of indeterminate cases (i.e., 51.53%). As in the case of the distribution of the adjectives across senses (cf. Section 4.4.1), neither *sweet-scented* nor *sweet-smelling* are particularly entrenched in any of the twelve semantic categories, a fact which is undoubtedly related to their low overall frequency in the corpus.

Figure 13 presents the diachronic evolution of the five adjectives across semantic categories. Once again, a separate graph is plotted for each of the four periods.

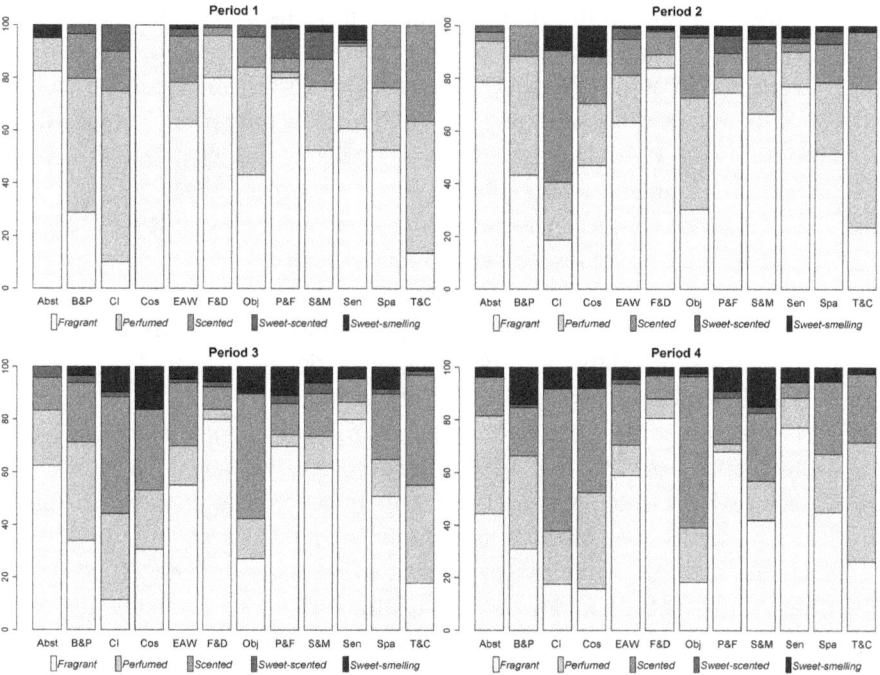

Figure 13: Percentages of the five near-synonyms in each semantic category across periods.

Two clear tendencies can be observed. On the one hand, as shown in the figure, in half of the semantic categories, the situation remains rather stable from P1 to P4. This is the case of the categories EARTH, ATMOSPHERE, AND WEATHER, FOOD AND DRINK, PLANTS AND FLOWERS, and SENSATION, where *fragrant* maintains a clear dominance over time with only a minimal decrease in some cases, mostly in favor of *scented*. Additionally, stability also applies to the distribution of the near-synonyms in the categories SPACE and TEXTILE AND CLOTHING. In SPACE, *fragrant* is the most common adjective throughout the period 1810–2009, but its dominance is not as clear as in the four semantic categories mentioned above, where the frequency of both *perfumed* and *scented* is much lower. In TEXTILE AND CLOTHING, *perfumed* and, to some extent, *scented* dominate the scene in all four periods, with only a slight increase of *fragrant* in P4.

On the other hand, diachronic tendencies can be observed as regards the remaining semantic categories:

(i) ABSTRACT shows a decrease of *fragrant* in favor of *perfumed*, so that in P4 the former is only marginally more frequent than the latter (44.44% vs. 37.04%).

(ii) Concerning BODY AND PEOPLE, *perfumed* loses its initial dominance in P1 (50.85%), as the frequencies of both *scented* and *sweet-smelling* increase over time. By P4, there exists a more balanced distribution of the adjectives in this category, with *perfumed* and *fragrant* outperforming the others (35.33% and 30.98%, respectively) but being rather closely followed by *scented* and *sweet-smelling* (18.48% and 14.13%, respectively).

(iii) In CLEANING, *scented* increases dramatically over time at the expense of *perfumed* and surpasses it already from P2 onwards.

(iv) As regards COSMETICS, from P2 onwards *perfumed* and *scented* gain more and more ground at the expense of *fragrant*, and in P4 they are the most frequent adjectives with nouns denoting cosmetic products, with 36.51% and 39.68%, respectively (vs. the 15.87% of *fragrant*).[47]

(v) With respect to the category OBJECT, in P1 *fragrant* and *perfumed* are clearly predominant (43.18% and 40.91%, respectively). However, over time, particularly from P2 to P3, there is a drastic increase of *scented*, which comes to represent 57.47% of the total data in P4, that is, more than double the amount of the second most frequent adjective (i.e., *perfumed*; 20.69%).

(vi) Lastly, in SUBSTANCE AND MATERIAL, although *fragrant* remains the most frequent adjective throughout the whole time span considered, *perfumed*

---

[47] Little can be said about the distribution of COSMETICS in P1, as there are only 4 cases in total, which correspond to instances of *fragrant*.

and *scented* invert positions over time: whereas *perfumed* is more frequent than *scented* in P1 and P2, *scented* is more common than *perfumed* in P3 and P4. In fact, by P4 the frequency of *perfumed* equals that of *sweet-smelling* (i.e., 14.81%), as the latter also increases substantially in the period 1810–2009 in this category.[48]

4.4.3 Interim summary and discussion

The results presented in this section regarding the onomasiological structure of the synonym set therefore demonstrate that *fragrant* is the most salient adjective in the natural sense across all five prototypically 'natural' categories, that is, EARTH, ATMOSPHERE, AND WEATHER, FOOD AND DRINK, PLANTS AND FLOWERS, SENSATION, and SPACE. Moreover, it maintains its pronounced dominance in all these contexts throughout the four periods, with only a slight decrease in frequency, mostly in favor of *scented*. On the contrary, all prototypically 'artificial' categories, except TEXTILE AND CLOTHING, do exhibit distributional changes over time. In particular, *scented* gains ground at the expense of *perfumed* and, to a certain extent, *fragrant*, and becomes the most salient adjective in the artificial sense by P4, more specifically in the semantic categories CLEANING, COSMETICS, and OBJECT. Additionally, changes are also identified in the figurative sense and, consequently, in the category ABSTRACT. In this case, *perfumed* increases considerably and becomes almost as salient as *fragrant* in P4. Finally, in the value 'indeterminate', *fragrant* decreases somewhat over time, mainly in favor of *sweet-smelling*, which increases considerably. In particular, this increase of *sweet-smelling* seems to have taken place with nouns belonging to BODY AND PEOPLE, which, as has been argued before, comprises a very high number of ambiguous examples classified here as indeterminate.

In sum, as was the case in the previous sections of this chapter, several diachronic changes also emerge if an onomasiological perspective is adopted, as proved by the rearrangement in the proportions of use of the different adjectives in several of the senses and semantic categories. In Section 4.1, it was shown that both *fragrant* and *sweet-scented* decreased in frequency over time, while *scented* and *sweet-smelling* increased, and *perfumed* remained relatively stable (cf. Table 8 and Figure 2). The results in Section 4.4 demonstrate that the

---

48 Nothing can be said about the diachronic evolution of *sweet-scented* across semantic categories when compared to the other four adjectives, as its frequency is almost negligible in all four periods, even in the category in which it is most frequent, i.e., PLANTS AND FLOWERS.

decrease of *fragrant* takes place mainly in the figurative sense and in indeterminate uses, and semantic categories associated with these two values, but that this adjective also undergoes a slight decline in 'natural' contexts of use. The increase of *scented*, in turn, affects mostly the artificial sense (i.e., CLEANING, COSMETICS, and OBJECT), with a minimal increase also in the natural one. In the case of *sweet-smelling*, it increases primarily in the indeterminate cases, particularly with nouns denoting BODY AND PEOPLE. Finally, regarding *perfumed* and *sweet-scented*, the former becomes more salient over time in the figurative sense, although it does not exhibit an overall increase in frequency, while the latter decreases mainly in the natural sense, that is, the only sense for which there is enough data to trace diachronic fluctuations for this adjective. Therefore, the changes in the frequency of the adjectives uncovered in Section 4.1 do not occur across the board, that is, in all contexts of use. On the contrary, they seem to be restricted to particular semantic functions.

4.5 Chapter summary and discussion

This chapter has been devoted to the analysis of the synonym set object of study from both semasiological and onomasiological perspectives. Both approaches are important to account for the semantics of the individual adjectives, the relation among them, and the concept they designate, given that they provide different viewpoints of the data. Despite the fact that the semantic relation studied in the present monograph is that of synonymy and, therefore, the main focus is on the onomasiological structure of the set, considering the semasiological structure of each adjective enabled us to conduct a more holistic analysis and thus explain some of the diachronic tendencies uncovered.

Section 4.1 proved the existence of several changes over time in the frequency of the five adjectives under analysis. Put briefly, *fragrant* and *sweet-scented* decreased considerably throughout the period 1810–2009, whereas *scented* and *sweet-smelling* increased. Interestingly, the increase of the latter two adjectives took place despite the overall downward tendency in the frequency of the concept PLEASANT SMELLING as a whole. A continuum of senses emerged from this analysis, with *fragrant* and *sweet-scented* being prototypically 'natural', thus occupying the natural end of the continuum, and *perfumed* being prototypically 'artificial'. *Scented* and *sweet-smelling*, on the other hand, occupied intermediate positions on this cline, as they occurred relatively frequently in both the natural and artificial senses. It therefore became evident that there exists a clear correspondence between the fluctuations in frequency over time and the continuum of senses postulated: the two adjectives which decreased in frequency are both prototypically 'natural', whereas the two that increased are relatively salient in both the artificial and the natural senses. On the contrary, the frequency of the prototypically 'artificial' adjective, namely *perfumed*, remained relatively stable diachronically.

Concerning changes in the semasiological structure of the near-synonyms, a common pattern was identified for all the adjectives except *sweet-scented*. Interestingly, despite their different degree of prototypicality, *fragrant*, *perfumed*, *scented*, and *sweet-smelling* all became increasingly more frequent to denote artificial aromas across periods, while they became less and less common in the natural sense, although to different degrees. This shared trend seems to point to a gradual convergence of these four adjectives concerning their semantic functions, whereby they become more similar rather than dissimilar over time. Additionally, the shared diachronic development of the four near-synonyms in this respect also becomes evident when examining the concept PLEASANT SMELLING as a whole (cf. Section 4.2), which also becomes more artificial over time.

Section 4.4 focused on the onomasiological structure of the synonyms, thus comparing their frequency in different contexts of use. This allowed us to zoom in on the competition between the five adjectives and to identify the exact semantic functions in which the frequency fluctuations took place. It was found that the increase of *scented* affected mostly the artificial sense and the semantic categories associated with it, whereas that of *sweet-smelling* took place mainly in the value 'indeterminate', particularly in the category BODY AND PEOPLE. On the contrary, *fragrant* decreased especially in the figurative sense and in indeterminate uses, but also to a certain extent in the natural sense. Therefore, not all contexts of use are equally affected by the general fluctuations in frequency uncovered in Section 4.1, as they seem to be limited to particular senses and semantic categories. In these contexts of use in which changes are identified, a rearrangement is often found in the onomasiological salience of the adjectives, so that in some of the senses and semantic categories the originally predominant adjective is ousted by another member of the set. This is, for instance, the case of the artificial sense and of some of the prototypically 'artificial' categories, namely CLEANING, COSMETICS, and OBJECT. On other occasions, the end result is a more equal distribution of the adjectives by P4, in such a way that none of the adjectives are clearly dominant, as happens in the figurative sense and in the value 'indeterminate' and the semantic categories ABSTRACT, BODY AND PEOPLE, and TEXTILE AND CLOTHING.

By taking into account the results of the different types of analyses conducted in the present chapter, we can characterize the semantic development of the synonyms object of study as one of attraction and ongoing substitution, at least in some contexts of use. As mentioned in Section 2.3, most studies on near-synonymy have resorted to a simplified theory of competition in which languages aim at an isomorphic state, mainly through the processes of differentiation and substitution. However, De Smet et al. (2018) argue that situations can be found in which near-synonymous expressions become over time more similar, rather than dissimilar, thus coming to share more semantic ground. The results presented throughout this chapter seem to point to the conclusion that at least four of the adjectives have undergone, and may still be undergoing, such a process of attraction. This was made evident in Section 4.3, in which it was shown that *fragrant*, *perfumed*, *scented*, and *sweet-smelling* follow a similar developmental path in semasiological terms, becoming more 'artificial' and less 'natural' across time. Moreover, this process of attraction seems to be accompanied by an ongoing process of substitution, whereby *scented* increases at the expense of both *perfumed* and *fragrant*, having already surpassed the former in terms of its overall frequency by P4 (cf. Section 4.1), and both *perfumed* and *fragrant* in particular semantic functions (cf. Section 4.4). It is not entirely surprising to find the processes of attraction and substitution operating at the same time, as they are not mutually exclusive: while the former is concerned with the functions of a set of competing expressions, the latter relates to their relative frequencies (De Smet et al. 2018: 205). In fact, a certain degree of attraction is probably a prerequisite for substitution, given that synonyms may need to be sufficiently functionally similar for one to be replaced by another. The interrelation between these two processes is further explored in the next chapter, where the onomasiological tendencies identified here are statistically tested by means of multivariate techniques and where further contexts of use are examined beyond the semantic ones considered up to now.

5 In-depth onomasiological analysis of the synonym set: A multivariate approach

Even though the five near-synonymous adjectives *fragrant*, *perfumed*, *scented*, *sweet-scented*, and *sweet-smelling* seem to be mostly interchangeable, their distribution, as shown in Chapter 4, depends largely on the sense in which they occur and the type of nouns with which they collocate. However, the evidence provided in the previous two chapters can be further refined by examining the competition between the adjectives in greater depth and with more sophisticated statistical techniques. Therefore, the focus of the present chapter is only on the onomasiological structure of the synonym set to discover the contexts of use in which speakers favor each adjective at the expense of the others and whether these preferences have changed over time. In particular, the preliminary findings of the onomasiological analysis in Section 4.4 are here tested for significance, and a larger number of variables, including further semantic but also morphosyntactic and extralinguistic ones, are examined. Moreover, the stylistic dimension is also considered here by taking into account the text-types in which the adjectives occur. Special attention is paid in this chapter to the diachronic tendencies of the adjectives by ascertaining whether their probability of occurrence in particular functions and contexts of use varies over time. The results will allow us to explore the processes at work in the diachronic evolution of the near-synonym set and thus confirm or refute the preliminary conclusion drawn in Chapter 4 that the adjectives are undergoing processes of attraction and substitution.

The present chapter is divided into four sections. Section 5.1 briefly summarizes the structure of the dataset employed and provides an explanation of the statistical methods applied to the data. Then, in Section 5.2, the results of the statistical analyses are presented: while Section 5.2.1 focuses on the effects of the variables Concreteness, Degree, Countability, Syntactic function, Text-type, Sense, Semantic category, and Period, Section 5.2.2. zooms in on the idiosyncratic collocational patterns of the adjectives. The results of the different analyses are jointly discussed in Section 5.3.

5.1 Data and methodology

The dataset used for the analyses in the present chapter is the first one explained in Section 3.2. Apart from the two semantic variables Sense and Semantic category, the instances of the adjectives in this dataset were also annotated for a series of additional language-internal variables, both semantic and non-semantic, and two language-external factors. These are Animacy, Concreteness (rating and binary), Countability, Syntactic function, Degree, Collocate, Period, and Text-type.[49] For reasons further explained below, only three of the adjectives were included in the analyses, namely *fragrant*, *perfumed*, and *scented*. On the other hand, *sweet-scented* and *sweet-smelling* had to be excluded due to their low frequency of occurrence, which makes it difficult to extract conclusions regarding their diachronic tendencies.

In order to account for the independent effects of each variable on the probabilities of the three adjectives, while at the same time controlling for the effects of the other variables, multivariate statistical tests were applied. First, the data was analyzed by means of multinomial logistic regression and, second, by means of binary mixed-effects logistic regression. Logistic regression analysis is a statistical technique that aims at predicting the probability of occurrence of the levels of a dependent or response variable on the basis of one or more independent variables, also called predictors (Speelman 2014: 488–489; Levshina 2015: 253–254). In turn, multinomial regression serves to model situations in which the response variable comprises more than two levels (Levshina 2015: 277), here the three near-synonyms *fragrant*, *perfumed*, and *scented*. Although several approaches exist to conduct this test, the polytomous package (Arppe 2013) in *R* was selected, given that it provides several goodness-of-fit statistics of the resulting model and easily interpretable coefficients. The heuristic used in this package is the so-called *one vs. rest* approach, in which the probabilities of each level of the dependent variable are compared with those of the other levels together (Levshina 2015: 277). Here, this implies comparing first the probability of *fragrant* vs. the joint probability of *perfumed* and *scented*, then that of *perfumed* vs. *fragrant* and *scented*, and finally that of *scented* vs. *fragrant* and *perfumed*. Two separate models were computed, with Synonym functioning as dependent variable and Sense/Semantic category, Countability, Concreteness rating, Syntactic function, Degree, Period, and Text-type as predictors, as well as the interactions between Period and the other variables, given that the main focus is on the diachronic development of the adjectives. An interaction between two variables entails that the effect of one of them on the response variable depends on the other (Levshina 2015: 162). For instance, a significant interaction between Period and Degree would mean that the influence of the degree of the adjectives on their probability of occurrence would vary across the four periods distinguished. Model A included Sense, not Semantic category, as a predictor of Synonym, while Model B included Semantic category, not Sense. Two separate

---

49 Cf. Table 7 in Section 3.3.5 for a summary of these variables and their values.

regression models were computed because, as previously mentioned in Section 3.3.2, Sense and Semantic category are strongly correlated, since there is often a one-to-one correspondence between their values (e.g., natural and PLANTS AND FLOWERS). Correlated predictors are problematic if added to the same model and, consequently, these predictors had to be kept apart (Levshina 2015: 272). Moreover, Animacy was not included in any of the models, since it is also too strongly correlated with Semantic category. This is so because the vast majority of animate referents occur in the semantic category BODY AND PEOPLE (88.54%), with only a few occurring in EARTH, ATMOSPHERE, AND WEATHER (9.48%) and PLANTS AND FLOWERS (1.58%), which correspond to highly poetic texts where natural phenomena such as weather terms and nouns denoting plants are personified, as in example (78) in Section 3.3.3, reprinted here as example (103):

(103) Ragged Ladies and **Marigolds** clustered together, And gossiped of scandal, the news, and the weather -- What dresses were worn at the wedding so fine Of sharp **Mr. Thistle** and sweet Columbine [. . .]. In a snug little nook sate the Jessamine pale, And that pure **fragrant Lily**, the gem of the vale. (*COHA*, 1834, FIC, Poems)

Given that concreteness was coded by means of two separate variables, one binary and one numerical (i.e., Concreteness binary and Concreteness rating; cf. Section 3.3.3), only one of them was finally included in the analyses, as they measure the same semantic feature in two different ways. By computing two separate models, each one with a different variable measuring concreteness, it was possible to identify that a model containing Concreteness rating performed significantly better (p <0.001) than a model with Concreteness binary. Therefore, the former variable was selected for inclusion in the final models.

To determine which predictors made a significant contribution to the models, a procedure known as *stepwise forward selection* was performed. This process consists in first computing a model without any predictors and then adding variables, one by one, until the addition of new variables does not lead to a significant improvement of the model (Levshina 2015: 149). First, the significance of each individual variable was ascertained and then the interactions between Period and the other predictors were tested for.

In order to interpret the results of the multinomial logistic regression models, the effects of the predictors were visualized by means of partial effect plots, which were carried out using the `ggplot2` package (Wickham 2016). Partial effect plots show the effects of each individual variable when the other variables remain constant.

The effect of the variable Collocate was measured by means of a different type of regression analysis, namely binary mixed-effects logistic regression. Mixed-effects models permit the inclusion of both fixed and random effects (Baayen 2008: 241–242; Tagliamonte and Baayen 2012: 143). The difference between these two kinds of effects lies in their repeatability. In the case of fixed effects, the levels of a predictor are repeatable, as happens with variables such as Sense: if we extracted a new sample of data of the adjectives under analysis from a different corpus, we would still annotate the resulting occurrences according to the values 'artificial', 'figurative', 'indeterminate', or 'natural'. On the contrary, random effects are open-ended, since there is not a limited number of values for such variables. This happens with variables such as Collocate, which only includes a subset of nouns out of all the potential nouns that could be modified by *fragrant*, *perfumed*, and/or *scented*. Therefore, if we extracted a new sample of the near-synonyms from a corpus other than *COHA*, it would inevitably contain individual noun collocates which do not appear in the current dataset. By including Collocate as a random effect, it is possible to identify particular lexical items that show a preference for one of the near-synonymous adjectives, thus accounting for their idiosyncratic collocational preferences. Mixed-effects models were computed by using the glmer function in the lme4 package (Bates et al. 2015).

All the resulting models are relatively complex, given that they include a large number of regressors. In logistic regression, each of the levels of a predictor counts as one regressor, excluding the reference value (Speelman 2014: 504). To illustrate this point, consider the predictor Countability. This variable contains three levels, namely, count, non-count, and other, which translates into two regressors. The most complex model, that is multinomial Model B, i.e., the one including Semantic category, contains 64 regressors. As a common rule of thumb, the number of instances of the least frequent level of the dependent variable should be at least ten to fifteen times larger than the total number of regressors (Baayen 2008: 195; Levshina 2015: 143–144). In the present dataset, the total number of instances of *sweet-scented* and *sweet-smelling*, the two least frequent near-synonyms, is 198 and 253, respectively (cf. Table 8 in Section 4.1). This implies that the maximum number of regressors allowed in a model with these two adjectives ranges between 13 and 19 in the case of *sweet-scented*, and between 16 and 25 in the case of *sweet-smelling*. Table 15 provides the overall frequency of the reduced dataset with the three near-synonyms *fragrant*, *perfumed*, and *scented*, as well as their distribution in absolute and relative frequencies, both generally and over time.

Table 15: Absolute and relative frequencies of *fragrant*, *perfumed*, and *scented*.

Period Synonym		P1 (1810–1859)	P2 (1860–1909)	P3 (1910–1959)	P4 (1960–2009)	Total
Fragrant	N	804	1291	712	588	3,395
	%	72.69	69.45	57.65	52.83	63.90
Perfumed	N	193	333	227	224	977
	%	17.45	17.91	18.38	20.13	18.39
Scented	N	109	235	296	301	941
	%	9.86	12.64	23.97	27.04	17.71
Total	N	1,106	1,859	1,235	1,113	5,313
	%	100	100	100	100	100

Finally, although logistic regression models can point to the relative importance of predictors to account for the choice between the levels of a dependent variable, another statistical test is more commonly used for this purpose, namely random forest analysis (Tagliamonte and Baayen 2012: 158–161; Levshina 2015: 297–299). This statistical test functions by computing many so-called conditional inference trees. Conditional inference trees, in turn, predict the probability of the values of a dependent variable by means of a series of binary splits in the data. The algorithm takes the predictor that is more strongly correlated with the dependent variable and considers whether dividing the data in two creates two new subsets of cases in which one of the values of the dependent variable is more probable than the rest. This process is then repeated until no further significant splits are identified (Tagliamonte and Baayen 2012: 159; Levshina 2015: 291–297). The individual trees in the forest are constructed on the basis of random samples of both predictors and instances of the dataset. Next, random forest analysis calculates the relative importance of predictors by arbitrarily changing the values of a given predictor. In this way, any discriminatory capacity that a particular predictor may have disappears. The test then compares the explanatory power of the original predictor with its reordered counterpart: if their explanatory power is the same, this means that the predictor does not have a significant effect on the choice between the levels of the dependent variable. On the contrary, if the explanatory power of the reordered predictor is worse than that of the original one, this implies that the latter has indeed a significant effect. The relative importance of a predictor is then calculated as the extent to which the model performs worse with the reordered version as opposed to the original one. Put simply, the worse the model becomes, the more important the effect of the predictor. The output of random forest analysis consists in a set of variable importance values which are usually interpreted as a ranking, where the predictor with the highest value is the most important and so on. Random forests were computed in *R* using the function `cforest()` in the `party` package (Hothorn et al. 2006; Strobl et al. 2007; Strobl et al. 2008).

5.2 Results

This section deals with the results obtained in the different regression models. While Section 5.2.1 presents the findings of the multinomial regression analyses, focusing on the fixed effect structures, Section 5.2.2 zooms in on the random effects of the variable Collocate, thus accounting for the outcome of the mixed-effects regression analyses.

5.2.1 Multinomial models: Fixed effect structure

As mentioned in the previous section, two multinomial regression models had to be computed separately to take the two variables Sense and Semantic category into consideration, as it is not possible to include both of them in the same model. The results of the two models, named 'Model A' and 'Model B', are here presented separately. However, given that besides the two highly correlated predictors Sense and Semantic category, the two models contain exactly the same significant predictors and predictor interactions, their effects are reported only once, as they are practically identical in Model A and Model B.

Starting with Model A, the following predictors and predictor interactions emerged as significant: Concreteness rating, Countability, Syntactic function, Degree, and the interactions between Period and Sense and between Period and Text-type. Table 16 displays the summary statistics of Model A, which provides several goodness-of-fit statistics, namely accuracy, McFadden R^2, Nagelkerke R^2, and likelihood ratio test.

Table 16: Model summary of multinomial logistic regression Model A (Sense).

Model summary	
accuracy	67.34% (baseline = 63.90%; $p < 0.001$)
McFadden R^2	0.1341
Nagelkerke R^2	0.2575
likelihood ratio test	1300.9 ($p < 0.001$)

The first row shows the accuracy, a reflection of the percentage of correct predictions of the model. Logistic regression predicts for each individual instance in the dataset whether it is most likely that one of the three adjectives occurs by using the information provided by the independent variables. In some cases, these predictions are correct, while in others they are not. For instance, the model may estimate on the basis of the predictors (i.e., their specific values) that a concrete example in the data should be realized as *perfumed*, when the actual observed near-synonym is either *fragrant* or *scented*. Therefore, it is possible to identify the amount of times that the predictions of the model are in line with the actual observed data. In Model A, the accuracy value is 67.34%. The baseline accuracy is 63.90%, which is equal to the total amount of the most frequent value of the dependent variable, namely *fragrant* (cf. Table 15 in Section 5.1). The accuracy value of Model A is therefore significantly better than the baseline value ($p < 0.001$), which means that the predictors included entail an improvement over a null model (i.e., a model with no predictors).

The following two rows in Table 16 presents the McFadden's R^2 and Nagelkerke's R^2, both of which are indications of how well the model fits the actual observed data. R^2 is an additional index of predictive power which, put simply, translates into the proportion of variance that the fitted model explains. As concerns McFadden R^2, values between 0.2 and 0.4 indicate a good fit of a model (Levshina, 2015: 280); therefore, the value obtained in Model A (i.e., 0.1341) signals that there is still some unexplained variance. The same holds for the obtained Nagelkerke R^2 index, the values of which range from zero, if a model has no predictive power, to 1, if a model achieves a perfect fit. In this case, the value 0.2575 points to a similar conclusion as the McFadden R^2. Finally, the last row displays the findings of the likelihood ratio test, which provide the overall significance of the model. As we can observe, this model is statistically significant ($p < 0.001$).

Continuing with Model B, the same predictors and predictor interactions are significant. The only difference concerns a significant interaction between Semantic category – as opposed to Sense – and Period. Table 17 displays the summary statistics of Model B. As shown in the table, the indexes are similar to those of Model A. There is, however, an improvement in the predictive power of the model, given that the accuracy, McFadden R^2, and Nagelkerke R^2 values are all higher than in Model A. In fact, Model B performs significantly better than Model A ($p < 0.001$). This was to be expected, given that Semantic category provides a more fine-grained division than Sense and therefore identifies differences between the preferences of the near-synonyms which may be obscured if only the sense in which they are used is considered. A likelihood ratio test indicates that Model B is also statistically significant ($p < 0.001$).

Table 17: Model summary of multinomial logistic regression Model B (Semantic category).

Model summary	
accuracy	69.13% (baseline = 63.90%; $p < 0.001$)
McFadden R^2	0.1754
Nagelkerke R^2	0.3250
likelihood ratio test	1702.5 ($p < 0.001$)

As regards the importance of the predictors to discriminate between the three adjectival near-synonyms, the variables of a semantic nature (i.e., Sense, Semantic category, Concreteness rating, and Countability) generally have a stronger explanatory power than the language-internal and language-external factors. This is confirmed by computing regression models with only the semantic variables and their significant interactions with Period, i.e., between Sense and Period and between Semantic category and Period, respectively, and comparing the resulting indexes with those obtained for Models A and B. The models with semantic variables only are displayed in Tables 18 and 19:

Table 18: Model summary of multinomial logistic regression with only semantic predictors (Sense).

Model summary	
accuracy	67.04 % (baseline = 63.90 %; $p < 0.001$)
McFadden R^2	0.1187
Nagelkerke R^2	0.2310
likelihood Ratio test	1146.1 ($p < 0.001$)

Table 19: Model summary of multinomial logistic regression with only semantic predictors (Semantic category).

Model summary	
accuracy	67.83 % (baseline = 63.90 %; $p < 0.001$)
McFadden R^2	0.1567
Nagelkerke R^2	0.2952
likelihood Ratio test	1514.6 ($p < 0.001$)

As can be seen here, the accuracy, McFadden R^2, and Nagelkerke R^2 in the models including only semantic variables are not much lower than their counterparts in Models A and B, respectively. For instance, while the accuracies of Models A and B are 67.34% and 69.13% (cf. Tables 16 and 17 above), respectively, that of their counterparts with only semantic variables are 67.04% (Table 18) and 67.83% (Table 19).

The greater importance of semantic variables is further supported by the findings of a random forest analysis, with all the independent variables in Models A and B as predictors.[50] Figure 14 displays the variable importance values of the eight predictors included in the model: the predictors are located on the vertical axis and their importance values are displayed on the horizontal axis.[51] Therefore, the longer the line of a predictor, the greater its importance in the model. As can be observed, all the semantic variables exhibit a higher importance value than the other predictors, with the exception of Period, which is ranked third, following Semantic category and Sense. This implies that the choice between the adjectives *fragrant*, *perfumed*, and *scented* is mostly determined by semantic features, especially the two highly correlated predictors Semantic category and Sense, but also by the extralinguistic factor Period. The fact that Period achieves such a high ranking already indicates that the synonym set object of study undergoes important changes over the time span analyzed.

Turning now to the predictions of multinomial regression Models A and B, these are displayed in tabular form in Tables 20 and 21.[52] In both tables the first column displays the regressors of the model. The first row provides the values for the intercept which represents the probability of each of the adjectives in the reference levels of each of the eight predictors, namely fiction (Text-type), positive (Degree), count (Countability), P2 (Period), natural (Sense), EARTH, ATMOSPHERE, AND WEATHER (Semantic category), and attributive (Syntactic function), as well as the mean value for the numerical variable Concreteness rating, which is 4.365. The rest of the regressors signal the probability of the

---

[50] The fact that the results of the random forest analysis are computed on the basis of random samples of data points and predictors makes it relatively immune to problems caused by highly correlated predictors such as Sense and Semantic category. This is the reason why these two variables can be included in the same random forest model (Tagliamonte and Baayen 2012: 161).
[51] Although not the focus of the present discussion, it is worth mentioning here that the random forest model achieves a fairly high prediction accuracy of 73.52%, which is again statistically significantly higher than the baseline accuracy of 63.90% ($p < 0.001$).
[52] Table 21 contains only the values of the predictors Semantic category and Period, and their interaction, given that the remaining independent variables behave very similarly in Models A and B.

adjectives when the level of a specific predictor changes, while the rest are kept at the reference level. To illustrate this point, the regressor called 'Degree = Comparative' (i.e., row five in Table 20) presents the probabilities of *fragrant*, *perfumed*, and *scented* when they occur in comparative, instead of positive degree and the other predictors are maintained at their reference level. The regressors which include more than one predictor provide the values of interactions. However, given the difficulty of interpreting interactions in this format, they are visualized below by means of partial effect plots. The remaining columns in Tables 20 and 21 offer the coefficients for each adjective. The first column presents the estimates, that is, the increases or decreases in probability of the adjectives as compared to the reference level. The estimates are measured in log odds: whereas positive values point to an increase in the probability of the adjectives, the reverse holds in the case of negative values, and the higher the absolute number, the larger the respective increase/decrease. Finally, the columns entitled '*p*-value' show whether the decreases or increases in probability are statistically significant or not.

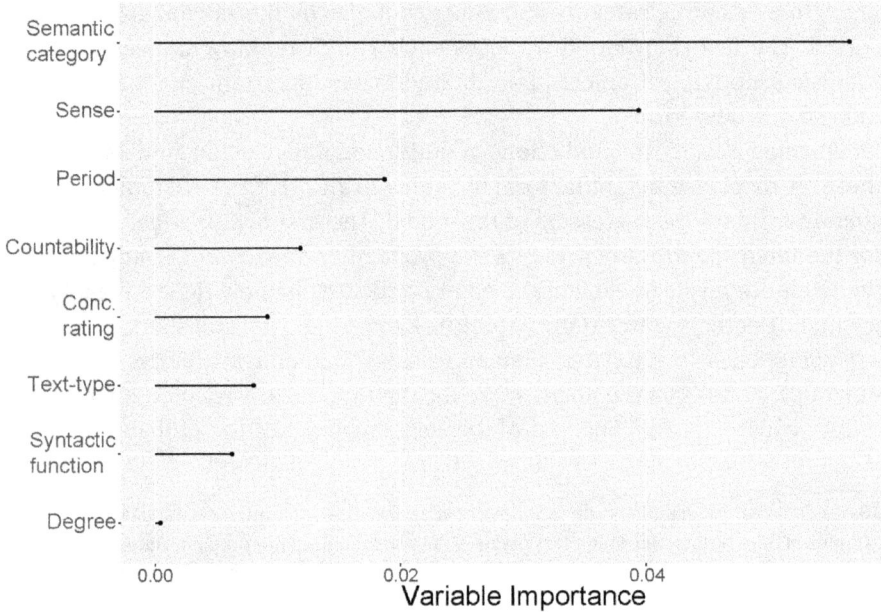

Figure 14: Variable importance of predictors according to random forest analysis.

Table 20: Model A coefficients (Sense).

Predictor	Fragrant		Perfumed		Scented	
	Estimate	p-value	Estimate	p-value	Estimate	p-value
Intercept	1.2100	< 0.001	−1.3180	< 0.001	−2.7950	< 0.001
Concreteness rating	−0.0007	0.989	−0.1541	0.005	0.1676	0.007
Text-type = Non-fiction	0.3321	0.053	−0.3221	0.127	−0.1967	0.383
Text-type = Periodicals	0.8170	< 0.001	−0.6296	0.020	−0.7541	0.020
Degree = Comparative	1.5910	< 0.001	−1.1300	0.001	−1.4980	0.001
Degree = Superlative	1.8500	0.020	−1.6270	0.120	−1.3700	0.1870
Countability = Non-count	−0.5127	< 0.001	0.1224	0.158	0.5617	< 0.001
Countability = Other	−0.1891	0.224	0.3368	0.051	−0.1025	0.587
Period = P1	0.4424	< 0.001	−0.3775	0.022	−0.3662	0.026
Period = P1: Text-type = Non-fiction	−1.002	< 0.001	1.213	< 0.001	0.2020	0.573
Period = P1: Text-type = Periodicals	−1.1160	0.006	1.1580	0.015	0.5480	0.385
Period = P1: Sense = Artificial	−0.8259	0.001	0.7340	0.004	0.2148	0.480
Period = P1: Sense = Figurative	0.3195	0.530	−0.4040	0.466	−0.2460	0.835
Period = P1: Sense = Indeterminate	−0.6112	0.134	0.5325	0.225	0.4072	0.478
Period = P3	−0.0855	0.470	−0.3866	0.022	0.4261	0.003
Period = P3: Text-type = Non-fiction	−0.4307	0.158	0.2767	0.480	0.3283	0.348
Period = P3: Text-type = Periodicals	−0.8875	0.002	0.7093	0.038	0.7639	0.041
Period = P3: Sense = Artificial	−0.1585	0.439	−0.1217	0.598	0.3882	0.091
Period = P3: Sense = Figurative	−0.3738	0.367	0.3794	0.422	0.9582	0.190
Period = P3: Sense = Indeterminate	−0.4491	0.104	0.3481	0.271	0.4532	0.200
Period = P4	−0.0075	0.955	−0.3995	0.035	0.3218	0.041
Period = P4: Text-type = Non-fiction	−1.425	<0.001	0.5223	0.212	1.156	0.002
Period = P4: Text-type = Periodicals	−0.8974	0.001	0.3521	0.305	1.0610	0.004

Table 20 (continued)

Predictor	Fragrant		Perfumed		Scented	
	Estimate	p-value	Estimate	p-value	Estimate	p-value
Period = P4: Sense = Artificial	−0.5440	0.011	−0.1306	0.589	0.7349	0.002
Period = P4: Sense = Figurative	−1.300	0.006	1.472	0.003	1.0750	0.169
Period = P4: Sense = Indeterminate	−0.5292	0.065	0.8371	0.010	−0.0587	0.879
Sense = Artificial	−1.7010	<0.001	1.7770	<0.001	0.5268	0.002
Sense = Figurative	0.0030	0.991	0.4098	0.172	−1.0550	0.078
Sense = Indeterminate	−0.8125	<0.001	1.094	<0.001	0.06071	0.827
Syntactic function = Other	−0.5313	0.001	0.8028	<0.001	−0.1603	0.431
Syntactic function = Postpositive	−0.2697	0.018	0.0711	0.603	0.3016	0.020
Syntactic function = Predicative	0.5007	<0.001	−0.4043	0.003	−0.3108	0.020

Table 21: Model B coefficients (Semantic category).

Predictors	Fragrant		Perfumed		Scented	
	Estimate	p-value	Estimate	p-value	Estimate	p-value
Intercept	1.3220	<0.001	−1.3550	<0.001	−2.8840	<0.001
Semantic category = ABS	0.3649	0.240	−0.0772	0.819	−1.0540	0.085
Semantic category = B&P	−0.9288	<0.001	1.2160	<0.001	−0.3052	0.371
Semantic category = CL	−1.9090	<0.001	0.2655	0.561	1.7720	<0.001
Semantic category = COS	−0.6148	0.262	0.5143	0.395	0.3477	0.607
Semantic category = F&D	1.167	<0.001	−1.415	0.001	−0.6243	0.065
Semantic category = OBJ	−1.562	<0.001	1.2500	<0.001	0.6869	0.040
Semantic category = P&F	0.9180	<0.001	−1.2380	<0.001	−0.3555	0.074
Semantic category = S&M	0.4714	0.049	−0.1651	0.556	−0.6100	0.075
Semantic category = SEN	0.8692	0.005	−0.4004	0.237	−1.4830	0.015
Semantic category = SPA	−0.5804	0.014	0.6255	0.016	0.1585	0.617

5.2 Results — 143

Table 21 (continued)

Predictors	Fragrant		Perfumed		Scented	
	Estimate	p-value	Estimate	p-value	Estimate	p-value
Semantic category = T&C	−1.8420	<0.001	1.613	<0.001	0.4606	0.127
Period = P1	−0.0084	0.964	−0.2352	0.314	0.2636	0.267
Period = P1: Semantic category = ABS	0.7757	0.196	−0.2968	0.636	−12.6400	0.957
Period = P1: Semantic category = B&P	−0.5832	0.154	0.4720	0.249	0.2063	0.695
Period = P1: Semantic category = CL	−0.5052	0.580	2.189	0.003	−2.2600	0.004
Period = P1: Semantic category = COS	12.5600	0.938	−12.4700	0.963	−14.4100	0.984
Period = P1: Semantic category = F&D	0.1407	0.735	1.0270	0.057	−1.709	0.016
Period = P1: Semantic category = OBJ	0.7663	0.099	0.0528	0.911	−1.2360	0.044
Period = P1: Semantic category = P&F	1.2140	<0.001	−1.2140	0.005	−1.0230	0.004
Period = P1: Semantic category = S&M	−0.4355	0.252	0.7135	0.102	−0.1737	0.749
Period = P1: Semantic category = SEN	−0.3858	0.366	0.8269	0.078	−1.6260	0.174
Period = P1: Semantic category = SPA	−0.2325	0.603	−0.1122	0.827	0.4285	0.426
Period = P1: Semantic category = T&C	−0.5138	0.462	−0.0584	0.913	0.3359	0.555
Period = P3	−0.295	0.079	−0.2503	0.240	0.6639	0.001
Period = P3: Semantic category = ABS	−0.1811	0.693	0.3652	0.482	0.5014	0.513
Period = P3: Semantic category = B&P	−0.0255	0.934	0.0186	0.955	0.2588	0.530
Period = P3: Semantic category = CL	−0.0326	0.961	0.7334	0.200	−1.0500	0.047
Period = P3: Semantic category = COS	−0.1401	0.831	0.1206	0.867	−0.0368	0.962
Period = P3: Semantic category = F&D	0.5336	0.209	−0.1604	0.812	−0.7309	0.149

Table 21 (continued)

Predictors	Fragrant		Perfumed		Scented	
	Estimate	p-value	Estimate	p-value	Estimate	p-value
Period = P3: Semantic category = OBJ	0.2959	0.505	−1.1420	0.021	0.5481	0.228
Period = P3: Semantic category = P&F	(0.2027)	0.444	−0.0274	0.947	−0.3799	0.225
Period = P3: Semantic category = S&M	0.1860	0.599	−0.1066	0.812	−0.0751	0.871
Period = P3: Semantic category = SEN	0.3468	0.514	−0.5778	0.415	0.4744	0.561
Period = P3: Semantic category = SPA	0.3739	0.270	−0.5692	0.173	0.0445	0.915
Period = P3: Semantic category = T&C	−0.0473	0.915	−0.3842	0.331	0.3312	0.424
Period = P4	−0.0309	0.878	−0.5064	0.066	0.4868	0.041
Period = P4: Semantic category = ABS	−1.1710	0.030	1.588	0.006	0.6324	0.455
Period = P4: Semantic category = B&P	−0.3808	0.253	0.4568	0.225	0.3217	0.462
Period = P4: Semantic category = CL	0.2573	0.669	0.3127	0.598	−0.6455	0.212
Period = P4: Semantic category = COS	−1.252	0.063	0.9308	0.187	0.2124	0.778
Period = P4: Semantic category = F&D	0.1191	0.763	0.9094	0.109	−0.8048	0.096
Period = P4: Semantic category = OBJ	−0.5303	0.232	−0.5626	0.221	0.9173	0.038
Period = P4: Semantic category = P&F	−0.0022	0.994	−0.2598	0.622	−0.0855	0.799
Period = P4: Semantic category = S&M	−0.8290	0.031	0.5555	0.255	0.7626	0.106
Period = P4: Semantic category = SEN	0.0541	0.926	0.3629	0.593	0.0370	0.970
Period = P4: Semantic category = SPA	−0.2695	0.462	0.2501	0.569	0.2234	0.612
Period = P4: Semantic category = T&C	0.4187	0.386	0.0982	0.834	−0.4794	0.340

The remainder of this section focuses on the effects of each of the predictors in Models A and B, starting with the main effects and then moving to the interactions of Period and Text-type, Period and Sense, and Period and Semantic category. As mentioned previously, the effects are visualized by means of partial effect plots, which are interpreted as follows: the levels of the predictors are shown on the horizontal axis and the probability of the adjectives in each level on the vertical axis. Each adjective is represented with a different shape, or line type in the case of the numerical variable Concreteness rating, as indicated in the legend to the right of the plots. Within the plots, whiskers, or a shaded grey area in the case of Concreteness rating, show the 95% confidence intervals. Confidence intervals constitute the range of values within which we can be 95% sure that the true values of the regressors are located (Levshina 2015: 98).

Figure 15 displays the effect of Concreteness rating on the choice between the near-synonyms. As is clearly observed in the figure, for *fragrant* no significant effect emerges, which means that it is more or less equally probable regardless of the degree of concreteness of the nominal elements it modifies, with all values ranging between 66% and 67%. Despite the lack of effect, *fragrant* is by far the most prominent adjective in all cases, which is not surprising, given its high overall frequency. On the contrary, both *perfumed* and *scented* are significantly influenced by the feature Concreteness. The former adjective is less likely as the rating increases, that is, the more concrete the modified nominal element, the lower the likelihood of encountering *perfumed*. On the other hand, *scented* exhibits the opposite trend, becoming more likely as the concreteness rating increases. However, for none of the two adjectives is the effect extremely pronounced: the probabilities of *perfumed* and *scented* are 23.46% and 10.03%, respectively, when they modify nouns with a rating of 1, and 15.21% and 17.52%, when they modify nouns with a rating of 5. This entails a decrease in probability of 8.25% in the case of *perfumed* and an increase of 7.49% in the case of *scented*. Moreover, the probabilities of the two adjectives are very similar when they collocate with highly concrete nouns (e.g., *lady* and *meadow*). This means that the main difference between the adjectives *perfumed* and *scented* lies in their frequency with more abstract nouns, especially those with a rating between 1 and 2 (e.g., *knowledge* and *regret*), in which case *perfumed* is more likely.

Continuing with the effect of Degree, the probabilities of the three adjectives are plotted in Figure 16. With respect to this variable, *fragrant* is again the dominant variant in all three levels but its dominance is more pronounced in the comparative and superlative degrees, with a probability of 90.84% and 92.37%, respectively. In fact, the high probability of *fragrant* in these two values, as compared to that for the positive degree, is statistically significant. In turn, both *perfumed* and *scented* are significantly less likely in the comparative and the superlative

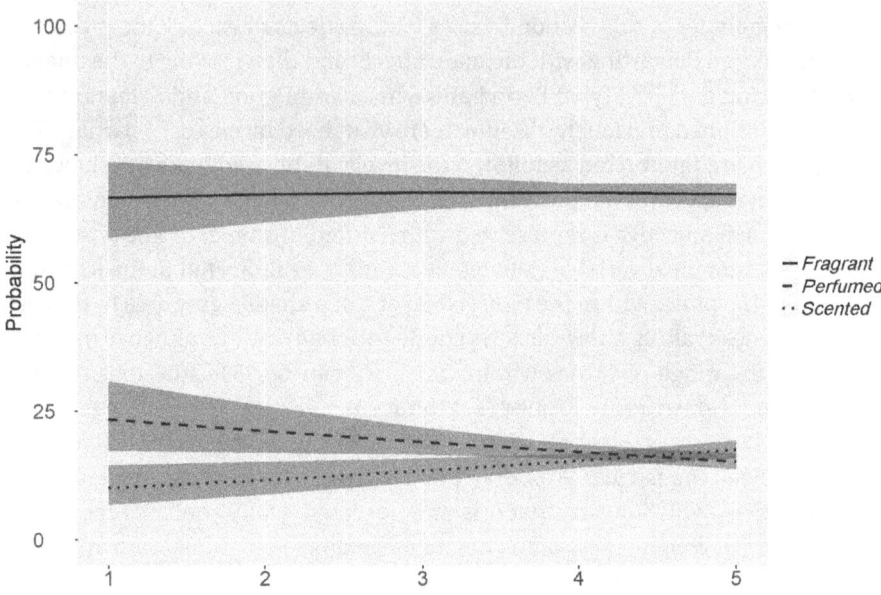

Figure 15: Effect of Concreteness rating on the probabilities of the adjectives *fragrant*, *perfumed*, and *scented*.

degrees, and more probable in the positive degree. As can be deduced from the large confidence intervals in this graph for the superlative degree, the number of instances corresponding to this level is very low, with a total of 22 instances. Therefore, the results for the superlative degree should be taken with caution.

In the case of Countability (cf. Figure 17), *fragrant* is once more the most likely choice with the three values. However, it is significantly less likely with non-count nouns (58.79%) than with count nouns (70.46%). On the other hand, *scented* exhibits the opposite effect, being significantly more likely with non-count (23.07%) than with count nouns (14.18%). Finally, the variable Countability does not have a significant effect on the probability of *perfumed*.

The last main effect is that of Syntactic function, which is visualized in Figure 18. The probabilities of the adjectives with respect to this variable follow the general tendency, with *fragrant* representing again the prevailing option in all levels. Nonetheless, some significant differences emerge. First, *fragrant* is less likely in postpositive and other minor functions (i.e., predicative adjunct, fused modifier-head, and predeterminer) than in attributive function, while it occurs more often as a predicative complement. Second, *perfumed* is more likely in the category 'other' if compared to attributive function, but less likely as a predicative complement. Similarly, *scented* is also less likely in predicative function, whereas

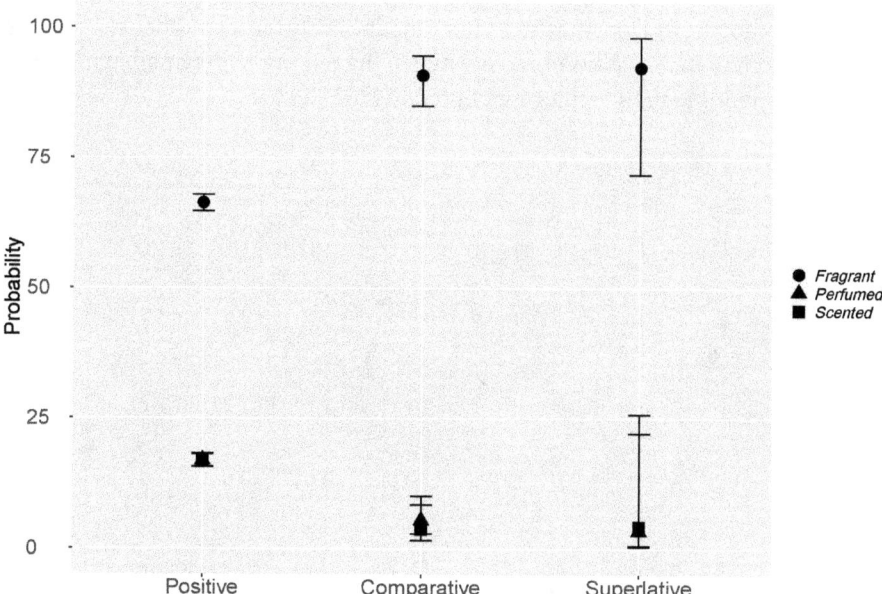

Figure 16: Effect of Degree on the probabilities of the adjectives *fragrant*, *perfumed*, and *scented*.

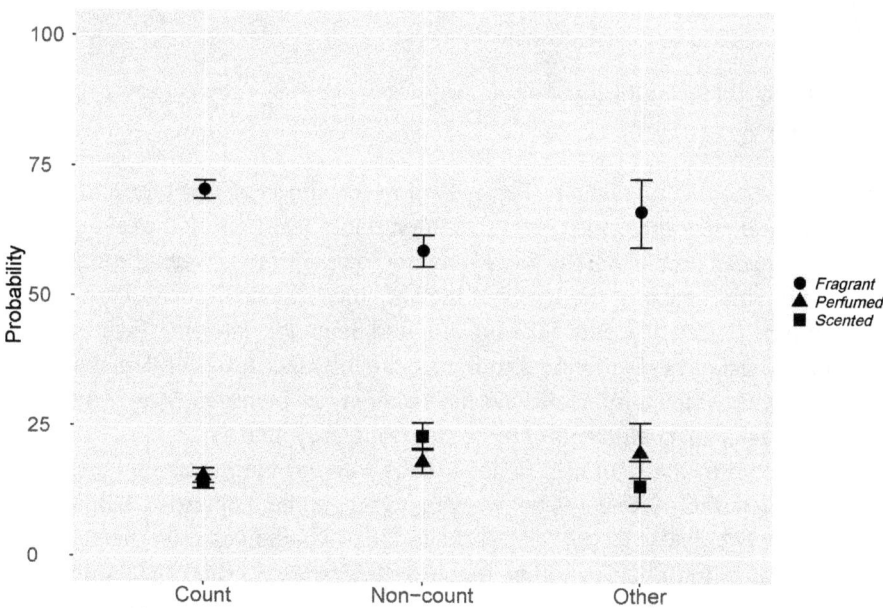

Figure 17: Effect of Countability on the probabilities of the adjectives *fragrant*, *perfumed*, and *scented*.

it is more probable as a postpositive modifier. The fairly large confidence intervals of the adjectives in the value 'other' are due to the relatively low number of examples corresponding to the minor functions.

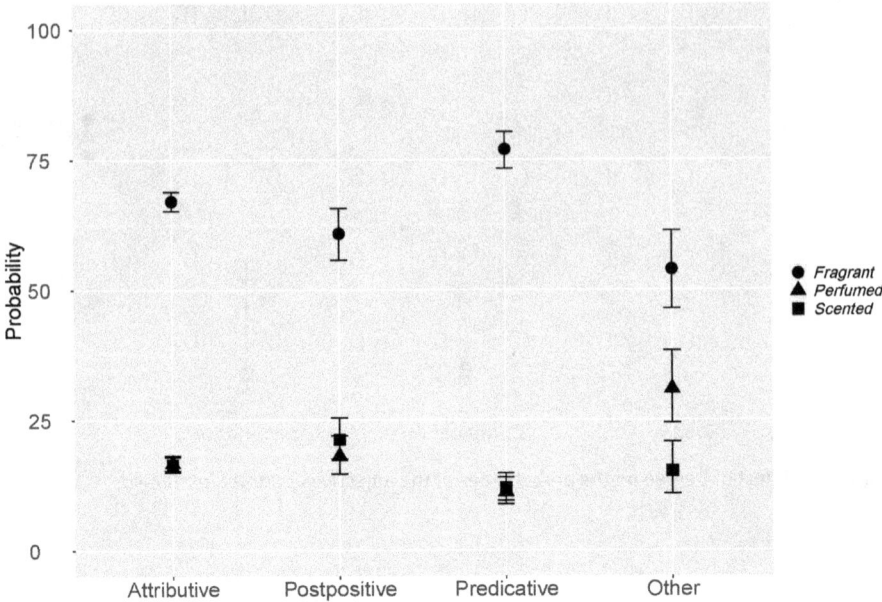

Figure 18: Effect of Syntactic function on the probabilities of the adjectives *fragrant*, *perfumed*, and *scented*.

Turning now to the interactions, Figure 19 plots the effects of Text-type and Period in three different graphs, one per level of the variable Text-type. In the case of interactions between predictors, the focus is on the competition between the adjectives over time within each of the levels of the variables interacting with Period, that is, Text-type (Figure 19), Sense (Figure 20), and Semantic category (Figure 21). To examine some of these additional contrasts, the reference levels of Period and the variables with which it interacts have been altered (cf. Tables 38–56 in the Appendix for the relevant coefficients of these supplementary models).

As shown in the figure, in fictional texts *fragrant* maintains its dominance through the period 1810–2009, but we witness a significant decrease of this adjective from P1 (72.77%) to P2 (67.79%). *Perfumed* also experiences a significant downward tendency in fiction over time from P2 (18.58%) to P3 (14.03%). Contrary to *fragrant* and *perfumed*, the likelihood of *scented* in fiction increases diachronically: it is more likely in P2 (13.62%) than in P1 (11.14%), and also in P3 (22.24%) and P4 (21.71%) than in P2.

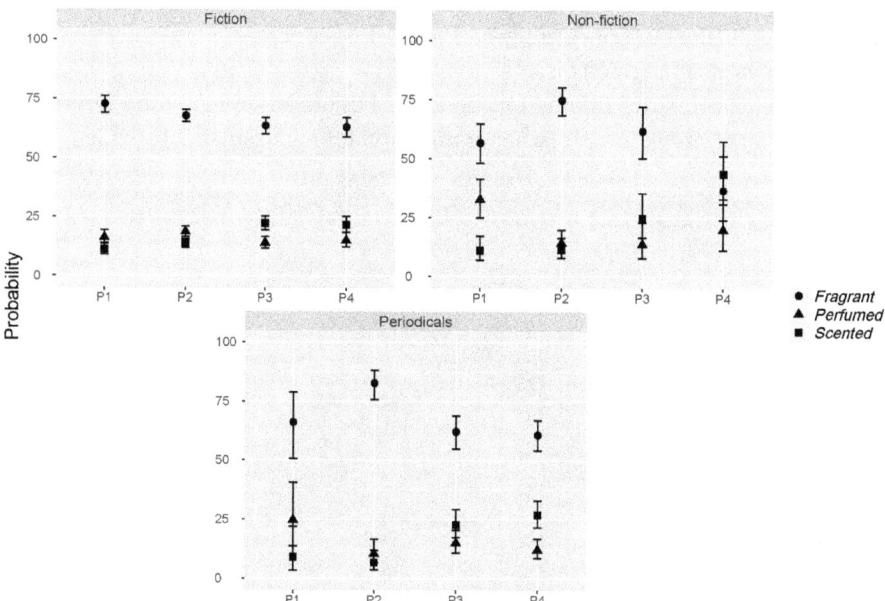

Figure 19: Effect of Text-type on the probabilities of the adjectives *fragrant*, *perfumed*, and *scented* across periods.

As regards non-fictional texts, the probability ranking of the adjectives changes over time. *Fragrant* is the most likely adjective in P1 (56.54%), P2 (74.58%), and P3 (61.65%), but then in P4 it is overthrown by *scented* (36.58% vs 43.56%, respectively). Although there is a significant increase of *fragrant* from P1 to P2 its probability drastically and significantly declines throughout the twentieth century (P3 and P4). Similarly, the likelihood of *perfumed* displays a significant downward tendency, particularly from P1 (32.53%) to P2 (14.11%). Since then, *perfumed* remains rather stable, with only a slight increase again in P4 (19.86%). The respective decreases of *fragrant* and *perfumed* in non-fictional texts seem to be in favor of *scented*, which increases significantly from P2 onwards: while it is the least probable adjective in this text-type in P1 (10.92%), it becomes the most likely choice one in P4 by first outperforming *perfumed* in P3 and then *fragrant* in P4.

Finally, in periodicals, the results for P1 are not entirely reliable due to the low number of instances of the adjectives in this text-type. From P2 onwards, a similar trend to that identified in non-fiction is followed by *fragrant* and *scented*, whereby the latter increases at the expense of the former. Nevertheless, in this case, although the probabilities of the two adjectives become more similar, *scented* does not surpass *fragrant* in P4, as the latter still clearly dominates (26.97% vs

60.85%, respectively). Concerning *perfumed*, no significant differences emerge from P2 onwards in periodicals.

Figure 20 plots the interaction between Period and Sense (i.e., Model A). Again, as in the previous case, a separate graph for each Sense is provided.

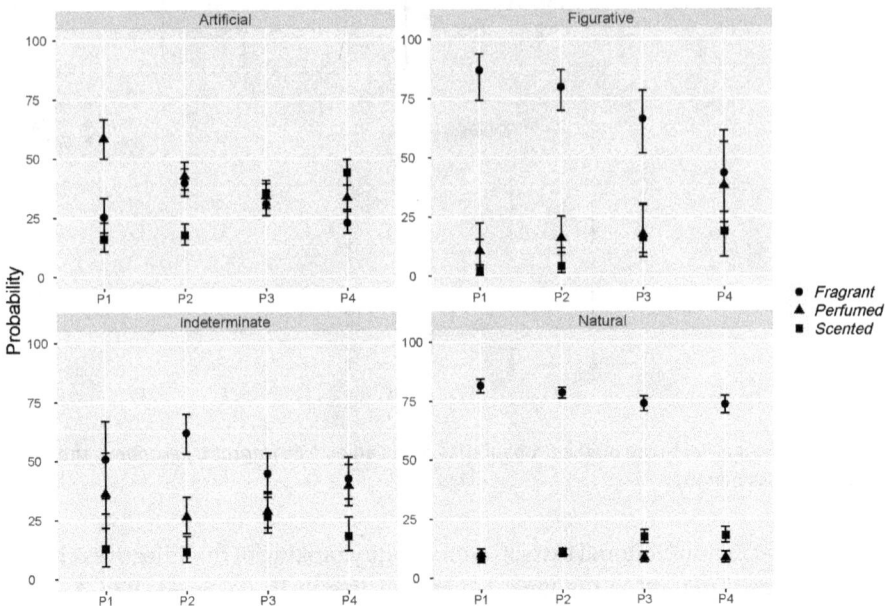

Figure 20: Effect of Sense on the probabilities of the adjectives *fragrant*, *perfumed*, and *scented* across periods.

As regards the artificial sense, various significant tendencies can be observed. The adjective *fragrant* displays a gradual downward tendency from P2 onwards, although the only significant contrast is that between P2 (39.80%) and P4 (22.74%). Similarly, although more drastically, *perfumed* also declines over time, particularly from P1 (58.61%) and P2 (42.55%) to P3 (33.93%) and P4 (33.30%). In fact, this adjective loses its initial clear dominance in this sense in favor of *scented* from P3 onwards: in P3 the probabilities of these two adjectives are very similar, 33.93% and 35.32%, respectively, but then *scented* becomes much more likely in P4. In fact, in this last period *scented* displays a likelihood of 43.96%, while that of *perfumed* is 33.30%. The increase in probability of *scented* just mentioned is particularly noticeable between P2 (17.74%) and P3 (35.32%), which coincides with the turn of the nineteenth to the twentieth century. In this specific sense, *scented*, the least likely adjective in P1 (16.07%), becomes the most probable choice in P4.

In the figurative sense, *fragrant* experiences a decrease from P2 onwards. In particular, the adjective occurs significantly less often in P3 (66.41%) and P4 (43.35%) than in P1 (86.98%), on the one hand, and in P4 than in P2 (79.94%), on the other. *Perfumed* shows the opposite trend, becoming more likely with time. In fact, it is significantly more likely in P4 (37.97%) than in P1 (10.60%), P2 (16.04%), and P3 (17.50%). As can be observed in Figure 20, the probabilities of *fragrant* (43.35%) and *perfumed* (37.97%) in the figurative sense are rather similar in P4. However, as the confidence intervals reflect, the number of instances of the adjectives in this sense at the end of the time span under analysis is considerably lower. Finally, as regards *scented*, no significant changes are observed for this adjective in the figurative sense.

In the value 'indeterminate', *fragrant* exhibits a downward tendency from P2 onwards, as it is significantly less likely in P3 (44.63%) and P4 (42.42%) than in P2 (61.82%). In turn, *scented* increases significantly from P2 (11.64%) to P3 (26.60%), but then decreases from P3 to P4 (18.17%) and *perfumed* does not display any significant changes. However, due to the decline of *fragrant*, the probabilities of *perfumed* and *fragrant* converge over time, and in P4 the two adjectives are almost equally likely (39.41% vs 42.42%, respectively).

Finally, in the natural sense, *fragrant* once again decreases significantly, particularly from P1 onwards, but it still remains by far the most likely variant in all four periods. *Perfumed* also decreases over time, but only from P2 onwards. In the case of *scented*, we witness an increase in this sense with each subsequent period, but although this upward trend is statistically significant, the probability of *scented* continues to be much lower than that of *fragrant*, even in P4 (18.02% vs 73.55%, respectively).

The last interaction, namely that between Period and Semantic category (i.e., Model B), is shown in Figure 21: twelve separate plots are given, one for each semantic category, and within each plot the probabilities of the three adjectives per period are provided.

Starting with the level ABSTRACT, Figure 21 shows a significant decrease of *fragrant* and an increase of *perfumed*. In both cases the diachronic trends appear gradually over the time span 1810–2009: *fragrant* is less likely in P3 (63.91%) and P4 (42.04%) than in P1 (85.41%), and in P4 than in P2 (77.05%); *perfumed*, in turn, is more likely in P4 (40.13%) than in P1 (14.59%) and P2 (17.91%). By P4, *perfumed* is almost as likely as *fragrant*, although the latter was clearly predominant at the beginning of the time span examined, being 70.82 percentual points more likely than *perfumed* in P1. No significant effect emerges for *scented* in this semantic category.

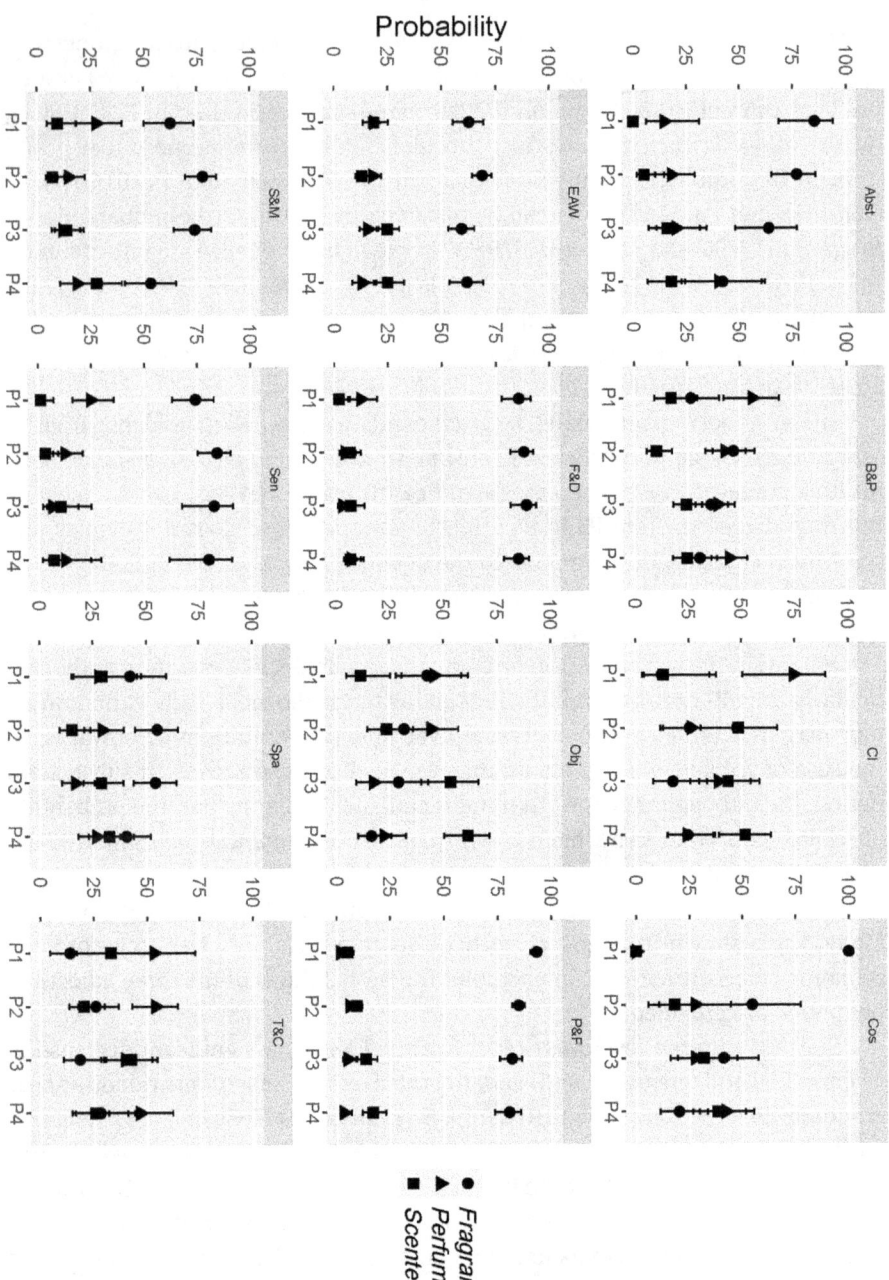

Figure 21: Effect of Semantic category on the probabilities of the adjectives *fragrant*, *perfumed*, and *scented* across periods.

In BODY AND PEOPLE, on the other hand, only *scented* exhibits a significant change diachronically, increasing in probability from P2 onwards: it is more likely in P3 (24.45%) and P4 (24.74%) than in P2 (10.43%).

With nouns belonging to the category CLEANING, *scented* increases significantly, while *perfumed* declines. For both adjectives, the significant change occurs from P1 onwards, and already in P2 *scented* becomes more likely than *perfumed* (48.56% vs. 26.09%), which was initially the most likely choice.

As concerns COSMETICS, the probabilities of the adjectives in P1 are meaningless, given that just 4 instances are attested in this period, all of which correspond to *fragrant*. From P2 onwards, only *fragrant* exhibits significant differences in probability as it is less likely in P4 (19.95%) than in P2 (54.54%): in P4 it loses its dominance and is surpassed by both *scented* (38.17%) and *perfumed* (41.88%).

In the category EARTH, ATMOSPHERE, AND WEATHER, the plot shows a significant increase of *scented*, which undergoes an upward tendency from P2 onwards: this adjective is significantly more likely in both P3 (24.79%) and P4 (24.92%) than in P2 (13.05%). Despite this increase of *scented*, *fragrant* maintains its dominance throughout the four periods.

Another semantic category in which *fragrant* remains the dominant variant over time is FOOD AND DRINK, and no significant contrasts are identified for this adjective. However, both *scented* and *perfumed* exhibit significant diachronic differences with this category of nouns: *scented* increases slightly, especially between P1 (2.11%) and P3 (7.41%), while *perfumed* decreases from 12.21% in P1 to 3.54% in P3. Nevertheless, neither *perfumed* nor *scented* are particularly likely in this category. This is so because these adjectives do not exceed the 12.21% likelihood of *perfumed* in P1 in any other period and *fragrant* always exhibits a probability of 85%–89%.

OBJECT is a semantic category in which all three adjectives undergo significant changes across time. While both *fragrant* and *perfumed* decrease in probability, the opposite tendency applies to *scented*. In the case of *fragrant*, the only contrast that reaches significance is that between P4 and P1, with the adjective being significantly less likely in the former (16.41%) than in the latter period (42.60%). As regards *perfumed* and *scented*, their respective decrease and increase occur from P2 onwards: in both cases a significant change is observed between P3/P4 and P2, on the one hand, and between P3/P4 and P1, on the other. In fact, in this category, *scented* starts out as the least probable adjective in P1 (11.61%) and P2 (23.77%), but already in P3 (53.30%) it is the most likely one. Finally, in P4 the distance between *scented* (61.35%) and the other two adjectives becomes more pronounced.

The category PLANTS AND FLOWERS displays a similar development to that of FOOD AND DRINK as concerns the clear dominance of *fragrant*, which is maintained throughout the period 1810–2009. However, *fragrant* does exhibit significant changes in this category, as its probability decreases from P1 (93.14%) to P4 (80.31%). Conversely, both *perfumed* and *scented* display a significant upward trend with these types of nouns, also from P1 onwards.

In SUBSTANCE AND MATERIAL, although *fragrant* is the dominant variant in all four periods, this predominance is not as clear in P4 as in the previous stages. In fact, the probability of this adjective in P4 (53.48%) is significantly lower than in P2 (77.78%) and P3 (74.07%). *Perfumed*, in turn, remains rather stable in this category, although it shows a considerable dip in probability from P1 (27.73%) to P3 (12.10%). Finally, *scented* increases significantly if we compare its likelihood in P4 (27.83%) to that of P1 (9.53%) and P2 (7.34%).

Turning now to SENSATION, once again, *fragrant* is the default choice in all four periods, and does not exhibit any significant diachronic trends. In the case of *perfumed*, a significant decrease emerges between P1 (24.74%) and P3 (6.68%), but the high probability of this adjective in P1 is, as mentioned earlier (cf. Section 4.3.2), a result of its very frequent use with the noun *flavor* in only three particular texts. *Scented*, despite its low likelihood in all four periods with SENSATION nouns, exhibits a slight increase from P1 (1.06%) to P3 (10.58%).

In the category SPACE, the only significant change concerns *perfumed*, which decreases from P2 (29.51%) to P3 (16.65%). Lastly, in TEXTILE AND CLOTHING, only the probability of *scented* experiences significant differences over time: it first increases from P2 (20.25%) to P3 (42.24%) and then decreases between P3 and P4 (25.51%).

As mentioned in Section 5.1, the effect of the predictor Collocate had to be measured by a different type of regression analysis. Therefore, before turning to the discussion of the findings obtained, the analyses comprising the variable Collocate are provided in the next section to determine whether the inclusion of this predictor significantly improves the models including only fixed effects that have been presented so far.

5.2.2 Mixed-effects models: The effects of individual noun collocates

The mixed-effects regression models were computed using the same heuristic employed in the multinomial models, namely one vs. rest. Three separate models were calculated, each one focusing on the collocational preferences of one of the three adjectives. The summary statistics of the models zooming in on the behavior of *fragrant*, *perfumed*, and *scented*, respectively, are presented in Tables 22–24.

Table 22: Model summary of the binary mixed-effects logistic regression (*fragrant*).

Model summary	
C-index of concordance	0.8417
accuracy	78.11% (baseline = 63.90%; $p < 0.001$)
Nagelkerke R^2 (marginal)	0.2106
Nagelkerke R^2 (conditional)	0.4053

Table 23: Model summary of the binary mixed-effects logistic regression (*perfumed*).

Model summary	
C-index of concordance	0.8349
accuracy	84.49% (baseline = 81.61%; $p < 0.001$)
Nagelkerke R^2 (marginal)	0.1538
Nagelkerke R^2 (conditional)	0.3683

Table 24: Model summary of the binary mixed-effects logistic regression (*scented*).

Model summary	
C-index of concordance	0.7903
accuracy	83.74% (baseline = 82.29%; $p < 0.01$)
Nagelkerke R^2 (marginal)	0.1508
Nagelkerke R^2 (conditional)	0.2775

In this case, the indexes differ somewhat from those presented for the multinomial regression analyses. First, in the upper row of each table we have the C-index of concordance, which is an indicator of how well the model discriminates between *fragrant* and the other two adjectives (i.e., *perfumed/scented*) in Table 22, between *perfumed* and the other two (i.e., *fragrant/scented*) in Table 23, and between *scented* and the other two (i.e., *fragrant/perfumed*) in Table 24. The values of this index range between 0.5 and 1, and the higher the value, the better the discrimination of the model. The following thresholds are commonly distinguished for the C-index: (i) $C = 0.5$ no discrimination, (ii) $C = 0.7–0.8$ acceptable discrimination, (iii) $C = 0.8–0.9$ excellent discrimination, and (iv) $C \geq 0.9$ outstanding discrimination (Speelman 2014: 514–515). Therefore, the values obtained in the models for *fragrant* and *perfumed* (i.e., 0.8417 and 0.8349, respectively) entail that these models exhibit an excellent discrimination capacity. However, the model for *scented* exhibits only an acceptable discrimination (i.e., 0.7903), as it does not reach the 0.8 threshold, although it is very close to it.

In the second row of Tables 22–24, the accuracies of the models are provided. As can be observed, the values for all three models point to an improvement with respect to the multinomial models A and B with only fixed effects presented in the previous section (i.e., 67.34% and 69.13%, respectively; cf. Tables 16 and 17). The *p*-values also confirm that these three accuracy values are significantly better than their respective baselines.

In the last two rows of the tables, two Nagelkerke R^2 values are shown, termed marginal and conditional. These values were retrieved by using the MuMIn package and, in particular, the r.squaredGLMM() function (Barton 2020). The marginal Nagelkerke R^2 indexes indicate the predictive power of the models accounting solely for the fixed effects. The conditional Nagelkerke R^2 indexes, in turn, signal the predictive power of the models considering both the fixed and the random effects. As can be observed in Tables 22–24, there is an important difference between the two values, as the latter is almost twice as large as the former in the models for *fragrant* and *scented* (cf. Tables 22 and 24, respectively) and more than twice as large in the model for *perfumed* (cf. Table 23). This means that the random effects of the variable Collocate are extremely important to discriminate between the near-synonymous adjectives.

The models achieved by means of mixed-effects regression analyses constitute a substantial improvement over the models including only fixed effects, given that all indexes reach values indicating a good fit, which was not the case in the models with fixed effects only (cf. Section 5.2.1 for more details). This highlights the importance of taking the individual collocates of the near-synonyms into consideration. In the remainder of this section, the idiosyncratic collocational preferences of the three adjectives are discussed in more depth by focusing on their most salient noun collocates.

Figures 22–24 plot the collocational behavior of the adjectives according to mixed-effects regression analysis. In these figures, each individual point in the plot represents one specific noun collocate. Vertical axes represent the adjustments to the intercept for each noun collocate, with positive values indicating collocates which are more strongly associated with the near-synonym of interest (*fragrant* in Figure 22, *perfumed* in Figure 23, and *scented* in Figure 24) and negative values indicating collocates which are more strongly associated with the other two adjectives combined (*perfumed* and *scented* in Figure 22, *fragrant* and *scented* in Figure 23, and *fragrant* and *perfumed* in Figure 24). Finally, horizontal axes plot the absolute adjustments to the intercept for each noun collocate, that is, the same values shown on the vertical axes but without considering whether they are positive or negative. In more conceptual terms, horizontal axes signal the strength of the association between the noun collocates and the adjectives: the higher the value, the stronger the association. For each adjective, the most prominent collocates have been included in the figures by selecting an arbitrary threshold value of 1.25. Given that the goal here is to offer only a bird's-eye-view of the general collocational tendencies of the near-synonymous items to show the importance of the idiosyncratic preferences of each adjective, the plots represent the tendencies in all four periods together. A more fine-grained diachronic analysis of the near-synonyms' collocational behavior is provided in Chapter 6.

Starting with *fragrant*, Figure 22 displays the nouns that are more strongly associated with this variant. In this particular case, positive values on the vertical axis indicate those collocates that are associated with *fragrant*, as opposed to *perfumed/scented*, whereas the values on the horizontal axis signal the strength of this association.

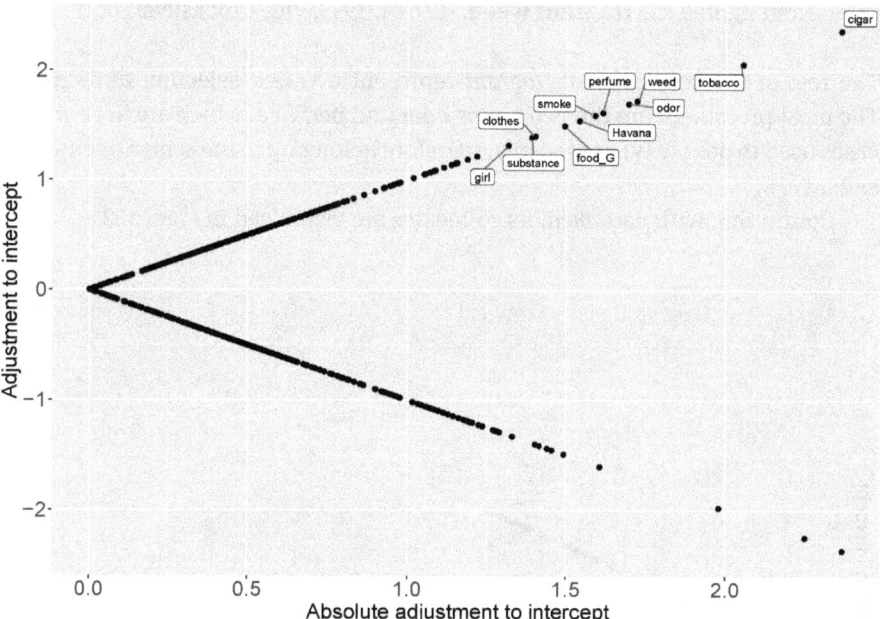

Figure 22: Collocational preferences of *fragrant*.

As can be observed, 11 collocates emerge as prominent and some interesting trends can be extracted from this figure. The specific noun collocates which are more strongly connected with *fragrant* are those located in the top right corner of the plot (e.g., *cigar*, *tobacco*, *weed*, and *odor*). Of the 11 collocates included in Figure 22, three are clearly related to the semantic domain of TOBACCO AND SMOKING, namely *cigar*, *tobacco*, and *Havana*. Moreover, two additional nouns, though polysemous, are also often used in this domain: *smoke* and *weed*. In fact, of the 42 total instances in *COHA* in which *fragrant* occurs as a modifier of *smoke*, 25 (59.53%) are of the type illustrated in example (104), and hence belong to the same semantic domain:

(104) He kicked the newspaper from his feet, sat back, and felt in his pocket for a cigar. It was a short thick one, and he lit it. and puffed out a cloud of blue and **fragrant smoke**. (*COHA*, 1951, FIC, GodsMen)

Similarly, of the 12 times *fragrant* co-occurs with *weed*, 8 (66.67%) are used to refer to a substance that is used for smoking, as in example (105):

(105) "He took the pipe down and packed it with tobacco, held a taper to the fire and lighted the **fragrant weed**. (*COHA*, 1955, FIC, QuicksilverPool)

The rest of the collocates of *fragrant* represent a varied selection of domains. The most prominent are the two nouns *odor* and *perfume*, which are in nearly all cases used to denote types of scents, therefore belonging to the semantic category SENSATION.

Continuing with *perfumed*, its collocates are visualized in Figure 23.

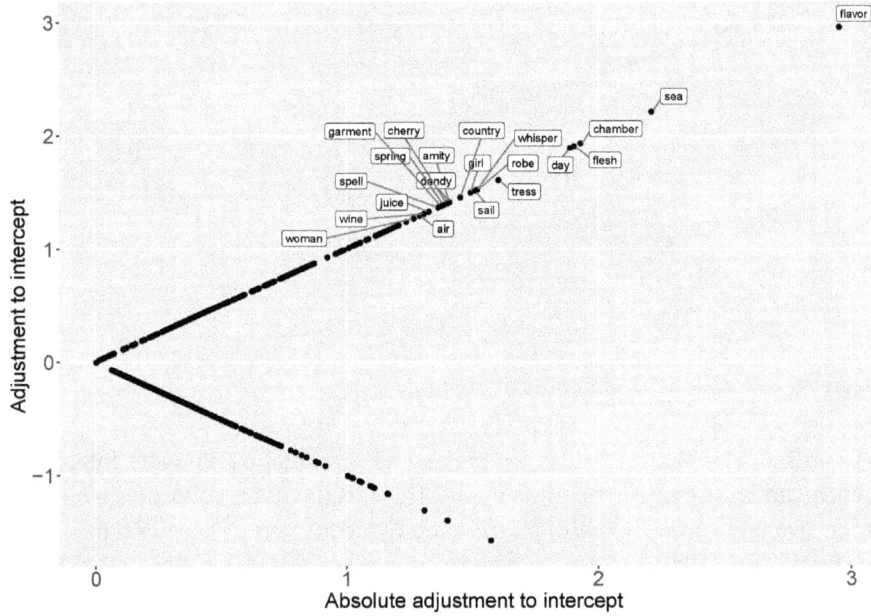

Figure 23: Collocational preferences of *perfumed*.

Again, some clear tendencies can be observed in the plot:
(i) Several of the most prominent nouns pertain to the semantic category BODY AND PEOPLE, a category in which *perfumed* is the preferred variant in most periods (cf. Figure 21 in Section 5.2.1); these are *flesh* (of a human body; cf. example (106)), *tress* (of hair), *girl*, *dandy*, and *woman*.

(106) But Alvin wasn't looking at anything. His nose was buried in the soft, **perfumed flesh** just below her left ear. (*COHA*, 1972, FIC, Clone)

(ii) More surprisingly, several collocates belonging to FOOD AND DRINK, to wit, *flesh* (of fruit; cf. example (107)), *cherry*, *juice*, and *wine*, are strongly associated with *perfumed*, although the probability of finding this adjective in this semantic category is relatively low (cf. Figure 21 above). In the case of *flesh*, most instances come from the same text (i.e., AmericanFruitCulturist). The noun *flavor*, belonging to SENSATION, is the most strongly associated collocate of *perfumed* according to the mixed-effects model. However, similarly to *flesh* (of fruit), this is due its high co-occurrence frequency with *perfumed* in three specific texts (cf. Section 4.3.2). Therefore, these two associations may be due to the idiosyncratic preferences of the authors of these texts.

(107) Large **Pears**. BEURRE BOSC. (Syn. Calebasse Bosc.) [...] body large oblate; surface nearly smooth, deep yellow, russeted in patches; stalk an inch and a half long, slender, curved; basin very shallow; **flesh** juicy, buttery, rich, perceptibly **perfumed**, sweet, excellent. (*COHA*, 1850, NF, American-FruitCulturist)

(iii) Three of the collocates that emerge as being highly associated with *perfumed* represent instantiations of this adjective being used in the figurative sense: *whisper*, *amity*, and *spell*. For an illustrative example, see (108). As in the case of the nouns belonging to BODY AND PEOPLE, this is not at all surprising, given that *perfumed* is relatively likely in the figurative sense, especially at the end of the time span examined (cf. Figure 20 above). The rest of the collocates mostly belong to the categories EARTH, ATMOSPHERE, AND WEATHER (e.g., *sea*, *spring*, and *country*) and TEXTILE AND CLOTHING (i.e., *garment* and *robe*), two categories in which *perfumed* is relatively productive.

(108) I much prefer the company of ploughboys and tin-peddlers to the silken and **perfumed amity** which celebrates its days of encounter by a frivolous display, by rides in a curricle and dinners at the best taverns. (*COHA*, 1841, FIC, Essays–FirstSeries)

Finally, Figure 24 plots the collocational preferences of *scented*.

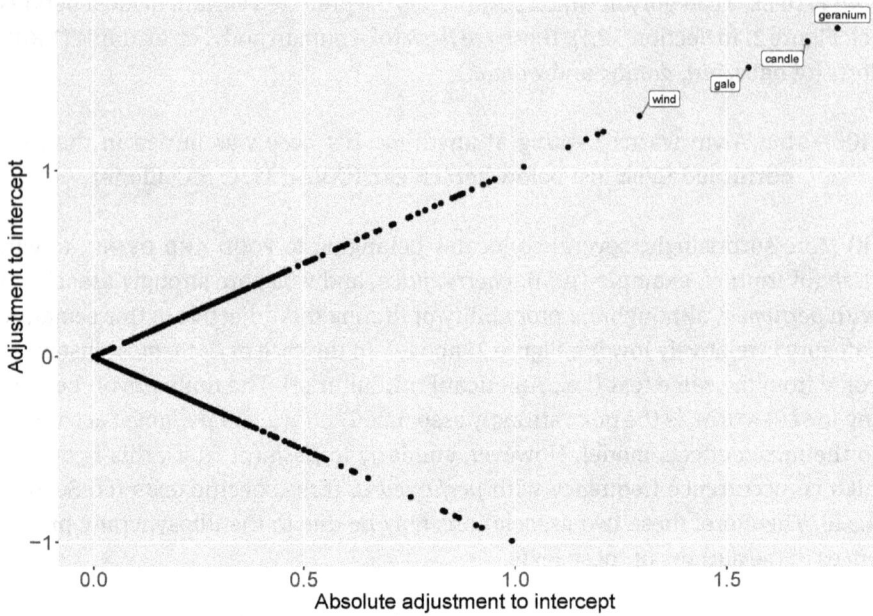

Figure 24: Collocational preferences of *scented*.

In this case, only 4 nouns are included in the plot, namely *geranium*, *candle*, *gale*, and *wind*. That a considerably lower number of collocates emerge for this adjective is probably due to the fact that the mixed-effects regression model for *scented* have a lower discriminatory power than those for *fragrant* and *perfumed* (cf. compare the first row in Tables 22–24 above). This, in turn, may be the result of the collocational preferences of *scented* being more similar to the collocational behavior of *fragrant* and *perfumed* than these two are with respect to each other. In Section 4.3, it was postulated that *fragrant* and *perfumed* are located on opposite ends of a continuum of senses, with the former closer to the natural end of the cline and the latter placed at the artificial end. *Scented*, on the other hand, occupied a more intermediate position, given that it seemed to be relatively salient in both the artificial and natural senses (cf. Figures 5 and 6 in Section 4.3.1). Therefore, it may well be the case that *scented* shares more semantic ground with *fragrant* and *perfumed*, than either of them does with one another. The fact that the model for *scented* performs worse than those of the other two adjectives may thus be a consequence of *scented* occupying a middle position between *fragrant* and *perfumed*. This is an issue which is further explored in Chapter 6.

Concerning the 4 noun collocates which are strongly associated with *scented*, the most prominent one is *geranium*. However, as in the case of *flesh* (of fruit) and *flavor* discussed above in relation to *perfumed*, this is probably also a corollary of the preferences of one particular author, as out of the 13 total instances in which *scented* modifies *geranium*, 11 appear in the same text in *COHA* (i.e., *Scan*: Homesteading). The second prominent noun collocate is *candle*, which represents a particularly interesting case. This is so because *scented* modifies this noun on 25 occasions in the corpus, but only from the 1950s onwards, and of these, 20 instances are dated from the 1990s onwards. Therefore, most occurrences of the collocation *scented candle* appear in P4. Moreover, the collocate *candle* is almost exclusively used with the adjective *scented*, as only two cases of this noun are found with *fragrant* and one with *perfumed* in *COHA*. These findings could point to *scented candle* nowadays being a compound or multiword unit (Liu 2010:64–66) rather than a noun phrase formed by an attributive adjective and a head noun. This is so because a scented candle is used to denote a particular concept, namely that of a candle which is used to perfume the air. This hypothesis is supported by the fact that *scented* is immediately followed by *candle* in 20 of the 25 cases (i.e., 80%) in *COHA* in which these two words co-occur (cf. example 109):

(109) His fireplace was of reasonable size, and when it was not in use, it held **scented candles** that he had selected for himself in the Perfumers' Market. This was the only room in the house that he ever felt warm in. (*COHA*, 2004, FIC, OutstretchedShadow).

In fact, the combination *scented candle* could be claimed to be in the early stages of *lexicalization*, understood as

> the change whereby in certain linguistic contexts, speakers use a syntactic construction or word formation as a new contentful form with formal and semantic properties that are not completely derivable or predictable from the constituents of the construction or word formation pattern. (Brinton and Traugott 2005: 96)

Whereas the main purpose of a candle is to function as a source of light (*OED*, s.v. *candle* n. 1a), a scented candle is, as mentioned above, most typically used to refresh or perfume the air of a place. In this sense, it is more similar to different types of air diffusers (e.g., electric plug-ins, mist dispensers and evaporating sprays) rather than to classical candles. This can be deduced from examples such as (110), where *scented candle* is in fact referred to as a type of air freshener delivery method:

(110) Many other **air freshener delivery methods** have become popular since, including **scented candles**, reed diffusers, potpourri, and heat release products. (*CD*, s.v. *candle* n. collocations)

The remaining two prominent collocates of *scented* are *gale* and *wind*, two related words, as the former is a hyponym of the latter, which belong to the semantic category EARTH, ATMOSPHERE, AND WEATHER.

5.3 Discussion

The analyses conducted in this chapter proved the adequacy of the set of variables selected for examination since they all emerged as significant predictors of the choice between the near-synonymous adjectives *fragrant*, *perfumed*, and *scented*. This indicates that variables of a varied nature should be considered to reach a better understanding of the variation between lexical near-synonyms. However, not all predictors play an equally important role according to the statistical methods employed here. In Section 5.2.1, both the multinomial regression models and the random forest analysis pointed to the conclusion that the intralinguistic semantic variables were stronger determinants for this particular synonym set, especially the two related predictors Semantic category and Sense, but also Countability and Concreteness. Similarly, the mixed-effects analyses computed in Section 5.2.2 indicated that the individual noun collocates considerably improved the performance of the regression models, as idiosyncratic collocational patterns explained a great amount of the variation existing between the near-synonyms. This is in line with previous research (cf. Section 2.2.2), which demonstrates that zooming in on the nouns that adjectives modify is a particularly effective approach to uncover their semantic structure (Geeraerts 1986: 282–284). On the other hand, the morphosyntactic variables Syntactic function and Degree, although significant, played a relatively minor role (cf. Figure 14). This finding highlights the importance of considering the POS of the near-synonyms object of study when selecting variables for the analysis: while morphosyntactic variables are indeed crucial for near-synonymous verbs (e.g., Divjak 2010: 183–193), their effect size is rather negligible in the case of adjectives, at least in the set examined here. This reminds us of Hank's (1996: 92; 96) and Liu's (2010: 61) arguments that, despite the similar goals of usage-based corpus research on near-synonymy, the micro-procedures that need to be employed in each study vary, since the ways in and the dimensions on which near-synonyms differ also vary from one set to another. Additionally, the extralinguistic variable Period also exerted a great influence on the distribution of the near-synonyms at stake, being ranked third in order of importance according to the random forest analysis. The fact that Period is a more powerful predictor than most of the other variables suggests that the diachronic dimension of lexical variation cannot be disregarded. As shown in Section 2.3, this issue has not received the attention it clearly deserves, as only a handful of diachronic distributional corpus-based studies on lexical near-synonyms exist to date.

Concerning the specific effects of the predictors, most of the diachronic onomasiological tendencies of Sense and Semantic category uncovered in Section 4.4 are confirmed by the regression analyses, as many of these trends reach statistical significance. Once again, *fragrant* emerges as the default choice in the natural sense and all five prototypically 'natural' semantic categories (i.e., EARTH, ATMOSPHERE, AND WEATHER, FOOD AND DRINK, PLANTS AND FLOWERS, SENSATION, and SPACE). We witness, however, a slight decrease in the probability of this adjective in most of these contexts, mainly in favor of *scented*, which increases significantly over time, although it does not threaten the prominence of *fragrant* with these types of nouns. On the other hand, some substantial changes do occur in the artificial sense and with most of the related semantic categories, namely, CLEANING, COSMETICS, OBJECT, and SUBSTANCE AND MATERIAL. In fact, we observe a reorganization of the near-synonyms in many of these contexts of use.

(i) The probability of *fragrant* decreases somewhat in the artificial sense, and that of *perfumed* does so more drastically. *Scented*, in turn, gains ground at the expense of the other two adjectives, particularly from P2 to P3, and becomes the default choice in this sense in P4.

(ii) With respect to specific semantic categories, the probability of *scented* increases particularly in CLEANING, COSMETICS, and OBJECT, but also somewhat in SUBSTANCE AND MATERIAL. In fact, in CLEANING and in OBJECT *scented* becomes the default choice, ousting *perfumed* in the former and both *fragrant* and *perfumed* in the latter. In COSMETICS and SUBSTANCE AND MATERIAL, *scented* converges in probabilities with *perfumed* and *fragrant*, respectively, although it does not surpass them.

Similarly, the internal structure of the set is also reorganized in the figurative sense and in the category ABSTRACT, where *fragrant* loses its dominance over time; by P4, *perfumed* and *fragrant* are almost equally likely. Finally, in the value 'indeterminate', *fragrant* also loses ground in favor of *scented*, while *perfumed* remains stable. This change seems to be restricted to BODY AND PEOPLE, where *scented* also displays a substantial upward tendency.

As in Chapter 4, the results of this chapter suggest the existence of a probably still ongoing process of substitution within the synonym set, whereby *scented* gains ground at the expense of *fragrant* and *perfumed*. Figure 25 depicts this process in a more visual manner, where both the overall frequencies of each adjective, as well as those within the artificial, indeterminate, and natural senses, are displayed.[53] Here, the vertical axis represents the percentages of use of the adjectives in each sense, whereas the horizontal axis shows the four historical periods. Within the plot, a different pattern is used to signal the frequencies of each adjective: squares are used to indicate those of *fragrant* and black diamonds those of *scented*, while the absence of a pattern in the middle area of the graph corresponds to *perfumed*. Additionally, a different color signals the frequencies of each sense: purple stands for the artificial sense, white for indeterminate uses, and green for the natural sense. Figure 25 combines the patterns and colors to portray the percentages of use of the three adjectives in each sense over time. By focusing exclusively on the patterns, the ongoing process of replacement can clearly be observed.

Overall, *fragrant* – located at the bottom of the figure – decreases considerably in frequency throughout the period 1810–2009, while the opposite tendency is true for *scented* – located at the top of the figure. However, while *fragrant* becomes less and less commonly selected over time in favor of *scented*, it still remains the dominant choice overall in P4.

Perfumed, in turn, does neither increase nor decrease substantially. In P4, the situation seems to be one of a greater degree of competition between the near-synonyms, with all three adjectives being more equally distributed than in P1. Nevertheless, this greater degree of competition between the variants does not appear to result in an increasingly higher degree of differentiation between the synonyms as time passes. In fact, the contrary tendency seems to hold in this particular case, namely attraction. This can be observed by focusing on the colors in Figure 25, that is, by zooming in on the frequencies of each adjective in the different senses. By P4, all three adjectives are much more frequently used in the artificial sense – the purple areas – than in earlier periods. On the contrary, none of the adjectives exhibit a substantial upward tendency in the natural sense – the green areas–: *fragrant* and *perfumed* both clearly decrease in this sense over time, and *scented* shows only a minor increase. Similarly to the development of the adjectives in the artificial sense, all of them also increase in the value 'indeterminate' – the white areas – from P1 to P4. Interestingly, the diachronic development of the adjectives in so-called indeterminate contexts is very similar to their evolution in the artificial sense. This could be taken as an indication that a

---

[53] The figurative sense is not included in this graph as the frequencies of the three adjectives in this sense are almost negligible.

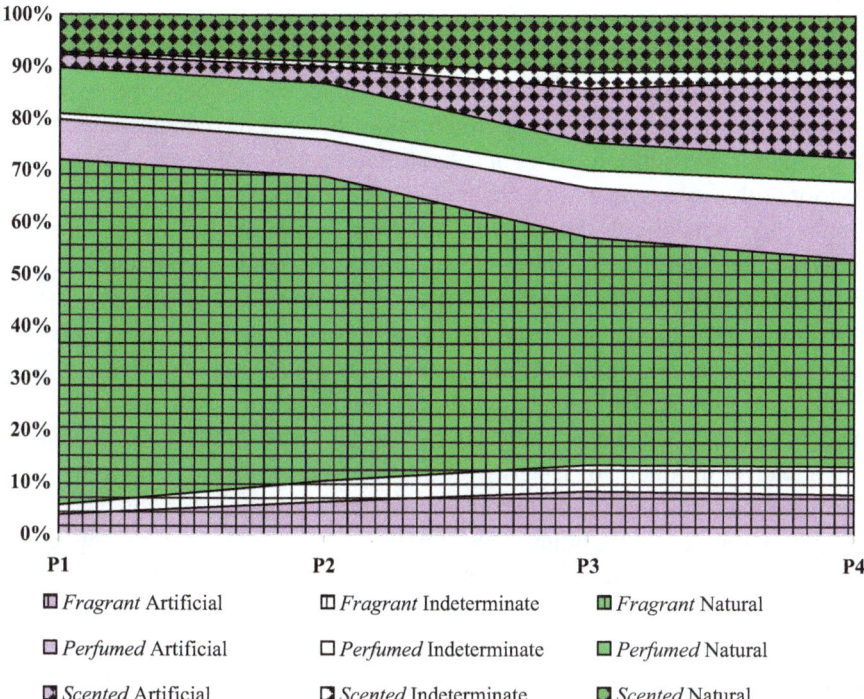

Figure 25: The use of *fragrant*, *perfumed*, and *scented* in the artificial, indeterminate, and natural senses over time.

relatively large amount of such ambiguous cases is, in fact, 'artificial', although this cannot be discerned in the actual instances in *COHA*. Moreover, more than half of the examples (56.96%) which are classified as indeterminate belong to the semantic category BODY AND PEOPLE. The reader may recall that a considerable increase over time of this particular semantic category emerged from the analysis (cf. Section 4.2.2), and that this upward tendency may have been the result of the growing availability and use of cosmetics and other personal care products applied to the. Therefore, it may well be the case that the general rise of the indeterminate sense is, at least in part, due to the increase of the category BODY AND PEOPLE and that of potential artificial uses of the adjectives which had to be categorized as 'indeterminate' due to a lack of sufficient evidence.

The end result of the frequency fluctuations described in the previous paragraph is a more even distribution of the adjectives in P4, both generally and across the different senses. In general terms, the overall frequencies of the adjectives are more similar in P4, although *fragrant* remains the dominant variant of the set. Additionally, their individual distribution across senses is also more similar at the end of the time span, with all three adjectives being more commonly used than before in both the artificial sense and in indeterminate cases, and less so in the natural sense, except in the case of *scented*, which does not recede from natural contexts of use. Therefore, the findings point to the conclusion reached in Chapter 4 that both processes of substitution and attraction are at play in the history of this synonym set. De Smet et al. (2018: 217) postulate that attraction results from analogical change, whereby functionally similar words or structures parallel each other's behavior through an interchange of characteristics, an explanation that would account, for instance, for near-synonymous expressions developing the same metaphorical mappings. However, a more likely explanation in this case is that the tendency of all three adjectives to denote more and more artificial aromas derives from extralinguistic forces. In particular, the underlying motivations for change may be related here to the socio-cultural and technological advances of American society over the time span 1810–2009, whereby these specific types of aromas have become increasingly prominent in the day-to-day life of the American population. This hypothesis is tested in Chapter 7 by means of two analyses focusing on the diachronic development of the collocates of the adjectives.

Turning now to the significant predictors which do not interact with Period, namely the semantic factors Concreteness rating and Countability and the morphosyntactic variables Degree and Syntactic function, *fragrant* is the default choice in all levels of the four predictors throughout 1810–2009. This is not surprising, given the much higher overall frequency of *fragrant* in COHA than that of the other adjectives. However, there are some contexts where *perfumed* and *scented* are more likely than expected, whereas the reverse is true for *fragrant*:

(i) *Perfumed* is more likely with highly abstract nouns than with more concrete nouns, while the opposite tendency holds for *scented*.
(ii) As concerns Countability, *fragrant* is dominant in all three levels (count, non-count, and other), but less so with non-count nouns, where *scented* is more probable than expected, and with pronouns and proper nouns ('other'), where *perfumed* is marginally more likely than expected.
(iii) In the case of the variable Degree, *fragrant* is again salient in all levels, but much more so in the comparative and superlative degrees, because *perfumed* and *scented* are hardly ever used in either comparative or superlative form in *COHA*.
(iv) Finally, as regards Syntactic function, *fragrant* outperforms the other two adjectives in all functions, especially as a predicative complement. However, in the postpositive use and in other minor functions its probability is not as pronounced: in the former, *scented* exhibits a higher probability than

expected, whereas the same is true for *perfumed* when serving as a predicative adjunct, fused-modifier head, or predeterminer.

These results entail that the overall prominence of *fragrant* is not threatened in any of these morphosyntactic or semantic contexts, and that this situation is maintained diachronically.

Some stylistic differences between the three near-synonyms also emerged from the regression analyses. Crucially, some diachronic changes can be said to exist as regards the probability of the adjectives in some text-types in *COHA*. An overall increase of *scented* is attested in all three text-types, but it is in non-fictional texts where this upward tendency is most pronounced. In fact, *scented*, the least probable adjective in non-fiction in P1, becomes the most likely choice in P4. In fiction and periodicals *scented* also increases and outperforms *perfumed* in P3 and P4, but it does not reach the probability of *fragrant* in any of these two text-types. Therefore, the overall increase of *scented* in frequency uncovered in Section 4.1 seems to occur across all text-types, though the increase is sharper in non-fictional texts. Thus, as in previous studies on the distribution of near-synonyms, stylistic differences also play a role on the choice between the three adjectives examined here (e.g., Kjellmer 2003; Liu and Espino 2012). However, it must be noted here that the categorization of text-types used in the present study is relatively coarse-grained and could be further refined in future research to pinpoint exactly in which particular subgenres each adjective is preferred (e.g., poetry, novels, movie scripts, editorials, advertisements, academic writing from different sciences).

Lastly, the goodness-of-fit indexes of the multinomial regression models provided in Section 5.2.1 signal that there is still room for improvement. As previously explained, the accuracy and the R^2 values of both Models A and B indicate that the set of predictors included in the analyses and their interactions are insufficient to explain all the variation in the data. Three possible reasons why these models are not optimal are postulated here. First, although a rather large number of predictors of different types has been examined, other variables may also play a role in the choice between the near-synonyms. Two factors which have been shown to influence linguistic variation in different dimensions of language are the opposing forces of *priming* (Gries 2005; Szmrecsanyi 2005) and the so-called *horror aequi* principle (e.g., Rohdenburg 2003). The former consists in the (explicit) repetition or reiteration of linguistic elements precisely because they have been employed in a recently produced utterance. The latter, in turn, implies the avoidance of the repeated use of "formally (near-) identical and (near-) adjacent [. . .]" linguistic elements (Rohdenburg 2003: 236). For instance, in example (111) *scented*, as opposed to *fragrant* or *perfumed*, may have been chosen as a modifier of the noun *fruit* precisely because it has already been used earlier in the same sentence (i.e., *scented bloom*), thus potentially constituting a case of priming. On the contrary, in (112) *fragrant* may have been selected as a modifier of the COSMETICS noun *oils* because *scented*, which is a more likely choice with this semantic category, has already been employed in the previous noun phrase (i.e., *scented soap*), hence a possible instance of *horror aequi*.

(111)   About me were miles on miles of apple orchards, and in our own I worked and played from the time of pink and **scented bloom** to that of **scented** and yellow **fruit**. (*COHA*, 1930, MAG, Atlantic)

(112)   "Everybody is waiting for it to happen down here, hoping every-thing will jell," said Sarah Laight, an ex-pat Brit who sells **scented soaps**, **fragrant oils** and summer-of-love dresses in her Life boutique. (*COHA*, 1994, NEWS, SanFran)

Moreover, the non-optimal values of the multinomial models may result from interactions between variables which were not tested for in the analyses. The reader may recall that only the interactions between the variable Period and the other predictors were included, as the main aim of this work is to examine the diachronic development of the adjectives. However, interesting findings may be revealed if a larger number of predictors, for instance, Text-type and Sense or Semantic category, are cross-cut to see whether functional differences exist between the near-synonyms in different genres. Nevertheless, the inclusion of additional variable interactions would require a larger dataset than the one used in the present monograph.

The second reason why the models with only fixed effects are not optimal could be that some of the variation in the data may be relatively random. After all, we are here dealing with the phenomenon of synonymy and semantically related terms need to exhibit a sufficiently high degree of interchangeability without a change in meaning to be considered near-synonyms. If this was not the case, language users would not be able to resort to near-synonyms for the purposes of avoidance of repetition and coherence in text production (Murphy 2013: 289–290).

Finally, and more importantly, the mixed-effects regression analyses in Section 5.2.2 highlighted the great importance of considering the idiosyncratic behavior of the near-synonyms. By including the specific noun collocates of the adjectives, a substantial improvement in model fit was achieved. The resulting models with both fixed and random effects (cf. Section 5.2.2) explained almost double the amount of variation than a model with only fixed effects (cf. Section 5.2.1). This means that, in this particular case, what really distinguishes between the adjectives are the specific nouns that they modify. Thus, Firth's (1957: 11) famous quote "you shall know a word by the company it keeps" (cf. Section 1.1), by means of which he emphasizes the importance of collocational patterns, seems to be an adequate description of this synonym set. Given the great importance of the individual noun collocates of the near-synonymous adjectives, the next chapter zooms in on their idiosyncratic collocational behavior throughout the period 1810–2009 by using different methodological approaches that are specifically geared towards analyses of this kind.

6 Idiosyncratic collocational preferences of the near-synonyms

The notion of collocation constitutes one of the central tenets of the distributional approach, being emphasized already in several of Firth's most important works (e.g., 1935; 1957). With the advent of corpora, the notion became even more essential in lexico-semantic analysis and, therefore, research on collocational behavior flourished. Similarly, advancements in the methods and statistical techniques used both to measure the degree of association between nodes and their collocates and to represent such associations led to an increasing interest in this phenomenon. In particular, the notion of collocation has figured prominently in research on near-synonymy as one of the types of contextual patterns used to quantify the degree of (dis)similarity between potentially near-synonymous expressions. In fact, many scholars argue that the more contextual ground two lexemes share, including specific collocates, the more similar they are (e.g., Rubenstein and Goodenough 1965; Miller and Charles 1991; Gries 2001; 2003; Gries and Otani 2010; Liu 2010). For instance, Gries (2001; 2003) examines the degree of collocate overlap between pairs of near-synonymous -*ic*/-*ical* adjectives by accounting for the amount of significant collocates they share, as well as the amount of significant collocates one near-synonym exhibits, but not the other.

Due to the broad application of the notion of collocation and the boost it received from the distributional corpus-based approach, it is not surprising that this term has been interpreted in various ways. For instance, Gries (2013: 138–139), in his overview of collocational research over the last 50 years, identified a series of parameters on which the notion has varied. Among these, he includes the nature of the linguistic items examined (e.g., POS), the frequency threshold for a co-occurring item to be considered a collocate, the distance between the items making up the collocation (i.e., context window), and the relation between the node and the collocate, that is, whether mere adjacency between the items in question suffices or whether the two items need to be syntactically or semantically related. Such variations in the use of the concept have logically resulted in the proposal of several definitions of the term in the specialized literature, namely the textual, the statistical, and the associative definitions. These definitions are not mutually exclusive and, in fact, in the present chapter both the textual and the statistical definitions are employed, as the latter can be seen as a refinement of the former with the addition of some frequency or associative thresholds.

Most research on near-synonyms reviewed in Chapter 2 analyzed collocational patterns in one way or another, either by considering specific collocates or more schematic classifications, that is, semantic preferences and/or semantic prosody, among others (e.g., Persson 1989; Gries 2001; 2003; Kjellmer 2003; Arppe and Järvikivi 2007; Primahadi-Wijaya-R and Rajeg 2014). The great majority of these studies are of a synchronic nature, thus measuring the contextual overlap of near-synonyms in, most commonly, Present-Day English (e.g., Persson 1989; Kjellmer 2003). However, a few studies examine how the collocational preferences of such related words have changed over time, thus offering a fine-grained perspective of how the relation between near-synonyms can vary from one period to another. Two cases in point are Primahadi-Vijaya-R. and Rajeg (2014) on the adjectives *hot* and *warm* and Baker (2017: 95–101) on the prepositional pairs *round/around* and *on/upon* (cf. Section 2.3). In the present work, the synonym set under examination exhibits important diachronic tendencies, with Period emerging as a particularly strong predictor which is involved in significant interactions with Sense and Semantic category, among others (cf. Section 5.2.1). Additionally, the idiosyncratic collocational patterns of the adjectives also play a crucial role in their choice, as confirmed by the mixed-effects regression analyses in Section 5.2.2. Nevertheless, changes over time in the collocational profiles of the adjectives were not analyzed in depth in Chapter 5, where only their general collocational tendencies were visualized (cf. Figures 22–24). The main aim of this chapter is therefore to determine whether these tendencies vary diachronically, much as in the case of the semantic preferences of the near-synonymous adjectives uncovered in the previous two chapters.

The structure of this chapter mirrors that of the preceding one. The dataset and the statistical techniques employed are first described in Section 6.1. Then, Section 6.2 focuses on the results of the different collocational analyses, with 6.2.1 providing a bird's-eye view of all noun collocates of the near-synonyms and 6.2.2 zooming in on just the most prominent ones. Finally, Section 6.3 offers a summary and a discussion of the main findings.

6.1 Data and methodology

Contrary to the first dataset which served as the basis for the analyses in Chapters 4 and 5, the second dataset does not comprise the actual instances of the near-synonymous adjectives, but instead their noun collocates in an L5–R5 context window (cf. Section 3.2). The collocates of the adjectives were extracted automatically from *COHA* by making use of the Collocates and POS-tag options available in the corpus. Additionally, to be able to provide the diachronic development of the collocational behavior of the adjectives, their collocates were retrieved per period. This allows us to compare (i) the collocational patterns of each adjective across periods (e.g., the collocates of *fragrant* in P1 with those of *fragrant* in P2) and (ii) the collocational patterns of the different adjectives (e.g., the collocates of *fragrant* in P1 with those of *scented* in P1). Table 25 displays six of the rows in the database to provide an overview of its structure. For instance, the lemma *afternoon* occurs in COHA as a collocate of *fragrant* zero times in P1, 3 in P2, and so on and so forth. Similarly, this particular noun only collocates with *perfumed* once, in P3. As further explained below, the adjectives *sweet-scented* and *sweet-smelling* were excluded also from the present analyses for similar reasons to those put forward in Section 5.1 above. The retrieval process resulted in a total of 10,740 tokens and 2,682 types of noun collocates, which were then submitted to two types of analyses so as to measure the (dis)similarities of the collocational preferences of the near-synonymous adjectives and, consequently, their semantic structure.

Table 25: Structure of the dataset.

Node Collocate	*Fragrant*				*Perfumed*				*Scented*			
	P1	P2	P3	P4	P1	P2	P3	P4	P1	P2	P3	P4
afternoon	0	3	3	0	0	0	1	0	0	0	1	0
age	0	1	0	0	0	0	0	0	0	0	0	0
air	33	74	44	34	11	28	9	7	8	17	15	21
aisle	0	3	0	1	0	0	0	0	0	0	0	0
alabaster	2	0	0	0	0	0	0	0	0	0	0	0
alcohol	0	0	0	0	0	1	0	0	0	0	0	0

First, the data was analyzed by means SVS modeling. This technique is specifically geared towards the comparison of the contexts of words or word senses. It is therefore a particularly suitable method to measure the semantic (dis)similarity between related words, such as near-synonyms, on the basis of their collocational profiles. Different types of SVS analyses exist depending on how context and the notion of collocation are conceived. If one adopts a more textual definition where all neighboring words in a specific context window (e.g., L5–R5) are considered collocates, a so-called *bag-of-words* SVS model is applied (Peirsman, Heylen, and Geeraerts 2008: 34–35; Levshina 2015: 323–324). If, on the contrary, only those context words which exhibit a specific syntactic relation with the node are accounted for, a so-called *dependency-based* SVS model is conducted (Padó and Lapata 2007; Heylen, Speelman, and Geeraerts 2012).

Additionally, another distinction is made between *type-* and *token-based* SVS. The former averages "collocate frequencies over many occurrences of the same word [. . .]", whereas the latter "operates at the level of word tokens, thus capturing meaning differences between individual occurrences of the same word" (Hilpert and Correia Saavedra 2020: 394; cf. also Heylen, Speelman, and Geeraerts 2012; Hilpert and Flach 2021). The dataset analyzed here and illustrated in Table 25 is an example of a data sample used for type-based SVS. This is so because the main units of analysis are the word types or lemmas *fragrant*, *perfumed*, and *scented* and the frequencies of occurrence of their collocates are averaged over all the instances of these lemmas in the corpus.

These various types of SVS, as well as the context windows selected, have different advantages, some of them being more appropriate for the study of specific semantic phenomena (for more information, cf. for instance, Padó and Lapata 2007; Peirsman, Heylen, and Geeraerts 2008). Thus, for instance, bag-of-words models are especially useful to uncover issues connected to particular discourse contexts and to semantic prosody. On the contrary, dependency-based models are claimed to perform better at measuring semantic relations between words or word senses (Padó and Lapata 2007). Moreover, as mentioned in Section 3.2, the size of the context window employed in bag-of-words models also affects the results of SVS modeling: while tighter windows of one or two words to the left and to the right typically retrieve near-synonyms or antonyms of the target word, somewhat looser windows (e.g., L5–R5) are more suitable to retrieve the most typical collocates of the node (Peirsman, Heylen, and Geeraerts 2008: 40). In the analyses conducted in the present chapter, the results of a restricted bag-of-words SVS with an L5–R5 context window are provided, focusing exclusively on the noun collocates of the adjectives. The decision to include only noun collocates was justified in Section 3.2 on the basis of findings of previous studies, which suggest that nouns are more informative than other POS when the semantic structure of adjectives is concerned (Geeraerts 1986; Gries 2001; 2003). Therefore, other content words (e.g., adjectives and verbs) and function words (e.g., prepositions and pronouns) were excluded. By means of illustration, in example (113) the square brackets delimit the L5–R5 collocation window and, within this span, only three nouns (i.e., *garden*, *roses*, and *orange-trees*) appear and are thus considered collocates of *fragrant* in the present analyses.

(113) [. . .] continued Miriam, glancing at Meschines, and then letting her eyes wander across the **[garden**, blooming with **roses** and **fragrant** with **orange-trees**, and so across**]** the trellised vines towards the soft outline of the mountains eastward. ". (*COHA*, 1892, FIC, GoldenFleeceRomance)

Nevertheless, it must be noted that two different SVS analyses were also conducted to determine their suitability for the present data. First, non-nominal content words were accounted for, thus including adjective, adverb, and verb, as well as noun, collocates of the adjectives (e.g., adding *blooming* in example (113)).

Despite the fact that a minimal improvement in the quality of the analysis was achieved when all content words were considered, the resulting patterns were not as elucidating as the ones obtained on the basis of the restricted SVS with only noun collocates. Second, a dependency-based SVS model was also computed by considering only those nouns that are semantically modified by the adjectives (e.g., *flower* in *the flower is fragrant*). In this case, however, the resulting SVS model performed much worse than the one with all noun collocates.[54] Furthermore, as explained above, a type-based, as opposed to a token-based, SVS was carried out here. Token-based SVS typically results in data sparseness, given that the database contains many more cells with zero than that for a type-based SVS. To solve this problem, token-based SVS models resort to *second-order collocates*, that is the collocates of the collocates of the node (Hilpert and Flach 2021: 308). This means that one would first search for the collocates of *fragrant* in each instance of this adjective in *COHA* (e.g., *flower* in *the flower is fragrant*) and then for the collocates of *flower*. This is indeed an interesting approach, but retrieving second-order collocates in a time-sensible manner requires access to the whole corpus. In addition, token-based SVS analysis is more typically employed to trace the existence of different senses (i.e., polysemy) within the same target word(s) in a data-driven fashion, whereas type-based SVS is more adequate when working with near-synonyms or other semantically related words (Heylen et al. 2015: 155). Given that the focus here is on the degree of (dis)-similarity of the adjectives rather than on the existence of different senses (e.g., natural, artificial, figurative), which was already established for this synonym set on the basis of reference materials in Section 3.1, type-based SVS modeling was chosen.

Regardless of the type of SVS one wants to conduct, a similar series of steps is typically followed to construe the models (cf. for instance, Levshina 2015: 326; Hilpert and Correia Saavedra 2020: 396–401):

(i) First, a table with the raw co-occurrence frequencies of the target words (i.e., the near-synonyms) and the context words (i.e., the noun collocates) is generated. In our case, given the strong focus on diachronic changes, the co-occurrence frequencies in the four periods distinguished were included in a separate column (cf. Table 25).

---

54 The stress values (cf. below for a definition of this term) of these three models are as follows: 0.19 (Bag-of-words SVS with all content words), 0.21 Bag-of-words SVS with only nouns, and 0.30 (Dependency-based SVS with modified nouns).

(ii) Second, a collocational strength value is calculated from the raw co-occurrence frequencies. Here, the association measure resorted to is PMI (e.g., Church and Hanks, 1990: 23) given that it is the standard one used in SVS analysis, since it works well with low co-occurrence frequencies (Levshina 2015: 327).

(iii) Finally, cosine similarity scores are computed (Levshina 2015: 328) between the collocational behavior of the node words (i.e., *fragrant*, *perfumed*, and *scented* in each period). Cosine values range between 0 and 1: the higher the value between two nodes (e.g., 'fragrant P1' and 'fragrant P2'), the higher their degree of similarity. The final result is a similarity matrix, shown in Table 26:

Table 26: Similarity matrix based on cosine similarity scores for the data.

		Fragrant				Perfumed				Scented			
		P1	P2	P3	P4	P1	P2	P3	P4	P1	P2	P3	P4
Fragrant	P1	1	0.76	0.59	0.53	0.83	0.47	0.34	0.37	0.71	0.58	0.53	0.47
	P2	0.76	1	0.71	0.42	0.43	0.57	0.34	0.36	0.48	0.48	0.39	0.36
	P3	0.59	0.71	1	0.79	0.32	0.45	0.39	0.40	0.43	0.42	0.70	0.49
	P4	0.53	0.42	0.79	1	0.25	0.36	0.43	0.56	0.20	0.40	0.42	0.45
Perfumed	P1	0.83	0.43	0.32	0.25	1	0.87	0.50	0.51	0.95	0.65	0.49	0.23
	P2	0.47	0.57	0.45	0.36	0.87	1	0.76	0.60	0.83	0.84	0.66	0.41
	P3	0.34	0.34	0.39	0.43	0.50	0.76	1	0.85	0.40	0.30	0.83	0.33
	P4	0.37	0.36	0.40	0.56	0.51	0.60	0.85	1	0.35	0.54	0.95	0.73
Scented	P1	0.71	0.48	0.43	0.20	0.95	0.83	0.40	0.35	1	0.78	0.61	0.22
	P2	0.58	0.48	0.42	0.40	0.65	0.84	0.30	0.54	0.78	1	0.59	0.42
	P3	0.53	0.39	0.70	0.42	0.49	0.66	0.83	0.95	0.61	0.59	1	0.66
	P4	0.47	0.36	0.49	0.45	0.23	0.41	0.33	0.73	0.22	0.42	0.66	1

The value in each cell in Table 26 represents the degree of similarity between a node in the columns and another one in the rows. For instance, the degree of similarity between 'fragrant P1' and 'fragrant P2' is 0.76. The series of cells with a value of 1 signal the degree of similarity of each node with itself. As mentioned above, a value of 1 represents complete collocate overlap between two nodes, which only occurs when a node is compared with itself. The diagonal line formed by the cells with a value of 1 separates the matrix into two identical halves, with the top right half reduplicating the values of the bottom left half.

The similarity scores obtained in this third and last step of the process were subsequently fed into cluster analysis and MDS, two different dimensionality reduction techniques used to explore and interpret the (dis)similarities between the adjectives in the different periods. For easier interpretability of the resulting cluster and MDS analyses, the similarity matrix was first transformed into a distance matrix by subtracting each of the similarity scores in Table 26 from 1. The distance matrix is shown in Table 27: in this case, distance values go from 0 to 1, and the higher the value between two nodes, the larger the semantic distance between them. In this case, the diagonal line of zero crossing Table 27, which stands for absolute similarity in terms of collocational behavior, divides the matrix into two identical halves.

Table 27: Distance matrix for the data.

		Fragrant				Perfumed				Scented			
		P1	P2	P3	P4	P1	P2	P3	P4	P1	P2	P3	P4
Fragrant	P1	0	0.24	0.41	0.47	0.17	0.53	0.66	0.63	0.29	0.42	0.47	0.53
	P2	0.24	0	0.29	0.58	0.57	0.43	0.66	0.64	0.52	0.52	0.61	0.64
	P3	0.41	0.29	0	0.21	0.68	0.55	0.61	0.60	0.57	0.58	0.30	0.51
	P4	0.47	0.58	0.21	0	0.75	0.65	0.57	0.44	0.80	0.60	0.58	0.55
Perfumed	P1	0.17	0.57	0.68	0.75	0	0.13	0.50	0.49	0.05	0.36	0.51	0.77
	P2	0.53	0.43	0.55	0.65	0.13	0	0.24	0.40	0.17	0.16	0.34	0.59
	P3	0.66	0.66	0.61	0.57	0.50	0.24	0	0.15	0.60	0.70	0.17	0.67
	P4	0.63	0.64	0.60	0.44	0.49	0.40	0.15	0	0.65	0.46	0.05	0.27
Scented	P1	0.29	0.52	0.57	0.80	0.05	0.17	0.60	0.65	0	0.22	0.39	0.78
	P2	0.42	0.52	0.58	0.60	0.35	0.16	0.70	0.46	0.22	0	0.41	0.58
	P3	0.47	0.61	0.30	0.58	0.51	0.34	0.17	0.05	0.39	0.41	0	0.34
	P4	0.53	0.64	0.51	0.55	0.77	0.59	0.67	0.27	0.78	0.58	0.34	0

Cluster analysis is a group of methods that helps to identify groups or clusters of objects on the basis of their (dis)similarities (Levshina 2015: 301). The objective of such methods is therefore to create groups comprising objects that are maximally similar to one another and maximally dissimilar to those objects in other groups, all this on the basis of the data at hand, in this case the distance matrix displayed in Table 27. Here, HAC analysis is used, which organizes the data into clusters and subclusters in a tree-like structure by first considering each individual node (here, 'fragrant P1', 'fragrant P2', etc.,) as one separate cluster, then continually merging those two which are most similar until there is only one macro cluster containing all nodes (Steinbach, Tan, and Kumar 2005: Chapter 8). MDS, in turn, is a technique that represents differences between a set of objects as distances in a two- or three-dimensional plot, typically referred to as an MDS map (cf. for instance, Levshina 2015: 336–337; van der Klis and Tellings 2022: 1–2). The input for this test is again the distance matrix shown in Table 27 above and the output consists in a spatial representation of the nodes so that the more similar two nodes are, the closer they are located in this spatial configuration. The goal of MDS is to shed light on the structure of the data in an easily understandable and visual manner (Kruskal and Wish 1978: 7; Wickelmaier 2003: 4). The two methods, HAC and MDS, are used here since they complement each other. HAC permits us to discover groups in the data which are coherent and clearly delineated by categorically splitting the data into separate clusters. MDS, in turn, provides a semantically more realistic visualization of the data by arranging data points along a continuum of semantic (dis)similarity, thus not forcing categorical either/or splits on the data (cf. Jansegers and Gries 2020: 158).

To supplement the findings of SVS modeling, the most prominent collocates of the synonyms were also examined to provide a more detailed picture of the collocational behavior of the adjectives. This is so because, as argued by Heylen et al. (2015: 154–155), "the technique [SVS] is too much of a black box to be suitable for in-depth lexical analysis [. . .]". In other words, SVS results in a series of distance values, but it averages over a great amount of individual collocates so that it is not always easy to determine exactly where the (dis)similarities in the data reside.

To identify the prominent collocates of the adjectives, the association measure employed was again PMI. Collocates were classified as prominent only if they complied with the following criteria (cf. Baker 2017: 98–100): (i) a raw co-occurrence frequency of 5 of more with the near-synonyms in each period and (ii) a collocational strength (i.e., PMI) value of 3 or higher in each period. Therefore, this analysis is based on a much lower number of collocates of the near-synonyms than that of the SVS analysis, which makes it possible to adopt a more qualitative perspective on the collocational behavior of the adjectives. At this point, it became evident that *sweet-scented* and *sweet-smelling* could not be included in the analysis of prominent collocates, as almost none of their collocates emerged as prominent after applying these two thresholds: only the noun *flower* complied with these criteria as a collocate of *sweet-scented* in P1 and *sweet-smelling* in P2. For this reason, the two adjectives were excluded from this fine-grained analysis and, for the sake of comparability, also from the SVS analysis. Establishing lower thresholds, that is a raw frequency lower than 5 and a PMI lower than 3, would not be a particularly effective solution, as these would include collocates which may not be especially prominent. Moreover, scholars such as Church and Hanks (1990) and Church et al. (1994), among others, have pointed out that a PMI of 3 or higher can be taken as an indication of two words collocating significantly more often than expected by chance. Therefore, lowering this threshold would result in non-significant collocates entering the analyses. Table 28 shows the settings used to identify prominent collocates, namely the PMI and frequency cut-off values, the context window, and some additional filters. The additional filter column makes it explicit that only noun collocates were considered, thus discarding other content and function words.

Table 28: Settings for the analysis of prominent collocates.

PMI threshold	Frequency threshold	Context window	Additional filters
3	5	L5–R5	Function words and content words other than nouns removed

To discuss the findings of the analysis of prominent collocates, the terminology proposed by McEnery and Baker (2017: 25–30) is employed. These authors distinguish between four types of collocates, namely, *consistent* (cf. also Gabrielatos and Baker 2008), *terminating, initiating*, and *transient*. The first type refers to those collocates which are relatively stable and thus appear with a node regularly over a period of time. Here, a collocate is considered consistent when it appears in at least three of the four periods. Initiating collocates, in turn, are words which occur for the first time in an intermediate period and then occur consistently throughout the time span analyzed. Terminating collocates show the opposite trend, i.e., occurring at the beginning of the time span, and disappearing in later periods. Here, those collocates which occur either only in the first two or only in the latter two periods (that is, P1/P2 or P3/P4) are considered terminating and initiating, respectively. Similarly, those which occur either only in P1 or only in P4 are considered potentially terminating and potentially initiating collocates, respectively. Finally, transient collocates are those that occur with a node only for a short period of time without gaining consistency. In this case, transient collocates are those which do not meet the criteria for any of the other three types, occurring in one or two intermediate periods or in a maximum of two non-continuous periods (e.g., in P2 and P4). McEnery and Baker's (2017) taxonomy is particularly appropriate to discuss the findings of in-depth collocational analysis from a diachronic perspective since it highlights the specific collocates of a word which are lost or gained over time. Therefore, this approach is a useful one for the purposes of the analyses carried out in this chapter as it allows us to zoom in on the evolution of the collocational behavior of *fragrant*, *perfumed*, and *scented* over time.

6.2 Results

As mentioned in the introductory section to this chapter, the results of the two methods employed to examine the idiosyncratic collocational behavior of the near-synonyms *fragrant*, *perfumed*, and *scented* are presented separately in what follows. First, in Section 6.2.1, the findings of SVS are provided through the two different visualizations techniques selected here, i.e., HAC and MDS. Then, Section 6.2.2 presents the most prominent collocates of each adjective and their classification according to McEnery and Baker's (2017: 25–30) taxonomy.

6.2.1 Semantic vector space modeling

Figure 26 displays the distance between the near-synonymous adjectives across periods according to HAC in the form of a dendrogram: the higher two nodes are merged, the more dissimilar they are.[55] The grey rectangles indicate the optimal number of clusters on the basis of the average silhouette width of this solution, an index which serves as an indicator of the internal coherence of the clusters. This index ranges from 0 to 1, with values higher than 0.2 signaling that clusters are well-formed (Levshina 2015: 311).

A HAC solution with five clusters obtains the highest average silhouette width, namely 0.49. The five clusters are the following (from left to right in Figure 26):
(i) Cluster 1: *perfumed* and *scented* in P1 and P2.
(ii) Cluster 2: *scented* in P4.
(iii) Cluster 3: *perfumed* in P3 and P4 and *scented* in P3.
(iv) Cluster 4: *fragrant* in P3 and P4.
(v) Cluster 5: *fragrant* in P1 and P2.

---

[55] An earlier version of the analyses presented in this chapter was published in Pettersson-Traba (2019). However, the analyses have been considerably modified and extended in the present monograph.

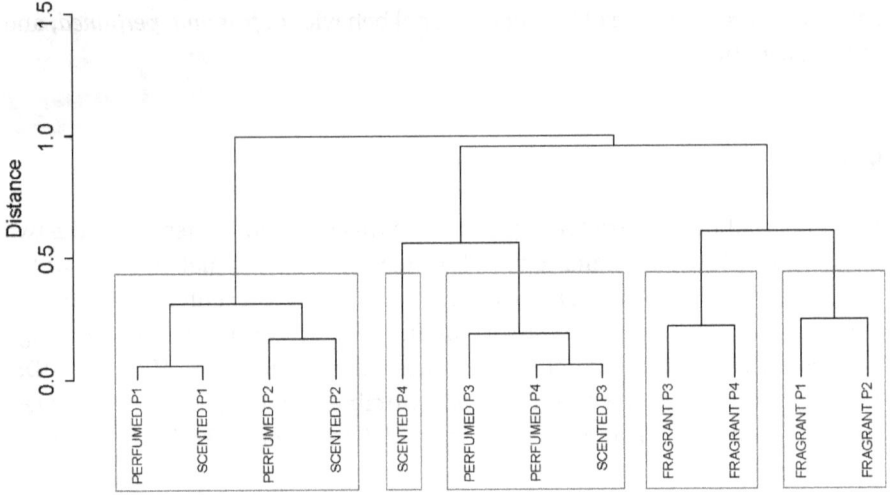

Figure 26: Dendrogram of the collocational preferences of *fragrant, perfumed*, and *scented* throughout the period 1810–2009.

The stability of the clusters obtained can be estimated by computing their Approximately Unbiased (AU) *p*-values, which determine how well supported they are by the data and thus also the chances of achieving the same clusters if a new data sample was to be analyzed. AU *p*-values range from 0 to 1 and the closer they are to 1, the more stable the clusters (Levshina 2015: 315–317). The AU *p*-values for the five clusters in Figure 26 are shown in Table 29:

Table 29: AU *p*-values for the five-cluster solution in Figure 26.

Cluster	AU *p*-value
1 (*perfumed* and *scented* in P1 and P2)	0.89
2 (*scented* in P4)	0.90
3 (*perfumed* in P3 and P4 and *scented* in P3)	0.93
4 (*fragrant* in P3 and P4)	0.88
5 (*fragrant* in P1 and P2)	0.78

Of the five clusters obtained, none reaches the traditional 0.95 significance threshold, but most of them are close to this value. The least stable cluster is that containing *fragrant* in P1 and P2 (i.e., cluster 5), which implies that if a new data sample was to be examined, these two nodes would possibly not be part of the same cluster. On the other hand, the cluster containing *perfumed* in P3 and P4 and that of *scented* in P3 (i.e., cluster 3) is almost statistically significant and therefore represents the most stable cluster. The remaining three clusters exhibit values that range from those obtained for cluster 5 to those for cluster 3, but they are closer to the latter.

Figure 26 above shows that the collocational profiles of the three adjectives seem to pattern according to period and near-synonym. First, the collocational profiles of the near-synonyms in P1 and P2 are grouped together (i.e., clusters 1 and 5), as well as those in P3 and P4 (i.e., clusters 3 and 4). Second, the collocational profiles of *fragrant* (i.e., clusters 4 and 5) differ from those of *perfumed* and *scented*, which are part of the same clusters (i.e., clusters 1 and 3). The only exception to this pattern is the collocational behavior of *scented* in P4, which forms its own cluster (i.e., cluster 2) and is thus kept apart from the nodes perfumed P3, perfumed P4, and scented P3 (i.e., cluster 3).

A semantically more realistic picture with no categorical either/or splits is provided by the MDS analysis of the data. Figure 27 plots a two-dimensional MDS solution of the collocational preferences of *fragrant*, *perfumed*, and *scented* across periods. This figure should be interpreted in the following way: each separate node in the graph represents the collocational behavior of one of the near-synonyms in a specific period and the closer two nodes are located on the MDS map, the more similar their collocational preferences. The quality of the MDS solution can be examined by computing the so-called stress value (Levshina 2015: 341): the smaller the stress, the better the performance of the model. As a rule of thumb, values higher than 0.2 indicate that the model can be further improved. The stress of the MDS solution visualized in Figure 27 is 0.21, indicating an almost acceptable fit.

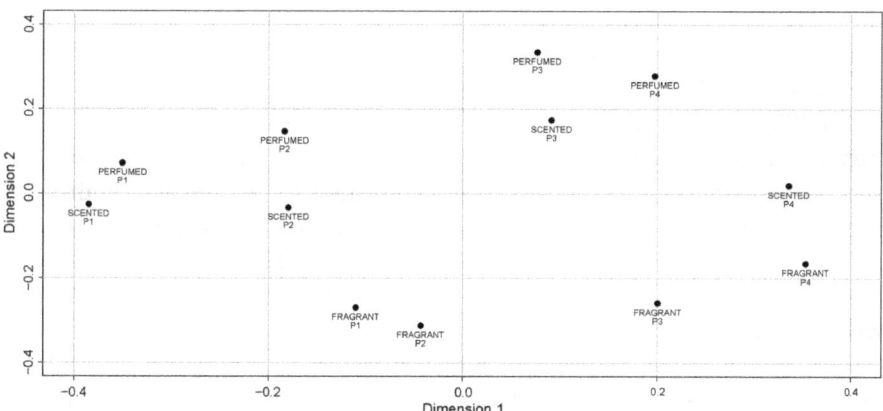

Figure 27: Two-dimensional MDS map of the collocational preferences of *fragrant*, *perfumed*, and *scented* throughout the period 1810–2009.

The vertical axis (Dimension 2) in Figure 27 organizes the nodes according to near-synonym, with *perfumed* being located at the top of the figure and *fragrant* at the bottom. *Scented*, in turn, occupies the middle ground but, overall, it is much closer to *perfumed* than to *fragrant*, with the exception of P4. In the horizontal axis (Dimension 1), on the contrary, the nodes are arranged from left to right representing a temporal continuum: negative values are assigned to P1 and P2, while positive values are assigned to P3 and P4. This visual interpretation of Figure 27 is confirmed by applying an independent one-way analysis of variance (i.e., ANOVA) to the values of the datapoints on the MDS map. ANOVA is a parametric statistical test, the aim of which is the comparison of the levels of a categorical variable that distinguishes between three or more groups (Levshina 2015: 172). In this case, we compare the mean MDS coordinates of the adjectives (i.e., *fragrant* vs. *perfumed* vs. *scented*) across periods but also the mean MDS coordinates of the periods (i.e., P1 vs. P2 vs. P3 vs. P4) across near-synonyms. The results of ANOVA consist in a global *p*-value that signals whether significant differences exist or not between the groups, but not where exactly those differences lie. As is often the case, only some of the levels of the categorical variable are significantly different from the others even though the global *p*-value reported by ANOVA reaches statistical significance. To identify which levels differ significantly from the rest, it is therefore necessary to conduct a so-called post hoc test. Here, the most common post hoc test was used, namely Tukey Honest Significant Differences or Tukey HSD for short (cf. for instance, Levshina 2015: 179). ANOVA and Tukey HSD were computed by means of the aov() and TukeyHSD() functions in *R*, respectively.

The results of an independent one-way ANOVA comparing the mean coordinates of the near-synonyms on Dimension 1, when averaged over the periods, show that the adjectives do not significantly differ on this dimension ($F = 0.446$, $df = 2$, $p > 0.05$). In other words, on the horizontal axis the datapoints on the MDS map are not arranged according to synonym. However, the synonyms do differ significantly on Dimension 2, i.e., the vertical axis ($F = 23.48$, $df = 2$, $p < 0.001$). A Tukey HSD test point to the significant differences being the following: *fragrant* behaves significantly different from both *perfumed* ($p < 0.001$) and *scented* ($p < 0.01$) while *perfumed* and *scented* do not significantly differ from one another ($p = 0.07$). In contrast, if the periods instead of the synonyms are compared, the nodes are not arranged according to period in Dimension 2 ($F = 0.329$, $df = 3$, $p > 0.05$) given that in this case the important dimension is Dimension 1, i.e., the horizontal axis ($F = 19.75$, $df = 3$, $p < 0.001$). A Tukey HSD test again serves as an indicator of which differences are significant. First, P1 differs significantly from P3 ($p < 0.01$) and P4 ($p < 0.001$). Second, P2 differs significantly from P4 ($p < 0.01$) and marginally so from P3 ($p = 0.054$). Finally and importantly for our purposes, P1 and P2 ($p > 0.05$), on the one hand, and P3 and P4 ($p > 0.05$), on the other, behave similarly according to the Tukey HSD test, which means that the significant split is that between P1/P2 and P3/P4.

Two main conclusions regarding the collocational behavior of the adjectives can be extracted from the two-dimensional MDS solution of the SVS analysis displayed in Figure 27 and aforementioned statistical results. First, *fragrant* behaves considerably differently from *perfumed* and *scented*, which are more similar to one another. Second, the collocational profiles of the three adjectives in the nineteenth century differ substantially from their profiles in the twentieth and twenty-first centuries. This finding is in line with those obtained in the previous chapters where important changes were also discovered at this particular point in time. However, as mentioned above, Heylen et al. (2015: 154–155) argue that SVS is "too much of a black box" to clarify the nature of the (dis)similarities uncovered. Therefore, to shed some light on such (dis)similarities, further analyses are required. Before turning to the more qualitative analysis carried out in Section 6.2.2, where the prominent collocates of the near-synonyms are examined, in the remainder of this section, quantitative techniques are applied to the results of the SVS to identify what the Dimensions (i.e., axes) in the MDS plot in Figure 27 stand for. To do so, *USAS* (cf. Section 3.3) was resorted to in order to group the 2,682 types of noun collocates included in the SVS analysis (cf. Section 6.1) into semantic categories.[56] Following *USAS* semantic classification for each near-synonym in each period (e.g., 'fragrant P1', 'fragrant P2'), a PMI score signaling their collocational strength with each semantic category in *USAS* was calculated. This was done with the aim of identifying whether there exist correlations between the MDS coordinates of the nodes and their PMI scores with the semantic categories. The significance of correlations was assessed by means of Pearson's product-moment correlation tests (Levshina 2015: 116–130). Besides a significance value, this test provides a correlation coefficient, represented by the letter *r*, which ranges from 0 to 1 and indicates the strength of the correlation: the higher the value, the stronger the correlation. Positive coefficients signal a positive correlation, which means that the values of the tested variables, here the MDS coordinates of the nodes and their PMI scores with the *USAS* semantic categories, jointly decrease and increase. In other words, if the values of one variable increase, so do the values of the other variable, and vice versa. On the contrary, negative coefficients signal a negative or inverse correlation, implying that the values go in opposite directions: if the values of one variable increase, the values

---

56 Given the data-driven nature of SVS analysis, the semantic classification of the noun collocates in this chapter was carried out automatically using *USAS*, instead of the *HTOED*. As mentioned in Section 3.3.2, despite being less precise, *USAS* allows researchers to automatically analyze strings of words according to their semantics and thus check the domains to which particular words belong.

of the other decrease, and vice versa. The eight correlations shown in Table 30 emerged as significant:

Table 30: Significant correlations between the dimensions in Figure 27 and semantic categories in USAS.

MDS dimension	USAS semantic category	Direction of correlation	Correlation coefficient (r)	p-value
Dimension 1	F4: FARMING AND HORTICULTURE	negative	−0.63	< 0.05
Dimension 1	W4: WEATHER	negative	−0.58	< 0.05
Dimension 2	B: THE BODY AND THE INDIVIDUAL	positive	0.88	< 0.001
Dimension 2	L3: PLANTS	negative	−0.54	0.06
Dimension 2	M3: MOVEMENT/TRANSPORTATION (LAND)	negative	−0.53	0.07
Dimension 2	Q1: COMMUNICATION	positive	0.77	< 0.01
Dimension 2	Q4: THE MEDIA	positive	0.69	< 0.05
Dimension 2	S2: PEOPLE	positive	0.80	< 0.01

Given that some of these semantic categories differ from those used in previous chapters, examples of nouns belonging to these categories that exhibit a significant correlation with any of the MDS dimensions are shown in Table 31:

Table 31: Examples of types of noun collocates in the semantic (sub)-categories in USAS.

Semantic category	Examples of types of noun collocates
B: THE BODY AND THE INDIVIDUAL	B1: *hand, hair, neck, shoulder, wrist* B4: *detergent, perfume, lotion, shampoo, soap* B5: *clothes, handkerchief, garment, glove, lace*
F4: FARMING AND HORTICULTURE	*crop, farm, farmhouse, field, mow, pasture, vineyard*
L3: PLANTS	*cactus, garden, magnolia, pollen, pumpkin, root, vine*
M3: MOVEMENT/ TRANSPORTATION (LAND)	*avenue, path, pathway, road, wayside*
Q1: COMMUNICATION	*draft, leaflet, letter, note, notepaper, stationery*
Q4: THE MEDIA	*article, book, edition, newspaper, paper*
S2: PEOPLE	*boy, child, gentleman, maiden, man, people, woman*
W4: WEATHER	*breeze, flood, fog, haze, mist, rain, storm, wind*

First, two semantic categories, namely F4: FARMING AND HORTICULTURE and W4: WEATHER, turn out to be significantly correlated with Dimension 1 of the MDS map, that is, the horizontal axis in Figure 27, which represents the collocational profiles of the near-synonymous adjectives over time. Importantly, this correlation is negative, which means that the higher the value of a node on Dimension 1, the lower its PMI score with these categories. Therefore, in P3 and P4 the adjectives occur with F4 and W4 nouns significantly less frequently than in P1 and P2. This change could again constitute a reflection of the transformation of American society, evolving from a preindustrial and mainly rural society in the nineteenth century to the world's major industrial and commercial power in the twentieth and twenty-first centuries (cf. Chapter 7). As a result of this process of modernization, the importance of farming and horticultural activities in the daily life of most American citizens has surely drastically declined over time, particularly after the First and Second Industrial Revolutions of the nineteenth century, which resulted in mass migration from the countryside to the cities. In a more indirect way, the importance of weather phenomena may also have decreased with time, as farming and horticultural activities rely greatly on the climate.

Second, another two semantic categories exhibit a significantly negative correlation with the MDS coordinates on Dimension 2 (vertical axis in Figure 27): L3: PLANTS and M3: MOVEMENT/TRANSPORTATION (LAND). Again, this finding implies that such types of nouns co-occur with the near-synonyms more often as their values on MDS Dimension 2 decrease. Such nouns are therefore more strongly associated with *fragrant* than with *perfumed* and *scented*. In all likelihood, nouns belonging to the categories L3 and M3 appear mostly in contexts where the near-synonyms are used in the natural sense. This is particularly true of nouns in category L3, in which plants generally (e.g., *bush*, *sapling*, and *blossom*), specific species of plants (e.g., *magnolia*, *pine*, and *rose*), and parts of plants (e.g., *bark*, *branch, and petal*) are included. Two examples in which some such nouns appear as collocates of *fragrant* are shown below in (114) and (115):

(114) Birds and fishes and reptiles disport themselves in the sunshine, and giant butterflies of the most marvellous colours flutter so bravely among the ferns and flowers. There are no tents here in our camp, but we are covered with the **fragrant branches** of the spicy **pines** and nutmeg trees. (*COHA*, 1909, FIC, AnAnarchistWoman)

(115) His own hand, (mid winter though it was,) was warm, moist with a light perspiration, and whiter than the milk of the cocoa-nut, or **petals** of the **fragrant magnolia**. (*COHA*, 1843, FIC, IdomenValeYumuri)

On the contrary, several categories display a significantly positive correlation with Dimension 2 of the MDS map, namely B: THE BODY AND THE INDIVIDUAL, Q1: COMMUNICATION, Q4: THE MEDIA, and S2: PEOPLE, which means that the higher the value of the adjectives on this dimension, the more often they collocate with nouns in these categories (e.g., *hair, soap, glove, note, newspaper*, and *child*). In the MDS map, this translates into *perfumed* and *scented* being more likely than *fragrant* to co-occur with nouns in these four categories. A large proportion of the occurrences of these nouns most probably correspond to uses of the near-synonyms in the artificial sense, particularly in the case nouns in the categories B4: CLEANING AND PERSONAL CARE and B5: CLOTHES AND PERSONAL BELONGINGS, which amount to 26 and 66 of the types in category B (49.2% of the total). The same is true of nouns in the categories Q1 and Q4. On the contrary, nouns belonging to category B1: ANATOMY AND PHYSIOLOGY, the most recurrent sub-class in category B (76 types; 40.6%), and those in S2: PEOPLE are more ambiguous, as it is not always clear whether the smell referred to by *fragrant, perfumed*, and *scented* in such contexts is either natural or artificial. As a matter of fact, as mentioned in Sections 3.3.1.1 and 4.2.2 above, a relatively large amount of such nouns was classified as indeterminate cases. Despite this high degree of ambiguity, many occurrences of the adjectives with B1 and S2 collocates correspond to the artificial sense, as in example (116), where the locks of the women emit a pleasant smell only because they have been impregnated by artificial perfumes:

(116) This is a great improvement on the Persian poets who go into raptures over the **fragrant locks of fair women**, not for their inherent sweetness, however, but for the **artificial perfumes** used by them, including the disgusting musk! (*COHA*, 1899, NF, PrimitiveLoveLove)

Figure 28 visualizes the significant correlations between the MDS dimensions and semantic categories in *USAS* just discussed.

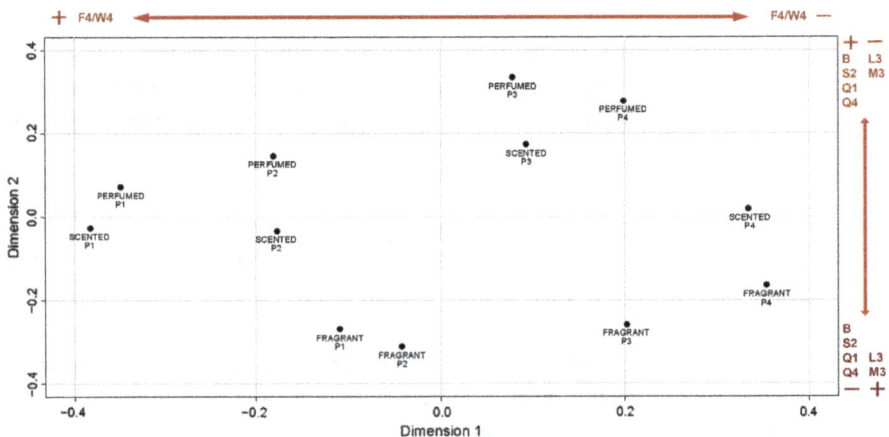

Figure 28: Significant correlations between MDS dimensions and semantic categories in *USAS*.

The diachronic development of the collocational behavior of the three near-synonymous adjectives across the four time periods, as shown by both the HAC solution and the MDS plot in Figures 26 and 27, respectively, can be summarized as follows.

In P1, the collocational preferences of *perfumed* and *scented* are very similar, while *fragrant* differs considerably from them, and does not change much from P1 to P2. Therefore, in P1 and P2, *perfumed* and *scented* are semantically closer to one another than either of them is to *fragrant*, as they seem to share a great deal of collocations and, therefore, considerable semantic space. This can be observed in the HAC solution and MDS map since, *perfumed* and *scented* are clustered together according to the former and are located in close proximity of one another on the latter. On the contrary, *fragrant* is part of a different cluster and is further removed from the other two adjectives in the MDS solution.

However, a substantial development is identified from P2 to P3 in the collocational behavior of the adjectives, as they all move considerably towards the right-hand side of the MDS map. This change is also reflected in the dendrogram in Figure 26, given that the P3 components of the adjectives are kept apart from their P1 and P2 components. Despite these changes, *perfumed* and *scented* are still closer to each other in P3 than they are to *fragrant*.

The collocational profiles of *fragrant* and *perfumed* remains rather stable from P3 to P4 but, by contrast, that of *scented* does indeed change. In fact, in P4 *scented* moves away from *perfumed* and occupies an intermediate position on the MDS map between *perfumed* and *fragrant*, which are located at opposite ends of Dimension 2 (i.e., the vertical axis). This change is again reflected in the dendrogram, given that, contrary to previous periods, *scented* in P4 does not form part of the same cluster as *perfumed*.

As in the analyses of the previous two chapters, the results of SVS indicate that most changes seem to take place from P2 to P3, i.e., in the transition from the nineteenth to the twentieth centuries. The changes identified here at level of individual collocates seem to replicate the tendencies uncovered in Chapters 4 and 5. This is so because, as shown by the interpretation of the MDS dimensions and their correlation with specific *USAS* semantic categories, changes along the vertical axis seem to correspond to changes in the frequency with which the adjectives are used in different senses. Again, *perfumed* and *fragrant* seem to be more closely associated with the artificial and natural senses, respectively, as proved by their positions on opposite ends of MDS Dimension 2, with *perfumed* at the top and *fragrant* at the bottom. In turn, *scented* occupies an intermediate position, with values close to 0 on this dimension in all periods except P3. Therefore, as already suggested, *scented* does not show a particularly clear preference for neither the artificial nor the natural sense. Finally, changes along the horizontal axis (i.e., Dimension 1) appear to correspond with some of the transformations of American society over the period analyzed.

This bird's-eye view of the evolution of the collocational preferences of *fragrant, perfumed,* and *scented* has enabled us to identify potential semantic changes concerning the collocational patterns of the synonyms. However, given the large number of collocates present in the dataset used for the SVS analysis (i.e., 2,682 types and 10,740 tokens), it has not yet been possible to identify the most prominent collocates of each near-synonym in a more qualitative fashion. This is the focus of Section 6.2.2, which zooms in on the top noun collocates of each adjective.

6.2.2 Prominent collocates

The most prominent collocates of *fragrant, perfumed,* and *scented*, that is, those occurring at least 5 times and displaying a PMI of 3 or higher in a given period, are shown in tabular form (cf. Tables 33–35), with a plus sign (+) indicating the occurrence of a particular collocate. These tables facilitate the task of identifying which collocates occur with the adjectives in all periods, and which ones are lost or gained at some point in time. By resorting to the collocational types distinguished by McEnery and Baker (2017: 25–30) explained above, namely consistent, initiating, terminating, and transient, it is possible to spot shifts in word meaning or in the productivity of particular senses of the three synonymous adjectives. Here, the focus is mainly on consistent, initiating, and terminating noun collocates, particularly on the last two types, as they are the most informative ones regarding possible diachronic fluctuations in collocational preferences. Transient collocates are disregarded, as they are basically indicative of transient or punctual changes (McEnery and Baker 2017: 28), while the focus here is on more stable diachronic tendencies or the lack of such trends.

Table 32 provides a summary of the absolute number and percentages of the different types of collocates of the three near-synonyms.

Table 32: Number and percentage of consistent, initiating, terminating, and transient noun collocates of *fragrant*, *perfumed*, and *scented*.

		Consistent	Initiating	Terminating	Transient	Total
Fragrant	N	27	12	22	35	96
	%	28.13	12.51	22.91	36.46	100
Perfumed	N	6	4	4	11	25
	%	24.00	16.00	16.00	44.00	100
Scented	N	3	9	1	13	26
	%	11.54	34.62	3.85	50.00	100

The adjectives *fragrant* and *perfumed* seem to be the most stable ones, with a much higher amount of consistent collocates, 28.13% and 24%, respectively. *Scented*, in turn, exhibits a lower rate of such collocates, namely 11.54%. If we consider the share of initiating and terminating collocates of the adjectives, an interesting picture emerges. *Fragrant* displays the largest amount of terminating collocates (22.91%) and the lowest amount of initiating ones (12.51%), which means that it loses more collocates over time than it gains. This finding replicates those of Section 4.1 (cf. Table 8 and Figure 2), where an overall decrease in frequency of this adjective was identified during the time span analyzed. Interestingly, some patterns can be deduced from the semantics of the noun collocates that *fragrant* gains and loses over time (cf. Table 33).[57]

Table 33: Consistent, initiating, terminating, and transient noun collocates of *fragrant*.

Collocate	P1	P2	P3	P4	Type	Collocate	P1	P2	P3	P4	Type
Air	+	+	+	+	Cons.	Hay	+	+	+		Cons.
Apple				+	Init.	Heat				+	Init.
Aroma			+	+	Init.	Herb	+	+	+		Cons.
Atmosphere		+	+		Tran.	Hillside			+		Tran.
Balsam		+			Tran.	Honeysuckle	+	+			Ter.
Basket		+			Tran.	Incense	+	+	+		Cons.
Berry		+			Tran.	Jasmine				+	Init.
Beverage		+			Tran.	June		+			Tran.
Bloom	+	+	+	+	Cons.	Leaf	+	+	+	+	Cons.
Blossom	+	+	+	+	Cons.	Lily		+	+		Tran.
Blush	+				Ter.	Liquid			+		Tran.
Bough		+	+		Tran.	Load		+			Tran.

---

[57] In Tables 33–35, the following abbreviations are used to refer to consistent, initiating, terminating, and transient collocates, respectively: cons., init., ter., and tran.

Table 33 (continued)

Collocate	P1	P2	P3	P4	Type	Collocate	P1	P2	P3	P4	Type
Bouquet		+	+		Tran.	Magnolia		+			Tran.
Bower	+	+			Ter.	Meadow	+	+			Ter.
Bowl		+			Tran.	Melody		+			Tran.
Bread				+	Init	Memory		+			Tran.
Breath	+	+	+		Cons.	Minute				+	Init.
Breeze	+	+	+	+	Cons.	Odor	+	+	+	+	Cons.
Bud	+	+			Ter.	Oil		+		+	Tran.
Bunch		+			Tran.	Orchard		+			Tran.
Cedar		+			Tran.	Perfume	+	+	+	+	Cons.
Chicken				+	Init.	Petal	+	+			Ter.
Cigar	+	+	+		Cons.	Pile			+		Tran.
Cigarette			+		Tran.	Pine		+	+	+	Cons.
Cloud		+	+		Tran.	Plant	+				Ter.
Clover		+	+		Tran.	Porch		+			Tran.
Cluster	+	+			Ter.	Rose	+	+	+	+	Cons.
Coffee	+	+	+		Cons.	Scent	+	+	+	+	Cons.
Cup	+	+	+	+	Cons.	Shade	+	+			Ter.
Curl	+				Ter.	Shrub	+	+		+	Cons.
Dew	+	+	+		Cons.	Sight	+				Ter.
Dusk		+			Tran.	Smell		+	+	+	Cons.
Fern		+			Tran.	Smoke		+	+	+	Cons.
Fir		+			Tran.	Spice	+	+			Ter.
Flesh				+	Init.	Spring		+			Tran.
Flower	+	+	+	+	Cons.	Steam		+	+	+	Cons.
Foliage	+	+			Ter.	Summer	+	+	+		Cons.
Forest			+	+	Init.	Sunshine		+			Tran.
Fruit	+	+			Ter.	Tea	+	+		+	Cons.
Gale	+				Ter.	Tobacco	+	+	+		Cons.
Garden	+	+	+	+	Cons.	Tree		+		+	Tran.
Garland	+				Ter.	Verdure		+			Tran.
Garlic				+	Init.	Vine	+	+			Ter.
Geranium		+			Tran.	Weed		+			Tran.
Goddess				+	Init.	Wind	+				Ter.
Grass	+	+	+	+	Cons.	Wine	+				Ter.
Grove	+	+			Ter.	Wood	+	+			Ter.
Gum		+			Tran.	Wreath	+	+			Ter.
Hair			+	+	Init.						

Terminating collocates correspond mostly with nouns belonging to the semantic categories L3: PLANTS (e.g., *bower*, *foliage*, *honeysuckle*, *petal*, and *plant*) and W4: WEATHER (e.g., *gale*, *meadow*, and *wind*), whereas initiating ones are concentrated mainly in categories F: FOOD AND FARMING (e.g., *apple*, *bread*, *chicken*, and *garlic*) and B1: ANATOMY AND PHYSIOLOGY (e.g., *flesh* [of body] and *hair*). As seen in Section 4.3.2, *fragrant* increased in P4 with nouns belonging to the semantic category FOOD AND DRINK; the findings obtained here point to a similar conclusion. However, it is worth mentioning that *fragrant* also gains some new L3 collocates (e.g., *forest* and *jasmine*) and loses some F collocates (e.g., *fruit*, *spice*, and *wine*), which suggests that its prototypical uses remain largely the same over time. This can also be observed by zooming in on the consistent collocates of this adjective, most of which are L3 nouns, especially basic level terms such as *bloom*, *blossom*, *flower*, *garden*, *grass*, and *leaf* and W4 nouns, such as *breeze*, *dew*, and *summer*. Many of the consistent collocates of *fragrant* correspond with those that exhibited a high degree of association with this adjective in the mixed-effects regression analysis carried out in Section 5.2.2. These are the three tobacco-related nouns *cigar*, *smoke*, and *tobacco*. In turn, the noun *weed*, which emerged as a prominent collocate of *fragrant* in the mixed-effects regression analyses, is here categorized as a transient collocate, occurring only in P2. This shows the importance of conducting a fine-grained qualitative analysis of the individual collocates in different periods, since some collocates are more informative than others, occurring continually over time. Finally, two other consistent collocates of *fragrant* are also in line with the results of the mixed-effects regression model. These are the two nouns *odor* and *perfume*, which belong to the sensory domain. While both lemmas appear as prominent collocates in all four periods, *odor* displays a downward tendency with *fragrant* in P4: out of its six occurrences in this period, five are dated before the 1980s, with only one example of this noun co-occurring with *fragrant* in the last 30 years in *COHA*. The decrease of *odor* as a collocate of *fragrant* may be related to the fact that this noun has undergone a process of pejoration in recent years, as explained in Section 2.3, being nowadays used mainly with a negative connotation to depict 'unpleasant smells', much as many of its related forms (e.g., *odorous*; cf. Section 3.1.2). On the contrary, *fragrant* and the other adjectives analyzed in the present work are explicitly used to denote pleasant smells, and no indication has been found in the corpus of their use to designate disagreeable ones. Therefore, it is not at all surprising that *odor*, which progressively becomes more strongly associated with negative smells, almost vanishes in the last decades in *COHA* as a collocate of *fragrant*.

As regards *perfumed*, its relative stability in terms of its overall frequency (cf. Section 4.1) seems to be reflected also in its proportion of initiating and terminating noun collocates. As can be seen in Table 32 above, these two types of collocates are evenly distributed, namely 16%. This indicates that, over time, *perfumed* has gained as many new prominent collocates as it has lost. As concerns the semantics of these collocates (cf. Table 34), three out of four initiating ones correspond to uses in the artificial sense and in indeterminate uses, namely *bath* and *soap*, i.e., category B4: CLEANING AND PERSONAL CARE, and *body*. i.e., category B1: ANATOMY AND PHYSIOLOGY. On the contrary, two of its terminating collocates belong to L3: PLANTS (*flower* and *tree*) and another one is the SENSATION noun *flavor*, which has already been commented on at several points in this monograph, as the use of *perfumed* with this noun is restricted to just a few particular texts in *COHA* in P1 (cf. Sections 4.3.2 and 5.2.2).

Table 34: Consistent, initiating, terminating, and transient noun collocates of *perfumed*.

Collocate	P1	P2	P3	P4	Type	Collocate	P1	P2	P3	P4	Type
Air	+	+	+	+	Cons.	Oil	+	+		+	Cons.
Bath			+	+	Init.	Pocket		+			Tran.
Blossom		+			Tran.	Powder			+		Tran.
Body				+	Init.	Rose		+			Tran.
Breath	+	+	+		Cons.	Silk		+	+		Tran.
Flavor	+				Ter.	Smell				+	Init.
Flower	+	+			Ter.	Smoke		+			Tran.
Garden		+			Tran.	Soap			+	+	Init.
Garment			+		Tran.	Spring		+			Tran.
Hair		+	+	+	Cons.	Tree	+				Ter.
Handker-chief	+		+	+	Cons.	Water	+	+	+	+	Cons.
Lace		+			Tran.	Wind			+		Tran.
Note	+	+			Ter.						

The consistent noun collocates of *perfumed* also speak to its prototypical use being that of denoting artificial aromas or those labeled here 'indeterminate': out of six consistent collocates, four are related to uses in the artificial sense and/or indeterminate uses, namely *hair, handkerchief, oil,* and *water*. Although the latter two nouns are highly polysemous, most of their instances co-occurring with *perfumed* in *COHA* clearly fall into the domains of PERSONAL CARE (*oil* and *water*) and CLEANING (*water*), as illustrated in examples (117) and (118):

(117) [. . .] he stopped at the barber in the straw market every morning before coming to work to be shaved and have his hair combed with a **perfumed oil**. (*COHA*, 1961, FIC, AgonyEcstasy)

(118) This morning, he spent more time than usual, being sure that no vestige of beard was left on his face, and that he was perfectly clean. He completed his bath by dashing **perfumed water** over his entire body. (*COHA*, 1955, FIC, Millenium)

The findings concerning *oil* and *water*, particularly the latter, often being used in a specialized sense with the near-synonymous adjectives with the meaning 'alcohol plus essential oils', are in line with Wright (2016; 2017), who pays close attention to the shifting names of perfumes in Late Modern English (1700-1900). In fact, many of the early examples of the near-synonyms in the semantic categories CLEANING and COSMETICS in the present data correspond to general nouns of this type in which they take on technical meanings related to the perfuming industry. However, *water* continues being used in this way as a noun collocate of *perfumed* throughout the whole period analyzed, occurring alongside other nouns (e.g., *deodorant* and *hair lacquer*) which refer to synthesized smells that became increasingly popular following the discoveries in chemical synthesis that took place during the Second Industrial Revolution (cf. Section 7.2). The early examples of *water* and similar nouns (e.g., *extract* and *essence*) in the data are difficult to categorize in either COSMETICS or CLEANING given that just as Wright (2016: 148) states, initially such "[. . .] perfumer's wares were not perfume in the modern sense but medicinal, used externally and internally" and often applied to the handkerchief people carried with them, not worn on the body, with the purpose of keeping out disagreeable smells and germs. In fact, this is easily observable in examples in which perfumed waters are available in fountains which were typical at public events in the mid-nineteenth century to refresh the air of the events and which attendees could use to dip their handkerchiefs in (cf. also Wright 2016: 155-156). One such example is given in (119) below:

(119)   Around the walls were Phoebus and Hermes in Parian marble, and the nine Muses in ivory. A **fountain** of **perfumed water** from the adjoining room diffused coolness and fragrance as it passed through a number of concealed pipes, and finally flowed into a magnificent vase, supported by a troop of Naiades. (*COHA*, 1836, FIC, Philothea)

Whenever *water* occurs modified by the adjectives in examples of the kind provided in (113) it has therefore been classified as a CLEANING noun. On the contrary, when waters are applied to the body in order to "enhance allure" (Wright 2017: 124), the noun has been classified as belonging to COSMETICS. Examples of *water* such as that in (120) in which it is massaged onto the body of the woman has thus been grouped into COSMETICS:[58]

---

58 *Messaged* in example (114) is in all likelihood a transcription error of the corpus and should be read *massaged*.

(120) But the night had turned tiresome – Jesus is worth only so much money – and all she wanted now was to get home and soak in her opulent Turkish bath, attended by her staff of servile Indian women who messaged her selfish **body** with **perfumed water** and exotic Amazonian oils. (*COHA*, 2001, FIC, Ploughshares)

The two remaining consistent noun collocates of *perfumed* are *air* and *breath*. The former also emerged as a prominent collocate of this adjective in the mixed-effects regression analysis (cf. Figure 23 in Section 5.2.2), while most other prominent collocates identified here are absent from the regression model, except the two transient collocates *garment* (in P3) and *spring* (in P2). This lack of consistency of the results between the present analysis and those of the mixed-effects regression again emphasize the need for careful in-depth qualitative analysis to distinguish the collocates which are truly informative from those that are only transient.

The significant upward tendency of *scented* in terms of its overall frequency (cf. Table 8 in Section 4.1) can also be observed in the results of the present analysis. In fact, *scented* is the adjective that exhibits the largest share of initiating collocates (34.62%) and the lowest amount of terminating ones (3.85%) (cf. Table 32 above). Hence, over time, *scented* gains more collocates than it loses, thus showing the opposite tendency to that of *fragrant*. Table 35 shows the consistent, initiating, terminating, and transient collocates of *scented* in *COHA*.

Table 35: Consistent, initiating, terminating, and transient noun collocates of *scented*.

Collocate	P1	P2	P3	P4	Type	Collocate	P1	P2	P3	P4	Type
Air	+	+	+	+	Cons.	Hair			+		Init.
Bath				+	Init.	Handkerchief		+			Tran.
Bloom		+			Tran.	Oil		+	+		Init.
Blossom		+			Tran.	Perfume			+		Init.
Breath		+	+		Tran.	Powder		+			Tran.
Breeze		+			Tran.	Sheet				+	Init.
Cake			+		Tran.	Smell				+	Init.
Candle				+	Init.	Smoke				+	Init.
Envelope			+		Tran.	Soap		+	+	+	Cons.
Flower	+	+	+	+	Cons.	Summer		+			Tran.
Garden			+		Tran.	Tree			+		Tran.
Geranium				+	Init.	Water		+		+	Tran.
Grass		+			Tran.	Wind	+				Ter.

As seen here, many of the initiating collocates of *scented* suggest that it came to be used more and more often in the artificial sense over time. In fact, out of its nine initiating collocates, more than half correspond to artificial smells, namely *bath*, *candle*, *oil*, *perfume*, and *sheet*. In Section 5.2.2, *scented candle* was already discussed as a plausible instance of a newly formed compound or a multiword unit or even as a case of lexicalization. By resorting to a contemporary corpus such as *COCA*, it can be ascertained that the degree of association between *scented* and *candle* keeps increasing in American English after the time span covered in *COHA*: in the 2010s, there are 72 occurrences of *candle* in the surrounding context of *scented* (i.e., L5–R5 window) and, out of these, 63 (87.5%) are instances of *scented* immediately preceding *candle* (i.e., *scented candle(s)*). Furthermore, the PMI score between *scented* and *candle* rises from 8.54 in P4 (1960–2009) to 11.04 in the 2010s, as calculated in *COCA*. The two initiating collocates *oil* and *perfume* behave in a similar way to *oil* and *water* as collocates of *perfumed* (cf. discussion above): although polysemous, most cases of these two nouns collocating with *scented* are used to denote artificial aromas. The remaining four initiating collocates of *scented*, that is, *hair*, *geranium*, *smell*, and *smoke*, represent a more varied picture. The nouns *hair*, *smell*, and *smoke* can be used together with *scented* in the natural or artificial senses and, on some occasions, it is not possible to identify the source of the aroma. On the contrary, all instances of *scented geranium* refer to natural uses of the adjective, but almost all these examples come from a single text in the corpus (cf. Section 5.2.2).

Out of the nine initiating collocates of *scented*, six are shared with *fragrant* and/or *perfumed*: *perfume* and *smoke* are shared with *fragrant*, *bath* with *perfumed*, and *hair*, *oil*, and *smell* with both *fragrant* and *perfumed*. Interestingly, several of these nouns become more closely associated with *scented* over time than with the other two adjectives. In other words, the PMI scores of these nouns are higher in P4 with *scented* than with *fragrant* or *perfumed*. This is the case of *hair*, *perfume*, and *smoke* for *fragrant*, *bath* for *perfumed* and *oil* for both (cf. Table 36 for the PMI score of these nouns with the three adjectives). This particular finding is in line with previous results (cf. Sections 4.4 and 5.2.1), where *scented* comes to occupy some of the semantic space previously belonging to *fragrant* and/or *perfumed*.

Table 36: PMI scores over time of *fragrant*, *perfumed*, and *scented* with shared collocates in P4.

COLLOCATE	FRAGRANT				PERFUMED				SCENTED			
	P1	P2	P3	P4	P1	P2	P3	P4	P1	P2	P3	P4
Bath	–	–	–	–	0	0	6.68	6.68	0	0	0	6.76
Hair	0	0	3.17	3.11	0	3.96	4.11	4.11	0	0	0	3.51
Oil	0	4.47	0	3.94	7.36	5.91	0	4.72	0	0	4.37	5.34

Table 36 (continued)

COLLOCATE	FRAGRANT				PERFUMED				SCENTED			
	P1	P2	P3	P4	P1	P2	P3	P4	P1	P2	P3	P4
Perfume	6.14	5.5	7.15	6.07	–	–	–	–	0	0	0	7.47
Smell	0	5.28	5.42	4.96	0	0	0	5.35	0	0	0	4.29
Smoke	0	4.54	5.19	3.93	0	4.79	0	0	0	0	0	4.48

The only terminating noun of *scented* is *wind*, belonging to category W4: WEATHER and thus to uses of the adjective in the natural sense. *Scented* exhibits three consistent collocates, namely *air*, *flower*, and *soap*, which point to the relative neutrality of this adjective in comparison to *perfumed* and *fragrant*. Note that one collocate is clearly 'natural' (*flower*), one is clearly 'artificial' (*soap*), and another one (*air*) can be used in both natural and artificial contexts.

Finally, out of the 4 noun collocates that emerged as being closely associated with *scented* in the mixed-effects regression analysis (cf. Section 5.2.2), three have also been discussed here, namely *candle*, *geranium*, and *wind*. Interestingly, none of these collocates is classified as consistent in the present analysis: whereas *candle* and *geranium* are initiating collocates, occurring only in P4, *wind* is a terminating collocate which occurs only in P1.

The more in-depth qualitative analysis carried out in this section by means of the classification of the most prominent collocates into consistent, initiating, terminating, and transient ones has served to confirm many of the tendencies identified in earlier sections and chapters. Among them, note the preference of *fragrant* for the natural sense, that of *perfumed* for the artificial one, and the relative neutrality of *scented*, although many of its initiating collocates (e.g., *bath*, *handkerchief*, and *soap*), seem to correspond to artificial rather than to natural uses of the adjective. This slight inclination of *scented* towards artificial contexts in later periods may go a long way towards explaining its closer similarity to *perfumed* than to *fragrant* observed in previous analyses, namely the regression analyses conducted in Chapter 5 and the SVS modeling discussed in Section 6.2.1. Similarly, the frequency fluctuations uncovered in Section 4.1. are also reflected in the qualitative analysis provided here: *fragrant* loses more collocates than it gains over time, *scented* gains more than it loses, and *perfumed* remains relatively stable, losing and gaining the same amount of collocates over time. However, the main findings of the qualitative analysis conducted in this section are the highly idiosyncratic collocational preferences of the adjectives, preferences which cannot be captured by methods which average over a very large amount of collocates (that is, SVS) or those which take into account more coarse-grained semantic categorizations (that is, the analyses in Chapters 4 and 5). Two idiosyncratic trends with important implications are the cases of *fragrant* and *odor*, on the one hand, and of *scented* and *candle*, on the other. The former suggests that the positive connotation of the adjective has probably not changed diachronically, as the noun *odor*, which has recently acquired a negative connotation, becomes a less and less likely collocate of *fragrant* over time. In turn, the combination *scented candle* may constitute a case of compounding or even of ongoing lexicalization, as it has become established in the language as a multiword unit over a relatively short period of time. Concrete examples such as these two demonstrate that examining the individual collocates of near-synonyms, as done in the present chapter, is an indispensable task to further uncover idiosyncratic distributional behavior of such semantically related words.

7 The concept PLEASANT SMELLING: A victim of societal change?

By applying corpus-based distributional methods and resorting to concepts such as prototypicality, salience, and entrenchment, which are key notions in cognitive semantics, it has been possible to identify changes over time in the internal semantic structure of the near-synonyms object of study in the present monograph and relate the findings obtained to a theoretical framework on language and human cognition, in general, and lexical semantics, in particular. Nevertheless, identifying the causes of lexico-semantic changes is often not a straightforward endeavor given that such changes are often considered to be more difficult to categorize than other types of linguistic changes (e.g., changes in pronunciation or morphology) in the sense that individual lexical items often follow idiosyncratic developmental patterns. Moreover, semantic developments are in many cases subject to a wider range of factors than other types of changes, including both intra- and extralinguistic ones.

With the increasing popularity of Cognitive Linguistics, the interest in semantic change is currently back on the agenda after having been disregarded in most structuralist and generative approaches. This renewed interest is mainly due to the appeal of issues regarding the relation between cognition and linguistics, the flexibility and dynamicity of meaning, and more importantly for our purposes in the present chapter, the relation of meaning with society and culture, which, as Kay and Allan (2015: 73) claim, "offer convincing ways of approaching the 'messiness' and unpredictability of lexical semantic change". Extralinguistic factors in fact play a major role in many instances of lexico-semantic change, which adds more complexity to the task of describing the evolution over time of particular lexical items (Kay and Allan 2015: 72–74). In the words of Durkin (2009: 222–223):

> Semantic changes are notoriously difficult to classify or systematize [. . .]. [A]lthough some semantic changes occur in clusters, with a change in one word triggering another, we do not find anything comparable to regular sound change [. . .]. Additionally, semantic change is much more closely connected with change in the external, non-linguistic world, especially with developments in the spheres of culture and technology.

As such, non-linguistic history, particularly technological, socio-political, and cultural transformations, must often be resorted to in order to explain the occurrence of semantic change. In fact, language-external pressures have been found in numerous occasions to lie at the root of change, which is perhaps unsurprising given that both language and society are ever evolving and often the change in one goes hand in hand with the change in the other. Cases in point are the reorganization of kinship terms in English after the Norman Conquest (Kay and Allan, 2015: 140–141) and the restructuring of French names for the meals of the day after the sixteenth century due to changes in lifestyle (Blank, 1999: 73). In fact, as Rautionaho, Nurmi, and Klemola (2020: ix) state, "[i]t is commonly accepted that changes in society are reflected as changes in language and vice versa". For instance, the emergence of new entities in the extralinguistic reality leads to new words being coined or new senses appearing for an already-existing word, often based on some perceived similarity between the newly introduced entity and an entity already designated by that word.

7.1 Exploring the interconnection between societal and linguistic developments

Recently, there has been an increased interest in the specialized literature in showing how extralinguistic changes at the cultural and social levels can be observed through the use of computerized linguistic corpora, which have by now been established as the default source of data in historical linguistics. In this vein, Baker (2017: 177) states that the frequencies of words in particular semantic domains reflect what "people actually write about at the conceptual level", thus uncovering aspects connected to "matters of culture and national identity" (cf. also Leech and Fallon 1992; Oakes 2003; Potts and Baker 2012). By drawing on data from corpora belonging to the Brown family (e.g., *The Lancaster-Oslo/Bergen Corpus (LOB)* and *The Freiburg-Brown Corpus of American English (FROWN)*), Leech and Fallon (1992), Oakes (2003), Potts and Baker (2012), and Baker (2017: Chapter 7) identify cultural and social differences between the United States and Great Britain from the 1930s to the 2000s. The frequencies of words belonging to various semantic domains are examined in the British and American components of the Brown family of corpora to determine social, political, and cultural aspects which are particularly salient in each society in different subperiods. These studies focus on general semantic domains like MASS MEDIA (e.g., *advertising, article, editor,* and *journal*) and SCIENCE AND TECHNOLOGY (e.g., *electronics, machine, scientific,* and *technical*), among others. In the case of these two domains, all four studies find a considerable increase in frequency over time in both varieties. These analyses demonstrate that corpus data can be used as an indicator, if not as conclusive evidence, of cultural and social changes.

Another clear example of the interest in the connection between linguistic and societal changes is the main theme of a recent edition of the *International Computer Archive of Modern English (ICAME)* conference, namely *Corpus Linguistics and the Changing Society* (i.e., *ICAME 39*, celebrated in Tampere in 2018).

This conference welcomed diachronic corpus-based research papers where the connection between linguistic changes and societal developments, both cultural and technological, was explicitly addressed. An edited monograph compiling studies presented at this conference which delves deeper into its main theme was recently published (Rautionaho, Nurmi, and Klemola 2020). Whereas several chapters included in this volume (i.e., Brooks and Wright 2020; Ratia 2020) focus precisely on linguistic changes which appear to respond to changes in the extra-linguistic reality, others (i.e., Hilpert 2020; Renouf 2020; Schneider 2020) adopt a more methodological orientation by testing the viability of corpora in general and/or specific corpus methods so as to explore the interrelation between language and society.

Much like several of the analyses in previous chapters of the present monograph, Brooks and Wright (2020) and Ratia (2020) examine changes over time through collocational patterns. In particular, they use collocational analyses in order to examine the changing representations of certain groups of people and how such representations are manifested through language. Brooks and Wright pay attention to the representation of non-native speakers of English living in Britain as reflected in the right leaning press. The period analyzed, namely 2005–2017, is both shorter and more recent than is typical in diachronic linguistic studies but reflects a time of heated debate regarding immigrants' knowledge and use of English. The authors examine the collocational behavior of the phrase *speak English* in different forms (e.g., *speaks English, speaking English, speaker of English*) by combining corpus data and Critical Discourse Analysis. The collocates of this phrase are grouped into four categories that represent the main themes of the "speak English" debate: (i) proficiency, (ii) multilingualism, (iii) learning English and integration, and (iv) public services and the private sector. The findings show that despite the fact that non-native speakers of English are consistently portrayed in a negative light over the 14 years examined, the picture worsens as time progresses. This can be observed in all the aforementioned categories. For example, regarding proficiency the focus shifts from specific individuals not being able to speak English well enough in the first years analyzed to the general immigrant population in later years. Therefore, the authors conclude that there has been a widening throughout the 2010s in terms of both the scope and targeting of the stigmatization of immigrants by the right-leaning British press.

Ratia (2020) focuses on the depiction of another group of people, in this case that of patients in medical discourse. She examines a period of 300 years (i.e., 1500–1800), spanning both the Early and Late Modern English Periods, which witnessed major developments in medicine and changes in moral values, moving towards a more polite and humane society. Ratia hypothesizes that the attitudes of physicians towards their patients might have been influenced by these developments, resulting in doctors becoming more concerned about the well-being of their patients. To test this hypothesis, the author examines the collocational behavior of the lemma *patient*. Ratia demonstrates that patients are mainly viewed as objects in Early Modern English whereas they are represented as experiencers in Late Modern English. This shift is made evident by the frequent occurrences of *patient* in the later period with collocates that have a clear negative connotation (e.g. *complains* and *aversion*). Such collocates point to a concern for the patients and their suffering on the part of their physicians. Another conclusion reached by Ratia is that while the singular and plural forms of the lemma analyzed behave similarly in the first 200 years of her corpus, the plural form increasingly appears with collocates related to hospital life (e.g., *hospital admission*) in later years, which leads to a difference in collocational behavior of the singular and plural forms. The frequent appearance of such collocates is believed to be a result of the increasing significance of hospitals and public health in the eighteenth century. Brooks and Wright (2020) and Ratia (2020) constitute instances of the usefulness of corpus data to uncover social changes and their reflection in language, in particular in the collocational behavior of word or larger linguistic units.

Schneider (2020) approaches the issue of the interconnection between linguistic and societal changes from a methodological perspective. By investigating the changing views to poverty in the period 1500–1920, that is, the attitudes towards it and the association the concept holds to other topics in the corpora, he puts three different methods to the test, namely a data-based dictionary approach and two data-driven distributional semantic approaches. The former attempts to identify social changes as a reflection of the changing frequencies of a series of pre-determined terms or concepts thought to reflect social or cultural issues, in the case of Schneider's (2020) study, poverty. The terms are chosen by the researcher and therefore consist in manually selected wordlists which range from a few terms to longer and more complete lists of concepts, all of which tend to be drawn from one or several dictionaries or other databases. For instance, Schneider (2020: 41–43) first conducts a dictionary-based analysis with only three terms that are considered to represent extreme forms of poverty, namely *famine*, *starvation*, and *starving*. Then, he resorts to the *OED* to compile a longer list by using the Historical Thesaurus to retrieve a whole set of words which are related to poverty (e.g., *feeble, indigent, pennyless, miserable*).[59] The frequencies of these selected words are then queried in different periods of the corpus used and are thought to reflect the development in frequency of the concept POVERTY. On the contrary,

---

[59] For the complete list of words selected for this more comprehensive dictionary-based analysis, see Schneider (2020: 42).

data-driven distributional semantic approaches allow for the relevant words and/or concepts to emerge from the data in an automatic way. The three methods all provide interesting findings regarding how the concept object of study develops from Early Modern English to the present-day. First, the dictionary-based approach shows that poverty seems to remain a constant problem over the period investigated with only minor and inconclusive increases and decreases of the words associated to it. Second, through the data-driven methods it is possible to observe that poverty is always related to religion in Early Modern English, being a consistent associated concept throughout this period, while other related subjects such as urbanization, war, and criminality become increasingly important over time. Another interesting finding is that in Early Modern English poverty is not seen so much as a "humanitarian problem" but rather as a "religious virtue" (Schneider 2020: 53). On the other hand, in Late Modern English, new topics emerge from the data as being closely linked to poverty, for instance, trade and seafaring. In sum, according to Schneider, the dictionary-based approach is not viable to draw conclusions about how attitudes towards poverty have developed over time given that in this particular case the frequencies of words connected to poverty did not fluctuate much over time. To dig deeper into the association of poverty with other concepts it is therefore necessary to resort to data-driven analytical procedures which complement the findings of the dictionary-based approach.

Although investigating the link between language and society is of course possible and indeed a fruitful endeavor, research on social change and its reflection in diachronic corpora needs to be approached with a certain caution. Hilpert (2020) in fact draws attention to several crucial problems to bear in mind when connecting corpus findings to extralinguistic developments in order to avoid offering inaccurate interpretations of the data. Three of these problems are directly related to corpus frequencies of words and can easily mislead scholars in their analysis of corpus findings. The first of these is that the frequencies of words do not always coincide with the frequencies of their denotatum in the extralinguistic world. As an example, Hilpert proposes a search of the verbal collocates of the prepositional phrase *with a screwdriver* in the *News on the Web* corpus (Davies 2013). Many of the top collocates of this phrase refer to violent uses, including verbs such as *stab*, *threaten*, and *attack*, which would not be representative of the typical day-to-day uses of a screwdriver. Instead, such collocates clearly reflect the genre the corpus is made up of, namely news articles, which tend to be about extraordinary rather than ordinary events. The second problem concerns the analysis of polysemous words since the frequencies of their different senses and uses need to be accounted for separately. For instance, if one does not examine the different senses of a highly polysemous verb such as *get* one might associate an increase in the overall frequency of this verb with an increase in individualist values such as selfishness (cf. Greenfield 2013). This is so because this verb is often associated with a focus on receiving something from another person or entity as in the example *I get more money now*, provided by Hilpert (2020: 9). However, this verb is often also used in passive (e.g., *she got hit*) or copular constructions (e.g., *I am getting ready*), which do not reflect any type of individualistic value (examples taken from Hilpert 2020: 9). Therefore, one cannot simply lump together all of the uses of *get* or any other polysemous word and draw spurious conclusions of the type just exemplified. Finally, to be able to accurately compare frequency trends over time, it is necessary to conduct some type of statistical analysis. This point of course does not just apply to the connection between linguistic and extralinguistic changes, but to distributions in general, be they across varieties, registers, or time periods, among others. If statistical analyses are not conducted, one runs the risk of drawing erroneous conclusions from the data. As a general conclusion, Hilpert encourages linguists to address the intersection between language and social change, but emphasizes the importance of doing so in a methodologically sound way.

All the recent studies surveyed in this section provide evidence of corpora being adequate resources to investigate socio-cultural changes and their effects on language, provided that corpus analyses are conducted using appropriate methods and procedures. In what follows, the insights from these studies are drawn on in order to test whether socio-cultural changes could lie behind the diachronic developments undergone by the concept PLEASANT SMELLING throughout 1810–2009.

7.2 Historical background: First and Second Industrial Revolutions

Many analyses in the previous chapters of this monograph have identified recurrent evolutionary trends as regards the concept PLEASANT SMELLING. First, it was seen that the concept as a whole (cf. Section 4.2) went from being used mostly to denote natural aromas to designating more and more artificial smells as time progressed. Similarly, in the semasiological analysis provided in Section 4.3, it became clear that all near-synonyms except *sweet-scented* showed the same tendency whereby they became more artificial over time and that this development occurred irrespectively of their prototypical uses. Not only *scented* and *perfumed*, which were initially already more prominent in the artificial sense, displayed such an evolution, but also *fragrant* and *sweet-smelling*, which were mainly used to refer to natural aromas in earlier periods. The same trend was identified in the onomasiological analyses (cf. Section 4.4 and Chapter 5): the findings suggested a convergence in frequencies in the artificial sense and several prototypically 'artificial' semantic categories (e.g., COSMETICS and OBJECT). Finally, the collocational analyses in Chapter 6 also pointed to the same conclusion, with the adjectives exhibiting an increase of noun collocates referring to artificial smells and a decrease of collocates designating natural aromas. That all the different analyses of the present monograph result in similar diachronic semantic developments suggest that these changes are not coincidental, but rather the consequence of some underlying motivation. In Chapter 4, it was hypothesized that these developments were due to extralinguistic factors, namely the socio-economic changes (i.e., industrialization and mass production) that American society underwent throughout the period examined.

It is well-known that important social and technological changes took place during the period examined in the present work (1810–2009), both around the globe and, in particular, in the United States of America. From a primarily pre-industrial economy in the nineteenth century, American society became throughout the twentieth century the world's major industrial and commercial power (Jones 1996: Chapter 16; Baker 2017: 193–194). In such a context, the social and technological changes experienced as a result of the First and Second Industrial Revolutions may well constitute the underlying motivations accounting for the rise in the use of the concept PLEASANT SMELLING in the artificial sense at the expense of the natural one. First, there has been an important upsurge in the production of goods with artificial aromas, including cosmetics and cleansing agents, which most certainly also led these products to be more readily available to the population. In the second half of the nineteenth century, developments in industrial manufacturing and, particularly, chemistry enabled the production of cosmetics so that by the 1920s the mass production of these commodities became much cheaper, which, together with the fall of traditional Victorian standards of beauty and the proliferation of marketing campaigns, allowed a larger number of people to access cosmetics and wear them in their daily life (Jones 1996: 308–309; Johnson 1997: 393, 476). Moreover, the growth of the advertising industry and the increased effect the advertisements featured in newspapers and magazines had on people's choices in all likelihood also helped making these kinds of goods more important and visible in people's daily lives. According to Wright (2016: 6), perfume products were in fact hardly advertised until after the 1820s. Throughout the time span 1880–1914, the increase in the number and importance of periodicals in the United States, both newspapers and magazines, went hand in hand with an increase in the number of American citizens having access to this type of publications (Johnson 1997: 397): in 1850, there were merely around 260 newspapers in circulation in the country, while only 60 years later, by 1910, approximately 2,600 different titles (i.e., ten times more) were published on a daily basis.

The diachronic development of the concept PLEASANT SMELLING throughout Late Modern and Present-day American English might hence constitute a reflection of language-external factors that were at play during the same period and which inevitably led to a growing need for *artificially* scented soaps and oils rather than for *naturally* fragrant flowers. As demonstrated by the works reviewed in the previous section, this hypothesis can be empirically tested by using corpora and well-established distributional corpus-based methods like collocational analyses, among others. This is precisely the aim of the analyses in the present chapter, which are explained in more detail in the following section.

7.3 Data and methodology

The effect of the aforementioned socio-economic changes on the usage patterns of the concept PLEASANT SMELLING in American English is here tested in two steps by employing two separate methods. First, a dictionary-based approach such as that in Schneider (2020) is used to identify whether the most prominent noun collocates of the near-synonyms in the prototypically artificial and natural semantic categories also increase and decrease in frequency, respectively, in general in *COHA*, and not only when co-occurring with the near-synonyms. This step is resorted to in order to provide a first approximation to the issue. Second, a more data-driven approach is employed to establish the associations that the noun collocates of the near-synonyms hold with other words in the corpus and whether these associations fluctuate diachronically. By doing so, it should be possible to uncover whether these noun collocates are talked about in more 'artificial' terms, just as has been shown to occur with the near-synonyms in previous analyses. This step is akin to the type of SVS modeling known as token-based SVS (cf. Section 6.1) which consists in examining so-called second-order collocates, that is, the collocates of the collocates of a node word (cf. for instance, Hilpert and Flach 2021: 308).

In the first step of the analysis, the distribution over time of the 15 most prominent collocates of the near-synonyms in the prototypically artificial and natural semantic categories are examined. These semantic categories are those in which there is a one-to-one correspondence with one of the levels of the variable Sense, in particular, the artificial and natural ones (cf. Section 3.3.2): (i) CLEANING, (ii) COSMETICS, and (iii) TEXTILE AND CLOTHING, on the one hand, and (i) EARTH, ATMOSPHERE, AND WEATHER, (ii) FOOD AND DRINK, and (iii) PLANTS AND FLOWER, on the other. As concerns the noun collocates within the three prototypically artificial semantic categories, many of them in all likelihood allude to products which have been greatly influenced by modernization and industrialization processes.

Therefore, if these nouns exhibit an overall increase in frequency, and not only when collocating with the near-synonyms, this could point to the conclusion that the transformation of American society from a pre-industrial to a fully industrialized nation constitutes one of the causes steering the diachronic developments identified in previous chapters. In addition, in line with the hypothesis, it could also be expected that the nouns in the prototypically natural semantic categories have decreased over time, thus reflecting the diminishing importance of nature and activities connected to it (e.g., farming and horticultural activities; cf. Section 6.2.1) in the daily life of most American citizens, primarily due to mass migrations from the countryside to the cities following the First and Second Industrial Revolutions of the nineteenth century.

The selected noun collocates in each of the six aforementioned semantic categories are the following:

(i) CLEANING: *bath, bathtub, cleaning, cleanliness, deodorant, detergent, disinfectant, gel, handkerchief, laundry, shampoo, soap, sponge, suds, tissue.*
(ii) COSMETICS: *body oil, brush, cologne, cosmetics, face cream, hairspray, haircut, lipstick, lotion, make-up, manicure, mascara, perfume, razor, shimmer.*
(iii) TEXTILE AND CLOTHING: *blouse, cambric, clothes, cushion, dress, flannel, garment, glove, lace, linen, sheet, shirt, silk, skirt, textile.*
(iv) EARTH, ATMOSPHERE, AND WEATHER: *breeze, dew, earth, forest, gale, garden, grove, hill, island, land, meadow, sea, shade, shadow, wind.*
(v) FOOD AND DRINK: *apple, berry, beverage, bread, broth, chocolate, coffee, fruit, pie, sauce, spice, stew, strawberry, tea, wine.*
(vi) PLANTS AND FLOWERS: *bloom, blossom, bud, flower, geranium, grass, hay, honeysuckle, leaf, lily, petal, rose, shrub, tree, vine.*

The collocates selected in each category included the 15 nouns most frequently modified by all five near-synonyms. However, some nouns were excluded in order to avoid highly polysemous words in which the various senses might belong to different semantic domains. As mentioned above (cf. Section 7.1), Hilpert (2020) cautions against the inclusion of highly polysemous lexical items in analyses of the interconnection between linguistic and social changes without first separating the frequencies of their different senses. To avoid this pitfall, here the decision was taken to exclude these nouns from the analysis because separating the senses would entail a great deal of manual pruning of the data without access to a semantically annotated version of *COHA*. Examples of highly polysemous nouns which appeared in the top 15 list includes *oil, water, air,* and *atmosphere*, among others. The case of *air* was previously discussed in Section 3.3.3, where it was stated that at least two of its senses recurrently appear in the data. Whereas one of its senses belongs to EARTH, ATMOSPHERE, AND WEATHER, being used as a synonym of *breeze* or *light wind* (cf. example (121)), another of its uses is classified in the category SPACE, designating '[a] special state, condition, or quality of the atmosphere, as affected by temperature, moisture, etc., or as modified by time or place' (*OED*, s.v. *air* n1. I. 4; cf. example (122)).

(121) **Scented airs** which had swept all the way from distant blue hills over countless orange, olive, and mulberry groves filled the room, and fluttered the paper upon which the girls were writing [. . .]. (*COHA*, 1899, FIC, BarbarasHeritage)

(122) At the town florist's he rapped a timid signal to the driver to stop, and, glowing with anticipation, spryly shuffled into the warm, **scented air** of the little shop. (*COHA*, 1913, FIC, UncleNoahsChristmas)

The lemma *air* occurs in *COHA* more than 141,000 times, which would make it extremely time consuming to disambiguate these two senses from each other and from other senses of the word.

Following the selection process, the normalized frequencies (NFs) per million words per decade of the 90 noun collocates were retrieved from *COHA*, and an average NF was computed for each semantic category.[60] These NFs were subsequently plotted by means of line graphs (cf. Figures 29–30 below in Section 7.4.1) to visualize the possible increases or decreases of the semantic categories in the period analyzed.

The second step of the analysis constitutes a data-driven approach in which the second-order collocates of the near-synonyms are examined to pinpoint whether the conceptualization of the semantic categories of noun collocates changes over time and whether these changes mirror those undergone by the concept PLEASANT SMELLING and the near-synonyms designating it. To this purpose, the noun collocates of the 15 most prominent noun collocates in all the semantic categories established in Chapter 3 (cf. Section 3.2.2 for more detailed information about these categories) were retrieved from *COHA*. The same 15 nouns of the categories CLEANING, COSMETICS, EARTH, ATMOSPHERE, AND WEATHER, FOOD AND DRINK, PLANTS AND FLOWERS, and TEXTILE AND CLOTHING that were analyzed in the first step of the analysis were examined in this second step. However, in this step it

---

60 The analyses in the present chapter are based on the newly updated version of *COHA*, released in 2021. As the decade 1810s has been eliminated in the new version, it is not featured in Figures 29 and 30 in Section 7.4.1.

was also necessary to identify the 15 most prominent collocates of the remaining categories.[61] The same criteria of selection were used.

(i) BODY AND PEOPLE: *beard, belly, body, cheek, girl, hair, hand, head, lady, maid, man, mother, skin, tress, woman.*
(ii) OBJECT: *bed, box, cage, candle, card, couch, drawer, envelope, jar, lamp, letter, note, page, paper, taper.*
(iii) SENSATION: *aroma, cord, flavor, music, odor, savor, scent, sigh, silence, smell, sweetness, taste, tone, voice, whiff.*
(iv) SPACE: *bedroom, boudoir, chamber, conservatory, floor, hall, house, kitchen, lane, path, road, room, street, temple, walk.*
(v) SUBSTANCE AND MATERIAL: *censer, cigar, cigarette, dust, ether, fire, fountain, fume, ink, light, smoke, snuff, steam, tobacco, vaper.*

To retrieve the noun collocates of these 180 nouns, the same criteria as that established for the analyses in Section 6.1 were used here, namely a minimum frequency of 5 in each period, a PMI threshold of 3, and an L5–R5 collocation window. The extracted collocates were subsequently semantically classified in an automatic way due to extensive number of collocates retrieved (more than 19,000) by resorting once again to *USAS* (cf. Section 3.2.2). The main aim of this step was to identify whether the 11 semantic categories become more natural or artificial over time in line with our hypothesis or whether they remain stable diachronically. The discussion of the results of this step of the analysis will focus only on those semantic domains in *USAS* which in one way or another represent instantiations of the artificial-natural continuum, some of which were already present in the analyses in Chapter 6. These categories along with examples of collocates belonging to each are illustrated in Table 37:

Table 37: Semantic classes in *USAS* representing the artificial-natural continuum.

Sense	Semantic category	Examples of noun collocates
artificial	B3: MEDICINE AND MEDICAL TREATMENT	*balm, balsam, bandage, medicine, pill, scalpel, stimulant, suture*
	B4: CLEANING AND PERSONAL CARE	*comb, eyeliner, lipstick, lotion, mascara, razor, shampoo, soap*

---

61 The category ABSTRACT was excluded because as previously mentioned in Section 3.2.2, there is a one-to-one correspondence between the category ABSTRACT and the figurative sense. Given that the focus here is on the natural and artificial senses, this category is not useful to this purpose.

Table 37 (continued)

Sense	Semantic category	Examples of noun collocates
	B5: CLOTHES AND PERSONAL BELONGINGS	bag, bracelet, fabric, garment, gown, lace, moccasin, umbrella
	F3: CIGARETTES AND DRUGS	cigar, cigarette, Havana, nicotine, puff, roll-up, snuff, tobacco
	H5: FURNITURE AND HOUSEHOLD FITTINGS	armchair, closet, curtain, cushion, mattress, pillow, rug, shelf
	I4: INDUSTRY	industry, mill, mineral
	O3: ELECTRICITY AND ELECTRICAL EQUIPMENT	bulb, electricity, generator
	Q1.2: PAPER DOCUMENTS AND WRITING	card, chart, clipboard, diary, folio, list, map, notebook
	Y: SCIENCE AND TECHNOLOGY	Y1: genetics, geology, lab, laboratory, observatory, radiation, reactor Y2: byte, megabyte, password, processor, software, spreadsheet
natural	F1: FOOD	Cabbage, cucumber, lettuce, lunch, meat, oatmeal, sauce, strawberry
	F2: DRINKS	brandy, tea, ale, cider, liquor, milk, rum, wine
	F4: FARMING AND HORTICULTURE	agriculture, cultivation, farm, farmland, harvest, livestock, pasture, plantation
	H3: AREAS AROUND OR NEAR HOUSES	backyard, garden, patio
	L: LIFE AND LIVING THINGS	L1/L2 LIFE, LIVING THINGS AND LIVING CREATURES: animal, ape, beaver, bison, dolphin, horse, leopard, otter L3: PLANTS: cedar, elm, flower, fir, grass, leaf, magnolia, tree
	W3: GEOGRAPHICAL TERMS	archipelago, bay, continent, creek, island, lagoon, mountain, peninsula
	W4: WEATHER	breeze, drought, gale, rainstorm, snow, weather, wind, whirlwind
	W5: GREEN ISSUES	conservancy, conservation, deforestation, ecology, ecosystem

The other categories in *USAS* cannot be used to shed light on the artificial-natural divide, at least not without analyzing example by example. Therefore, they are excluded from the discussion of the findings in the next section.

7.4 Results

The results of the two methods described in the previous section, namely a dictionary-based approach and a data-driven approach, are presented separately. The former is the focus of Section 7.4.1, while the latter is dealt with in Section 7.4.2. No statistical tests are conducted in this chapter for two reasons. First, in the dictionary-based approach NFs are displayed and discussed. NFs cannot be the input of statistical tests like chi-square, used in previous analyses (cf. Chapter 4), given that absolute frequencies are required to conduct this type of test. Second, in the data-driven approach the actual number of second-order collocates that are relevant for the natural-artificial divide is rather low in some periods and semantic categories. Data sparseness, as discussed previously in Chapter 4, constitutes a problem for statistical tests. Consequently, the analyses conducted in this chapter are more exploratory in nature than those presented in Chapters 4–6.

7.4.1 Dictionary-based approach

In Figure 29, the mean NFs per million words of the three prototypically artificial semantic categories are shown. It can be clearly observed that CLEANING, COSMETICS, and TEXTILE AND CLOTHING all increase over the period 1820–2009, but more dramatically so at the end of the nineteenth century and the beginning of the twentieth century, coinciding with the moment in time in which the concept PLEASANT SMELLING as a whole becomes more prominent to denote artificial aromas (cf. Section 4.2). The semantic category TEXTILE AND CLOTHING, the most frequent of the three, exhibits a much lower NF in the 1820s than at the end of the period analyzed. Two peaks in frequency are clearly noticeable, one in the 1870s, before the category undergoes a sharp decrease until the 1890s, and another in the 1940s, again previous to a substantial decline taking place between the 1950s and the 1970s. Following the 1970s, the category rises again and reaches another high point in the 2000s. It is perhaps not at all surprising that TEXTILE AND CLOTHING displays a peak in frequency before the turn of the century, increasing progressively from the 1820s onward. This is probably because the manufacturing of textile products, including cotton, was one of the most important activities already during the First Industrial Revolution which took place in the United States in the late eighteenth and early nineteenth centuries (Jones 1996: 117–123). It is not until the Second Industrial Revolution that that industry turned to the production of goods derived from chemicals and petroleum. For this reason, the increase in frequency of CLEANING and COSMETICS does not take place until the late nineteenth or early twentieth centuries, as displayed in Figure 29. In the case of CLEANING, there is a steep increase between the 1890s and the 1910s, after which the category continues rising but in a more gradual manner. The growth in frequency of COSMETICS, in turn, occurs a couple of decades later, namely from the 1910s onwards, reaching a peak in the 1990s. Surprisingly, in the 2000s, there is a drastic decline and the domain falls to frequencies which are similar to those that it showed in the 1820s.⁶² Despite this decline, it is safe to state that the general trend of COSMETICS is similar to those of TEXTILE AND CLOTHING and CLEANING, that is, exhibiting a general increase in frequency over time.

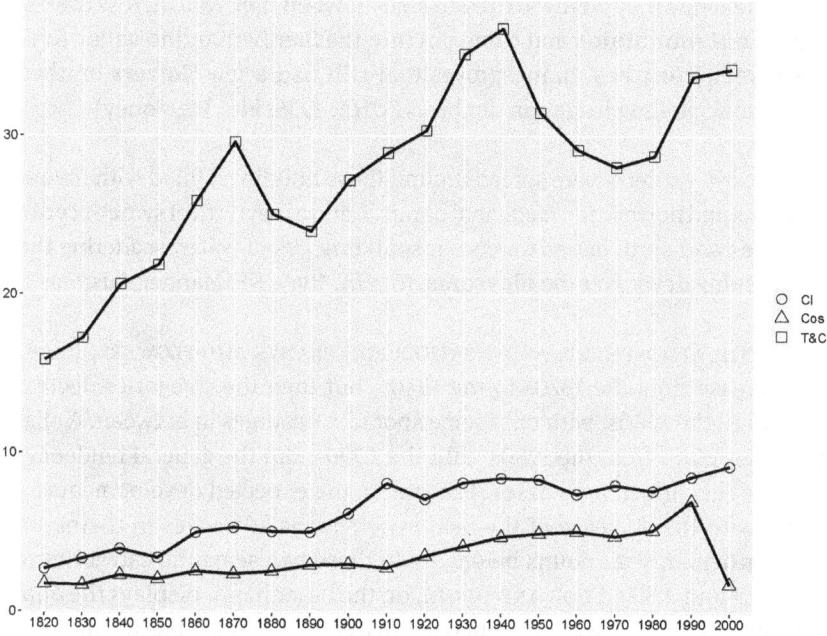

Figure 29: Mean NFs of the prototypically artificial semantic categories (1820s–2000s).

Turning now to Figure 30 and the prototypically natural semantic categories EARTH, ATMOSPHERE, AND WEATHER, FOOD AND DRINK, and PLANTS AND FLOWERS, the first and the last of these domains exhibit comparable developments, which in all likelihood point to the semantic similarity of these two categories, sometimes

---

62 As argued by Schneider (2020: 42), one of the disadvantages of the dictionary-based method is that there are often sharp increases and decreases from one period to the next, especially if one resorts to short time intervals such as years or decades, as is done here. The reason for this, according to Schneider, is that individual words may occur on very few occasions or even fall out of use in a particular year or decade.

overlapping with one another. This is so because, on occasions when some of the nouns in EARTH, ATMOSPHERE, AND WEATHER are referred to (e.g., *forest*, *garden*, *meadow*, and *mountain*), plants and flowers of different kinds are probably included in their denotation, as they are a crucial part of these areas of land. For instance, consider examples (123) and (124) in which *fragrant* and *sweet-scented*, respectively, modify nouns in EARTH, ATMOSPHERE, AND WEATHER (i.e., *mountains* and *groves*), but where several noun collocates belonging to PLANTS AND FLOWERS (i.e., *fruittrees*, *flowers*, and *blossoms*) also occur in the extended context:

(123) The next day they were too tired to enjoy it when they went across the high **fragrant mountains** and came out into the San Bernardino valley full of wellkept **fruittrees**, orangegroves that still had a few **flowers** on them, and coolsmelling irrigation ditches. (*COHA*, 1936, FIC, BigMoney)

(124) Extensive gardens were spread around these buildings, filled with fragrant shrubs and flowers and medicinal plants. Amid a labyrinth of **sweet-scented groves** and shrubberies were seen sparkling jets of water, scattering their refreshing dews over the **blossoms**. (*COHA*, 1849, NF, MannersCustoms)

In both EARTH, ATMOSPHERE, AND WEATHER and PLANTS AND FLOWERS, there is a sharp increase from the 1820s to the 1840s, but then the categories decrease gradually until the 1980s, with only some sporadic upsurges in between. A slight increase takes place from the 1980s until the 2000s, but the general tendency is clearly one of decline in both cases. These were the expected developments and are in line with the decrease of the near-synonymous adjectives in the natural sense, in particular, with nouns belonging to these two semantic categories (cf. Sections 4.2.2 and 4.3.2). FOOD AND DRINK, on the other hand, displays the opposite development, that is, a gradual increase in frequency, much like the prototypically artificial semantic categories in Figure 29. The reader might recall here that in Section 4.2.2, it was pointed out that FOOD AND DRINK was one of the natural semantic categories that did not follow the general downward trend exhibited by the other natural domains when modified by the adjectives. In fact, it was argued in that section that food and drinks have perhaps also been affected by the increased use of chemical compounds, with culinary products being altered through the addition of food coloring, sweeteners, and preservatives, among others. Additionally, *fragrant*, the prototypical adjective to denote natural smells, in fact, went from being used mostly with nouns denoting plants and flowers and other natural phenomena to becoming more and more frequent with food and drink nouns, particularly in Period 4 (i.e., 1960–2009). Therefore, the increase of FOOD AND DRINK also mirrors previous findings described in this monograph.

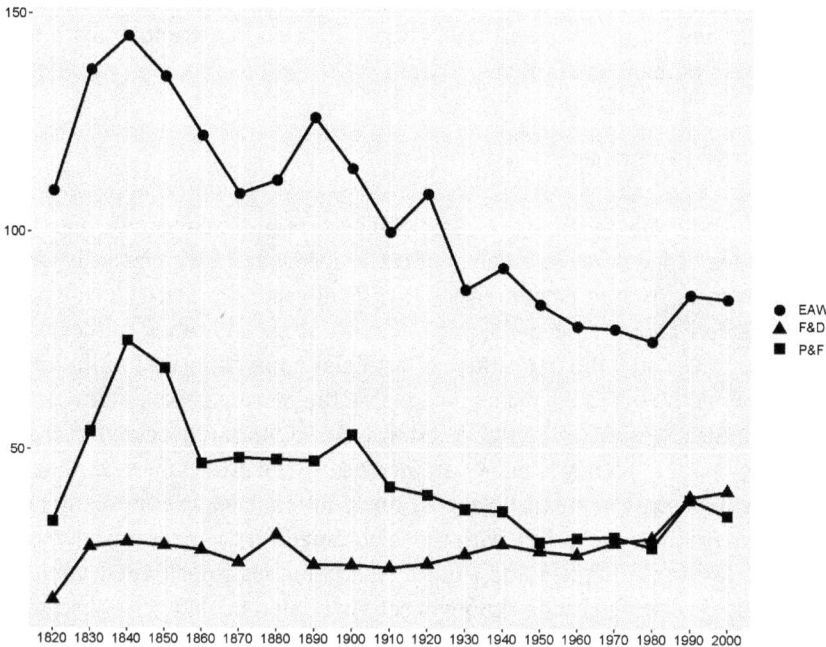

Figure 30: Mean NFs of the prototypically natural semantic categories (1820s–2000s).

In sum, the findings obtained regarding the evolution of the prototypically artificial and natural semantic domains provided in this section point to the existence of a change at the conceptual level in American English, which might well reflect the socio-economic transformations in American society explained in Section 7.2. It is likely that technological and scientific advancements, which increasingly affected and permeated the day-to-day life of American people, implied that the three prototypically artificial semantic domains became more frequent topics of conversation at the expense of the prototypically natural ones, some of which decreased in importance with respect to previous periods. Consequently, it is probably safe to assume that these social, economic, and technological advancements influenced the way in which the concept PLEASANT SMELLING developed over time, from primarily denoting natural smells to also referring frequently to artificial ones.

However, the growing importance of synthetic substances might not be reflected only in the frequency of the semantic domains, but also in the way in which these domains themselves are conceptualized over time, in which case they would be discussed in more 'artificial' terms. This can be investigated by examining the second-order collocates of the adjectives, not only in the prototypically artificial and natural semantic categories, but also in the remaining ones. This is the focus of the next section.

7.4.2 Data-driven approach

Figures 31–33 show the percentage of artificial second-order collocates (i.e., the noun collocates of the noun collocates) of the adjectives in each semantic category. In each category, the percentages of artificial second-order collocates are to be understood against the percentage of natural second-order collocates.[63] For instance, in Period 3 the percentage of artificial noun collocates of the category BODY AND PEOPLE is 53.05, which means that the percentage of natural noun collocates in this category in the same period is 46.95. As can observed in these figures, the general tendency is one of an increase in the artificial sense, that is, most categories become more artificial over time, although some only slightly so. Therefore, the findings are in line with those obtained for the near-synonymous adjectives in previous chapters and support the hypothesis postulated, namely that the changes observed in the synonym set are related to changes in extralinguistic reality.

Focusing first on the three prototypically artificial semantic categories CLEANING, COSMETICS, and TEXTILE AND CLOTHING (cf. Figure 31), no changes are observed in TEXTILE AND CLOTHING, which is overall mostly artificial in all periods, with more than 80% of artificial noun collocates. There is a marginal move towards the artificial end of the semantic continuum, but the picture is still one of stability overall. As concerns CLEANING, the change towards the artificial end of the spectrum is only visible from P2 onwards, because from P1 to P2 there is a decrease in the percentage of artificial collocates with this category. Nevertheless, the change is not considerable, and in general the category remains an artificial one throughout the whole time span analyzed, with around 70% of nouns belonging to artificial semantic classes in *USAS*. The category COSMETICS, in turn, is a particularly interesting case given that it changes dramatically over time. Whereas in P1 and P2, noun collocates mainly belong to natural semantic classes in *USAS*, for instance L2: LIVING CREATURE GENERALLY, L3: PLANTS, W3: GEOGRAPHICAL TERMS, and W4: WEATHER (e.g., *fox*, *feather*, *bloom*, *blossom*, and *creek*), in P3 and P4, more than 60% of collocates belong to artificial classes, particularly B4: CLEANING AND PERSONAL CARE and B5: CLOTHES AND PERSONAL BELONGINGS

---

63 The exact figures of noun collocates in the artificial and natural semantic classes in *USAS* in each period are displayed in Tables 57–67 in the Appendix.

(e.g., *broom*, *brush*, *lipstick*, *mascara*, *clothes*, *dress*, and *handkerchief*). The considerable development undergone by noun collocates in COSMETICS probably corresponds to developments in chemistry that took place primarily during the Second Industrial Revolution. As Wright (2016; 2017) points out, many chemical compounds were produced throughout the nineteenth century and this led to the need to name new perfumes, dyes, and drugs, among other products, that saw the light owing to these newly synthesized smells. To name just a few, coumarin, ionone, and citronellol were compounds that were synthesized in the nineteenth century and which became frequent ingredients in cosmetic products throughout this period (for a more comprehensive list of early synthesized smell compounds, cf. Table 3 in Wright (2016: 17), which is adapted from Sell (2006: 21)).

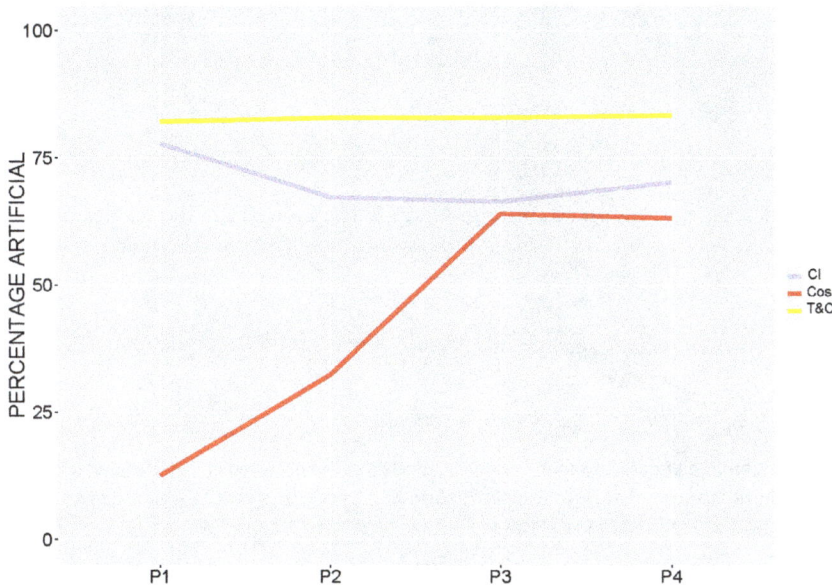

Figure 31: Percentage of artificial second-order collocates in the prototypically artificial semantic categories CLEANING, COSMETICS, and TEXTILE AND CLOTHING.

In the case of the three prototypically natural semantic categories EARTH, ATMOSPHERE, AND WEATHER, FOOD AND DRINK, and PLANTS AND FLOWERS, they all become slightly more artificial over time (cf. Figure 32). However, they still retain their natural character with around 90% or more second-order collocates belonging to natural semantic classes (cf. Tables 60, 61, and 63 in the Appendix), in particular in the *USAS* semantic classes L3: PLANTS, W3: GEOGRAPHICAL TERMS, F1: FOOD, and F2: DRINKS, which is unsurprising given that these are the *USAS* classes to which the second-order collocates themselves belong. In other words, the nouns collocate mostly with other nouns that belong to their category (e.g., a noun such as *blossom* collocates often with the nouns *clover*, *bud*, and *foliage*). The artificial semantic classes of nouns with which the prominent nouns in these three categories collocate more often in later periods are H5: FURNITURE AND HOUSEHOLD FITTINGS in the case of all three and B5: CLOTHES AND PERSONAL BELONGINGS in the case of EARTH, ATMOSPHERE, AND WEATHER and FOOD AND DRINK.

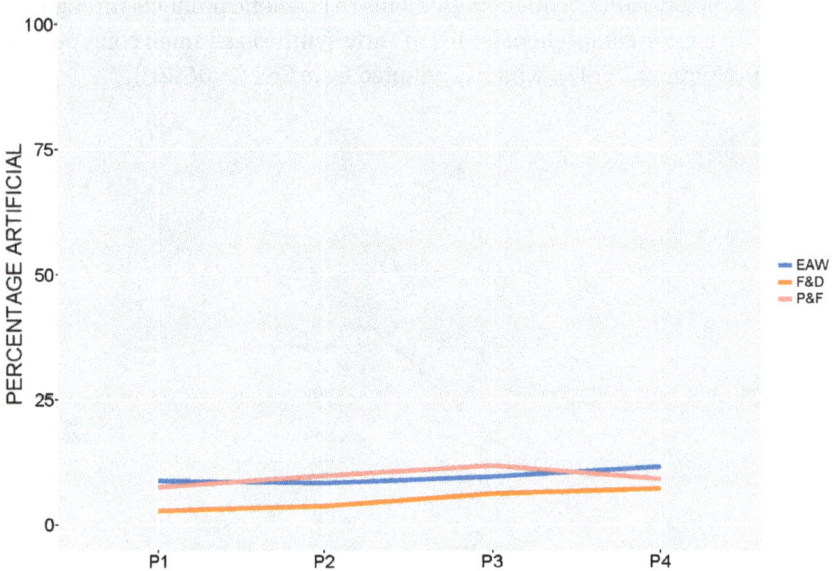

Figure 32: Percentage of natural second-order collocates in the prototypically natural semantic categories EARTH, ATMOSPHERE, AND WEATHER, FOOD AND DRINK, and PLANTS AND FLOWERS.

In the remaining five categories which include examples of the adjectives in both the artificial and natural senses, as well as that labeled indeterminate, several also display an increase with artificial classes of nouns at the end of the period analyzed (cf. Figure 33). BODY AND PEOPLE, SUBSTANCE AND MATERIAL, and SPACE all exhibit considerable changes. The first of these goes from being used almost 55% of the time in P1 with natural classes in *USAS* (e.g., F1: FOOD, L2: ANIMALS, and L3: PLANTS), to collocating in over 60% of the cases with artificial classes in P4. In particular, the rise with artificial classes in *USAS* is located in B3: MEDICINES AND MEDICAL TREATMENT, B4: CLEANING AND PERSONAL CARE, and B5: CLOTHES AND PERSONAL BELONGINGS. This finding seems to support the claim made in Section 4.2.2, namely that the upward tendency of the near-synonymous adjectives with BODY AND PEOPLE nouns is related to the growing use of lotions, perfumes and other cosmetic products that are often applied to the body, among other artificial goods. In the case of both SUBSTANCE AND MATERIAL and SPACE similar developments are observed. This is so because nouns in these two categories go from collocating mostly with natural semantic classes of nouns in P1, with figures amounting to between 60% and 70%, to being used more or less equally frequently with natural and artificial semantic classes of nouns in P4 (cf. Tables 64 and 66 in the Appendix for exact figures). The most prominent noun collocates in SENSATION also become more commonly used with artificial semantic classes in *USAS* over time, but the category still remains being mostly natural in all periods. The increase in the artificial sense is mainly located with B4: CLEANING AND PERSONAL CARE nouns, whereas there is a decrease with nouns in the natural classes L2: LIVING CREATURE GENERALLY, W3: GEOGRAPHICAL TERMS, and W4: WEATHER. Finally, OBJECT is the only category which goes against the general tendency given that the prominent nouns in this category become slightly more common with nouns in natural semantic classes in *USAS*, particularly those belonging to F1: FOOD (e.g., *asparagus*, *biscuit*, *bread*, and *breakfast*). However, the change is not substantial, and OBJECT overall retains its artificial character throughout the whole time span examined, with around 60% of noun collocates belonging to artificial classes.

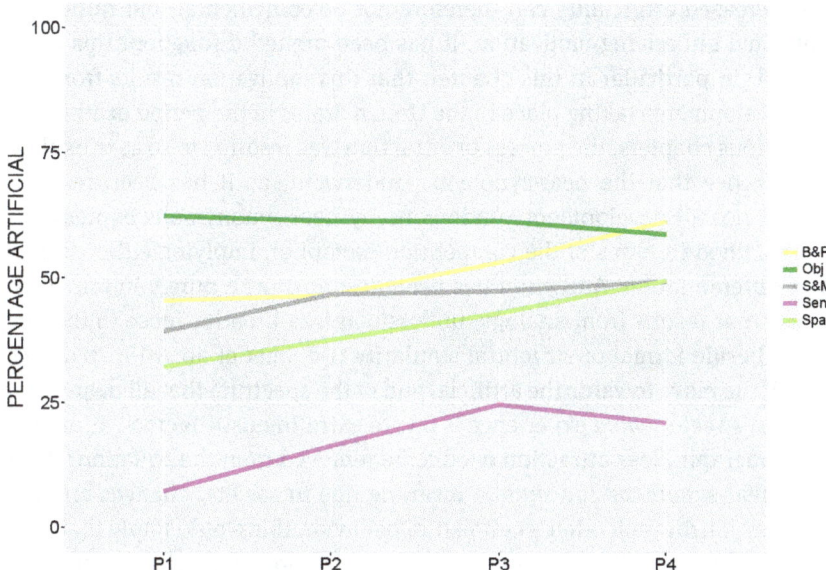

Figure 33: Percentage of artificial second-order collocates in the semantic categories BODY AND PEOPLE, OBJECT, SUBSTANCE AND MATERIAL, SENSATION, and SPACE.

7.5 Discussion

The findings presented in this chapter offer support to the hypothesis that semantic change within the synonym set analyzed in the present monograph is influenced by extralinguistic factors, namely the increased presence of artificial smells in people's daily lives as a result of the modernization of American society. The analyses conducted in Section 7.4.1 showed that the prototypically artificial semantic categories CLEANING, COSMETICS, and TEXTILE AND CLOTHING increased in frequency over time at the expense of two of the prototypically natural ones, namely EARTH, ATMOSPHERE, AND WEATHER and PLANTS AND FLOWERS. In Section 7.4.2., it was shown that extralinguistic factors are not only reflected in the rise and decline of the prototypically artificial and natural semantic categories, respectively, but also in the conceptualization of many of the semantic categories. In fact, out of the eleven semantic categories examined, eight of them clearly become increasingly associated with nouns located towards the artificial end of the continuum. Therefore, overall the findings of the present chapter are in line with those uncovered in previous analyses in this monograph and it appears to be the case that the semantic categories of nouns that the synonymous adjectives collocate with experience a move towards the artificial end of the continuum not only when being modified by the adjectives but in general. This general move towards increased artificiality can therefore not be coincidental, but rather the result of some underlying motivation. It has been argued throughout this monograph and, in particular in this chapter, that this motivation results from the societal developments taking place in the United States in the period examined.

In previous chapters, the process of attraction was resorted to so as to explain the convergence that the near-synonyms underwent, as it has been recently shown that not all developments undergone by near-synonymous expressions can be explained in terms of the competition metaphor, implying either substitution or differentiation. Attraction has been described as a purely intralinguistic process that results from analogy, understood in a broader sense to include functional beside formal or structural similarity (De Smet et al. 2018: 204, 217). However, if the move towards the artificial end of the spectrum that all near-synonyms except *sweet-scented* experience is due to extralinguistic factors, as argued in this monograph, does attraction need to be removed from the equation? After all, if the near-synonyms converge in meaning due to societal changes and not because they mirror each other's contextual behavior, this would imply that they are not really "attracted" to one another, but simply undergoing similar but independent processes which in the end result in semantic and functional convergence. It could of course be the case that both extralinguistic and intralinguistic processes are at work at the same time, in which case attraction could still play a role in the semantic convergence uncovered here. In fact, it was shown in the onomasiological analyses in Section 4.4. and Chapter 5, as well as in the analysis of prominent collocates in Section 6.2.2, that *scented* has come to displace both *fragrant* and *perfumed* in some contexts of use, becoming more frequent in particular semantic categories and more strongly associated with specific noun collocates than the other two adjectives at the end of the period analyzed. For this reason, it was argued that besides attraction, a process of substitution was also ongoing (cf. Section 6.2.2). If only extralinguistic processes were involved and the development of each adjective occurred independently of one another, *scented* would not need to encroach upon the semantic space of the other adjectives. Extralinguistic processes cannot help answering why *scented* is the adjective that gains ground at the expense of the others, and not *fragrant* or *perfumed*. In fact, *perfumed* was the default adjective to denote artificial aromas until the rise of *scented* and therefore we would have expected this adjective to be the one to have risen in frequency and not *scented*. However, *perfumed* does not increase in frequency, but remains rather stable across the period examined (cf. Section 4.1). Therefore, besides extralinguistic factors steering the change, there appear to be also purely intralinguistic developments going on within the synonym set, with a process of ongoing substitution of *fragrant* and *perfumed* by *scented*, and as a consequence, attraction cannot be ruled out entirely. It is worth recalling at this point De Smet et al's (2018: 229) claim that attraction may well be a prerequisite for substitution to occur, since synonyms need to share enough semantic ground for one to replace another.

Disentangling intra- and extralinguistic processes is not a straightforward endeavor because in many cases both types of processes are simultaneously at play and the motivations underlying specific linguistic developments are often multifactorial. A case in point is Brinton's (2020) analysis of the non-inference marker *that is not to say (that)*. Brinton concludes that the diachronic development of this marker constitutes an instance of grammaticalization, as it fulfils many of the criteria for this process (e.g., desemanticization, decategorization, and (inter)subjectification). Nevertheless, she also claims that some of the recent changes of *that is not to say (that)*, namely the loss of the final *that* complementizer and the increase of contracted forms (e.g., *that ain't to say* and *that isn't to say*), could be attributed to a process of colloquialization rather than one of grammaticalization, thus showing a possible interplay between intra- and extralinguistic processes. The concept PLEASANT SMELLING might be in a similar situation, its developments being steered by both intra- and extralinguistic processes.

8 Concluding remarks and suggestions for future research

The semantic relation of synonymy is a topic with a fairly long research tradition in lexical semantics, especially since the structuralist movement brought to the fore a focus on onomasiological structures in the language (cf. Section 1.1). Synonymy, as well as other lexico-semantic relations, was considered by structuralists to be of crucial importance for the delineation of meaning and the organization of lexical knowledge. The perspective adopted by structuralists was paradigmatic in nature, as priority was given to the language system —as opposed to language use— and therefore to the identification of different types of semantic relations existing in language. Neostructuralist approaches, particularly the distributional corpus-based one, moved away from this excessive emphasis on the system to a focus on language use by adopting a syntagmatic perspective. In this way, research on synonymy widened in scope and the interest shifted from the mere classification of semantic relations in general, and types of synonyms in particular, to an in-depth analysis of the factors that determine the choice between near-synonymous expressions. One of the main tenets of distributional semantics was the great importance of collocations in language knowledge and language use. Collocations, in their different forms (e.g., semantic preference and semantic prosody), have been repeatedly found to influence the use of alternative expressions such as near-synonyms and the notion is still widely used in linguistics. In particular, cognitive semantics continued along the lines set out by distributional semantics and largely converged with many of the principal foundations of this neostructuralist approach, mainly due to its strong usage-based orientation. Additionally, research on synonymy within cognitive semantics benefitted from the theoretical apparatus of cognitive linguistics, thus improving the distributional method.

Despite the prominence of synonymy in previous research in the field, both within the (neo)structuralist schools and, more recently, within cognitive semantics, a dimension which has been overlooked is that of the diachronic development of particular sets of lexical near-synonyms (but cf. Section 2.3 for some diachronic approximations). The overarching aim of the present monograph was therefore to partially fill this gap in the specialized literature by analyzing a set of near-synonymous adjectives from the relatively little studied semantic domain of SMELL in nineteenth- and twentieth-century American English, namely, *fragrant, perfumed, scented, sweet-scented,* and *sweet-smelling*, which designate the concept PLEASANT SMELLING. An in-depth description of the semantics of the near-synonyms was provided in Section 3.1 on the basis of both present-day and historical dictionaries and thesauri, followed by an explanation of the data retrieval process (Section 3.2). Drawing on historical data from *COHA*, the main focus was on the contextual behavior of the five selected lexical items, that is, their degree of (dis)similarity was quantified in terms of their distributional patterns operationalized through a series of variables from different linguistic domains —semantic, lexical, morphosyntactic, and stylistic— and levels of granularity —i.e., from more abstract semantic preferences to individual collocates (cf. Section 3.3). To this purpose, state-of-the-art methods used in synchronic corpus-based studies on synonymy were applied to the data in subsequent chapters (cf. Chapters 4–7) and their usefulness for diachronic research on this same phenomenon was tested.

Chapter 4 offered descriptive univariate analyses concerning both the semasiological and the onomasiological structures of the near-synonymous expressions at issue, as well as their overall frequency and frequency development over the time span examined. The results suggested the existence of a large difference between the items in the set in terms of their frequency of use, with one clearly dominant adjective, namely *fragrant*, which accounted for more than half of the total data (cf. Section 4.1). With a frequency of approximately 17% each, *perfumed* and *scented* were ranked second and third in the frequency cline, respectively. Lastly, *sweet-smelling* and *sweet-scented* were far less common in the corpus, each amounting to less than 5% of the data.

Interesting developments over time regarding the frequency of the near-synonyms emerged from the data, given that whereas *fragrant* and *sweet-scented* both decreased significantly from the 1810s to the 2000s, *scented* and *sweet-smelling* increased. In turn, *perfumed* remained relatively stable diachronically. These frequency fluctuations led to a reorganization of the members of the synonym set: although *fragrant* remained the most common adjective throughout the nineteenth and twentieth centuries, *scented* displaced *perfumed* and *sweet-smelling* outperformed *sweet-scented*. Interestingly, the concept PLEASANT SMELLING as a whole, that is, as designated by all five adjectives, decreased considerably in frequency over time, which makes the increase of *scented* and *sweet-smelling* even more striking. The semantics of the concept also exhibited diachronic trends (cf. Section 4.2). Although overall it was used mostly to qualify natural aromas —and the associated semantic categories of nouns—, a shift towards artificial smells was observed, particularly at the turn of the nineteenth to the twentieth century. A hypothesis was put forward in Chapter 4 to explain this diachronic development on the basis of extralinguistic forces, namely the sociocultural and technological transformations experienced by American society following the First and Second Industrial revolutions. In a nutshell, it was argued that the increasing need to refer to artificial —as opposed to natural— smells sprang from the growing availability of synthetic products and goods, as well as from their presence in the daily life of American people. This hypothesis was empirically tested in Chapter 7.

However, one of the main goals of Chapter 4 was to confirm or refute the information provided by the reference material introduced in Section 3.1.2 concerning the semantics of the five near-synonyms. This was done by examining their semasiological structures (cf. Section 4.3). The distribution of each of the synonyms across senses and semantic categories of modified nouns confirmed most of the information available in the reference material, with *perfumed* and *scented* being used more often to qualify artificial aromas, as opposed to the other three adjectives. However, the actual state of affairs was somewhat more nuanced than that represented in the dictionaries consulted. First, although for *fragrant* and *sweet-scented* most dictionaries provided only the general basic sense 'having a sweet pleasant smell', both adjectives were found to be prototypically 'natural', as the great majority of the occurrences of these two adjectives in the corpus corresponded to the natural sense and its associated semantic categories. Second, *sweet-smelling*, although more common also in the natural sense, exhibited a fairly large amount of 'artificial' uses. In addition, although not specified in the dictionaries, important differences regarding the use of the adjectives across semantic categories of modified nouns emerged from the corpus. This finding highlighted valuable usage differences which might have been overlooked if only the sense in which the adjectives are used were considered. For instance, although both *perfumed* and *scented* were common to qualify artificial aromas, the former was more prominent with nouns belonging to the categories BODY AND PEOPLE and TEXTILE AND CLOTHING, while the latter was more prominent with those in the category OBJECT.

As concerns diachronic patterns in semasiological terms, similar trends arose for all adjectives except *sweet-scented*, namely an increase over time in their frequency of use in the artificial sense and most of its corresponding semantic categories. The importance of this finding resided in the fact that, irrespective of their prototypicality, be it natural or artificial, most near-synonyms in the set ended up being more 'artificial' at the end of the time span examined, hence suggesting that these changes are not coincidental, but rather the result of some underlying motivation, which, as suggested in Chapter 4 and further tested in Chapter 7, could be related to language-external forces, in particular the modernization of American society from a preindustrial to a fully industrialized nation.

Finally, a first glimpse into the onomasiological structure of the synonym set was provided by zooming in on the competition between the five semantically related adjectives across senses and semantic categories (cf. Section 4.4). This analysis allowed us to determine which adjectives were the most likely in different contexts of use in comparison with the other members of the set. It was shown that, despite the much higher overall frequency of *fragrant*, this adjective was not the most likely one in the artificial sense and some of its associated semantic categories, where it was outperformed by *perfumed* and/or *scented*. In addition, a change over time in the proportions of use of the near-synonyms in some senses and semantic categories was identified. First, *scented* displaced *perfumed* and, to a certain extent, *fragrant* in several of the 'artificial' semantic categories and, second, in the figurative sense and in indeterminate uses *fragrant* lost its initial clear dominance over time. All this brought about a more balanced distribution of the adjectives at the end of the time span analyzed.

The separate analyses carried out in Chapter 4 offered different but complementary interpretations of the data in as much as the results of one type of analysis aided in the interpretation of other findings. This resulted in a more holistic approach to the study of the five near-synonyms. First, a correlation was observed between the frequency fluctuations of the adjectives and their semasiological salience: the adjectives which decreased in frequency over time were those which were prototypically 'natural' (i.e., *fragrant* and *sweet-scented*), while those that increased (i.e., *scented* and *sweet-smelling*) occupied an intermediate position on the continuum of senses postulated in Section 4.3.3. In turn, *perfumed*, that is, the prototypically 'artificial' adjective, remained relatively stable. Second, the onomasiological analyses uncovered the specific contexts of use in which each of the five adjectives increased and decreased in frequency. For instance, it became clear that *fragrant* decreased primarily in the figurative sense and in indeterminate uses, but also somewhat in the natural sense. On the contrary, the increase of *scented* occurred mainly in the artificial sense and its associated semantic categories, while that of *sweet-smelling* was located mainly in indeterminate uses, particularly with BODY AND PEOPLE nouns. Lastly, the analysis of the concept PLEASANT SMELLING as a whole suggested the existence of some external motivations underlying most of the diachronic trends identified in Chapter 4, namely the increasing tendency to qualify more and more artificial aromas as time passed, a trend which was common to four out of the five adjectives object of study, with the exception of *sweet-scented*.

Chapter 5 delved deeper into the onomasiological organization of the synonym set by analyzing the competition between the three most common adjectives (i.e., *fragrant*, *perfumed*, and *scented*) across a wider range of internal and external variables. To this purpose, a series of multivariate statistical techniques were applied to the data to quantitatively measure the degree of (dis)similarity between the adjectives. The variables included semantic (Sense, Semantic category, Concreteness, and Countability) and non-semantic determinants (Collocate, Degree, and Syntactic function), as well as extralinguistic factors (Period and Text-type). The main goals of this chapter were to determine which variables exerted a stronger influence on the choice between the near-synonyms and to identify in which contexts of use the relation between the three adjectives changed over time. The findings confirmed most of the tendencies uncovered in Chapter 4 regarding the competition between the adjectives across senses and semantic categories, but it also shed new and valuable light on other patterns. All the other semantic and non-semantic linguistic factors played a significant role on the choice between the alternative expressions, but the adjectives did not display diachronic tendencies in any of these contexts of use. The extralinguistic predictor Text-type also affected the alternation between the near-synonymous expressions and, in fact, significant changes over time emerged with respect to this variable, which indicated that the increase of *scented* took place in all text-types, but that it was particularly pronounced in non-fiction.

Although all the variables included in the analyses in Chapter 5 played a significant role on the choice between the adjectives, some of them were found to have a stronger impact. In particular, the semantic variables outperformed all the non-semantic ones except Period, the latter being of crucial importance in the present data. This specific finding was in line with previous research in the field (e.g., Gries 2001; Liu 2010; Liu and Espino 2012), which indicated that semantic factors, particularly those relating to modified nouns, are stronger determinants of the alternation between adjectival near-synonyms. Despite the fact that all variables included in the analyses turned out to be significant, the goodness-of-fit statistics of the multinomial logistic regression models conducted in Section 5.2.1 showed that these predictors were not enough to explain all the variance in the data. The effects of the individual noun collocates of the adjectives were assessed in Section 5.2.2, and the results of these analyses demonstrated that the variable Collocate significantly improved the quality of the models: almost double the amount of variance in the data was explained when this particular predictor was considered, hence proving the great importance of idiosyncratic collocational preferences in lexical choice.

Given that the individual collocates of the adjectives were found to exert such a strong influence on the alternation between *fragrant*, *perfumed*, and *scented*, Chapter 6 set out to examine the collocational preferences of the three adjectives in more detail by means of methods specifically geared towards this type of analysis. First, Section 6.2.1 offered a bird's-eye view of the collocational behavior of the near-synonyms by averaging over all individual collocates. The findings again confirmed many of the tendencies identified on the basis of more schematic semantic preferences (that is, senses and semantic categories): *fragrant* collocated more frequently with nouns located at the natural end of the semantic spectrum, whereas the opposite tendency was observed for *perfumed*. In turn, *scented* occupied an intermediate position, showing no strong association with any of the two senses and thus being more neutral in this respect. The results of Section 6.2.1 also pointed to a similar conclusion regarding the influence of extralinguistic forces on the diachronic evolution of the near-synonymous adjectives as that reached in Chapter 6. The three adjectives were found to co-occur significantly more often with nouns in 'natural' semantic categories in the nineteenth century (i.e., P1 and P2) than in the twentieth century (i.e., P3 and P4). This again seemed to indicate a process of convergence regarding the diachronic patterns of the adjectives, all of them becoming less and less common to denote natural smells as time passed. Second, Section 6.2.2 provided a more qualitative examination of the collocational preferences of the near-synonyms by zooming in on their most prominent noun collocates. The tendencies identified in previous chapters received further support by many of the patterns uncovered by means of this fine-grained qualitative analysis. Nevertheless, by far the most important finding of Section 6.2.2 was that, regardless of any diachronic abstract semantic trends shared by the adjectives, the three of them exhibited rather idiosyncratic collocational behaviors when their most prominent individual collocates were accounted for.

The results of Chapters 4–6 suggested that two diachronic processes were at work in this particular synonym set, namely those of attraction and substitution. As mentioned in Section 2.3, a common assumption in the specialized literature is that languages work against absolute synonymy. In other words, if two or more synonyms come to exist in the language, either they become increasingly differentiated over time, or one or more of them eventually drop out of use. The present study revealed, however, that only the process of substitution seemed to be partially at work in the synonym set object of study, with *scented* increasing in frequency over time, particularly at the expense of *fragrant*, the predominant member of the set. The outcomes of the increases and decreases in frequency of these two adjectives were twofold. First, a much more balanced picture was identified in many of the contexts of use in Present-Day American English, which no longer shows a clearly dominant option. Second, a rearrangement took place concerning the likelihood of the adjectives in some contexts, with *scented* ousting *fragrant* and/or *perfumed* and hence becoming the default option in such cases. Therefore, the development of the near-synonyms cannot be characterized as one of differentiation, since they do not become more dissimilar throughout the period 1810–2009. Rather, the reverse process, namely that of attraction, was observed in the present data, given that all adjectives except *sweet-scented* came to be used more and more frequently in the artificial sense and its associated semantic categories, irrespective of whether they were semasiologically more salient in the natural or in the artificial sense. This finding is in line with recent theories of language change, which claim that attraction is a far more common development than previously assumed (De Smet et al. 2018: 201–202).

Chapter 7 focused on the hypothesis postulated in Chapter 4, namely that extralinguistic developments undergone by American society throughout the First and Second Industrial Revolutions steered many of the semantic changes uncovered in the analyses in Chapters 4–6. In line with recent research which has demonstrated that corpus data can be used to investigate the connection between extra- and intralinguistic changes, the analyses in this chapter resorted to dictionary-based and more data-driven approaches to empirically test the hypothesis previously proposed. The findings showed that not only have the prototypically artificial and natural semantic categories of nouns increased and decreased respectively in frequency over time when collocating with the near-synonymous adjectives, but they have also increased and decreased in general terms. Moreover, by examining the second-order collocates of the adjectives, it was possible to identify that the majority of the semantic categories analyzed in this monograph, not only those which lie more towards the artificial end of the continuum, have become conceptualized in more artificial terms in later periods, thus collocating increasingly more frequently with nouns in artificial semantic domains as time progressed. Consequently, the findings of Chapter 7 provided support to the hypothesis that extralinguistic changes indeed influenced the semantic developments undergone by the near-synonyms and by the concept PLEASANT SMELLING as a whole. The question was raised of whether these extralinguistic forces underlying the change ruled out the intralinguistic process of attraction also playing a role in the reorganization of the concept and the synonyms designating it. It was argued that some of the developments identified, in particular the partial and probably still ongoing substitution of *fragrant* and *perfumed* by *scented*, could not be explained by the changes undergone by American society as a result of the First and Second Industrial Revolutions. Therefore, attraction could not be entirely discarded as one of the forces at play in this particular case. In fact, most lexico-semantic developments, as well as other linguistic changes, are probably multifactorial in nature, with many processes converging —and sometimes also probably conflicting— in one and the same development.

From a theoretical perspective, therefore, the findings of the present work provide further support to the claim that the process of attraction figures more prominently in language change than has been assumed in most previous work on synonymy. This, in turn, implies that the forces behind the diachronic evolution of semantically related words and expressions such as near-synonyms is more complex than originally believed, given that, besides differentiation and substitution, other processes such as attraction and convergence due to extralinguistic forces may be at work. Additionally, the fact that both attraction and substitution seem to be at play in the case of the selected synonym set again corroborates De Smet et al.'s (2018: 229) hypothesis that attraction may well be a prerequisite for substitution to occur, since synonyms need to share enough semantic ground for one to replace another.

From a methodological point of view, the analyses conducted in this monograph show that the methods used in synchronic research on synonymy can be successfully applied to diachronic data. The techniques employed for the analyses of the concept PLEASANT SMELLING uncover insightful diachronic patterns and demonstrate that such methods are not only useful to measure the (dis)similarities between the members of a synonym set at a particular point in time, but also the potential diachronic changes in the use of a given near-synonym in successive periods. Therefore, assuming a historical viewpoint allows for the visualization of the changing relation of an entire set of related words or expressions, hence making it possible to observe potential diachronic rearrangements concerning their frequency and saliency in particular contexts of use. In sum, the present monograph offers a significant methodological contribution by proving the usefulness of big data for diachronic lexico-semantic and lexicological research.

The contributions discussed in the previous paragraphs serve to fill an important gap in the specialized literature on lexical near-synonymy. However, it is necessary to mention some issues that could benefit from further investigation, hence improving and expanding the present piece of research. First of all, the hypothesis put forward regarding the influence of extralinguistic motivations on the diachronic changes observed was tested through two different approaches. Though showing that the hypothesis is on the right track, additional research could help reinforcing the claims made here. One way in which this hypothesis could be further examined is by undertaking a cross-linguistic study of the equivalent terms of *fragrant*, *perfumed*, *scented*, *sweet-scented*, and *sweet-smelling* in other languages spoken in societies which experienced similar sociocultural and technological developments as American society (e.g., Spanish *bienoliente*, *fragante*, *perfumado*, and *odorífero*). If the concept PLEASANT SMELLING and the terms denoting it in other languages follow identical or similar diachronic patterns as those uncovered here and the changes go hand in hand with language-external developments in the technological sphere, this could provide further validation to the hypothesis postulated in the present work. Moreover, the levels of the variable Period used here (i.e., four 50-year periods) could be rearranged to make the time division coincide with changes in the extralinguistic reality that may have affected the evolution of the use of the near-synonyms at issue. For instance, the variable could be modified so that its levels reflect, instead of arbitrary 50-year periods, times of economic growth vs. times of economic recession or other important moments in the history of industrialization and other modernization processes in American society.

In the multivariate analyses in Chapter 5 and 6 it became clear that the number of examples of two of the five near-synonyms, namely *sweet-scented* and *sweet-smelling*, was not enough to warrant their inclusion. This is far from being an extraordinary situation as it in fact reflects the day-to-day of a scholar working with diachronic corpus data: even though *COHA* is one of the largest diachronic corpora available, it is still not always large enough to retrieve sufficient examples of low-frequency items, at least not if one wants to conduct multivariate statistical tests which require sizeable datasets. To overcome this difficulty, it might sometimes be necessary to resort to additional corpora. For instance, a fairly compatible corpus is *COCA*, which covers the time span 1990–2019 and contains data from the same variety of English as *COHA*, as well as from many of the genres featured in the latter corpus (e.g., fiction and magazines). Drawing on *COCA* would allow us to trace the development of the near-synonyms in more contemporary sources and extract a larger amount of data from the 1990s and 2000s. However, *COCA* also contains spoken material and texts from genres not found in *COHA* (e.g., blogs and TV/movies), which would make it difficult to identify whether the (dis)similarities in the use of the adjectival near-synonyms between *COHA* and *COCA* are actual diachronic changes or, on the contrary, respond to stylistic patterns. Besides *COCA*, other diachronic corpora from earlier periods in the history of English could also be used. For instance, *Early English Books Online Corpus 1.0* (*EEBOCorp 1.0*) would enable the analysis of the five near-synonyms examined here in previous stages, thus making it possible to extract a larger number of attestations of these adjectives, but also of other near-synonyms which were not discussed in the present study. As we saw in Section 3.1.2, some of the semantically related adjectives from the same semantic domain (e.g., *balmy, odorous*, and *redolent*) were discarded here due to the fact that in Present-Day English they are no longer used predominantly in the sense 'having a sweet pleasant smell', as they have undergone processes of specialization and pejoration and came to be differentiated from *fragrant, perfumed, scented, sweet-scented*, and *sweet-smelling*. If one goes back to earlier historical periods, it might be worth including a larger set of adjectives from the domain of SMELL to pinpoint when and why they became differentiated from the five lexical items at issue here. An additional advantage of employing a corpus such as *EEBOCorp 1.0* is the fact that several of the adjectives of the synonym set examined in this work, namely, *fragrant, perfumed*, and *scented*, were borrowed into English in the first half of the sixteenth century. Given that this particular corpus goes back to the fifteenth century, it would give us the opportunity to trace the history of this synonym set from the time that it originated in the English language.

Finally, the multinomial regression models carried out in Section 5.2.1 made it evident that if the individual noun collocates of the near-synonyms were not taken into account, the set of language-internal and language-external variables examined in Chapter 5 still left some unexplained variance. It was there argued that enlarging the set of variables to include factors such as priming and *horror aequi*, among others, might alleviate this problem. In addition, a level of co-occurrence which was only briefly touched upon in the analysis of one of the prominent noun collocates of *fragrant*, namely *odor*, is that of semantic prosody and, more generally, connotation. Given that neither the reference material discussed in Section 3.1.2 nor impressionistic observations of the data seem to point to a loss of the positive connotation of the adjectives in the synonym set, semantic prosody was not considered in depth in the present monograph. However, it may be worth examining this issue in more detail, particularly if other adjectives belonging to the same semantic domain are included (e.g., *odorous*). This would allow us to identify whether differences also exist between the near-synonyms as regards this dimension of meaning, which, as has been shown in the specialized literature, often influences lexical choice (cf. Section 2.1). One relatively straightforward way in which the potential effects of semantic prosody could be uncovered is to submit the collocates in a determinate context window of the near-synonyms in the corpus to automatic sentiment analysis using, for instance, software such as *Linguistic Inquiry and Word Count 2015* (Pennebaker et al. 2015). This tool automatically assigns words to one or more grammatical, semantic, and punctuation categories from among 90 different ones (e.g., negative emotion and positive emotion). Therefore, if one near-synonym co-occurs significantly more often with words with a negative connotation than another near-synonym, this may suggest the existence of a difference in semantic prosody between them. Nonetheless, this particular issue as well as those discussed in the previous paragraphs must be left for future research. I hope that the present monograph serves as inspiration for other scholars working in diachronic semantics, especially regarding how big data can be used to shed light on changes in meaning which cannot entirely be uncovered by more traditional philological methods.

List of references and sources

References

Allan, Kathryn. 2014. An inquest into metaphor death: Exploring the loss of literal senses of conceptual metaphors. *Cognitive Semiotics* 5(1–2). 291–311.
Allan, Kathryn. 2015a. Education in the *Historical Thesaurus of the Oxford English Dictionary*. In Jocelyne Daems, Eline Zenner, Kris Heylen, Dirk Speelman & Hubert Cuyckens (eds.), *Change of paradigms – new paradoxes: Recontextualizing language and linguistics* (Applications of Cognitive Linguistics 31), 81–95. Berlin/Boston: De Gruyter Mouton.
Allan, Kathryn. 2015b. Lost in transmission? The sense development of borrowed metaphor. In Javier E. Diaz-Vera (Ed.), *Metaphor and metonymy across time and cultures*: Perspectives on the sociohistorical linguistics of figurative language (Cognitive Linguistics Research 52), 31–50. Berlin/Boston: De Gruyter Mouton.
Allan, Kathryn. 2021. Metaphor, metonymy and polysemy. A historical perspective. In Augusto Soares da Silva (Ed.), *Figurative language – intersubjectivity and usage* (Figurative Thought and Language 11), 287–306. Amsterdam: John Benjamins.
Arppe, Antti. 2002. The usage patterns and selectional preferences of synonyms in a morphologically rich language. In Annie Morin & Pascale Sébillot (eds.), *JADT-2002. 6th international conference on textual data statistical analysis*. Vol. 1, 21–32. Rennes: INRIA.
Arppe, Antti. 2008. *Univariate, bivariate, and multivariate methods in corpus-based lexicography: A study of synonymy*. Helsinki: University of Helsinki dissertation.
Arppe, Antti. 2013. *Polytomous: Polytomous logistic regression for mixed and fixed effects*.
Arppe, Antti & Juhani Järvikivi. 2007. Every method counts: Combining corpus-based and experimental evidence in the study of synonymy. *Linguistic Theory* 3(2). 131–159.
Atkins, Beryl T.S. 1987. Semantic ID tags: Corpus evidence for dictionary senses. In *Proceedings of the third annual conference of the UW centre for the New Oxford English Dictionary*, 17–36. Waterloo: University of Waterloo.
Atkins, Beryl T.S & Beth Levin. 1995. Building on a corpus: A linguistic and lexicographical look at some near-synonyms. *International Journal of Lexicography* 8(2). 85–114.
Baayen, R. Harald. 2008. *Analyzing linguistic data: A practical introduction to statistics using R*. Cambridge/New York: Cambridge University Press.
Bagli, Marco. 2021. *Tastes we live by. The linguistic conceptualization of taste in English* (Applications of Cognitive Linguistics 50). Berlin/Boston: De Gruyter Mouton.
Baker, Paul. 2005. *Public discourses of gay men*. Abington: Routledge.
Baker, Paul. 2011. Times may change but we'll always have money: A corpus driven examination of vocabulary change in four diachronic corpora. *Journal of English Linguistics* 39. 65–88.
Baker, Paul. 2017. *American and British English: Divided by a common language?* Cambridge: Cambridge University Press.
Baldinger, Kurt. 1980. *Semantic theory*. Oxford: Basil Blackwell.
Barton, Kamil. 2020. *MuMIn: Multi-model inference*. https://CRAN.R-project.org/package=MuMIn.
Bates, Douglas, Martin Maechler, Ben Bolker & Steve Walker. 2015. Fitting linear mixed-effects models using lme4. *Journal of Statistical Software* 67(1). 1–48.

Berg, Thomas. 2014. Competition as a unifying concept for the study of language. *The Mental Lexicon* 9(2). 338–370.
Bergenholtz, Henning & Rufus Gouws. 2012. Synonymy and synonyms in Lexicography. *Lexicographica: International Annual for Lexicography* 28(1). 309–336.
Berlin, Brent & Paul Kay. 1969. *Basic color terms: Their universality and evolution*. Berkeley/Los Angeles: University of California Press.
Biber, Douglas, Susan Conrad & Randi Reppen. 1998. *Corpus linguistics: Investigating language structure and use* (Cambridge Approaches to Linguistics). Cambridge: Cambridge University Press.
Biber, Douglas, Stig Johansson, Geoffrey Leech, Susan Conrad & Edward Finegan. 1999. *Longman Grammar of Spoken and Written English*. London: Longman.
Biggam, Carol P. 2012. *The semantics of colour. A historical approach*. Cambridge: Cambridge University Press.
Blank, Andreas. 1999. Why do new meanings occur? A cognitive typology of the motivations for lexical semantic change. In Andreas Blank & Peter Koch (eds.), *Historical semantics and cognition*, 61–89. Berlin/New York: Mouton de Gruyter.
Bolinger, Dwight. 1977. *Meaning and form*. London: Longman.
Bréal, Michel. 1897. *Essai de sémantique: science des significations*. Paris: Hachette.
Brezina, Vaclav, Tony McEnery & Stephen Wattam. 2015. Collocations in context. A new perspective on collocation networks. *International Journal of Corpus Linguistics* 20(2). 139–173.
Brinton, Laurel J. 2020. The development and pragmatic function of a non-inference marker: *That is not to say (that)*. In Paula Rautionaho, Arja Nurmi & Juhani Klemola (eds.), *Corpora and the changing society: Studies in the evolution of English* (Studies in Corpus Linguistics 96), 251–275. Amsterdam/Philadelphia: John Benjamins.
Brinton, Laurel J. & Elizabeth Closs Traugott. 2005. *Lexicalization and language change*. Cambridge/New York: Cambridge University Press.
Brookes, Gavin & David Wright. 2020. From burden to threat: A diachronic study of language ideology and migrant representation in the British Press. In Paula Rautionaho, Arja Nurmi & Juhani Klemola (eds.), *Corpora and the changing society: Studies in the evolution of English* (Studies in Corpus Linguistics 96), 113–140. Amsterdam/Philadelphia: John Benjamins.
Brown, Gillian & George Yule. 1983. *Discourse analysis*. Cambridge/New York: Cambridge University Press.
Brysbaert, Marc, Amy Beth Warriner & Victor Kuperman. 2014. Concreteness rating for 40 thousand generally known English word lemmas. *Behavior Research Methods* 46(3). 904–911.
Bushdid, Caroline, Marcelo O. Magnasco, Leslie B. Vosshall & Asaf Keller. 2014. Humans can discriminate more than 1 trillion olfactory stimuli. *Science* 343(6177): 1370–1372.
Carnoy, Albert. 1927. *La science des mots: Traité de sémantique*. Leuven: Editions Universitas.
Chadwyck Healey Literature Online. 1996–2020. Cambridge: Chadwyck Healey Ltd. (Bell & Howell Information and Learning Company). http://collections.chadwyck.com/marketing/list_of_all.jsp
Chomsky, Noam. 1965. *Aspects of the theory of syntax*. Cambridge, MA: Massachusetts Institute of Technology Press.
Chung, Siaw-Fong. 2011. A corpus-based analysis of "create" and "produce." *Chang Gung Journal of Humanities and Social Sciences* 4(2). 399–425.

Church, Kenneth W., William Gale, Patrick Hanks & Donald Hindle. 1991. Using statistics in lexical analysis. In Uri Zernik (ed.), *Lexical Exploiting On-line resources to build a lexicon*, 115–164. New Jersey, Hove, and London: Lawrence Erlbaum.

Church, Kenneth W., William Gale, Donald Hindle & Rosamund Moon. 1994. Lexical Substitutability. In Beth Levin & Antonio Zampolli (eds.), *Computational approaches to the lexicon*, 153–177. Oxford/New York: Oxford University Press.

Church, Kenneth W. & Patrick Hanks. 1990. Word association norms, mutual information, and lexicography. *Computational Linguistics* 16. 22–29.

Clear, Jeremy. 1993. From Firth principles: computational tools for the study of collocation. In Mona Baker, Gill Francis & Elena Tognini-Bonelli (eds.), *Text and Technology: In honour of John Sinclair*, 271–292. Amsterdam: John Benjamins.

Cole, Peter & Jerry Morgan (eds.). 1975. *Syntax and semantics, Vol 3: Speech acts*. New York: Academic Press.

Croft, William. 2000. *Explaining language change. An evolutionary approach*. Essex: Pearson Education.

Cruse, D. Alan. 1986. *Lexical semantics*. Cambridge: Cambridge University Press.

Cruse, D. Alan. 2000. *Meaning in language: An introduction to semantics and pragmatics*. Oxford/New York: Oxford University Press.

Cruse, D. Alan. 2002. Paradigmatic relations of inclusion and identity III: Synonymy. In D. Alan Cruse, Franz Hundsnurcher, Michael Job & Peter Wolf Lutzeier (eds.), *Lexicology. An international handbook on the nature and structure of words and vocabularies*, 485–497. Berlin: Mouton.

Culy, Christopher. 1996. Null objects in English recipes. *Language Variation and Change* 8(1). 91–124.

Davies, Mark. 2012. Expanding horizons in historical linguistics with the 400-million word Corpus of Historical American English. *Corpora* 7(2). 121–157.

Davies, Mark. 2013. *Corpus of News on the Web (NOW)*: +3 Billion words from 20 countries, updated every day <https://corpus.byu.edu/now/>.

Davies, Mark. 2019. Corpus-based studies of lexical and semantic variation: The importance of both corpus size and corpus design. In Carla Suhr, Terttu Nevalainen & Irma Taavitsainen (eds.), *From data to evidence in English language research* (Language and Computers: Studies in Digital Linguistics 83), 29–65. Leiden/Boston: Brill.

De Smet, Henrik, Frauke D'hoedt, Lauren Fonteyn & Kristel Van Goethem. 2018. The changing functions of competing forms: Attraction and differentiation. *Cognitive Linguistics* 29(2). 197–234.

Desagulier, Guillaume. 2014. Visualizing distances in a set of near-synonyms: *rather, quite, fairly*, and *pretty*. In Dylan Glynn & Justyna A. Robinson (eds.), *Corpus methods for semantics. Quantitative studies in polysemy and synonymy*, 145–178. Amsterdam/Philadelphia: John Benjamins.

Desagulier, Guillaume. 2017. *Corpus linguistics and statistics with R: Introduction to quantitative methods in linguistics*. Cham: Springer.

Digonnet, Rémi. 2018. The linguistic expression of smells: from lack to abundance. In Annalisa Baicchi, Rémi Digonnet & Jodi. L Sandford (eds.), *Sensory perceptions in language, embodiment and epistemology*, 177–192. Cham: Springer.

Divjak, Dagmar. 2006. Ways of intending: Delineating and structuring near synonyms. In Stefan Th. Gries & Anatol Stefanowitsch (eds.), *Corpora in cognitive linguistics: Corpus-based approaches to syntax and lexis*, 19–56. Berlin/New York: Mouton de Gruyter.

Divjak, Dagmar. 2010. *Structuring the lexicon: A clustered model for near-synonymy*. Berlin/New York: Mouton de Gruyter.

Divjak, Dagmar & Stefan Th. Gries. 2006. Ways of trying in Russian: Clustering behavioral profiles. *Corpus Linguistics and Linguistic Theory* 2(1). 23–60. https://doi.org10.1515/CLLT.2006.002.

Divjak, Dagmar & Stefan Th. Gries. 2008. Clusters in the mind? Converging evidence from near synonymy in Russian. *The Mental Lexicon* 3(2). 188–213. doi:doi:10.1075/ml.3.2.03div.

Durkin, Philip. 2009. *The Oxford guide to etymology*. Oxford: Oxford University Press.

Durkin, Philip. 2014. *Borrowed words: A history of loanwords in English*. Oxford: Oxford University Press.

Durkin, Philip & Kathryn Allan. 2016. Borrowing and copy: A philological approach to Early Modern English lexicology. In Anita Auer, Victorina González-Díaz, Jane Hodson & Violeta Sotirova (eds.), *Linguistics and Literary History. In honour of Sylvia Adamson*, 71–86. Amsterdam/Philadelphia: John Benjamins.

Early English Books Online. Chadwyck Healey. 2003–2020. Available at: http://eebo.chadwyck.com/home.

Edmonds, Philip. 1999. *Semantic representations of near-synonyms for automatic lexical choice*. Toronto: University of Toronto dissertation.

Edmonds, Philip & Graeme Hirst. 2002. Near-Synonymy and Lexical Choice. *Computational Linguistics* 28(2). 105–144.

Erdmann, Karl-Otto. 1910. *Die Bedeutung des Wortes: Aufsätze aus dem Grenzgebiet der Sprachpsychologie und Logik*. Leipzig: Avenarius.

Evert, Stefan. 2005. *The statistics of word cooccurrences: Word pairs and collocations*. Stuttgart: University of Stuttgart dissertation.

Fillmore, Charles J. 1968. The case for case. In Emmon Bach & Robert Thomas Harms (eds.), *Universals in Linguistic Theory*, 1–88. New York: Holt Rinehart & Winston.

Firth, John R. 1935. The technique of semantics. *Transactions of the Philological Society* 36–72.

Firth, John R. 1957. A synopsis of linguistic theory 1930–1955. In John R. Firth (ed.), *Studies in linguistic analysis*, 1–32. Oxford: Philological Society.

Gablasova, Dana, Vaclav Brezina & Tony McEnery. 2017. Collocations in corpus-based language learning research: Identifying, comparing, and interpreting the evidence. *Language Learning* 67. 155–179.

Gabrielatos, Costas & Paul Baker. 2008. Fleeing, sneaking, flooding: A corpus analysis of discursive constructions of refugees and asylum seekers in the UK press 1996–2005. *Journal of English Linguistics* 36(1). 5–38.

Geeraerts, Dirk. 1986. On necessary and sufficient conditions. *Journal of Semantics* 5(4). 275–291.

Geeraerts, Dirk. 1988. Where does prototypicality come from? In Brygida Rudzka-Ostyn (ed.), *Topics in Cognitive Linguistics*, 207–229. Amsterdam/Philadelphia: John Benjamins.

Geeraerts, Dirk. 1997. *Diachronic prototype semantics*. Oxford: Clarendon Press.

Geeraerts, Dirk. 2006. Prototype theory. In Dirk Geeraerts (ed.), *Cognitive Linguistics: Basic readings*, 141–165. Berlin: Mouton de Gruyter.

Geeraerts, Dirk. 2010. *Theories of lexical semantics*. Oxford: Oxford University Press.

Goossens, Louis. 1990. Metaphtonymy: The interaction of metaphor and metonymy in expressions for linguistic action. *Cognitive Linguistics* 1(3). 323–340.

Greenfield, Patricia M. 2013. The changing psychology of culture from 1800 through 2000. *Psychological Science* 24. 1722–1731.

Gries, Stefan Th. 2001. A corpus-linguistic analysis of English *-ic* vs *-ical* adjectives. *ICAME Journal* 25. 65–108.
Gries, Stefan Th. 2003. Testing the sub-test: An analysis of *-ic* and *-ical* adjectives. *International Journal of Corpus Linguistics* 8(1). 31–60.
Gries, Stefan Th. 2005. Syntactic priming: A corpus-based approach. *Journal of Psycholinguistic Research* 34(4). 365–399.
Gries, Stefan Th. 2010. Behavioral profiles: A fine-grained and quantitative approach in corpus-based lexical semantics. *The Mental Lexicon* 5(3). 323–346.
Gries, Stefan Th. 2013. 50-something years of work on collocations: what is or should be next. *International Journal of Corpus Linguistics* 18(1). 137–166.
Gries, Stefan Th. & Dagmar Divjak. 2009. Behavioral profiles: A corpus-based approach to cognitive semantic analysis. In Vyvyan Evans & Stéphanie Pourcel (eds.), *New directions in cognitive linguistics*. Amsterdam/Philadelphia: John Benjamins.
Gries, Stefan Th. & Naoki Otani. 2010. Behavioral profiles: corpus-based perspective on synonymy and antonymy. *ICAME Journal* 34. 121–150.
Grondelaers, Stefan & Dirk Geeraerts. 2003. Towards a pragmatic model of cognitive onomasiology. In Hubert Cuyckens, René Dirven & John R. Taylor (eds.), *Cognitive approaches to lexical semantics*, 66–92. Berlin: Mouton de Gruyter.
Grondelaers, Stefan, Dirk Speelman & Dirk Geeraerts. 2007. Lexical variation and change. *The Oxford Handbook of Cognitive Linguistics*, 988–1011. Oxford/New York: Oxford University Press.
Hanks, Patrick. 1996. Contextual dependency and lexical sets. *International Journal of Corpus Linguistics* 1. 75–98.
Hanks, Patrick. 2013. *Lexical analysis: Norms and exploitations*. Cambridge, MA: The MIT Press.
Heylen, Kris, Yves Peirsman, Dirk Geeraerts & Dirk Speelman. 2008. Modelling word similarity: An evaluation of automatic synonymy extraction algorithms. In Nicoletta Calzolari, Khalid Choukri, Bente Maegaard, Joseph Mariani, Jan Odijk, Stelios Piperidis & Daniel Tapias (eds.), *Proceedings of the sixth International conference on language resources and evaluation*, 3243–3249. Marrakech: European Language Resource Association.
Heylen, Kris, Dirk Speelman & Dirk Geeraerts. 2012. Looking at word meaning. An interactive visualization of semantic vector spaces for dutch synsets. In *Proceedings of the EACL-2012 joint workshop of LINGVIS & UNCLH: Visualization of language patterns and uncovering language history from multilingual resources*, 16–24. Stroudsburg: Association for Computational Linguistics.
Heylen, Kris, Thomas Wielfaert, Dirk Speelman & Dirk Geeraerts. 2015. Monitoring polysemy: Word space models as a tool for large-scale lexical semantic analysis. *Lingua* 157. 153–172.
Hilpert, Martin. 2011. Dynamic visualizations of language change: Motion charts on the basis of bivariate and multivariate data from diachronic corpora. *International Journal of Corpus Linguistics* 16(4). 435–461.
Hilpert, Martin. 2013. *Constructional change in English: Developments in allomorphy, word formation, and syntax*. Cambridge: Cambridge University Press.
Hilpert, Martin. 2016. Change in modal meanings: Another look at the shifting collocates of *may*. *Constructions and Frames* 8(1). 66–85.
Hilpert, Martin. 2020. The great temptation: What diachronic corpora do and do not reveal about social change. In Paula Rautionaho, Arja Nurmi & Juhani Klemola (eds.), *Corpora and the changing society: Studies in the evolution of English* (Studies in Corpus Linguistics 96), 3–27. Amsterdam/Philadelphia: John Benjamins.

Hilpert, Martin. 2021. Differentiation and attraction in constructional change. In Martin Hilpert (ed.), *Ten lectures on diachronic construction grammar* (Distinguished Lectures in Cognitive Linguistics 26), 174–198. Leiden: Brill.
Hilpert, Martin & David Correia Saavedra. 2020. Using token-based semantic vector spaces for corpus-linguistic analyses: From practical applications to tests of theoretical claims. *Corpus Linguistics and Linguistic Theory* 16(2). 393–424.
Hilpert, Martin & Susanne Flach. 2021. Disentangling modal meanings with distributional semantics. *Digital Scholarship in the Humanities* 36(2). 307–321.
Hoey, Michael. 1991. *Patterns of lexis in text*. Oxford: Oxford University Press.
Hoffmann, Sebastian. 2004. Using the *OED* quotations database as a corpus – a linguistic appraisal. *ICAME Journal* 28. 17–30.
Hopper, Paul J. & Elizabeth Traugott. 2003. *Grammaticalization* (Cambridge Textbooks in Linguistics). 2nd edn. Cambridge: Cambridge University Press.
Hothorn, Torsten, Peter Buehlmann, Sandrine Dudoit, Annette Molinaro & Mark Van Der Laan. 2006. Survival ensembles. *Biostatistics* 7(3). 355–373.
Huddleston, Rodney, Geoffrey Pullum, Laurie Bauer, Betty Birner, Ted Briscoe, Peter Collins, David Denison, et al. 2002. *The Cambridge grammar of the English language*. Cambridge/New York: Cambridge University Press.
Ibarretxe-Antuñano, Iraide. 1996. Semantic extensions in the sense of smell. *Anuario del Seminario de Filología Vasca 'Julio de Urquijo'* XXX (2). 631–643.
Ibarretxe-Antuñano, Iraide. 1999. Metaphorical mappings in the sense of smell. In Raymond W. Gibbs Jr. & Gerard J. Steen (eds.), *Metaphor in cognitive linguistics*, 29–45. Amsterdam/Philadelphia: John Benjamins.
Inkpen, Diana & Graeme Hirst. 2006. Building and using a lexical knowledge base of near-synonym differences. *Computational Linguistics* 32(2). 223–262.
Jackson, Howard. 1988. *Words and their meanings*. London: Longman.
Jansegers, Marlies & Stefan Th. Gries. 2020. Towards a dynamic behavioral profile: A diachronic study of polysemous *sentir* in Spanish. *Corpus Linguistics and Linguistic Theory* 16 (1). 145–187.
Jędrzejowski, Łukasz & Przemysaw Staniewski. 2020. *The linguistics of olfaction. Typological and diachronic approaches to synchronic diversity* (Typological Studies in Language 131). Amsterdam/Philadelphia: John Benjamins.
Jędrzejowski, Łukasz & Przemysaw Staniewski. 2020. Rendering what the nose perceives: An Introduction. In Łukasz Jędrzejowski & Przemysaw Staniewski (eds.), *The linguistics of olfaction. Typological and diachronic approaches to synchronic diversity* (Typological Studies in Language 131), 1–34. Amsterdam/Philadelphia: John Benjamins.
Johnson, Paul. 1997. *A history of the American people*. New York: Harper Collins.
Jones, Maldwyn A. 1996. *Historia de Estados Unidos 1607–1992*. Translated by Carmen Martínez Gimeno. Madrid: Cátedra.
Kaunisto, Mark. 2001. Nobility in the history of adjectives ending in *-ic* and *-ical*. In Ruth Brend, Alan K. Melby & Arle R. Lommel (eds.), *LACUS Forum XXVII: Speaking and comprehending*, 35–46. Fullerton: LACUS.
Kay, Christian. 2010. What is the *Historical Thesaurus of the OED*? In *Oxford English Dictionary*. Oxford: Oxford University Press. https://www.oed.com/public/whatishtoed/what-is-the-historical-thesaurus/loginpage (24 April, 2020).

Kay, Christian. 2012. Developing *The Historical Thesaurus of the OED*. In Kathryn Allan & Justyna A. Robinson (eds.), *Current methods in historical semantics*, 41–58. Berlin/Boston: De Gruyter Mouton.

Kay, Christian & Kathryn Allan. 2015. *English historical semantics*. Edinburgh: Edinburgh University Press.

Kennedy, Graeme. 1991. *Between* and *through*: The company they keep and the function they serve. In Karin Aijmer & Bengt Altenberg (eds.), *English corpus linguistics: Studies in honour of Jan Svartvik*, 95–110. London: Longman.

Kjellmer, Göran. 2003. Synonymy and corpus work: On *almost* and *nearly*. *ICAME Journal* 27. 19–27.

Klenová, Dominika. 2010. *The language of cookbooks and recipes*. Brno: Masaryk University MA thesis.

Kornexl, Lucia & Ursula Lenker. 2011. Culinary and other pairs: Lexical borrowing and conceptual differentiation in Early English food terminology. In Renate Bauer & Ulrike Krischke (eds.), *More than words: English lexicography and lexicology – past and present – Essays presented to Hans Sauer on the occasion of his 65th birthday – Part I*, 179–206. Frankfurt am Main: Peter Lang.

Kövecses, Zoltan. 2010. *Metaphor: A practical introduction*. Oxford: Oxford University Press.

Kövecses, Zoltan. 2019. Perception and metaphor: The case of smell. In Laura J. Speed, Carolyn O'Meara, lila San Roque & Asifa Majid (eds), *Perception Metaphors*, 327–346. Amsterdam/Philadelphia: John Benjamins.

Krawczak, Karolina. 2014. *Shame* and its near-synonyms in English: A multivariate corpus-driven approach to social emotions. In Iva Novakova, Peter Blumenthal & Dirk Siepmann (eds.), *Les émotions dans le discourse / Emotions in discourse*, 83–94. Frankfurt am Main: Peter lang.

Krawczak, Karolina. 2018. Reconstructing social emotions across languages and cultures: A multifactorial account of the adjectival profiling of SHAME in English, French and Polish. *Review of Cognitive Linguistics* 16(2). 455–493.

Kruskal, Joseph B. & Myron Wish. 1978. *Quantitative applications in the social sciences: Multidimensional scaling*. Thousand Oaks, CA: SAGE Publications.

Lakoff, George. 1970. Linguistics and natural logic. *Synthese* 22. 151–271.

Lakoff, George. 1993. The contemporary theory of metaphor. In Andrew Ortony (ed.), *Metaphor and thought*, 202–251. 2nd edn. Cambridge: Cambridge University Press.

Lakoff, George & Mark Johnson. 2003. *Metaphors we live by*. Chicago/London: The University of Chicago Press.

Landes, Shari, Claudia Leacock & Christiane Fellbaum. 1998. Building semantic concordances. In Christiane Fellbaum (ed.), *WordNet: An electronic lexical database*, 199–216. Cambridge, MA: Massachusetts Institute of Technology Press.

Langacker, Ronald W. 1987. *Foundations of cognitive grammar. Theoretical prerequisites*. Vol. 1. Stanford CA: Stanford University Press.

Leech, Geoffrey. 1974. *Semantics: The study of meaning*. 2nd edn. London: Penguin Books.

Leech, Geoffrey & Roger Fallon. 1992. Computer corpora – what do they tell us about culture? *ICAME Journal* 16. 29–50.

Lehrer, Adrienne. 1969. Semantic cuisine. *Journal of Linguistics* 5. 39–55.

Lehrer, Adrienne. 1974. *Semantic fields and lexical structure*. Amsterdam/London: North Holland.

Leith, Dick. 1983. *A social history of English*. London/Boston: Routledge & Kegan Paul.

Levshina, Natalia. 2011. Doe wat je niet laten kan: *A usage-based analysis of Dutch causative constructions*. Leuven: KU Leuven dissertation.
Levshina, Natalia. 2015. *How to do linguistics with R: Data exploration and statistical analysis*. Amsterdam/Philadelphia: John Benjamins.
Lewandowska-Tomaszcyk, Barbara. 2007. Polysemy, prototypes, and radial categories. In Dirk Geeraerts & Hubert Cuyckens (eds.), *The Oxford Handbook of Cognitive Linguistics*, 139–169. Oxford/New York: Oxford University Press.
Liu, Dilin. 2010. Is it a *chief, main, major, primary* or *principal concern*? A corpus-based behavioral profile study of the near-synonyms. *International Journal of Corpus Linguistics* 15(1). 56–87. doi:10.1075/ijcl.15.1.03liu.
Liu, Dilin. 2013. Salience and construal in the use of synonymy: A study of two sets of near-synonymous nouns. *Cognitive Linguistics* 24(1). 67–113.
Liu, Dilin & Maggie Espino. 2012. *Actually, genuinely, really*, and *truly*. A corpus-based behavioral profile study of the near-synonymous adverbs. *International Journal of Corpus Linguistics* 17. 198–228. https://doi.orgdoi:10.1075/ijcl.17.2.03liu.
Liu, Dilin & Shouman Zong. 2016. L2 vs L1 use of synonymy: An empirical study of synonym use/acquisition. *Applied Linguistics* 37(2). 239–261.
Lyons, John. 1963. *Structural semantics*. Oxford: Blackwell.
Lyons, John. 1968. *Introduction to theoretical linguistics*. Cambridge: Cambridge University Press.
Lyons, John. 1977. *Semantics*. Cambridge: Cambridge University Press.
Lyons, John. 1981a. *Language and linguistics*. Cambridge: Cambridge University Press.
Lyons, John. 1981b. *language, meaning, and context*. Bungay: Fontana.
Lyons, John. 1995. *Linguistic semantics*. Cambridge: Cambridge University Press.
MacLaury, Robert E. 1997. *Color and cognition in Mesoamerica: Constructing categories as vantages*. Austin: Texas University Press.
Majid, Asifa & Niclas Burenhult. 2014. Odors are expressible in language, as long as you speak the right language. *Cognition* 130(2). 266–270.
Martin, Marylin. 1984. Advanced vocabulary teaching: The problem of synonyms. *The Modern Language Journal* 68(2). 130–137.
McEnery, Tony. 2006a. *Swearing in English: Bad language, purity and power from 1586 to the present*. Abington: Routledge.
McEnery, Tony. 2006b. The moral panic about bad language in England, 1691–1745. *Journal of Historical Pragmatics* 7(1). 89–113.
McEnery, Tony & Helen Baker. 2017. *Corpus linguistics and 17th-century prostitution: Computational linguistics and history*. London: Bloomsbury Academic.
McGann, John P. 2017. Poor olfaction is a 19th-century myth. *Science* 356 (6338):eaam7263. https://doi.org/10.1126/science.aam7263
Miller, George A. & Walter G. Charles. 1991. Contextual correlates of semantic similarity. *Language and Cognitive Processes* 6(1). 1–28.
Mondorf, Britta. 2010. Variation and change in English resultative constructions. *Language Variation and Change* 22(3). 397–421.
Murphy, M. Lynne. 2003. *Semantic relations and the lexicon: Antonymy, synonymy, and other paradigms*. Cambridge: Cambridge University Press.
Murphy, M. Lynne. 2013. What we talk about when we talk about synonyms (and what it can tell us about thesauruses). *International Journal of Lexicography* 26(3). 279–304.

Nuyts, Jan & Pieter Byloo. 2015. Competing modals: Beyond (inter)subjectification. *Diachronica* 32(1). 34–68. https://doi.org10.1075/dia.32.1.02nuy.

Nyrop, Kristoffer. 1913. *Grammaire historique de la langue française IV: Sémantique.* Copenhagen: Gyldendalske Boghandel Nordisk Forlag.

Oakes, Michael P. 2003. Contrasts between US and British English in the 1991. In Elzbieta H. Oleksy & Barbara Lewandowska-Tomaszcyk (eds.), *Research and scholarship in integration processes*, 213–222. Lódz: Lódz University Press.

Padó, Sebastian & Mirella Lapata. 2007. Dependency-based construction of Semantic Space Models. *Computational Linguistics* 33(2). 161–199.

Panther, Klaus-Uwe & Günther Radden. 1999. *Metonymy in language and thought.* Amsterdam: John Benjamins.

Partington, Alan. 1998. *Patterns and meanings: Using corpora for English language research and teaching* (Studies in Corpus Linguistics). Amsterdam/Philadelphia: John Benjamins.

Paul, Hermann. 1920. *Prinzipien der Sprachgeschichte.* Halle: Niemeyer.

Peirsman, Yves, Kris Heylen & Dirk Geeraerts. 2008. Size matters. Tight and loose context definitions in English word space models. In Marco Baroni, Stefan Evert & Alessandro Lenci (eds.), *Proceedings of the ESSLLI workshop on distributional lexical semantics: Bridging the gap between semantic theory and computational linguistics*, 34–41. Hamburg.

Pennebaker, James W., Roger J. Booth, Ryan L. Boyd & Martha E. Francis. 2015. *Linguistic Inquiry and Word Count: LIWC2015.* Austin: Pennebaker Conglomerates. https://liwc.wpengine.com/.

Persson, Gunnar. 1989. Deep *and* profound: *A study in so-called synonymy.* Umeå: Printing office of Umeå University.

Pettersson-Traba, Daniela. 2019. Measuring semantic distance across time: An analysis of the collocational profiles of a set of near-synonyms in American English. *Journal of Research Design and Statistics in Linguistics and Communication Science* 6(2). 138–165.

Pettersson-Traba, Daniela. 2021. A diachronic perspective on near-synonymy: The concept of sweet-smelling in American English. *Corpus Linguistics and Linguistic Theory* 17(2). 319–349.

Phillips, Martin. 1985. *Aspects of text structure: An investigation of the lexical organisation of text.* Amsterdam: North-Holland.

Phillips, Martin. 1989. *Lexical structure of text* (Discourse Analysis Monograph). Vol. 12. Birmingham: University of Birmingham.

Potts, Amanda & Paul Baker. 2012. Does semantic tagging identify cultural change in British and American English? *International Journal of Corpus Linguistics* 17(3). 295–324.

Primahadi-Wijaya-R, Gede & I Made Rajeg. 2014. Visualising diachronic change in the collocational profiles of lexical near-synonyms. In I Nengah Sudipa & Gede Primahadi-Wijaya-R (eds.), *Cahaya bahasa: A Festschrift in honour of Prof. I Gusti Made Sutjaja*, 247–258. Denpasar: Swasta Nulus.

Quirk, Randolph, Sydney Greenbaum, Geoffrey Leech & Jan Svartvik. 1985. *A comprehensive grammar of the English language.* London/New York: Longman.

R Core Team. 2017. *R: A language and environment for statistical computing.* Vienna: R Foundation for Statistical Computing. https://www.R-project.org/.

Ratia, Maura. 2020. Finding evidence for a changing society: A collocational study of medical discourse in 1500–1800. In Paula Rautionaho, Arja Nurmi & Juhani Klemola (eds.), *Corpora and the changing society: Studies in the evolution of English* (Studies in Corpus Linguistics 96), 57–78. Amsterdam/Philadelphia: John Benjamins.

Rautionaho, Paula, Arja Nurmi & Juhani Klemola (eds.). 2020. *Corpora and the changing society: Studies in the evolution of English* (Studies in Corpus Linguistics 96). Amsterdam/Philadelphia: John Benjamins.

Renouf, Antoinette. 2019. Big data: Opportunities and challenges for English corpus linguistic. In Carla Suhr, Terttu Nevalainen & Irma Taavitsainen (eds.), *From data to evidence in English language research* (Language and Computers: Studies in Digital Linguistics 83), 29–65. Leiden/Boston: Brill.

Renouf, Antoinette. 2020. Semantic neology: Challenges in matching corpus-based semantic change to real-world change. In Paula Rautionaho, Arja Nurmi & Juhani Klemola (eds.), *Corpora and the changing society: Studies in the evolution of English* (Studies in Corpus Linguistics 96), 79–112. Amsterdam/Philadelphia: John Benjamins.

Rohdenburg, Günter. 2003. Cognitive complexity and horror aequi as factors determining the use of interrogative clause linkers in English. In Günter Rohdenburg & Britta Mondorf (eds.), *Determinants of grammatical variation in English* (Topics in English Linguistics 43), 205–249. Berlin/New York: Mouton de Gruyter.

Rosch, Eleanor. 1973. Natural categories. *Cognitive Psychology* 4. 328–350.

Rosenbach, Anette. 2008. Animacy and grammatical variation – Findings from English dative variation. *Lingua* 118. 151–171.

Rubenstein, Herbert & John B. Goodenough. 1965. Contextual correlates of synonymy. *Communications of the ACM* 8(10). 627–633.

Sahlgren, Magnus. 2006. *The word-space model. Using distributional analysis to represent syntagmatic and paradigmatic relations between words in high-dimensional vector spaces*. Stockholm: Stockholm University dissertation.

Samuels, Michael L. 1972. *Linguistic evolution with special reference to English*. London/New York: Cambridge University Press.

Sandford, Jodi L. 2016. Color entrenchment in middle-school English speakers: Cognitive Salience Index applied to color listing. *Folklore: Electronic Journal of Folklore* 64. 91–108.

Sandford, Jodi. L. 2018. Redder than red, and turning redder. Color term form and conceptualisation in English. In Dorota Gonigroszek (ed.), *Discourse on Colour*, 61–96. Poland: Uniwersytet Jana Kochanowskiego w Keilcach.

Sandford, Jodi L. 2021. *The sense of color: A cognitive linguistic analysis of color words*. Perugia: Aguaplano.

Saussure, Ferdinand de. 1916. *Course in general linguistics*. (Trans.) Roy Harris. London: Duckworth.

Schmid, Hans-Jörg. 2007. Entrenchment, salience, and basic levels. In Dirk Geeraerts & Hubert Cuyckens (eds.), *The Oxford Handbook of Cognitive Linguistics*, 117–138. Oxford/New York: Oxford University Press.

Schneider, Gerold. 2020. Changes in society and language: Charting poverty. In Paula Rautionaho, Arja Nurmi & Juhani Klemola (eds.), *Corpora and the changing society: Studies in the evolution of English* (Studies in Corpus Linguistics 96), 29–56. Amsterdam/Philadelphia: John Benjamins.

Schulz, Philip & Wilker Aziz. 2016. Fast collocation-based Bayesian HMM word alignment. In Yuji Matsumoto & Rashmi Prasad (eds.), *Proceedings of COLING 2016, the 26th International Conference on Computational Linguistics: Technical Papers*, 3146–3155. Osaka: COLING 2016 Organizing Committee.

Sell, Charles (ed.). 2006. *The chemistry of fragrances: From perfumer to consumer.* The Royal Society of Chemistry: Cambridge.
Shank, Christopher, Koen Plevoets & Hubert Cuyckens. 2014. A diachronic corpus-based multivariate analysis of "I think *that*" vs. "I think zero". In Dylan Glynn & Justyna A. Robinson (eds.), *Corpus methods for semantics: Quantitative studies in polysemy and synonymy*, 279–303. Amsterdam/Philadelphia: John Benjamins.
Sinclair, John M. 1966. Beginning the study of lexis. In Charles E. Bazell (ed.), *In memory of J.R. Firth*, 410–429. Harlow: Longman.
Sinclair, John M. 1987. Collocation: A progress report. In Ross Steele & Terry Threadgold (eds.), *Language topics: Essays in honor of Michael Halliday.* Vol. 2, 319–332. Amsterdam/Philadelphia: John Benjamins.
Sinclair, John M. 1991. *Corpus, concordance, collocation.* Oxford: Oxford University Press.
Sinclair, John M. 1996. The search for units of meaning. *Textus* 9. 75–106.
Sinclair, John M. 2004. *Trust the text: Language, corpus and discourse.* London: Routledge.
Smith, Barry C. 2015. The chemical senses. In Mohan Matthen (ed.), *The Oxford Handbook of Philosophy of Perception*, 314–353. Oxford: Oxford University Press.
Soares da Silva, Augusto. 2015. Competition of synonyms through time: Conceptual and social salience factors and their interrelations. *Catalan Journal of Linguistics* 14. 199–218.
Speelman, Dirk. 2014. Logistic regression: A confirmatory technique for comparisons in corpus linguistics. In Dylan Glynn & Justyna A. Robinson (eds.), *Corpus Methods for Semantics: Quantitative studies in polysemy and synonymy*, 487–533. Amsterdam/Philadelphia: John Benjamins.
Speelman, Dirk, Stefan Grondelaers & Dirk Geeraerts. 2003. Profile-based linguistic uniformity as a generic method for comparing language varieties. *Computers and the Humanities* 37. 317–337.
Sperber. 1975. *Rethinking symbolism.* Cambridge: Cambridge University Press.
Stefanowitsch, Anatol. 2008. Words and their metaphors: A corpus-based approach. In Anatol Stefanowitsch & Stefan Th. Gries (eds.), *Corpus-based approach to metaphor and metonymy.* Berlin/New York: Mouton de Gruyter.
Steinbach, Michael, Pang-Ning Tan & Vipin Kumar. 2005. *Introduction to data mining.* Boston: Longman.
Stern, Gustaf. 1931. *Meaning and change of meaning, with special reference to the English language.* Gothenburg: Elanders Bocktryckeri Aktiebolag.
Storjohann, Petra. 2009. Plesionymy: A case of synonymy or contrast? *Journal of Pragmatics* 41. 2140–2158.
Strobl, Carolin, Ann-Laure Boulesteix, Thomas Kneib, Thomas Augustin & Achim Zeileis. 2008. Conditional variable importance for random forests. *BMC Bioinformatics* 9(307). http://www.biomedcentral.com/1471-2105/9/307.
Strobl, Carolin, Ann-Laure Boulesteix, Achim Zeileis & Torsten Hothorn. 2007. Bias in random forest variable importance measures: Illustrations, sources and a solution. *BMC Bioinformatics* 8(25). http://www.biomedcentral.com/1471-2105/8/25
Stubbs, Michael. 2002. *Words and phrases: Corpus studies of lexical semantics.* Oxford: Blackwell.
Szmrecsanyi, Benedikt. 2005. Language users as creatures of habit: A corpus-based analysis of persistence in spoken English. *Corpus Linguistics and Linguistic Theory* 1(1). 113–149.

Tagliamonte, Sali A. & R. Harald Baayen. 2012. Models, forests, and trees of York English: *was/were* variation as a case study for statistical practice. *Language Variation and Change* 24(2). 135–178.

Taylor, John R. 1995. *Linguistic categorization*. 2nd edn. Oxford/New York: Oxford University Press.

Taylor, John R. 2003. Near synonyms as co-extensive categories: 'high' and 'tall' revisited. *Language Sciences* 25(3). 263–284. https://doi.org10.1016/S0388-0001(02)00018-9.

Trask, Robert L. 2007. *Language and linguistics: The key concepts*. 2nd edn. Abingdon/New York: Routledge.

Turkkila, Kaisa. 2014. Do near-synonyms occur with the same metaphors: A comparison of anger terms in American English. *Metaphorik* 25. 129–154.

Ullmann, Stephen. 1957. *The principles of semantics*. 2nd edn. Oxford: Basil Blackwell.

Ullmann, Stephen. 1962. *Semantics: An introduction to the science of meaning*. Oxford: Blackwell.

van der Klis, Martijn & Jos Tellings. 2022. Generating semantic maps through multidimensional scaling: linguistic applications and theory. *Corpus Linguistics and Linguistic Theory*. 1–39. Published ahead of print.

Wickelmaier, Florian. 2003. *An introduction to MDS*. Aalborg: Aalborg Universitetsforlag.

Wickham, Hadley. 2016. *ggplot2: Elegant graphics for data analysis*. New York: Springer-Verlag.

Wierzbicka, Anna. 1988. *The semantics of grammar*. Amsterdam: John Benjamins.

Wierzbicka, Anna. 1992. Defining emotion concept. *Cognitive Science* 16(4). 539–581.

Wierzbicka, Anna. 1999. Emotional universals. *Language Design* 2. 23–69.

Winter, Bodo. 2019. *Sensory Linguistics: Language, perception and metaphor*. Amsterdam/Philadelphia: John Benjamins.

Wright, Laura. 2011. Semantic of the colour-terms maroon and magenta in British Standard English. *Revista de Lengua para Fines Específicos* 17. 341–374.

Wright, Laura. 2016. From Lavender Water to *Kiss Me, You Dare*!: Shifting linguistic norms in the perfume industry, 1700–1900. In Giovanni Iamartino & Laura Wright (eds.), *Textus: English Studies in Italy. Late Modern English Norms and Usage*, 147–176. Rome: Carroci

Wright, Laura. 2017. *Kiss Me Quick*: On the naming of commodities in Britain, 1650 to the First World War. In Esther-Miriam Wagner, Bettina Beinhof & Ben Outhwaite (eds.), *Merchants of Innovation: The Language of Traders* (Studies in Language Change 15), 108–131. Berlin: De Gruyter Mouton.

Xiao, Richard & Tony McEnery. 2006. Collocation, semantic prosody, and near synonymy: A cross-linguistic perspective. *Applied Linguistics* 27(1). 103–129.

Yamamoto, Mutsumi. 1999. *Animacy and reference: A cognitive approach to corpus linguistics*. Amsterdam/Philadelphia: John Benjamins.

Yatandu Uba, Sani. 2015. A corpus-based behavioural profile study of near-synonyms: *Important, essential, vital, necessary* and *crucial*. *International Journal of English Language and Linguistics Research* 3(5). 9–17.

Yeshurun, Yara & Noam Sobel. 2010. An odor is not worth a thousand words: From multidimensional odors to unidimensional odor objects. *Annual Review of Psychology* 61. 219–241.

Sources

AHDOE = *The American Heritage Dictionary of the English Language.* 2016–. Houghton Mifflin Harcourt. https://ahdictionary.com/ (December 16, 2020)

CD = *Cambridge Dictionary.* 2016–. Cambridge University Press. Available at: https://dictionary.cambridge.org/ (December 16, 2020)

COCA = Davies, Mark. 2008–. *The Corpus of Contemporary American English (COCA): 520 million words, 1990-present.* Available at: http://corpus.byu.edu/coca/.

CoD = *Collins COBUILD Dictionary.* 2012–. Collins. Available at: https://www.collinsdictionary.com/ (December 16, 2020)

COHA = Davies, Mark. 2010–. *The Corpus of Historical American English (COHA): 400 Million Words, 1810–2009.* Available at: https://corpus.byu.edu/coha/.

LDOCE = *Longman Dictionary of Contemporary English.* 1996–2020. Pearson. Available at: https://www.ldoceonline.com/ (December 16, 2020)

Lexico. 2019. Oxford University Press. Available at: https://www.lexico.com/ (December 16, 2020)

MD = *Macmillan Dictionary.* 2009–2020. Macmillan Education Limited. Available at: https://www.macmillandictionary.com/ (December 16, 2020)

MW = *Merriam-Webster Dictionary and Thesaurus.* 2017–. Merriam-Webster. Available at: https://www.merriam-webster.com/ (December 16, 2020)

NHDAE = *Newbury House Dictionary of American English.* 2018–. Heinle. Available at: http://nhd.heinle.com/home.aspx (December 16, 2020)

OED = *Oxford English Dictionary Online.* 3rd edn. 2000–. Oxford University Press. Available at: <http://www.oed.com/> (December 16, 2020)

USAS = Archer, Dawn, Andrew Wilson & Paul Rayson. 2002. Introduction to the USAS category system. *Benedict Project Report* 1–37.

USAS = Rayson, Paul, Dawn Archer, Scott Piao & Tony McEnery. 2004. The UCREL semantic analysis system. In Louise Guthrie, Roberto Basili, Eva Hajicova & Frederick Jelinek (eds.), *Proceedings of the workshop on beyond named entity recognition semantic labelling for NLP tasks*, 7–12. Lisbon: LREC.

Appendix

Table 38: Period contrasts in fiction.

Reference values: Fiction and P1						
Predictor	*Fragrant*		*Perfumed*		*Scented*	
	Estimate	p-value	Estimate	p-value	Estimate	p-value
Intercept	3.2430	< 0.001	−2.8250	< 0.001	−4.6590	< 0.001
Period = P2	−0.4424	< 0.001	0.3775	0.022	0.3662	0.026
Period = P3	−0.5278	< 0.001	−0.0091	0.963	0.7923	< 0.001
Period = P4	−0.4498	0.003	−0.0220	0.919	0.6880	< 0.001
Reference values: Fiction and P2						
Predictor	*Fragrant*		*Perfumed*		*Scented*	
	Estimate	p-value	Estimate	p-value	Estimate	p-value
Intercept	1.2100	< 0.001	−1.3180	< 0.001	−2.7950	< 0.001
Period = P1	0.4424	< 0.001	−0.3775	0.022	−0.3662	0.026
Period = P3	−0.0855	0.470	−0.3866	0.022	0.4261	0.003
Period = P4	−0.0075	0.955	−0.3995	0.035	0.3218	0.041
Reference values: Fiction and P3						
Predictor	*Fragrant*		*Perfumed*		*Scented*	
	Estimate	p-value	Estimate	p-value	Estimate	p-value
Intercept	2.7150	< 0.001	−2.8340	< 0.001	−3.8670	< 0.001
Period = P1	0.5278	< 0.001	0.0091	0.963	−0.7923	< 0.001
Period = P2	0.0855	0.470	0.3866	0.022	−0.4261	0.003
Period = P4	0.0780	0.597	−0.0129	0.953	−0.1043	0.531
Reference values: Fiction and P4						
Predictor	*Fragrant*		*Perfumed*		*Scented*	
	Estimate	p-value	Estimate	p-value	Estimate	p-value
Intercept	2.7930	< 0.001	−2.8470	< 0.001	−3.9710	< 0.001
Period = P1	0.4498	0.003	0.0220	0.919	−0.6880	< 0.001
Period = P2	0.0075	0.955	0.3995	0.035	−0.3218	0.041
Period = P3	−0.0780	0.597	0.0129	0.953	0.1043	0.531

Table 39: Period contrasts in non-fiction.

Reference values: Non-fiction and P1						
Predictor	*Fragrant*		*Perfumed*		*Scented*	
	Estimate	*p*-value	Estimate	*p*-value	Estimate	*p*-value
Intercept	2.5730	< 0.001	−1.9340	< 0.001	−4.6540	< 0.001
Period = P2	0.5594	0.016	−0.8356	0.003	0.1643	0.620
Period = P3	0.0432	0.883	−0.9456	0.013	0.9187	0.011
Period = P4	−0.8726	0.013	−0.7128	0.082	1.6420	< 0.001
Reference values: Non-fiction and P2						
Predictor	*Fragrant*		*Perfumed*		*Scented*	
	Estimate	*p*-value	Estimate	*p*-value	Estimate	*p*-value
Intercept	3.1330	< 0.001	−2.7700	< 0.001	−4.4890	< 0.001
Period = P1	−0.5594	0.016	0.8356	0.003	−0.1643	0.620
Period = P3	−0.5162	0.078	−0.1099	0.777	0.7544	0.025
Period = P4	−1.4320	< 0.001	0.1228	0.769	1.4770	< 0.001
Reference values: Non-fiction and P3						
Predictor	*Fragrant*		*Perfumed*		*Scented*	
	Estimate	*p*-value	Estimate	*p*-value	Estimate	*p*-value
Intercept	2.6170	< 0.001	−2.8800	< 0.001	−3.7350	< 0.001
Period = P1	−0.0432	0.883	0.9456	0.013	−0.9187	0.011
Period = P2	0.5162	0.078	0.1099	0.777	−0.7544	0.025
Period = P4	−0.9158	0.020	0.2327	0.636	0.7230	0.064
Reference values: Non-fiction and P4						
Predictor	*Fragrant*		*Perfumed*		*Scented*	
	Estimate	*p*-value	Estimate	*p*-value	Estimate	*p*-value
Intercept	1.7010	< 0.001	−2.6470	< 0.001	−3.0120	< 0.001
Period = P1	0.8726	0.013	0.7128	0.082	−1.6420	< 0.001
Period = P2	1.4320	< 0.001	−0.1228	0.769	−1.4770	< 0.001
Period = P3	0.9158	0.020	−0.2327	0.636	−0.7230	0.064

Table 40: Period contrasts in periodicals.

Reference values: Periodicals and P1						
Predictor	*Fragrant*		*Perfumed*		*Scented*	
	Estimate	p-value	Estimate	p-value	Estimate	p-value
Intercept	2.9440	< 0.001	−2.2970	< 0.001	−4.8650	< 0.001
Period = P2	0.6740	0.088	−0.7803	0.092	−0.1818	0.768
Period = P3	−0.2989	0.414	−0.4576	0.291	1.0080	0.071
Period = P4	−0.2308	0.520	−0.8277	0.056	1.2010	0.029
Reference values: Periodicals and P2						
Predictor	*Fragrant*		*Perfumed*		*Scented*	
	Estimate	p-value	Estimate	p-value	Estimate	p-value
Intercept	3.6180	< 0.001	−3.0770	< 0.001	−5.0470	< 0.001
Period = P1	−0.6740	0.088	0.7803	0.092	0.1818	0.768
Period = P3	−0.9730	< 0.001	0.3227	0.346	1.1900	0.001
Period = P4	−0.9049	0.001	−0.0475	0.890	1.3830	< 0.001
Reference values: Periodicals and P3						
Predictor	*Fragrant*		*Perfumed*		*Scented*	
	Estimate	p-value	Estimate	p-value	Estimate	p-value
Intercept	2.6450	< 0.001	−2.7550	< 0.001	−3.8570	< 0.001
Period = P1	0.2989	0.414	0.4576	0.291	−1.0080	0.071
Period = P2	0.9730	< 0.001	−0.3227	0.346	−1.1900	0.001
Period = P4	0.0681	0.753	−0.3701	0.218	0.1931	0.415
Reference values: Periodicals and P4						
Predictor	*Fragrant*		*Perfumed*		*Scented*	
	Estimate	p-value	Estimate	p-value	Estimate	p-value
Intercept	2.7130	< 0.001	−3.1250	< 0.001	−3.6640	< 0.001
Period = P1	0.2308	0.520	0.8277	0.056	−1.2010	0.029
Period = P2	0.9049	0.001	0.0475	0.890	−1.3830	< 0.001
Period = P3	−0.0681	0.753	0.3701	0.218	−0.1931	0.415

Table 41: Period contrasts in the artificial sense.

Reference values: Artificial and P1

Predictor	Fragrant		Perfumed		Scented	
	Estimate	p-value	Estimate	p-value	Estimate	p-value
Intercept	−0.8748	0.003	0.8153	0.008	−2.4200	< 0.001
Period = P2	0.3836	0.092	−0.3565	0.087	0.1515	0.566
Period = P3	0.1396	0.541	−0.8649	< 0.001	0.9657	< 0.001
Period = P4	−0.1680	0.468	−0.8866	< 0.001	1.2080	< 0.001

Reference values: Artificial and P2

Predictor	Fragrant		Perfumed		Scented	
	Estimate	p-value	Estimate	p-value	Estimate	p-value
Intercept	−0.4912	0.055	0.4587	0.102	−2.2680	< 0.001
Period = P1	−0.3836	0.092	0.3565	0.087	−0.1515	0.566
Period = P3	−0.2439	0.172	−0.5083	0.004	0.8143	< 0.001
Period = P4	−0.5515	0.003	−0.5301	0.002	1.0570	< 0.001

Reference values: Artificial and P3

Predictor	Fragrant		Perfumed		Scented	
	Estimate	p-value	Estimate	p-value	Estimate	p-value
Intercept	−0.7351	0.004	−0.0496	0.860	−1.4540	< 0.001
Period = P1	0.1396	0.541	0.8649	< 0.001	−0.9657	< 0.001
Period = P2	0.2439	0.172	0.5083	0.004	−0.8143	< 0.001
Period = P4	−0.3076	0.092	−0.0218	0.900	0.2424	0.145

Reference values: Artificial and P4

Predictor	Fragrant		Perfumed		Scented	
	Estimate	p-value	Estimate	p-value	Estimate	p-value
Intercept	−1.0430	< 0.001	−0.0714	0.803	−1.212	< 0.001
Period = P1	0.1680	0.468	0.8866	< 0.001	−1.208	< 0.001
Period = P2	0.5515	0.003	0.5301	0.002	−1.057	< 0.001
Period = P3	0.3076	0.092	0.0218	0.900	−0.2424	0.145

Table 42: Period contrasts in the figurative sense.

Reference values: Figurative and P1						
Predictor	Fragrant		Perfumed		Scented	
	Estimate	p-value	Estimate	p-value	Estimate	p-value
Intercept	1.9750	< 0.001	−1.6900	0.001	−4.4620	< 0.001
Period = P2	−0.7619	0.128	0.7815	0.148	0.6122	0.603
Period = P3	−1.2210	0.019	0.7742	0.181	1.9960	0.069
Period = P4	−2.0690	< 0.001	1.8540	0.002	2.0090	0.077
Reference values: Figurative and P2						
Predictor	Fragrant		Perfumed		Scented	
	Estimate	p-value	Estimate	p-value	Estimate	p-value
Intercept	1.2130	< 0.001	−0.9084	0.006	−3.8500	< 0.001
Period = P1	0.7619	0.128	−0.7815	0.148	−0.6122	0.603
Period = P3	−0.4593	0.255	−0.0072	0.987	1.3840	0.055
Period = P4	−1.3070	0.004	1.073	0.024	1.3960	0.071
Reference values: Figurative and P3						
Predictor	Fragrant		Perfumed		Scented	
	Estimate	p-value	Estimate	p-value	Estimate	p-value
Intercept	0.7539	0.025	−0.9157	0.018	−2.4660	< 0.001
Period = P1	1.2210	0.019	−0.7742	0.181	−1.9960	0.069
Period = P2	0.4593	0.255	0.0072	0.987	−1.3840	0.055
Period = P4	−0.8477	0.079	1.0800	0.037	0.0121	0.985
Reference values: Figurative and P4						
Predictor	Fragrant		Perfumed		Scented	
	Estimate	p-value	Estimate	p-value	Estimate	p-value
Intercept	−0.0938	0.817	0.1643	0.696	−2.4540	< 0.001
Period = P1	2.0690	< 0.001	−1.8540	0.002	2.0090	0.077
Period = P2	1.3070	0.004	−1.0730	0.024	−1.3960	0.071
Period = P3	0.8477	0.079	−1.0800	0.037	−0.0121	0.985

Table 43: Period contrasts in the indeterminate value.

Reference values: Indeterminate and P1						
Predictor	*Fragrant*		*Perfumed*		*Scented*	
	Estimate	*p*-value	Estimate	*p*-value	Estimate	*p*-value
Intercept	0.2288	0.576	−0.0688	0.875	−2.6930	< 0.001
Period = P2	0.1689	0.667	−0.1550	0.708	−0.0410	0.941
Period = P3	−0.3658	0.346	−0.1936	0.637	0.8383	0.111
Period = P4	−0.3678	0.348	0.2826	0.489	0.2221	0.684
Reference values: Indeterminate and P2						
Predictor	*Fragrant*		*Perfumed*		*Scented*	
	Estimate	*p*-value	Estimate	*p*-value	Estimate	*p*-value
Intercept	0.3977	0.152	−0.2238	0.464	−2.7340	< 0.001
Period = P1	−0.1689	0.667	0.1550	0.708	0.0410	0.941
Period = P3	−0.5346	0.036	−0.0386	0.889	0.8793	0.008
Period = P4	−0.5366	0.039	0.4376	0.108	0.2631	0.464
Reference values: Indeterminate and P3						
Predictor	*Fragrant*		*Perfumed*		*Scented*	
	Estimate	*p*-value	Estimate	*p*-value	Estimate	*p*-value
Intercept	−0.1369	0.616	−0.2624	0.385	−1.8550	< 0.001
Period = P1	0.3658	0.346	0.1936	0.637	−0.8383	0.111
Period = P2	0.5346	0.036	0.0386	0.889	−0.8793	0.008
Period = P4	−0.0020	0.994	0.4761	0.074	−0.6162	0.048
Reference values: Indeterminate and P4						
Predictor	*Fragrant*		*Perfumed*		*Scented*	
	Estimate	*p*-value	Estimate	*p*-value	Estimate	*p*-value
Intercept	−0.1389	0.614	0.2138	0.474	−2.4710	< 0.001
Period = P1	0.3678	0.348	−0.2826	0.489	−0.2221	0.684
Period = P2	0.5366	0.039	−0.4376	0.108	−0.2631	0.464
Period = P3	0.0020	0.994	−0.4761	0.074	0.6162	0.048

Table 44: Period contrasts in the natural sense.

Reference values: Natural and P1						
Predictor	*Fragrant*		*Perfumed*		*Scented*	
	Estimate	p-value	Estimate	p-value	Estimate	p-value
Intercept	1.6530	< 0.001	−1.6960	< 0.001	−3.1610	< 0.001
Period = P2	−0.4424	< 0.001	0.3775	0.022	0.3662	0.026
Period = P3	−0.5278	< 0.001	−0.0091	0.963	0.7923	< 0.001
Period = P4	−0.4498	0.003	−0.0220	0.919	0.6880	< 0.001
Reference values: Natural and P2						
Predictor	*Fragrant*		*Perfumed*		*Scented*	
	Estimate	p-value	Estimate	p-value	Estimate	p-value
Intercept	1.2100	< 0.001	−1.3180	< 0.001	−2.7950	< 0.001
Period = P1	0.4424	< 0.001	−0.3775	0.022	−0.3662	0.026
Period = P3	−0.0855	0.470	−0.3866	0.022	0.4261	0.003
Period = P4	−0.0075	0.955	−0.3995	0.035	0.3218	0.041
Reference values: Natural and P3						
Predictor	*Fragrant*		*Perfumed*		*Scented*	
	Estimate	p-value	Estimate	p-value	Estimate	p-value
Intercept	1.1250	< 0.001	−1.7050	< 0.001	−2.3690	< 0.001
Period = P1	0.5278	< 0.001	0.0091	0.963	−0.7923	< 0.001
Period = P2	0.0855	0.470	0.3866	0.022	−0.4261	0.003
Period = P4	0.0780	0.597	−0.0129	0.953	−0.1043	0.531
Reference values: Natural and P4						
Predictor	*Fragrant*		*Perfumed*		*Scented*	
	Estimate	p-value	Estimate	p-value	Estimate	p-value
Intercept	1.2030	< 0.001	−1.718	< 0.001	−2.4730	< 0.001
Period = P1	0.4498	0.003	0.0220	0.919	−0.6880	< 0.001
Period = P2	0.0075	0.955	0.3995	0.035	−0.3218	0.041
Period = P3	−0.0780	0.597	0.0129	0.953	0.1043	0.531

Table 45: Period contrasts in the semantic category ABSTRACT.

Reference values: ABSTRACT and P1						
Predictor	*Fragrant*		*Perfumed*		*Scented*	
	Estimate	*p*-value	Estimate	*p*-value	Estimate	*p*-value
Intercept	3.9710	< 0.001	−2.9840	< 0.001	−17.8300	0.939
Period = P2	−0.7673	0.182	0.5320	0.368	12.3800	0.958
Period = P3	−1.2430	0.036	0.6469	0.299	13.5400	0.954
Period = P4	−1.9690	0.002	1.6130	0.014	13.4900	0.954
Reference values: ABSTRACT and P2						
Predictor	*Fragrant*		*Perfumed*		*Scented*	
	Estimate	*p*-value	Estimate	*p*-value	Estimate	*p*-value
Intercept	3.2040	< 0.001	−2.4520	< 0.001	−5.4530	< 0.001
Period = P1	0.7673	0.182	−0.5320	0.368	−12.380	0.958
Period = P3	−0.4761	0.270	0.1149	0.812	1.1650	0.117
Period = P4	−1.2020	0.017	1.0810	0.038	1.1190	0.171
Reference values: ABSTRACT and P3						
Predictor	*Fragrant*		*Perfumed*		*Scented*	
	Estimate	*p*-value	Estimate	*p*-value	Estimate	*p*-value
Intercept	2.7270	< 0.001	−2.3370	< 0.001	−4.2880	< 0.001
Period = P1	1.2430	0.036	−0.6469	0.299	−13.540	0.954
Period = P2	0.4761	0.270	−0.1149	0.812	−1.1650	0.117
Period = P4	−0.7255	0.167	0.9665	0.083	−0.0460	0.949
Reference values: ABSTRACT and P4						
Predictor	*Fragrant*		*Perfumed*		*Scented*	
	Estimate	*p*-value	Estimate	*p*-value	Estimate	*p*-value
Intercept	2.0020	< 0.001	−1.3700	0.016	−4.3340	< 0.001
Period = P1	1.9690	0.002	−1.6130	0.014	−13.490	0.954
Period = P2	1.2020	0.017	−1.0810	0.038	−1.1190	0.171
Period = P3	0.7255	0.167	−0.9665	0.083	0.0461	0.949

Table 46: Period contrasts in the semantic category BODY AND PEOPLE.

Reference values: BODY AND PEOPLE and P1						
Predictor	*Fragrant*		*Perfumed*		*Scented*	
	Estimate	*p*-value	Estimate	*p*-value	Estimate	*p*-value
Intercept	1.3180	0.006	−0.9218	0.072	−4.2350	< 0.001
Period = P2	0.5917	0.106	−0.2369	0.487	−0.4698	0.322
Period = P3	0.2712	0.435	−0.4686	0.145	0.4528	0.262
Period = P4	0.1799	0.608	−0.2864	0.375	0.3387	0.408
Reference values: BODY AND PEOPLE and P2						
Predictor	*Fragrant*		*Perfumed*		*Scented*	
	Estimate	*p*-value	Estimate	*p*-value	Estimate	*p*-value
Intercept	1.9100	< 0.001	−1.1590	0.015	−4.7050	< 0.001
Period = P1	−0.5917	0.106	0.2369	0.487	0.4698	0.322
Period = P3	−0.3204	0.225	−0.2317	0.373	0.9227	0.011
Period = P4	−0.4117	0.126	−0.0495	0.850	0.8085	0.029
Reference values: BODY AND PEOPLE and P3						
Predictor	*Fragrant*		*Perfumed*		*Scented*	
	Estimate	*p*-value	Estimate	*p*-value	Estimate	*p*-value
Intercept	1.5890	< 0.001	−1.3900	0.003	−3.7820	< 0.001
Period = P1	−0.2712	0.435	0.4686	0.145	−0.4528	0.262
Period = P2	0.3204	0.225	0.2317	0.373	−0.9227	0.011
Period = P4	−0.0913	0.707	0.1822	0.438	−0.1142	0.676
Reference values: BODY AND PEOPLE and P4						
Predictor	*Fragrant*		*Perfumed*		*Scented*	
	Estimate	*p*-value	Estimate	*p*-value	Estimate	*p*-value
Intercept	1.4980	< 0.001	−1.2080	0.010	−3.8960	< 0.001
Period = P1	−0.1799	0.608	0.2864	0.375	−0.3387	0.408
Period = P2	0.4117	0.126	0.0495	0.850	−0.8085	0.029
Period = P3	0.0913	0.707	−0.1822	0.438	0.1142	0.676

Table 47: Period contrasts in the semantic category CLEANING.

Reference values: CLEANING and P1						
Predictor	*Fragrant*		*Perfumed*		*Scented*	
	Estimate	*p*-value	Estimate	*p*-value	Estimate	*p*-value
Intercept	0.4160	0.626	−0.1547	0.826	−4.6240	< 0.001
Period = P2	0.5136	0.565	−1.9540	0.005	1.9970	0.008
Period = P3	0.1861	0.832	−1.4710	0.017	1.6110	0.023
Period = P4	0.7400	0.366	−2.1480	< 0.001	1.8380	0.007
Reference values: CLEANING and P2						
Predictor	*Fragrant*		*Perfumed*		*Scented*	
	Estimate	*p*-value	Estimate	*p*-value	Estimate	*p*-value
Intercept	0.9297	0.131	−2.1090	0.001	−2.6270	< 0.001
Period = P1	−0.5136	0.565	1.9540	0.005	−1.9970	0.008
Period = P3	−0.3276	0.615	0.4831	0.368	−0.3859	0.434
Period = P4	0.2264	0.692	−0.1937	0.715	−0.1587	0.733
Reference values: CLEANING and P3						
Predictor	*Fragrant*		*Perfumed*		*Scented*	
	Estimate	*p*-value	Estimate	*p*-value	Estimate	*p*-value
Intercept	0.6021	0.309	−1.6260	0.003	−3.0130	< 0.001
Period = P1	−0.1861	0.832	1.4710	0.017	−1.6110	0.023
Period = P2	0.3276	0.615	−0.4831	0.368	0.3859	0.434
Period = P4	0.5539	0.310	−0.6768	0.118	0.2272	0.567
Reference values: CLEANING and P4						
Predictor	*Fragrant*		*Perfumed*		*Scented*	
	Estimate	*p*-value	Estimate	*p*-value	Estimate	*p*-value
Intercept	1.1560	0.023	−2.3030	< 0.001	−2.7860	< 0.001
Period = P1	−0.7400	0.366	2.1480	< 0.001	−1.8380	0.007
Period = P2	−0.2264	0.692	0.1937	0.715	0.1587	0.733
Period = P3	−0.5539	0.310	0.6768	0.118	−0.2272	0.567

Table 48: Period contrasts in the semantic category COSMETICS.

Reference values: COSMETICS and P1						
Predictor	Fragrant		Perfumed		Scented	
	Estimate	p-value	Estimate	p-value	Estimate	p-value
Intercept	14.770	0.927	-14.560	0.957	-18.200	0.980
Period = P2	-12.550	0.938	12.700	0.962	14.150	0.984
Period = P3	-12.980	0.936	12.570	0.963	14.780	0.984
Period = P4	-13.830	0.932	13.120	0.961	14.850	0.984
Reference values: COSMETICS and P2						
Predictor	Fragrant		Perfumed		Scented	
	Estimate	p-value	Estimate	p-value	Estimate	p-value
Intercept	2.2240	0.001	-1.8600	0.012	-4.0520	< 0.001
Period = P1	12.550	0.938	-12.700	0.962	-14.150	0.984
Period = P3	-0.4351	0.495	-0.1297	0.852	0.6271	0.400
Period = P4	-1.2830	0.047	0.4244	0.518	0.6992	0.331
Reference values: COSMETICS and P3						
Predictor	Fragrant		Perfumed		Scented	
	Estimate	p-value	Estimate	p-value	Estimate	p-value
Intercept	1.7890	0.001	-1.9900	0.001	-3.4250	< 0.001
Period = P1	12.980	0.936	-12.570	0.963	-14.780	0.984
Period = P2	0.4351	0.495	0.1297	0.852	-0.6271	0.400
Period = P4	-0.8477	0.086	0.5540	0.227	0.0722	0.870
Reference values: COSMETICS and P4						
Predictor	Fragrant		Perfumed		Scented	
	Estimate	p-value	Estimate	p-value	Estimate	p-value
Intercept	0.9410	0.074	-1.4360	0.007	-3.3530	< 0.001
Period = P1	13.830	0.932	-13.120	0.961	-14.850	0.984
Period = P2	1.2830	0.047	-0.4244	0.518	-0.6992	0.331
Period = P3	0.8477	0.086	-0.5540	0.227	-0.0722	0.870

Table 49: Period contrasts in the semantic category EARTH, ATMOSPHERE, AND WEATHER.

Reference values: EARTH, ATMOSPHERE, AND WEATHER and P1						
Predictor	*Fragrant*		*Perfumed*		*Scented*	
	Estimate	*p*-value	Estimate	*p*-value	Estimate	*p*-value
Intercept	2.8300	< 0.001	−2.6100	< 0.001	−4.1360	< 0.001
Period = P2	0.0084	0.964	0.2352	0.314	−0.2636	0.267
Period = P3	−0.2866	0.155	−0.0151	0.954	0.4003	0.094
Period = P4	−0.0225	0.922	−0.2712	0.386	0.2233	0.408

Reference values: EARTH, ATMOSPHERE, AND WEATHER and P2						
Predictor	*Fragrant*		*Perfumed*		*Scented*	
	Estimate	*p*-value	Estimate	*p*-value	Estimate	*p*-value
Intercept	1.3220	<0.001	−1.3550	<0.001	−2.8840	<0.001
Period = P1	−0.0084	0.964	−0.2352	0.314	0.2636	0.267
Period = P3	−0.295	0.079	−0.2503	0.240	0.6639	0.001
Period = P4	−0.0309	0.878	−0.5064	0.066	0.4868	0.041

Reference values: EARTH, ATMOSPHERE, AND WEATHER and P3						
Predictor	*Fragrant*		*Perfumed*		*Scented*	
	Estimate	*p*-value	Estimate	*p*-value	Estimate	*p*-value
Intercept	2.5440	< 0.001	−2.6250	< 0.001	−3.7360	< 0.001
Period = P1	0.2866	0.155	0.0151	0.954	−0.4003	0.094
Period = P2	0.2950	0.079	0.2503	0.240	−0.6639	0.001
Period = P4	0.2641	0.217	−0.2561	0.389	−0.1771	0.459

Reference values: EARTH, ATMOSPHERE, AND WEATHER and P4						
Predictor	*Fragrant*		*Perfumed*		*Scented*	
	Estimate	*p*-value	Estimate	*p*-value	Estimate	*p*-value
Intercept	2.8080	< 0.001	−2.881	< 0.001	−3.9130	< 0.001
Period = P1	0.0225	0.922	0.2712	0.386	−0.2233	0.408
Period = P2	0.0309	0.878	0.5064	0.066	−0.4868	0.041
Period = P3	−0.2641	0.217	0.2561	0.389	0.1771	0.459

Table 50: Period contrasts in the semantic category FOOD AND DRINK.

Reference values: FOOD AND DRINK and P1						
Predictor	*Fragrant*		*Perfumed*		*Scented*	
	Estimate	*p*-value	Estimate	*p*-value	Estimate	*p*-value
Intercept	4.1380	< 0.001	−2.9980	< 0.001	−6.4690	< 0.001
Period = P2	−0.1323	0.726	−0.7915	0.109	1.4460	0.033
Period = P3	0.1063	0.798	−1.2020	0.044	1.3790	0.049
Period = P4	−0.0441	0.906	−0.3885	0.379	1.1280	0.095
Reference values: FOOD AND DRINK and P2						
Predictor	*Fragrant*		*Perfumed*		*Scented*	
	Estimate	*p*-value	Estimate	*p*-value	Estimate	*p*-value
Intercept	4.0060	< 0.001	−3.7890	< 0.001	−5.0240	< 0.001
Period = P1	0.1323	0.726	0.7915	0.109	−1.4460	0.033
Period = P3	0.2386	0.547	−0.4107	0.526	−0.0670	0.887
Period = P4	0.0882	0.802	0.4030	0.427	−0.3179	0.464
Reference values: FOOD AND DRINK and P3						
Predictor	*Fragrant*		*Perfumed*		*Scented*	
	Estimate	*p*-value	Estimate	*p*-value	Estimate	*p*-value
Intercept	4.2450	< 0.001	−4.2000	< 0.001	−5.0910	< 0.001
Period = P1	−0.1063	0.798	1.2020	0.044	−1.3790	0.049
Period = P2	−0.2386	0.547	0.4107	0.526	0.0670	0.887
Period = P4	−0.1504	0.701	0.8137	0.181	−0.2509	0.593
Reference values: FOOD AND DRINK and P4						
Predictor	*Fragrant*		*Perfumed*		*Scented*	
	Estimate	*p*-value	Estimate	*p*-value	Estimate	*p*-value
Intercept	4.0940	< 0.001	−3.3860	< 0.001	−5.3420	< 0.001
Period = P1	0.0441	0.906	0.3885	0.379	−1.1280	0.095
Period = P2	−0.0882	0.802	−0.4030	0.427	0.3179	0.464
Period = P3	0.1504	0.701	−0.8137	0.181	0.2509	0.593

Table 51: Period contrasts in the semantic category OBJECT.

Reference values: OBJECT and P1

Predictor	Fragrant		Perfumed		Scented	
	Estimate	p-value	Estimate	p-value	Estimate	p-value
Intercept	2.0350	< 0.001	−1.3070	0.018	−4.6850	< 0.001
Period = P2	−0.7578	0.075	0.1823	0.657	0.9720	0.086
Period = P3	−0.7569	0.088	−1.2100	0.013	2.1840	< 0.001
Period = P4	−1.3190	0.002	−0.8866	0.035	2.3760	< 0.001

Reference values: OBJECT and P2

Predictor	Fragrant		Perfumed		Scented	
	Estimate	p-value	Estimate	p-value	Estimate	p-value
Intercept	1.2770	0.007	−1.1250	0.029	−3.7130	< 0.001
Period = P1	0.7578	0.075	−0.1823	0.657	−0.9720	0.086
Period = P3	0.0009	0.998	−1.3920	0.002	1.2120	0.003
Period = P4	−0.5613	0.161	−1.0690	0.004	1.4040	< 0.001

Reference values: OBJECT and P3

Predictor	Fragrant		Perfumed		Scented	
	Estimate	p-value	Estimate	p-value	Estimate	p-value
Intercept	1.2780	0.010	−2.5170	< 0.001	−2.5010	< 0.001
Period = P1	0.7569	0.088	1.2100	0.013	−2.1840	< 0.001
Period = P2	−0.0009	0.998	1.3920	0.002	−1.2120	0.003
Period = P4	−0.5622	0.181	0.3230	0.484	0.1922	0.599

Reference values: OBJECT and P4

Predictor	Fragrant		Perfumed		Scented	
	Estimate	p-value	Estimate	p-value	Estimate	p-value
Intercept	0.7156	0.133	−2.1940	< 0.001	−2.3080	< 0.001
Period = P1	1.3190	0.002	0.8866	0.035	−2.3760	< 0.001
Period = P2	0.5613	0.161	1.0690	0.004	−1.4040	< 0.001
Period = P3	0.5622	0.181	−0.3230	0.484	−0.1922	0.599

Table 52: Period contrasts in the semantic category PLANTS AND FLOWERS.

Reference values: PLANTS AND FLOWERS and P1

Predictor	Fragrant		Perfumed		Scented	
	Estimate	p-value	Estimate	p-value	Estimate	p-value
Intercept	4.9620	< 0.001	−5.0610	< 0.001	−5.5150	< 0.001
Period = P2	−1.2050	< 0.001	1.4490	< 0.001	0.7598	0.006
Period = P3	−1.2970	< 0.001	1.1710	0.011	1.0440	0.001
Period = P4	−1.2380	< 0.001	0.6825	0.211	1.1610	< 0.001

Reference values: PLANTS AND FLOWERS and P2

Predictor	Fragrant		Perfumed		Scented	
	Estimate	p-value	Estimate	p-value	Estimate	p-value
Intercept	3.7570	< 0.001	−3.6120	< 0.001	−4.7550	< 0.001
Period = P1	1.2050	< 0.001	−1.4490	< 0.001	−0.7598	0.006
Period = P3	−0.0923	0.671	−0.2777	0.439	0.2840	0.260
Period = P4	−0.0331	0.888	−0.7662	0.097	0.4013	0.119

Reference values: PLANTS AND FLOWERS and P3

Predictor	Fragrant		Perfumed		Scented	
	Estimate	p-value	Estimate	p-value	Estimate	p-value
Intercept	3.6640	< 0.001	−3.8900	< 0.001	−4.4710	< 0.001
Period = P1	1.2970	< 0.001	−1.1710	0.011	−1.0440	0.001
Period = P2	0.0923	0.671	0.2777	0.439	−0.2840	0.260
Period = P4	0.0592	0.831	−0.4885	0.359	0.1173	0.696

Reference values: PLANTS AND FLOWERS and P4

Predictor	Fragrant		Perfumed		Scented	
	Estimate	p-value	Estimate	p-value	Estimate	p-value
Intercept	3.7240	< 0.001	−4.3790	< 0.001	−4.3540	< 0.001
Period = P1	1.2380	< 0.001	−0.6825	0.211	−1.1610	< 0.001
Period = P2	0.0331	0.888	0.7662	0.097	−0.4013	0.119
Period = P3	−0.0592	0.831	0.4885	0.359	−0.1173	0.696

Table 53: Period contrasts in the semantic category SUBSTANCE AND MATERIAL.

Reference values: SUBSTANCE AND MATERIAL and P1

Predictor	Fragrant		Perfumed		Scented	
	Estimate	p-value	Estimate	p-value	Estimate	p-value
Intercept	2.8660	< 0.001	−2.0610	< 0.001	−4.9200	< 0.001
Period = P2	0.4440	0.182	−0.4783	0.199	−0.0899	0.855
Period = P3	0.3350	0.332	−0.8351	0.045	0.4990	0.292
Period = P4	−0.4159	0.247	−0.4292	0.312	1.1600	0.013

Reference values: SUBSTANCE AND MATERIAL and P2

Predictor	Fragrant		Perfumed		Scented	
	Estimate	p-value	Estimate	p-value	Estimate	p-value
Intercept	3.3100	< 0.001	−2.5400	< 0.001	−5.0090	< 0.001
Period = P1	−0.4440	0.182	0.4783	0.199	0.0899	0.855
Period = P3	−0.1089	0.731	−0.3568	0.374	0.5888	0.160
Period = P4	−0.8599	0.009	0.0491	0.904	1.2490	0.002

Reference values: SUBSTANCE AND MATERIAL and P3

Predictor	Fragrant		Perfumed		Scented	
	Estimate	p-value	Estimate	p-value	Estimate	p-value
Intercept	3.2010	< 0.001	−2.8970	< 0.001	−4.4210	< 0.001
Period = P1	−0.3350	0.332	0.8351	0.045	−0.4990	0.292
Period = P2	0.1089	0.731	0.3568	0.374	−0.5888	0.160
Period = P4	−0.7509	0.029	0.4059	0.367	0.6606	0.091

Reference values: SUBSTANCE AND MATERIAL and P4

Predictor	Fragrant		Perfumed		Scented	
	Estimate	p-value	Estimate	p-value	Estimate	p-value
Intercept	2.4500	< 0.001	−2.4910	< 0.001	−3.7600	< 0.001
Period = P1	0.4159	0.247	0.4292	0.312	−1.1600	0.013
Period = P2	0.8599	0.009	−0.0491	0.904	−1.2490	0.002
Period = P3	0.7509	0.029	−0.4059	0.367	−0.6606	0.091

Table 54: Period contrasts in the semantic category SENSATION.

Reference values: SENSATION and P1						
Predictor	Fragrant		Perfumed		Scented	
	Estimate	p-value	Estimate	p-value	Estimate	p-value
Intercept	3.3140	< 0.001	−2.1830	< 0.001	−7.2450	< 0.001
Period = P2	0.3943	0.310	0.5917	0.154	1.362	0.246
Period = P3	0.4461	0.364	−1.4200	0.032	2.5000	0.029
Period = P4	0.4175	0.439	−0.7352	0.224	1.8860	0.134
Reference values: SENSATION and P2						
Predictor	Fragrant		Perfumed		Scented	
	Estimate	p-value	Estimate	p-value	Estimate	p-value
Intercept	3.7080	< 0.001	−2.7750	< 0.001	−5.8820	< 0.001
Period = P1	−0.3943	0.310	0.5917	0.154	−1.3620	0.246
Period = P3	0.0518	0.919	−0.8281	0.224	1.1380	0.152
Period = P4	0.0232	0.967	−0.1435	0.819	0.5238	0.582
Reference values: SENSATION and P3						
Predictor	Fragrant		Perfumed		Scented	
	Estimate	p-value	Estimate	p-value	Estimate	p-value
Intercept	3.7600	< 0.001	−3.6030	< 0.001	−4.7440	< 0.001
Period = P1	−0.4461	0.364	1.4200	0.032	−2.5000	0.029
Period = P2	−0.0518	0.919	0.8281	0.224	−1.1380	0.152
Period = P4	−0.0286	0.964	0.6846	0.398	−0.6145	0.501
Reference values: SENSATION and P4						
Predictor	Fragrant		Perfumed		Scented	
	Estimate	p-value	Estimate	p-value	Estimate	p-value
Intercept	3.7310	< 0.001	−2.9190	< 0.001	−5.3590	< 0.001
Period = P1	−0.4175	0.439	0.7352	0.224	−1.8860	0.134
Period = P2	−0.0232	0.967	0.1435	0.819	−0.5238	0.582
Period = P3	0.0286	0.964	−0.6846	0.398	0.6145	0.501

Table 55: Period contrasts in the semantic category SPACE.

Reference values: SPACE and P1						
Predictor	Fragrant		Perfumed		Scented	
	Estimate	p-value	Estimate	p-value	Estimate	p-value
Intercept	2.0170	< 0.001	−2.0970	< 0.001	−3.5490	< 0.001
Period = P2	0.2409	0.555	0.3474	0.453	−0.6921	0.156
Period = P3	0.3199	0.435	−0.4721	0.340	0.0164	0.972
Period = P4	−0.0594	0.887	0.0912	0.850	0.0181	0.969
Reference values: SPACE and P2						
Predictor	Fragrant		Perfumed		Scented	
	Estimate	p-value	Estimate	p-value	Estimate	p-value
Intercept	2.2580	< 0.001	−1.7490	< 0.001	−4.2410	< 0.001
Period = P1	−0.2409	0.555	−0.3474	0.453	0.6921	0.156
Period = P3	0.0789	0.793	−0.8195	0.025	0.7085	0.054
Period = P4	−0.3004	0.335	−0.2563	0.463	0.7102	0.060
Reference values: SPACE and P3						
Predictor	Fragrant		Perfumed		Scented	
	Estimate	p-value	Estimate	p-value	Estimate	p-value
Intercept	2.3370	< 0.001	−2.5690	< 0.001	−3.5320	< 0.001
Period = P1	−0.3199	0.435	0.4721	0.340	−0.0164	0.972
Period = P2	−0.0789	0.793	0.8195	0.025	−0.7085	0.054
Period = P4	−0.3793	0.226	0.5633	0.148	0.0017	0.996
Reference values: SPACE and P4						
Predictor	Fragrant		Perfumed		Scented	
	Estimate	p-value	Estimate	p-value	Estimate	p-value
Intercept	1.9580	< 0.001	−2.0050	< 0.001	−3.5310	< 0.001
Period = P1	0.0593	0.887	−0.0912	0.850	−0.0181	0.969
Period = P2	0.3004	0.335	0.2563	0.463	−0.7102	0.060
Period = P3	0.3793	0.226	−0.5633	0.148	−0.0017	0.996

Table 56: Period contrasts in the semantic category TEXTILE AND CLOTHING.

Reference values: TEXTILE AND CLOTHING in P1

Predictor	Fragrant		Perfumed		Scented	
	Estimate	p-value	Estimate	p-value	Estimate	p-value
Intercept	0.4743	0.521	−1.055	0.093	−3.3390	<0.001
Period = P2	0.5223	0.438	0.2935	0.542	−0.5995	0.248
Period = P3	0.1800	0.798	−0.3410	0.496	0.3957	0.442
Period = P4	0.9101	0.206	−0.1147	0.830	−0.5920	0.303

Reference values: TEXTILE AND CLOTHING and P2

Predictor	Fragrant		Perfumed		Scented	
	Estimate	p-value	Estimate	p-value	Estimate	p-value
Intercept	0.9966	0.034	−0.7612	0.131	−3.939	<0.001
Period = P1	−0.5223	0.438	−0.2935	0.542	0.5995	0.248
Period = P3	−0.3423	0.405	−0.6345	0.060	0.9951	0.006
Period = P4	0.3878	0.378	(0.4082	0.288	0.0075	0.987

Reference values: TEXTILE AND CLOTHING and P3

Predictor	Fragrant		Perfumed		Scented	
	Estimate	p-value	Estimate	p-value	Estimate	p-value
Intercept	0.6543	0.200	−1.3960	0.008	−2.9440	<0.001
Period = P1	−0.1800	0.798	0.3410	0.496	−0.3957	0.442
Period = P2	0.3423	0.405	0.6345	0.060	−0.9951	0.006
Period = P4	0.7301	0.131	0.2263	0.580	−0.9877	0.025

Reference values: TEXTILE AND CLOTHING and P4

Predictor	Fragrant		Perfumed		Scented	
	Estimate	p-value	Estimate	p-value	Estimate	p-value
Intercept	−0.1327	0.765	−0.1497	0.731	−2.4160	<0.001
Period = P1	−0.9101	0.206	0.1147	0.830	0.5920	0.303
Period = P2	−0.3878	0.378	0.4082	0.288	−0.0075	0.987
Period = P3	−0.7301	0.131	−0.2263	0.580	0.9877	0.025

Table 57: Number and percentage of artificial and natural second-order collocates in the semantic category BODY AND PEOPLE.

Sense	P1	P2	P3	P4	Total
Artificial	53 (45,30%)	72 (46.45%)	113 (53.05%)	114 (61.30%)	379 (53.01%)
Natural	64 (54.70%)	53.55%	46.95%	38.70%	336 (46.99%)
Total	117 (100%)	155 (100%)	213 (100%)	230 (100%)	715 (100%)

Table 58: Number and percentage of artificial and natural second-order collocates in the semantic category CLEANING.

Sense	P1	P2	P3	P4	Total
Artificial	21 (77.78%)	37 (67.27%)	81 (66.39%)	87 (70.16%)	226 (68.90%)
Natural	6 (22.22%)	18 (32.73%)	41 (33.61%)	37 (29.84%)	102 (31.10%)
Total	27 (100%)	55 (100%)	122 (100%)	124 (100%)	328 (100%)

Table 59: Number and percentage of artificial and natural second-order collocates in the semantic category COSMETICS.

Sense	P1	P2	P3	P4	Total
Artificial	2 (12.50%)	11 (32.35%)	48 (64.00%)	60 (63.16%)	121 (55.00%)
Natural	14 (87.50%)	23 (67.65%)	27 (36.00%)	35 (36.84%)	99 (45.00%)
Total	16 (100%)	34 (100%)	75 (100%)	95 (100%)	220 (100%)

Table 60: Number and percentage of artificial and natural second-order collocates in the semantic category EARTH, ATMOSPHERE, AND WEATHER.

Sense	P1	P2	P3	P4	Total
Artificial	18 (8.70%)	23 (8.27%)	33 (9.54%)	45 (11.48%)	119 (9.73%)
Natural	189 (91.30%)	255 (91.73%)	313 (90.46%)	347 (88.52%)	1,104 (90.27%)
Total	207 (100%)	278 (100%)	346 (100%)	392 (100%)	1,223 (100%)

Table 61: Number and percentage of artificial and natural second-order collocates in the semantic category FOOD AND DRINK.

Sense	P1	P2	P3	P4	Total
Artificial	7 (2.75%)	11 (3.69%)	20 (6.17%)	34 (7.17%)	72 (5.33%)
Natural	248 (97.25%)	287 (96.31%)	304 (93.83%)	440 (92.83%)	1,279 (94.67%)
Total	255 (100%)	298 (100%)	324 (100%)	474 (100%)	1,351 (100%)

Table 62: Number and percentage of artificial and natural second-order collocates in the semantic category OBJECT.

Sense	P1	P2	P3	P4	Total
Artificial	81 (62.31%)	133 (61.29%)	187 (61.31%)	209 (58.71%)	610 (60.52%)
Natural	49 (37.69%)	84 (38.71%)	118 (38.69%)	147 (41.29%)	398 (39.48%)
Total	130 (100%)	217 (100%)	305 (100%)	356 (100%)	1,008 (100%)

Table 63: Number and percentage of artificial and natural second-order collocates in the semantic category PLANTS AND FLOWERS.

Sense	P1	P2	P3	P4	Total
Artificial	18 (7.44%)	34 (9.71%)	41 (11.75%)	37 (9.07%)	130 (9.64%)
Natural	224 (92.56%)	316 (90.29%)	308 (88.25%)	371 (90.93%)	1,219 (90.36%)
Total	242 (100%)	350 (100%)	349 (100%)	408 (100%)	1,349 (100%)

Table 64: Number and percentage of artificial and natural second-order collocates in the semantic category SUBSTANCE AND MATERIAL.

Sense	P1	P2	P3	P4	Total
Artificial	38 (39.18%)	69 (46.62%)	95 (47.26%)	103 (49.28%)	305 (46.56%)
Natural	59 (60.82%)	79 (53.38%)	106 (52.74%)	106 (50.72%)	350 (53.44%)
Total	97 (100%)	148 (100%)	201 (100%)	209 (100%)	655 (100%)

Table 65: Number and percentage of artificial and natural second-order collocates in the semantic category SENSATION.

Sense	P1	P2	P3	P4	Total
Artificial	3 (7.14%)	12 (16.22%)	26 (24.53%)	39 (20.97%)	80 (19.61%)
Natural	39 (92.86%)	62 (83.78%)	80 (75.47%)	147 (79.03%)	328 (80.39%)
Total	42 (100%)	74 (100%)	106 (100%)	186 (100%)	408 (100%)

Table 66: Number and percentage of artificial and natural second-order collocates in the semantic category SPACE.

Sense	P1	P2	P3	P4	Total
Artificial	26 (32.10%)	51 (37.50%)	75 (42.86%)	89 (49.44%)	241 (42.13%)
Natural	55 (67.90%)	85 (62.50%)	100 (57.14%)	91 (50.56%)	331 (57.87%)
Total	81 (100%)	136 (100%)	175 (100%)	180 (100%)	572 (100%)

Table 67: Number and percentage of artificial and natural second-order collocates in the semantic category TEXTILE AND CLOTHING.

Sense	P1	P2	P3	P4	Total
Artificial	92 (82.14%)	170 (82.93%)	234 (82.98%)	271 (83.38%)	767 (83.01%)
Natural	20 (17.86%)	35 (17.07%)	48 (17.02%)	54 (16.62%)	157 (16.99%)
Total	112 (100%)	205 (100%)	282 (100%)	325 (100%)	924 (100%)

Index

ambiguity 59, 63, 66, 69–70, 84, 106, 108, 118, 127, 165, 186
amelioration 44
analogy 46, 166, 218
animacy 27, 32, 34, 68, 85–86, 95, 133
ANOVA 182
antonymy 4, 52, 58, 64, 72, 173
association measure 6, 17, 25, 28–29, 175, 177, 188, 208
attraction 2, 11, 45–47, 129–131, 164, 166, 218–219, 225–226

Behavioral Profile approach 31–32, 35, 41
borrowing 42, 44, 48, 52–53, 119, 228

Chi-Square 98, 101, 210
cognitive semantics 2–4, 6–8, 10, 15, 32, 37–38, 198, 220
COHA 10, 48, 57, 61–62, 64, 94, 171, 228
colligation 17, 28–29, 71
collocation
– collocate vs. node word 16
– collocation window 16, 28, 64, 170, 172–173, 178, 208, 229
– collocational meaning 15–18
– collocational network 40
– collocational preference 18, 29, 196
– collocational range 17
– collocational strength 6, 25, 28–29, 175, 177, 183
– consistent collocates 178
– definition of 5, 16–17, 29, 170
– initiating collocates 178, 188
– prominent collocates 177–178
– terminating collocates 178, 188
– transient collocates 178, 188
competition 2, 11–12, 40, 42, 44–45, 98–99, 101, 120, 129–131, 148, 164, 218, 222–223
concreteness 32, 34, 68, 85, 87, 95, 133, 138, 145, 146, 162, 166

connotation 14, 15, 18, 22, 23, 43, 58, 61, 191, 197, 201, 229
context window. *see collocation: collocation window*
contextual normality 21
cosine similarity 175
countability 35, 68, 85, 88, 89, 95, 134, 138, 146, 147, 162, 166

data-driven 174, 201, 202, 205, 207
degree 67, 89, 92, 93, 95, 132, 140, 145, 147, 162, 166
denotation 18, 20, 23, 212
denotational meaning 15, 18–22, 45
dictionary-based approach 201, 205, 210
differentiation 2, 11, 39, 44–47, 58, 129, 164, 218, 225–226, 228
distributional corpus-based approach 5–6, 9, 14, 24, 32–33, 37–38, 41–42, 163, 170, 198, 201–202, 205, 220

Early Modern English 43, 45, 48, 52–53, 200–202
ellipsis 91, 94
entrenchment 7–8, 37, 98, 120, 198
expressive meaning 15, 18–19, 44, 229

family resemblance 7
French 36, 43–45, 48, 51–52, 199

generalization 43
generativism 3, 6, 198
Germanic 37, 43, 50
gradience 7

Hierarchical Agglomerative Cluster analysis 32, 35, 41, 176, 179, 187
Historical Thesaurus of the Oxford English Dictionary (HTOED) 72–74
historical-philological semantics 3–4, 8, 97
horror aequi 167–168
hyperonymy 87, 98
hyponymy 43, 98, 162

Industrial Revolution 13, 110, 185, 193, 204, 206, 210, 215, 221, 226
interpretative indeterminacy 70
isomorphic 21, 42, 129

Late Modern English 51, 193, 200, 202, 205
Latin 48, 51–53
loanword 45, 51–53
logical synonymy. *see synonymy: cognitive synonymy*
logistic regression 25, 32, 36, 132–133, 135, 137–139, 154, 156

metaphor
- conceptual metaphor theory 7
- conventional metaphor 74, 82
- metaphorical extension 27, 30, 39, 56, 74, 76, 84, 97
- metaphorical mapping 46, 77, 166
- PLEASURE IS SWEET 54, 56, 74
- STATES ARE LOCATIONS 77, 80, 82
- synesthetic metaphor 79

metonymy
- CHARACTERISTIC FOR CHARACTERIZED ENTITY 79, 83
- conceptual metonymy theory 7
- CONTAINER FOR CONTENTS 76, 78, 83–84
- metonymical extension 76, 79, 83
- OBJECT USED FOR USER 75
- PIECE OF CLOTHING FOR PERSON 75
- SWEET FOR PLEASANT 54, 56, 74
- TIME PERIOD FOR A CHARACTERISTIC ACTIVITY IN THAT PERIOD 77

Middle English 43–45
Multidimensional Scaling 32, 41–42, 176–177, 181–185, 187

neostructuralist semantics 2–3, 5, 9–10, 14, 220
non-discreteness 7
non-equality. *see gradience*

Old English 37, 43, 53
onomasiology 3, 5, 6, 97
Oxford English Dictionary (OED) 52

participial adjective vs. past participle 66–67
pejoration 44, 57, 191, 228
period 94, 96, 139, 162
plesionymy. *see synonymy: near-synonymy*
Polish 36
polysemy 17, 24, 31–32, 41–42, 57–58, 97, 157, 174, 192, 195, 202, 206
Present-Day English 38–39, 43–44, 51–52, 54, 57–58, 60, 97, 102, 171, 205, 225, 228
priming 167, 168
prototype theory 7, 70, 84
prototypicality 7–8, 22, 37, 55, 97–98, 120, 129, 198, 222

random forest analysis 135, 139
relational semantics 4
Russian 27, 31

salience
- onomasiological salience 8, 55, 98, 120, 129
- semasiological salience 97–98, 223
semantic category 68, 70–72, 74–76, 78–85, 95, 133, 136–139, 151, 153–154, 162
- ABSTRACT 74, 81, 83, 163
- BODY AND PEOPLE 75, 81–82, 106, 108, 165
- CLEANING 75–76, 81, 83–84, 193
- COSMETICS 75, 81, 84, 193
- EARTH, ATMOSPHERE, AND WEATHER 76, 80–82, 206, 211–212
- FOOD AND DRINK 78, 81, 84, 109, 211
- OBJECT 78, 81, 83
- PLANTS AND FLOWERS 78, 81–84, 86, 211–212
- SENSATION 79–82, 85
- SPACE 77, 79–81, 207
- SUBSTANCE AND MATERIAL 80–81
- TEXTILE AND CLOTHING 81
semantic preference 17–18, 28–29, 33, 71, 170–171, 220–221, 224
semantic prosody 17–18, 29, 57, 71, 171, 173, 220, 229

semantic relation. *see antonymy, hyperonymy, hyponymy, polysemy, synonymy*
Semantic Vector Space modeling 32, 172–174, 177, 183
semasiology 3, 6, 97
sense 68–71, 85, 95, 133–134, 136–139, 150–151, 162, 205
SMELL
– *aromatic* 50, 57, 59, 92
– *balmy* 50, 57, 59, 228
– *fragranced* 57, 59
– *fragrant* 52–57
– *odor* 44, 57, 92, 157, 191, 197, 229
– *odoriferous* 50, 57, 59
– *odorous* 50, 57, 59, 191, 228
– *perfume* (n.) 58, 158, 191, 195
– *perfume* (v.) 52, 55–66
– *perfumed* 52–55, 57
– *perfumy* 50, 57, 59
– *redolent* 50, 57–59, 228
– *scent* (n.) 79
– *scent* (v.) 52, 66
– *scented* 53–55, 57
– *smell* (n.) 44, 60, 195
– *smell* (v.) 53
– *stench* (n.) 44
– *sweet* 50, 53, 57, 58
– *sweet-scented* 53, 55–57
– *sweet-smelling* 53, 55–57
social change 199, 201–203, 206, 218
Spanish 41, 227
specialization 22, 42–44, 45, 57, 228
structuralist semantics 3–5, 15, 24, 97, 198, 220
style 1, 14, 22, 45, 61
stylistic meaning 15, 18, 30, 45
substitution 2, 11, 43, 45–46, 129–131, 163, 164, 166, 218–219, 225–226
synonymy
– absolute synonymy 1, 2, 15, 19, 21, 22, 23, 42, 44, 45, 48, 225
– *almost* vs. *nearly* 21, 28, 29
– *around* vs. *round* 40, 171
– *ashamed* vs. *embarrassed* vs. *humiliated* 36
– *ask* vs. *demand* 45
– *autumn* vs. *fall* 22
– *bad* vs. *substandard* 17
– *beef* vs. *cow* 45
– *begin* vs. *commence* vs. *start* 21, 26, 45
– *big* vs. *great* vs. *large* 28, 35, 48
– *bird* vs. *fowl* 43
– *brave* vs. *courageous* 22
– *calm* vs. *placid* 23
– *chief* vs. *main* vs. *major* vs. *primary* vs. *principal* 31, 34
– cognitive synonymy 15, 19–23
– *cordial* vs. *hearty* 45
– *couch* vs. *sofa* 20
– *deep* vs. *profound* 28
– definition of 1, 14, 15
– *die* vs. *kick the bucket* vs. *pass away* 22
– *drunk* vs. *inebriated* 20
– *drunk* vs. *pissed* 22
– *encourage* vs. *incite* vs. *urge* 29
– *firm* vs. *stubborn* 22
– *fog(gy)* vs. *mist(y)* 20, 22
– full synonymy 20
– *giggle* vs. *laugh* 22
– *groundhog* vs. *woodchuck* 20
– *guard* vs. *ward* 43
– *happiness* vs. *joy* 46
– *high* vs. *tall* 30, 37–38, 48
– *hot* vs. *warm* 39, 40, 171
– *-ic* vs. *-ical* adjectives 28–30, 34, 38–39, 48, 86, 170
– *lady* vs. *woman* 18
– *little* vs. *small* vs. *tiny* 35, 48
– *mutton* vs. *sheep* 45
– near-synonymy 1, 15, 19–23, 48, 68, 93, 129–130, 162, 166, 170–171, 218, 220, 226, 227
– no synonymy rule 2, 21, 42
– *on* vs. *upon* 40, 171
– partial synonymy 19
– *pig* vs. *pork* 45
– *powerful* vs. *strong* 28
– *quean* vs. *queen* 44

– sense synonymy 20
– *skinny* vs. *slender* vs. *slim* 23
syntactic function 30, 35, 39, 89, 92, 95, 146, 148, 162, 166

text-type 22, 31, 61–62, 94, 96, 148, 149, 167, 202, 224, 228

UCREL Semantic Analysis System (USAS) 71–74

vagueness 70

www.ingramcontent.com/pod-product-compliance
Lightning Source LLC
Chambersburg PA
CBHW060351190426
43201CB00044B/1998